MW01102593

An American Political Archives Reader

Edited by
Karen Dawley Paul
Glenn R. Gray
L. Rebecca Johnson Melvin

THE SCARECROW PRESS, INC.
Lanham, Maryland • Toronto • Plymouth, UK
2009

SCARECROW PRESS, INC.

Published in the United States of America
by Scarecrow Press, Inc.
A wholly owned subsidiary of
The Rowman & Littlefield Publishing Group, Inc.
4501 Forbes Boulevard, Suite 200, Lanham, Maryland 20706
www.scarecrowpress.com

Estover Road
Plymouth PL6 7PY
United Kingdom

British Library Cataloguing in Publication Information Available

Library of Congress Cataloging-in-Publication Data

An American political archives reader / edited by Glenn R. Gray, L. Rebecca
Johnson Melvin, Karen Dawley Paul.
    p. cm.
  Consists largely of papers originally presented at conferences of the
Congressional Papers Roundtable.
  Includes bibliographical references and index.
  ISBN 978-0-8108-6746-8 (cloth : alk. paper) — ISBN 978-0-8108-6747-5
(ebook)
  1. United States. Congress–Archives–Management–Congresses. 2. United States.
Congress–Records and correspondence–Management–Congresses. 3. United
States–Politics and government–Archival resources–Management–Congresses.
4. Archives–United States–Administration–Congresses. 5. Records–United
States–Management–Congresses. I. Gray, Glenn R., 1970- II. Melvin, L. Rebecca
Johnson. III. Paul, Karen Dawley. IV. Congressional Papers Roundtable (Society
of American Archivists)
  CD3043.A83 2009
  025.17'14–dc22   2008054581

♾ ™ The paper used in this publication meets the minimum requirements of
American National Standard for Information Sciences—Permanence of Paper
for Printed Library Materials, ANSI/NISO Z39.48-1992.
Manufactured in the United States of America.

Contents

Contents
v

Preface

> These papers and their contents separately may tell us very little about the
> place and time in which they were created, but they are the threads that,
> when woven together, create the fabric of our democracy.
>
> —Representative Vernon J. Ehlers, March 5, 2008, *Congressional Record*

In 1984, the Society of American Archivists (SAA) met in Washington, D.C.,
and following a presentation on congressional papers, a group of archivists
decided to form a Congressional Papers Roundtable to further discussions
on preserving these resources. A year later, the Dirksen Congressional
Center and the National Historical Publications and Records Commission
(NHPRC) sponsored a conference to explore minimum standards for these
collections. The Roundtable grew to become a vibrant network of archivists
from across the country who collect and preserve congressional papers.
Members organized special presentations at annual SAA meetings that were
designed to address various congressional papers issues. Sessions on appraisal, outreach, acquisitions, electronic records, records management, and
documentation reflected and addressed the concerns of the group. Some of
the papers from these sessions were published. Others were not, but they
were retained by the Senate Historical Office, where they became a reliable
resource when specific questions about management and appraisal arose.

It was editor Glenn Gray's move from the Senate Finance Committee
in Washington, D.C., to California State University, Fresno, in 2002 that
prompted the idea for this reader. Well versed in the archival practices of
Senate committees, Glenn found that he quickly needed to acquire additional background to administer and build congressional papers collections at his new institution. He further discovered that relevant readings

were scattered in various journals and out-of-print books. His proposal to compile an anthology of relevant articles was endorsed by Rountable members, and he secured a publisher. Glenn sought the assistance of two additional editors. With a range of experience and perspective, the editorial team selected material from previously published articles and other professional papers delivered at SAA (since the 1980s) and the Association of Centers for Congress (since 2004). New chapters were solicited as well, from archivists, political scientists, and those in the growing field of players who manage the collections and benefit from the rich content of American political archives. The result is the reader you see. It does not claim to be comprehensive nor definitive; the complexity of the subject defies such limitation and definition. New frontiers in such areas as electronic records are still open, and the challenges of these archives stimulate new issues and debates for archivists and researchers alike.

From the establishment of the Roundtable in 1984 to the founding of the Association of Centers for the Study of Congress in 2003, there has been a growing number of archival institutions that specialize in congressional documentation. This trend is widely applauded by congressional archivists, who see it as a way to improve the quality and availability of historical documentation of Congress and the political process. This reader is a resource for institutions developing their expertise in congressional holdings. It also should serve as a convenient reference for repositories that have only one or two political collections to manage. Finally, it should encourage historians, political scientists, and other scholars to consider the value of these primary sources toward understanding and teaching the fundamental structure of our American government.

The Congressional Papers Roundtable and the Society of American Archivists have issued *Managing Congressional Collections*, a publication funded by the NHPRC. Those management guidelines and this reader should assume places on the basic reference shelf of archival administrators who deal with the special challenges and idiosyncrasies of collecting and managing political and congressional collections.

It is the hope of the editors that this volume will inspire and encourage repositories to preserve the history of Congress and the American political process more fully than has been the case to date. It is also hoped that these essays will foster continued progress in making these resources available to an expanding community of scholars and students of all ages.

Introduction

Anniversaries have a way of focusing attention on their subjects, and the bicentennial of Congress was no exception. To prepare for a series of commemorative events, the Senate established its Historical Office in 1975 and the House established its Office of the Bicentennial in 1983. Conferences on congressional archives were held in 1976 by the Dirksen Congressional Center and in 1978 by the Senate Historical Office. In 1982, the National Archives was asked to loan an archivist to the Senate, and this became a permanent position in 1984. The House Office of the Bicentennial included an archivist on its staff. Fortunately, the bicentennial of Congress encouraged closer attention to preserving the history and records of Congress.

Thus began a steady march toward promoting preservation of the records of Congress. The collaborative patterns established during preparations for the bicentennial were maintained and evolved along two fronts: projects aimed at improving records management within the Congress and activities aimed at encouraging research institutions to develop an interest in collecting congressional sources. In the first category, records management handbooks, guidelines, and checklists were promulgated for committees and for members. Over the years, they have become increasingly effective because they have helped reinforce an appreciation for the documentation and have removed the discussion from the partisan realm. In addition, e-mail and listservs have increased archivists' ability to communicate more effectively within the Congress.

To facilitate scholarly research use of existing collections and to encourage current members to join their predecessors by donating their own collections, the House and Senate created guides to the locations of member's papers (no small feat in the days before the Internet). The establishment of the Congressional Papers Roundtable was part of this effort to reach beyond the Beltway by creating a national forum for archivists to discuss congressional papers issues. In addition, award-winning guides to the research collections of the House and Senate were produced by the Center for Legislative Archives.

A major turning point occurred in 1990 when P.L. 101-509 established the Advisory Committee on the Records of Congress and simultaneously improved the status of the Center for Legislative Archives at the National Archives. This committee broadened regular discussions about the records of Congress still further by including the clerk of the House, the secretary of the Senate, appointees of House and Senate leadership, and the archivist of the United States. Its accomplishments can be traced through the four *Reports* that are reproduced on the Center for Legislative Archives Web site. Many of the specific projects described in these reports were first articulated in *The Documentation of Congress*, published in 1992 (S. Pub. 102-20). This report was the product of the Congressional Papers Roundtable and its Documentation Task Force headed by the Senate archivist.

Another important building block was the establishment of the Association of Centers for the Study of Congress (ACSC) in 2003, testimony to the fact that research institutions were beginning to focus energies on building better documentation of the Congress. Through its 501(c)(3) status and its annual meetings, it has again broadened the discussion by including historians and political scientists to further illuminate what to preserve and how best to make it available. The ACSC is exploring various options to make congressional sources available through the Internet.

While much progress has been made in the over 30 years since the initiation of efforts to better manage these invaluable historical resources, there remains much to do. Preserving and making available the records of Congress and the political process is an enormous undertaking, requiring enormous resources that are efficiently managed. It requires continued coordination among numerous individuals and groups, including those who create, collect, preserve, use, and finance the preservation of congressional collections. This volume is designed to inspire those who are interested in participating in this fascinating endeavor. It also sheds light on where we started and where we have come. Together, we may create even more effective ways to manage this important segment of the historical record. Like the history of Congress itself, progress happens when many come together for a common goal. In this case, it is the documentation of our political process.

1

Reflections on the Modern History of Congressional History

Richard A. Baker
U.S. Senate Historian

HOUSE RESOLUTION 307

On March 5, 2008, within minutes of accepting an invitation to prepare an address on "the modern history of congressional history" to the annual meeting of the Association of Centers for the Study of Congress (ACSC), I received an urgent message. "Turn on C-SPAN to watch what's happening on the floor of the House of Representatives!" As the image flickered onto my computer monitor, I heard Representative Robert Brady (D-PA), chair of the Committee on House Administration, say, "[This legislation] reminds members of the importance of maintaining and archiving their papers so that future leaders and citizens may learn and understand the decisions that we have made." The camera then shifted to Brady's Republican counterpart, Vernon Ehlers of Michigan. "As members of Congress," said Ehlers, "we are routinely faced with an abundance of notes, letters, and other papers that cross our desk each day. For each of us, there is the temptation to rid ourselves of today's notes and papers and begin each day anew, free of the scourge of clutter." He continued, "It would be easiest to discard these items along with the rest of the day's castoffs, but, as history has shown us, it is often those mundane items that have painted the most accurate and detailed picture of our nation's history. These papers and their contents separately may tell us very little about the place and time in which they were created, but they are threads that, when woven together, create the fabric of our democracy."[1] The House then proceeded to adopt a resolution "expressing the sense of Congress that Members' Congressional papers should be properly

---

Presented at the Association of Centers for the Study of Congress, May 2008.

maintained and encouraging Members to take all necessary measures to manage and preserve their papers." Several months later, on June 20, the Senate unanimously joined the House in awarding its approval.[2]

Senate Archivist Karen Paul and I do not usually do a lot of dancing in the office. But, on any list of euphoric days in the modern history of congressional history, the morning of March 5, 2008, would surely be near the top. In 33 years as Senate historian, I have come to appreciate the potency of three simple words when strung together in a paragraph: "Congress," "democracy," and "history."

HISTORICAL FRAMEWORKS FOR STUDY OF CONGRESS

As the existence of the recently established Association of Centers for the Study of Congress affirms, history-based programs and agencies designed to explore the role of Congress in our democratic republic exist in an abundance unimaginable just a generation ago. Today, Congress employs close to 40 historians, archivists, and curators. This strong cadre is enhanced by 15 professionals at the National Archives Center for Legislative Archives. Staff at the center preserve and interpret House and Senate holdings amounting to 180,000 cubic feet of bills, resolutions, memoranda, and correspondence. The recent explosive growth of electronic records has added a new unit of measure to the center's holdings, which now include between five and six terabytes of data. Prior to 1975, with the exception of small curatorial programs, none of these staff positions existed.

How do we account for this remarkable burst of institutional support for the organized study of congressional history?

To frame an answer to that question, we must look at "The Scandal," "The Celebrations," and "The Dividend."

THE SCANDAL

Nixon

At the center of the scandal is President Richard M. Nixon. In response to revelations of the break-in at the Watergate headquarters of the Democratic National Committee, the Senate in 1973 created its Select Committee on Presidential Campaign Activities. That panel held 47 days of hearings and set in motion the process that led to Nixon's resignation. Nixon's efforts to withhold and destroy presidential records raised a long-deferred question: "Who owns the papers of federal officials, including those of U.S. senators and representatives?" The congressionally mandated National Study Commission on Records and Documents of Federal Officials—known as the

Public Documents Commission—concluded in 1977 that presidential and congressional papers, then considered the private property of those who possessed them, should be defined by statute as public property.[3] Congress considered that recommendation but chose only to deal with the papers of the nation's future chief executives by passing the 1978 Presidential Records Act. The prevailing sentiments among legislators regarding the remainder of the Public Documents Commission's proposal seemed to be "Who would want our papers?" and "Think how much they would cost to archive!"[4]

The Public Documents Commission had based its recommendations, in part, on testimony at a forum on congressional papers in December 1976. University of Michigan historian Robert Warner had commented, "In a sense, the problem of the papers of members of Congress is very great, indeed perhaps more considerable than either the Supreme Court or the presidency." He continued, "We have [had] 37 presidents and 102 Supreme Court Justices, but we have had almost 11,000 members of Congress."[5] Warner underscored complex issues of ownership, inadvertent loss, and the huge volume associated with these papers. Several years later, as archivist of the United States, he used that position to support major improvements in the preservation of congressional archival materials.

The aftershocks of the Watergate affair rumbled across the political landscape of the 1974 congressional election campaigns. Newly elected members, dubbed "Watergate Babies," arrived in Washington committed to inaugurating a more transparent government. In 1975, this spirit moved the Senate to create two reform-oriented, temporary panels: the Commission on the Operation of the Senate and the Select Committee to Study the Senate Committee System. The latter panel recommended that the Senate institute arrangements for timely and equitable access to its records.[6] The Senate responded and in 1980 mandated that most of its confidential records be opened 20 years after their creation.[7]

In this post-Watergate reform climate, and on the eve of the bicentennial celebration of the American Revolution, historian Arthur Schlesinger reminded Senate Majority Leader Mike Mansfield (D-MT) that most executive branch departments have historical offices. "Why should not the Senate have one? I need not add that Congress would be in a much stronger position when it complains about executive secrecy if it at least kept pace with the executive in opening up its own files."[8] Senator Mansfield and Minority Leader Hugh Scott (R-PA) successfully sponsored legislation establishing the Senate Historical Office, which opened in September 1975.[9]

New Harmony

The major historical and archival professional groups took note of these Watergate-inspired developments. In October 1976, they invited to a strategy session 41 historians and archivists concerned with the recent papers of still-active public figures. This gathering at the restored historic Indiana village of New Harmony proved to be anything but harmonious. The historians emphasized timely access, while the archivists counseled patience to ensure that the "chilling effect" of premature disclosure would not impel the creators of public papers to withhold, destroy, or place excessive restrictions on them.[10] Despite the conclave's contentiousness, the acquaintances forged there helped to shape the discussion for years to come.

Dirksen Center

The mid-1970s also witnessed the earliest moves toward the creation of congressional research centers. In 1976, President Gerald Ford traveled to the hamlet of Pekin, Illinois, to dedicate the Everett Dirksen Congressional Center. He made this trip out of affection for his one-time partner in the Capitol Hill Republican leaders' news conferences dubbed the "Ev and Jerry Show." An unfortunate side effect of that visit occurred when a zealous squad of Secret Service agents ripped open sealed boxes of unprocessed records in a futile search for explosive materials. Perhaps they were looking for evidence of a Dirksen plot to make the marigold the national flower. Only Dirksen Center Director Frank Mackaman would know if there are still any bombshells hidden among the Dirksen papers.

Later that spring, the Dirksen Center conducted an inaugural symposium that attracted 60 historians, archivists, and librarians curious about this new facility and concerned about mounting problems of conserving congressional papers. Dirksen Center Board Chair James Unland noted the late senator's dream "to humanize the history of the legislative process." Unland prophetically noted, "This [conference] is the beginning of his dream."[11] In his keynote address, Archivist of the United States James B. Rhoads—a member of the Public Documents Commission—observed that in the aftermath of the Watergate affair, "we see a growing interest in the Congress as a countervailing force to the executive branch." He warned, however, of the great costs of preservation, the expense to researchers of traveling to such widely dispersed resources, and the privacy concerns raised by opening relatively recent materials.[12] Weeks later, Senator Roman Hruska of Nebraska, a Dirksen protégé, inserted the conference proceedings in the *Congressional Record* so that, as he put it, "Senators who are considering disposition of their own papers may have some understanding of the considerations involved."[13]

Funding

The challenges expressed by archivist Rhoads signaled the need for significant funding. A pioneering federal grant to a congressional papers repository came in 1974—$1 million to process the papers of former House Speaker Sam Rayburn.[14] In 1978, following the death of former Vice President and Senator Hubert Humphrey, Congress appropriated $5 million to the Humphrey Institute of Public Affairs at the University of Minnesota. In an emerging tradition of balancing such grants between Democratic and Republican honorees at the same time, Senate Republican Leader Howard Baker of Tennessee inserted another $2.5 million for the Dirksen Center.[15] He honored his father-in-law and predecessor as Senate GOP leader, joking that Republicans could do the job for half of what the Democrats required for Humphrey. Sixteen years later, in 1994, the Dirksen Center made up that discrepancy by obtaining a further federal grant of $2 million to process the papers of former House Republican Leader Robert Michel. This second Dirksen grant came as part of a package that awarded $2 million to Boston College to manage the records of former Democratic House Speaker Thomas O'Neill. Other such bicameral and bipartisan pairings would follow.[16]

1978 Conference on Senators' Papers

In September 1978, Watergate, the New Harmony Conference, and expanding precedents for providing federal funds to process the papers of former members inspired the Senate to conduct a symposium on "The Research Use and Disposition of Senators' Papers." Senate leaders Robert Byrd (D-WV) and Howard Baker, both displaying increasing interest in management of the historical record, welcomed the 250 historians, archivists, and congressional staffers to the historic Senate Caucus Room. Throughout the two-day gathering, participants struggled to identify common ground. Historians who preferred to save everything, and archivists who insisted on having the final say about what to discard, had their eyes opened by Senate staff members who cited mail deliveries to member offices as high as 10,000 letters per week. This staggering volume in those pre-terabyte days created pressures for quick disposal of seemingly less significant items. "The scourge of clutter!" Participants noted that senators in 1978 would accumulate more paper in a single year than their predecessors of 30 years earlier would have amassed in an entire career on Capitol Hill. The 180-page conference proceedings included the first checklist of "Steps Toward Establishing a Records Disposition Program [for members of Congress]."[17]

Professional Endorsement

This fertile environment of the late 1970s produced two significant new historical membership associations: the Society for History in the Federal Government and the National Council on Public History. Working with

established historical and archival organizations, both created committees on government records. Simultaneously, an informal organization
of Washington-area historians, dormant for a quarter-century, resurfaced.
Soon, the "D.C. Historians' Group" was attracting more than 120 academic
and federal historians, archivists, and librarians to its semiannual lun-
cheons at the George Washington University faculty club. A by-product of
the Nixon scandal, a splendid network was now in place!

THE CELEBRATIONS

Bicentennial Fever

On Capitol Hill in 1977, Robert Byrd became majority leader of the
Senate. A longtime believer in historical knowledge as the firmest pillar
for a representative democracy, Senator Byrd, together with Howard Baker
and other congressional leaders, contracted "Bicentennial Fever." From a
legislative branch perspective, there was a great deal to celebrate. Congress
recently had been instrumental in bringing down an "imperial president."
It had also overridden a presidential veto to enact legislation reasserting
its constitutional war-making powers and had strengthened its role in the
nation's budgeting process.

The 1976 American Revolution Bicentennial commemoration provided
the motivation for the Senate to complete a grand restoration to their 1850s
splendor of the Capitol's former Senate and Supreme Court chambers.
Used for events associated with the Senate's institutional history, the Old
Senate Chamber reminded audiences of the "Golden Age" of the "World's
Greatest Deliberative Body."[18] Yet, the 1976 bicentennial disappointed
those who had hoped it would spur creation of projects and programs with
an enduring impact. Congressional leaders vowed not to miss the next opportunity: the forthcoming bicentennial of the Constitution and the resulting federal government.

In 1981, the Senate, under Republican leadership for the first time in
26 years, began some serious long-range planning. Previously, "long-range
planning" for history-related events on Capitol Hill usually amounted to a
short-range "quick fix" of hastily arranged ceremonies. American University
historian Anna Nelson called this "history without historians." Howard
Baker, the new majority leader, established the Senate Bicentennial Study
Group. Senator Baker selected as chair his predecessor, the former Senate
Republican leader Hugh Scott—a cofounder of the Senate Historical Office.
The Study Group included eight current and former senators, the librarian
of Congress, the archivist of the United States, and noted constitutional
scholars. It met three times over the following two years. The panel's five-

year game plan included revival of the long-out-of-print *Biographical Directory of the American Congress* and compilation of a guide to the papers of all former senators. Numbered among other projects were the first comprehensive finding aid for the historical records of the Senate at the National Archives, narrative histories of the Senate and its committees, a documentary film, and commemorative postage stamps.[19]

House Historical Office

These recommendations begged a large question. "Who would undertake companion projects for the House of Representatives?" Although the House had taken the initiative in the mid-1970s to create a joint congressional committee on the American Revolution Bicentennial, that panel's staff had long since departed. As the Senate Bicentennial Study Group was preparing its final report, key House members began to pay attention. Most notable among them were House Speaker Thomas P. "Tip" O'Neill (D-MA) and Rules Committee Chair Richard Bolling (D-MO). Representative Bolling, one of the institutionally oriented "wise men" of the House, sponsored legislation to create a House Historical Office, and Speaker O'Neill appointed a national panel of distinguished scholars to guide that office.

Then, without warning, on September 24, 1982, a small band of fiscally conservative House members struck. Interpreting this initiative as merely a gimmick to improve the public image of the House, they offered as their best argument against such an office the fact that the Senate had one. To the acute embarrassment of Speaker O'Neill, who was out of town, they mustered the votes on a quiet Friday morning to kill the plan. This prompted Representative Newt Gingrich, a Ph.D. in history, to lament,

—If my colleagues think the organization of ideas, the organization of our history as an institution is irrelevant;
—if my colleagues think the people's house deserves less than the White House mess or the limousine cost for the State Department;
—if my colleagues think it does not matter that young historians and political scientists are going to learn early in their careers it is pointless to study the institution of the House because you can not find the papers, you can not get the documents and you might as well go down to the White House because that is where the action is, that is what you can write about easily;
—if my colleagues want to vote for self-contempt and for ignorance, they have a chance. Walk in and vote 'no.'[20]

Ultimately, the House took the advice of Gingrich, who would become its speaker in the following decade. In place of a permanent historical office, members created a temporary House Bicentennial Office. Speaker O'Neill organized a national talent search and appointed as head of that

new office University of Maryland historian Raymond Smock. The new director wisely organized a bipartisan steering committee of House members,
with Representative Lindy Boggs (D-LA) as chair.[21]

Congress Returns to Philadelphia

Within months, Smock had assembled a staff and set to work—along
with the Senate Historical Office—on a full bicentennial agenda. The highlight of that agenda was a ceremonial meeting of Congress in Philadelphia
on July 6, 1987, to commemorate the 200th anniversary of the Constitutional Convention's Great Compromise. That agreement provided for states
to be represented equally in the Senate and in proportion to their respective
populations in the House. With a joint congressional meeting at Independence Hall and separate sessions in the Senate and House chambers
of Congress Hall, the event drew more than 200 members of Congress. A
picture-perfect day and thousands of spectators inspired members to enjoy
the occasion and to anticipate similar programs over the coming two years,
culminating in a 1989 celebration of the bicentennial of Congress.

Harpers Ferry Conference

Creation of the House Bicentennial Office spurred efforts—initiated at
the Senate's 1978 conference—to provide members of Congress and legislative committees with a full range of archival services. In 1984, the Senate
hired Karen Paul to be its first professional archivist. Previously archivist at
the University of Virginia and a National Archives staffer on loan for two
years to the Senate Historical Office, Karen, with her House counterparts,
helped to organize the Congressional Papers Roundtable within the Society
of American Archivists (SAA). Karen and her colleagues also worked with
Frank Mackaman of the Dirksen Center and the National Historical Publications and Records Commission (NHPRC) to organize a three-day conference in 1985 at Harpers Ferry, West Virginia. In its report to Congress,
the conference highlighted "the often severe problems of space, money,
and staffing encountered by libraries and historical agencies that acquire,
arrange, and describe these important historical materials." Noting the approach of the congressional bicentennial, the report emphasized "the need
for improved records management techniques in congressional offices" and
called for establishment of minimum standards for the collections themselves and for the archival repositories that accept them.[22]

1989 Bicentennial Events

The 1989 congressional bicentennial year featured what came to be seen
as a never-ending round of ceremonial activities. Early one bright spring

morning, trucks from the U.S. Mint lumbered into the Capitol Building's east front plaza bearing mammoth coin striking machines. On June 14, House and Senate leaders, members, and favored staff lined up for the opportunity to strike commemorative five-dollar gold pieces. Congress had authorized a three-coin bicentennial set, the sales of which ultimately contributed $30 million to underwrite costs of the Capitol Visitor Center.

In separate ceremonies, the Senate and House unveiled bicentennial first-class postage stamps. Planning for that event sparked a search for an object to serve as an iconic representation of each body. The Senate selected the golden eagle and shield that surmounted the presiding officer's dais in the Old Senate Chamber. From the former House Chamber, now Statuary Hall, the House chose sculptor Carlo Franzoni's magnificent *Car of History*. This work in marble depicts Clio, the muse of history, riding in a chariot, looking over her shoulder to record in a ledger events of the past. The chariot's visible wheel houses an ornate clock.

In a March 4, 1989, appearance before a joint meeting of Congress, historian David McCullough used Franzoni's masterwork as a stage-setter. In remarks entitled, "Time and History on the Hill," he began and ended with a vignette about early nineteenth-century clockmaker Simon Willard. McCullough lamented the popularity of the modern digital clock. He termed it "a perfect symbol for much that is out of balance in our day. It tells only what time it is now, at this instant, as if that were all that anyone would wish to know, or needs to know." Franzoni's clock, however, "with two hands and an old-fashioned face . . . tells us what time it is now, what time it used to be, and what time it will become."

At work on the biography of Harry Truman that would earn him a Pulitzer Prize, McCullough enumerated the outstanding members of past Congresses for whom no adequate life accounts existed. His list included House Speakers Joseph Cannon and Thomas Reed, and Senators Carl Hayden, Joseph T. Robinson, and George Aiken. "[C]ompared to what has been published about presidents and the presidency," he said, "we have hardly begun. The field [of congressional biography] is wide open. The opportunity for a new generation of outstanding congressional scholars couldn't be greater. . . . We are all of us so accustomed to seeing our history measured by the presidency that we forget the extent to which the real story of the country can be found here [on Capitol Hill]. . . . Above all, we need to know more about Congress because we are Americans. We believe in governing ourselves."[23]

Ken Burns's Film

The 1989 bicentennial production that reached the largest audience was Ken Burns's 90-minute Public Broadcasting Service film *The Congress: The*

History and Promise of Representative Government. Narrated by David Mc-
Cullough, this work premiered on March 13, 1989, at Washington's National Theater before an audience of several hundred members of Congress.
Produced concurrently with Burns's *Civil War* series, and using the same
fiddle music and some of the talking heads, *The Congress* was quickly over-
shadowed by its more heart-wrenching co-creation. Its greatest impact was
most likely felt in schools throughout the Midwest, thanks to free distribution by a regional phone company, but it continues to be seen on television
and DVD. This film represented the first comprehensive effort to assemble
visual material to support a major documentary on Congress.[24]

Capitol Bicentennial

The congressional bicentennial of 1987 to 1991 merged smoothly into
the U.S. Capitol bicentennial of 1993 to 2000. In 1992, the Office of the
Architect of the Capitol and the private U.S. Capitol Historical Society announced plans to commemorate the 200th anniversary of the 1793 placement of the Capitol's first cornerstone. A highlight of the Capitol bicentennial was the May 9, 1993, helicopter removal of the Statue of Freedom from
its perch atop the dome to the Capitol's east front plaza. Workers labored
for nearly six months to reverse the effects of 130 years of acid rain and
lightning strikes. On a spectacularly beautiful October 23 morning, congressional leaders welcomed President Bill Clinton at the west front to deliver remarks on the history of Congress and the Capitol. Then the intrepid
chopper hoisted the gleaming statue back to its accustomed platform.[25]

Over the next seven years, the Capitol bicentennial fostered projects of
enduring value. The Office of the Architect of the Capitol produced a richly
illustrated, 500-page history of the construction of the Capitol, by its architectural historian William Allen.[26] That office also published a collection of
essays by Capitol Curator Barbara Wolanin and other scholars on the Ital-
ian fresco artist Constantino Brumidi—the "Michelangelo of the Capitol."[27]
The Capitol Historical Society sponsored an annual symposium featuring
experts on the building's art, architecture, and political history, with proceedings published by the Ohio University Press.[28]

The Senate Historical Office obtained the long-obscured shorthand journals of the U.S. Army engineer Montgomery C. Meigs, who from 1853 to
1861 directed construction of the Capitol's House and Senate extensions
and dome. The Historical Office arranged for the translation of that obsolete system of shorthand and produced a 900-page, award-winning volume
entitled *Capitol Builder.* Meigs offered a daily accounting that extended
beyond construction issues to include detailed accounts of daily life in
pre–Civil War Washington.[29]

The Capitol bicentennial culminated in the year 2000 with a ground-
breaking ceremony for a long-needed Capitol Visitor Center.

THE DIVIDENDS

Numerous tangible dividends emerged from the commemorations that extended from the mid-1980s through 2000.

National Archives Independence

In 1985, Congress granted the National Archives independence from its unhappy status as a subordinate unit of the General Services Administration. Archivist of the United States Robert Warner had privately promised that one of the first fruits of independence would be a separate division devoted to managing the long-neglected records of the U.S. Congress. Congress did its part by enacting legislation adding funding and staff to the newly organized Center for Legislative Archives. The center eventually grew from three overburdened custodians to an exceptional cadre of 15 historians and archivists. They have produced useful finding aids, including the first comprehensive guides to the official records of the Senate and House, and notable exhibitions.[30]

In the statute that expanded the Legislative Archives Center, Congress created the permanent Advisory Committee on the Records of Congress.[31] That 11-member panel, meeting twice each year since 1991, is chaired by the secretary of the Senate and the clerk of the House. It includes the archivist of the United States, the historians of the House and Senate, and six outside professionals in the fields of history, political science, and archival management. Over nearly two decades, the Advisory Committee has proven to be a potent engine for keeping issues concerning the documentary record of Congress sharply in focus for that institution's officers and leaders. The value of such a structure is becoming increasingly evident as we confront the myriad challenges of preserving electronic records.[32]

In 1991, the archivist of the United States selected Michael Gillette to direct the Center for Legislative Archives. Formerly head of oral history programs for the Lyndon B. Johnson Presidential Library, Gillette brought a welcome fund of energy and creativity to the center.

The Encyclopedia of Congress

Preeminent among Gillette's contributions was the four-volume *Encyclopedia of Congress*, published by Simon and Schuster in 1995. An editorial team, comprised of a journalist, a political scientist, and a historian, recruited more than 500 scholars, members of Congress, journalists, and others with practical experience and theoretical knowledge on the workings of this complex institution. This project evolved into a robust network of experts, most of whom would never otherwise have had reason to communicate with one another, let alone to read one another's work. The

Encyclopedia of Congress, with its 1,000 separate entries, stands as a singular achievement in recent congressional history.

A Century of Lawmaking

As the *Encyclopedia* was going to press in 1995, the Library of Congress formed a team of congressional documents specialists and information technology experts to produce a new resource, unprecedented in scope. Their goal was to provide online access to the official printed records of Congress's first century. The project, "A Century of Lawmaking for a New Nation: Congressional Documents and Debates," now includes searchable text of a linked set of congressional journals and floor proceedings for the century between the First Continental Congress of 1774 and the 43rd Congress of 1875. By the year 2000, this vast documentary treasure had become available to anyone with Internet access.[33] Since then, subscription services have evolved to offer fully searchable content of the Congressional Serial Set from 1817 to 1980, including 12 million pages of legislative reports and documents. Soon the *Congressional Record*, electronically available for proceedings since 1989, will be fully accessible through the Internet, back to its first volume in 1873.

C-SPAN

The experts who worked on many of the above-mentioned projects included individuals who were becoming increasingly familiar to the public thanks to the cable network C-SPAN. The development of C-SPAN, from its founding in the mid-1970s to the advent of gavel-to-gavel televised coverage of House and Senate floor proceedings by 1986, paralleled and reinforced the growth of historical programs on Capitol Hill. Throughout those years, C-SPAN Chair Brian Lamb had contemplated an extended series of programs on the history, art, and architecture of the U.S. Capitol. His dream finally came true in May 2006 with a nine-hour series, *The Capitol*. In a review, *American Heritage Magazine* observed that "*The Capitol* proved as enthralling a history lesson as TV has ever offered—and a dazzling art and architecture survey in the bargain [that guided] viewers where tourists never tread."[34]

Capitol Visitor Center

Thirty years of focused study on Congress and the Capitol culminated in December 2008 with the opening of the $621 million, 580,000 square-foot Capitol Visitor Center. Since the 1980s, private financial contributions and sales of bicentennial coins produced significant revenues to defray the cost of exhibitions in a gallery that spans the length of two football fields. Unlike the bicentennial of 1976, however, Visitor Center planners did not have to search for resident experts. Three decades of growth in congressional history offices and expertise proved invaluable. Just as historians and archivists enjoyed the dividends of "bicentennial fever," now Congress and its leaders reaped the benefits of its well-established historical offices. Staffs of the House, Senate, and Architect of the Capitol's historical and curatorial programs joined with congressional specialists from the Library of Congress, the National Archives, and the Smithsonian Institution. They also worked closely with academic scholars in the fields of women's history, African American studies, and Native American culture to develop detailed exhibition scripts. In this, the team was guided by Ralph Appelbaum Associates, museum exhibit designers, whose deeply impressive work can be viewed at Washington's recently opened Newseum and the Holocaust Museum. For the first time, Congress will have a user-friendly visitor center, accessible to people of all ages, to promote inquiry and discussion surrounding the nation's "first branch" of government. The center's gift shops will expand the reach of the center's exhibitions, films, and interactive features by offering a range of educational materials conveniently available under one roof. The existence of these commercial outlets, patronized annually by an anticipated 3 million visitors, is likely to attract the attention of authors and publishers ready to exploit this newly energized market.[35]

Congressional scholars now have access to a vast public. C-SPAN routinely features the writers of books about Congress in its various book programs. DVDs of its recent series on the Capitol sell by the thousands. Historians employed by the Senate, House, Architect of the Capitol, and the National Archives Center for Legislative Archives create interpretive text for publications—both printed and Web based—that reach an audience numbering in the multiple millions. The Web pages of the nation's congressional research centers have a correspondingly wide reach.

Over the past third of a century, resources and networks for the study of Congress have expanded far beyond Everett Dirksen's dream "to humanize the history of the legislative process." For congressional studies centers, however, this expansion presents significant challenges. To remain vital, centers and collections initiated in a burst of enthusiasm with the high-profile donation of a single member's collection must maintain long-term reliable funding sources, shape programs attractive to ever more diverse audiences, and refresh their principal holdings with collections of subsequent generations of former members. The future will not smile on centers devoted to just one former member, no matter how prominent or accomplished.

Ensuring continued vibrancy for the study of Congress is the public's insistence on the right to know about the processes by which the nation sets its priorities. David McCullough got it exactly right. "Above all, we need to know more about Congress because we are Americans. We believe in governing ourselves."

NOTES

1. *Congressional Record,* 110th Congress, 2nd sess., H-1254-55 (daily edition) March 5, 2008.
2. *Congressional Record,* 110th Congress, 2nd sess., S-5947 (daily edition) June 20, 2008.
3. National Study Commission on Records and Documents of Federal Officials. *Final Report, March 13, 1977.*
4. Anna Kasten Nelson, ed. *The Records of Federal Officials: A Selection of Materials from the National Study Commission on Records and Documents of Federal Officials* (New York: Garland Publishing, 1978), 111–72.
5. Nelson, ed. *The Records of Federal Officials,* 113–18.
6. U.S. Congress, Senate, "Disposition of Committee Records," *Second Report with Recommendations of the Temporary Committee to Study the Senate Committee System,* Committee Print, (Washington, GPO, 1977), 22–23.
7. Senate Resolution 474, 96th Congress, 2d sess., "Relating to Public Access to Senate Records at the National Archives," Senate Report 96-1042, December 1, 1980, 1–4.
8. Arthur M. Schlesinger, Jr. to Mike Mansfield, May 6, 1974, collections of the U.S. Senate Historical Office.
9. See "Legislative Branch Appropriations, 1976," Senate Report 94-262, 94th Congress, 1st sess., 11; U.S. Senate, Committee on Appropriations, *Legislative Branch Appropriations for Fiscal Year 1976, H.R. 6950,* 1258–59.
10. Alonzo L. Hamby and Edward Weldon, *Access to the Papers of Recent Public Figures: The New Harmony Conference* (Bloomington, Ind.: Organization of American Historians, 1977), 1-8.
11. U.S. Congress, *Congressional Record,* 94th Congress, 2nd sess., 15290, May 25, 1976.
12. U.S. Congress, *Congressional Record,* 94th Congress, 2nd sess., 15290–92.
13. U.S. Congress, *Congressional Record,* 94th Congress, 2nd sess., 15290.
14. Public Law 93-441, October 11, 1974.
15. Public Law 95-270, April 27, 1978.
16. See "A Chronology of Successful and Unsuccessful Efforts to Fund Projects Related to Senators' and Representatives' Papers and Archival Repositories," by Karen D. Paul, U.S. Senate Historical Office, updated regularly.
17. U.S. Congress, Senate, *Conference on the Research Use and Disposition of Senators' Papers: Proceedings, September 14–15, 1978* (Washington: GPO, 1978).
18. *New York Times,* June 17, 1976; Stephen Goodwin, "Safeguarding the Senate's Golden Age," *Historic Preservation* (November/December 1983), 19–23.
19. U.S. Congress, Senate, *Final Report of the Study Group on the Commemoration of the United States Senate Bicentenary,* 98th Congress, 1st sess., Senate Document 98-13.

20. *Chronicle of Higher Education,* October 6, 1982; *New York Times,* October 13, 1982; U.S. Congress, *Congressional Record,* 97th Congress, 2nd sess., pp. 25029–32, September 24, 1982; 31951–58, December 17, 1982.

21. *Roll Call–The Newspaper of Capitol Hill,* October 6, 1983; *New York Times,* October 30, 1984.

22. National Historical Publications and Records Commission, *Congressional Papers Project Report, July 15–November 15, 1985, Grant No. 85-110* (Washington, DC, 1986), 7.

23. U.S. Congress, *Congressional Record,* 101st Congress, 1st sess., 3215-17, March 2, 1989; *Washington Post,* March 3, 1989.

24. *New York Times,* March 20, 1989.

25. *Washington Post,* October 24, 1993.

26. U.S. Congress, Senate, *History of the United States Capitol: A Chronicle of Design, Construction, and Politics,* by William C. Allen, 106th Congress, 2nd sess., 2001, Senate Document 106-29.

27. U.S. Congress, Senate, *Constantino Brumidi: Artist of the Capitol,* by Barbara A. Wolanin, 103rd Congress, 2nd sess., 1998, Senate Document 103-27.

28. Donald R. Kennon, ed., *The United States Capitol: Designing and Decorating a National Icon* (Athens, Ohio: Ohio University Press, 2000).

29. U.S. Congress, Senate, *Capitol Builder: The Shorthand Journals of Montgomery C. Meigs, 1853–1859, 1861,* edited by Wendy Wolff, 106th Congress, 2nd sess., 2001, Senate Document 106-20.

30. U.S. Congress, Senate, *Guide to the Records of the United States Senate at the National Archives, 1789–1989,* 100th Congress, 1st sess, 1989, Senate Document 100-42; U.S. Congress, House of Representatives, *Guide to the Records of the United States House of Representatives at the National Archives, 1789–1989,* 100th Congress, 1st sess., 1989, House Document 100-245; Jessie Kratz and Martha Grove, *Running for Office: Candidates, Campaigns, and the Cartoons of Clifford Berryman* (Washington, DC: Foundation for the National Archives, 2008).

31. Public Law 101-509, November 5, 1990.

32. U.S. Congress, House of Representatives, *Advisory Committee on the Records of Congress, Fourth Report, December 31, 2006,* 109th Congress, 2nd sess., House Document 109-156.

33. http://lcweb2.loc.gov/ammem/amlaw (17 Oct. 2008).

34. http://www.c-span.org/capitolhistory/index.asp (17 Oct. 2008).

35. http://www.aoc.gov/cvc/index.cfm (17 Oct. 2008).

Part I

ACQUIRING POLITICAL COLLECTIONS

2

Present at the Tenth Hour: Appraising and Accessioning the Papers of Marjorie S. Holt

Lauren R. Brown

For one interested in acquiring congressional papers, it might be called an archivist's dream. A call came through to my office one morning in October 1985 from the chief administrative aide of Congresswoman Marjorie S. Holt, at that time a U.S. representative from Maryland who was planning to retire in 1986. The aide, who said they were looking for a repository for Representative Holt's papers, asked these questions: Are you interested? Could you give us some advice on what types of material in our office are worth assembling for transfer to your repository? Can you work up a gift agreement for us to review? When can you come down to Washington in order to discuss this proposed donation and to review our files?[1]

The person I was speaking with is one of the more enlightened administrative aides that I have encountered during my visits to congressional offices on the Hill. Not all congressional staff members can be expected to have an informed idea of the research potential of the papers of a representative or senator. Nor does a typical staff assistant have any particular interest in meeting with an archivist who is interested in working out a deposit agreement with a congressional office. Fortunately, the U.S. Senate Historical Office and the Office for the Bicentennial of the House of Representatives are accomplishing a great deal on a daily basis in educating staffs on the Hill regarding the historical worth and proper handling of congressional papers.[2]

Previously published as "Present at the Tenth Hour: Appraising and Accessioning the Papers of Congresswoman Marjorie S. Holt" in *Rare Books and Manuscripts Librarianship*, vol. 2, issue 2 (fall 1987). Reprinted with permission.

The experience I had with Marjorie Holt and her staff, by and large a cordial and productive one, was not however entirely free of worries, difficulties, and disappointments. My observations are intended to convey a sense of this and to suggest what might be done to ensure that a congressional collection being accessioned has at least the prospect of containing documentation that is desirable and is free of boxes of unwanted material.

A few facts are needed to set the scene of my work with members of Representative Holt's staff. The University of Maryland, College Park, has been involved in collecting the papers of Maryland political leaders for at least several decades. Previous years have witnessed the collecting of papers relating to Maryland governors from the late nineteenth century to the present era. A number of important mid-twentieth-century Maryland politicians such as Senator Millard Tydings (who served prominently on the Senate Foreign Relations and Armed Services Committees during the 1930s and 1940s) and Spiro Agnew (who resigned as vice president due to questions regarding his conduct while governor of Maryland) have deposited their papers at College Park. The Historical Manuscripts and Archives Department administers the files of five former House members and four U.S. senators. Collections dealing with regional political concerns, such as the archives of the Maryland League of Women Voters, the Maryland Municipal League, and the Chesapeake Bay Foundation, serve to complement the papers of political leaders. The University of Maryland has an ongoing interest in this area, even to the point of occasionally collecting papers relating to state or county officials and political activists. This interest is tempered, however, with an acute awareness of the difficulty in adequately documenting political activity merely by the collecting of twentieth-century paper files. We are also very much aware of the danger of being swamped with a mountain of cartons during a time when the university libraries can ill afford to house massive collections needlessly.

Marjorie S. Holt, representing the 4th Congressional District in Maryland, was a formidable candidate who enjoyed increased margins of victory in elections from her first campaign in 1972 until her decision to retire after being reelected for the sixth time in 1984. She served on the House Armed Services Committee, was involved in a number of important Chesapeake Bay initiatives, and in 1978 proposed the Holt substitute budget amendment, calling for reduced spending and a cut in taxes. The Holt amendment, while not passed by Congress that year, became the model for Republican alternatives in the budget conflicts of ensuing years. Holt was not known to be at the top level of the U.S. House leadership, but her longevity in office and her longtime involvement in federal government projects relating to the Chesapeake Bay made the acquisition of her congressional papers a desirable objective for the University of Maryland. It can be difficult at times to carry out an appraisal of congressional papers created by a very junior member of the U.S. House who has served only one term; that particular problem did not apply in this instance.

I enjoyed the advantage when working in Representative Holt's office of being a person who would be listened to and who was in a position to guide Holt and her senior staff in making proper appraisal decisions. This is not always possible. Another member of the Maryland delegation to the U.S. Congress, with whom I made no headway, seemed to be concerned only with the creation of a permanent exhibit of his memorabilia at a small college. Another wanted to take most of his files home in order to assist himself in writing a book. I was fortunate to have the cooperation of Representative Holt's staff, as there was little I could say about making the office operation more efficient or effective from a records management standpoint. The office was closing down and, if anything, I was probably going to make that work more complicated than it might be otherwise.

In this office environment, where I could be expected to receive some measure of attention and cooperation, it became clear that my strategy should incorporate several basic features. One of these was whenever possible to remind the chief administrative assistant and others that they should be congratulated for their enlightened decision to offer congressional papers to a repository, that this activity was in support of a larger enterprise—the world of historical research—and that they should be justly proud of making a contribution to that enterprise. It was even more important to demonstrate from the first phone conversation that I was familiar with the way a typical congressional office operates, with the varieties of files that are generated there, such as legislative assistants' files or military academy files, and with the prevailing opinions expressed in the archival literature on how those files are appraised. Fortunately in recent years, there has been a dramatic growth in the literature regarding appraisal of congressional collections; I found it very helpful to share this printed information with staff members rather than forcing the staff, somewhat unrealistically, to remember what I was telling them verbally. I found especially useful the employment of a triad of publications of increasing complexity that served this need: (1) a six-page handout issued by Raymond Smock of the U.S. House Office for the Bicentennial of the Congress; (2) a publication written by Judy Carlile in 1981 entitled "Closing a Congressional Office: A Brief Overview"; and (3) Patricia Aronsson's article entitled "Appraisal of Twentieth-Century Congressional Collections," which appeared in *Archival Choices: Managing the Historical Record in an Age of Abundance* (an anthology of archival writings edited by Nancy Peace).[3] I might also add that the U.S. Senate Historical Office's records management manual, written by Karen Paul, was very helpful in clarifying certain appraisal issues and in providing information on the handling of machine-readable records in congressional offices.[4]

I soon discovered that appraisal decisions needed to be clearly resolved and documented and that this work needed to be completed as soon as possible. Time passes quickly in the last year of a congressional office, and a harried staff that is busily wrapping up its work and looking for employment elsewhere cannot always be expected to remember agreements reached or to follow through on them. My biggest fear was that the senior member of Representative Holt's office staff would leave for another position before all the arrangements for appraising and accessioning the Holt papers were made. For these reasons, I created a log book that contained a record of appraisal decisions and indicated what files were involved, with whom I had consulted about these decisions, on what dates the decisions were made, and when any follow-up work was scheduled to be completed.

In the case of the Holt papers acquisition, it was a matter of enlisting the staff's cooperation in surveying the contents of the files and resolving sticky issues that inevitably developed. One of the first of these issues that I broached with the staff was that of case files generated from constituent concerns and requests. It became clear that Representative Holt had made up her mind to return noncurrent files back to her constituents and, as is commonly done, to forward active files to her successor. I decided that the fate of these massive files was likely to be resolved according to her line of thinking, partly because I was ambivalent myself about the research potential of these files, and partly because it was clear that the reservoir of good will I enjoyed with the staff could be far better expended on other issues. We came to an amicable agreement that the University of Maryland would not receive these case files and that I did not have any particular concern about their disposition.

The issue of constituent mail, especially mail coming into the office on particular political issues and Representative Holt's response to this mail, was explored in some depth. In this instance, the congresswoman had for better or worse failed to preserve most of the documentation in this area. I was able to ask for and received a printout of the 150-odd standard responses to issue mail that had been prepared by Representative Holt's staff and located in a computer database—but it was too late to capture the actual flavor of the correspondence itself due to previous disposition decisions. In this instance, as with other groupings of material, one often comes into a congressional office prepared to deal with a number of complicated appraisal decisions, only to discover that major decisions have been made by the staff before your arrival and at times all you are able to do is to pick up off the table the remaining crumbs of documentation.

Another decision was reached—one that no doubt will horrify some manuscript collectors but also one I'm convinced was a satisfactory arrangement for future researchers using the Holt papers. Marjorie Holt had assembled over the years a separate collection of letters and notes written by U.S. presidents, secretaries of state and defense, and notable political leaders around the world. She was reluctant to surrender these items to the University of Maryland due to the interest expressed by her children and grandchildren in keeping these papers in the family. After some negotiation, a decision was made to present a full set of the letters and notes in facsimile to the university and to have the Holt family retain those originals that they prized most highly. To some extent, this policy was followed in the acquisition of original political cartoons involving Holt and with photographic material. The university received a substantial portion of original material and in all cases obtained in the form of photocopies the informational value contained in these items.

Political memorabilia in collections present a host of housing and access problems. Although I don't want to suggest that the acquisition of memorabilia should be ruled out altogether, I would not recommend devoting substantial archival storage space to this type of material unless one's repository has a formal policy of active collecting in this area. I was consequently delighted with the senior administrative assistant's most generous offer: to place all of Representative Holt's framed documents, plaques, statues, paperweights, and other memorabilia on a number of large tables and let the University of Maryland take away those items that were considered desirable but without being obliged to accept anything. (As an archivist, I recommend this procedure to all congressional staffs.) As it turned out, this "exhibition" did not actually occur; I toured the various areas of the office complex with an administrative aide, and a very limited number of items were set aside for the University of Maryland. Photocopies were taken of citations and plaques that were not scheduled to come to College Park.

It proved easier to find files that were not needed for the permanent collection than to locate desirable records that were possibly located in some unknown area of the office. A good example of this was my attempt, often unsuccessful, to find adequate documentation on the work of key legislative and administrative assistants on Representative Holt's staff.

As the year 1986 progressed, a deed of gift was drafted, approved with some modifications by the campus legal office, and endorsed by Representative Holt after review by her own legal counsel. During the same time, files selected for permanent retention were transferred into record-center cartons by Holt's staff. After the gift agreement was signed by both parties, the collection, consisting of 28 boxes, was shipped to the University of Maryland at College Park. The collection included speeches by Representative Holt, copies of bills sponsored or co-sponsored by her in the U.S. Congress, legislative files, project files, public relations files, her appointment books, and photographs. The University of Maryland Libraries' nonprint media department assisted in augmenting the collection by recording onto videotape a Baltimore public television program which dealt with Marjorie Holt's life and political career. Plans were made for a series of oral history interviews with Holt and her colleagues.

In terms of bulk, the Holt papers take on the appearance of a very trim collection compared to several earlier accessions of political papers in the Historical Manuscripts and Archives Department. The collections of U.S. House members at the University of Maryland range from 60 to 350 linear feet. Several of these previously acquired accessions are slated for review, as it is obvious in some cases that no significant appraisal work was done at the time the papers were acquired.

My story does not have an entirely happy ending. A reception and exhibit honoring Marjorie Holt and celebrating the acquisition of her papers at College Park was held in December 1986. I was responsible for mounting the exhibit, and it was at this time that I was able to inspect in depth the material that had been assembled and shipped out by the Holt office staff as the result of the appraisal decisions mentioned earlier.

Opening and reviewing the boxes was not a completely enjoyable experience. One source of irritation was that the overall integrity of the series that were established seemed to be in place, but the numbering of the boxes, or even the way the material was placed in the boxes, was done in a very haphazard fashion. One was forced to hop around from box to box in order to obtain a full view of the files on political campaigns, or project files on the Chesapeake Bay, or to locate photographic material. But even more serious was the fact that expected documentation was deficient in some areas. For example, legislative files covered a smaller span of years than expected, and Holt newsletters for the early years were scarce. One of the bright spots perhaps was the absence (as expected) of any committee files that might be considered alienated from the National Archives grouping of congressional committee records.

By this time, the Holt office had been completely vacated. In my search for answers to these puzzling holes in documentation, I investigated the possibility of additional boxes being located at the Washington National Records Center at Suitland. Previously I had relied on Representative Holt's office to tell me about the nature of her shipments to the center and what was being brought back to the office from the center as Holt's tenure on the Hill was ending in late 1986. I had two conversations with a member of the Records Center staff who was able to give me a far clearer idea of what was obviously a congressional papers holocaust. In December 1982, Representative Holt authorized the destruction of 13 early accessions into the Records Center. Also in December 1982, files described as personal records created before April 1979 were destroyed. In April 1984, parts of seven other accessions were destroyed. During May 1986, older case files that were previously maintained in Representative Holt's regional offices, amounting to 46 linear feet, were also tossed.[5]

Interestingly enough, there was clear evidence that Holt had ordered boxes to be brought back to her office in the spring of 1986, and some of this material was placed in the shipment slated for the University of Maryland. The most important pieces in this grouping, now part of the permanent collection, are her schedule books, dating from her first four years in Congress (1973–1977). I was at least partially reassured that my suggestions to her office staff had been carried out. However, it was also very disheartening to realize that possibly a large number of files of high research value had been permanently lost.

In retrospect, I can think of two aspects of the appraisal and accessioning process that I would have handled differently, given the insights that I now have. One would be to devote more attention to hands-on work with the congressional files in the office at the time they were being assembled for transfer to College Park. Although I did devote significant time in discussing appraisal decisions with the staff, in surveying files in the office, and in helping to assemble several file series, it would have paid off in the long run to have spent more time with the staff in supervising the actual physical work involved in packing the boxes. I should have spent more time also in investigating the full history of the disposition of the files created by Holt's office throughout her career as a member of the U.S. House. In this case, the damage of previous dispositions had already occurred before I arrived. However, gaining complete and in-depth knowledge as soon as possible of what exactly had happened to boxes sent to the off-site storage facility could have sharpened documentation and appraisal strategies.

There are obvious advantages in being in an active mode rather than agreeing to accept a congressional collection and then passively waiting to see what arrives at your archival doorstep. By securing access to the office and actively assembling the collection on the Hill, you are assured that the accession will have a low ratio of dross material. You have an opportunity to get acquainted with the staff that has created the files you are collecting. Questions about holes in the documentation can be addressed to that staff, and series within the collection can be well established and defined by the time the boxes arrive at your repository. Arrangements can be made for acquiring supplementary information through oral history interviews with the representative or senator and his or her staff. And it is also quite certain that the archivist should attempt to secure a deposit agreement as early in the career of a member of Congress as possible—in order to ensure that any paper holocausts are those of your own choosing.

NOTES

1. Phone conversation with Keith Berger, administrative assistant to U.S. Representative Marjorie S. Holt, October 23, 1985.

2. Those interested in the work of these offices can contact the Office of History and Preservation, Office of the Clerk at 202-226-1300 or history@mail.house.gov and the Senate Historical Office at 202-224-6900 or historian@sec.senate.gov.

3. Raymond Smock, *Disposal of Congressional Papers* (Washington, D.C: Office for the Bicentennial of the House of Representatives, n.d.); Judy Carlile, *Closing a Congressional Office: A Brief Overview* (Washington, D.C: Congressional Research Service, 1981); Nancy Peace, ed., *Archival Choices: Managing the Historical Record in an Age of Abundance* (Lexington, Mass.: Lexington Books, 1984), 81–101.

4. Karen Dawley Paul, *Records Management Handbook for United States Senators and Their Repositories* (Washington, D.C: U.S. Senate, 1985).

5. Phone conversations with Michael Leahy, April 20 and May 4, 1987.

3

A Repository Archivist
on Capitol Hill

Connell B. Gallagher

The receipt of large twentieth-century political collections can be a crippling experience for a moderately sized archival repository. A proactive approach can, however, soften the blow by permitting the archivist to (1) understand a working congressional office and (2) appraise the papers *en scene* before they are packed. As a result, the repository will receive a smaller, more organized collection with a preliminary finding aid, and the archivist will be in a better position to provide service on the papers sooner.

The University of Vermont began its manuscript-collecting program in 1962 with the creation of the Special Collections Department.[1] Little collecting was being done in twentieth-century manuscripts in Vermont, so this became the obvious focus for the program. By 1970, the university had acquired over 3,000 feet of manuscripts, with approximately 25 percent in political papers. The single largest collection was the papers of Senator Warren R. Austin, approximately 100 feet of material covering Austin's 15 years in the U.S. Senate (1931–1946) and six years as ambassador to the United Nations (1947–1953).

This proportion changed to 50 percent with the receipt of 450 feet of papers in 1972 following the death of Senator Winston L. Prouty, and 800 feet of papers in 1974 following the retirement of Senator George D. Aiken. Together, the Prouty and Aiken papers represented 53 years of combined service in Congress. It was reasonable to assume that with files inflation, we could expect to receive 1,000 feet or more just from Senator Robert T. Stafford, who was scheduled to retire in 1988 after 28 years in Congress.[2]

Previously published as "A Repository Archivist on Capitol Hill" in *Midwestern Archivist* xiv:1 (1991), 49–58. Reprinted with permission.

The manuscript collection was, from the beginning, a Vermont collection; congressional papers were acquired for their Vermont content and for their role in documenting Vermont legislators at the national level, rather than for tracking national issues or the functioning of Congress. These subjects are, however, by-products, and the collections have been used in many ways. Though congressional papers are primarily local in content, they provide much of the source material for national history. Senator Aiken's attempt to improve rural electrification in Vermont resulted in the construction of the St. Lawrence Seaway in 1959, and Senator John J. Williams's clean-up of corruption in Delaware tax collection resulted in the first publication of the Internal Revenue Code in 1954.[3]

PLANNING THE PROJECT

The idea of going to Washington to work in the office of a U.S. senator occurred to me during the Congressional Papers Project Conference sponsored by the Dirksen Congressional Center and the National Historical Publications and Records Commission (NHPRC), held in Harpers Ferry, West Virginia, in the summer of 1985.[4] This was my first opportunity to meet with many colleagues who also were responsible for the care of congressional collections. It was at this time, too, that a Society of American Archivists (SAA) Congressional Papers Group was established, and I was asked to be the first chair and to usher the group through the process of becoming an SAA roundtable.[5]

Robert Blesse of the University of Nevada, one of the Harpers Ferry conference participants, had just returned from a stint in the office of Senator Paul Laxalt, where he packed and shipped the senator's papers to the University of Nevada for deposit.[6] Patricia Aronsson had recommended this approach in 1984:

> Only by thoroughly understanding the context in which the records are created can the archivist be certain of the validity of his appraisal decisions. The ideal time for an archivist to gain these insights is while the senator or representative is still in office. Then the archivist can observe the operation of the congressional office, learn from congressional staff members what issues are of special importance to the member of Congress, and inquire about the value of particular categories of information.[7]

Blesse had spent five weeks dealing with seven years of Laxalt's papers, but I was looking at a longer stay to handle the accumulation of 28 years for Senator Robert T. Stafford. Time and cost would make such an approach prohibitive for most repository archivists under normal conditions, but the project seemed perfect for a sabbatical. Because Vermont is a small state with only three members of Congress, I had the opportunity to cover the whole delegation—if the members could somehow contribute to my travel and living expenses in Washington.

On my return from Harpers Ferry, I wrote to Senators Stafford and Patrick J. Leahy and Congressman James V. Jeffords to apprise them of my sabbatical plans. I hoped to come to Capitol Hill to learn about the workings of Congress firsthand in order to better understand congressional collections, and to advise staff on the organization and disposition of files. All were interested in the proposition, and I was invited to visit and meet with appropriate staff to flesh out my ideas. I did this in the summer of 1986. Neal Houston, Senator Stafford's administrative assistant, was most interested in my coming to help because the senator had just announced that he would retire at the end of the 100th Congress and that his papers would go to the university. Houston pretty much hired me on the spot.

Congressman Jefford's administrative assistant was also interested because her boss was planning to run for Stafford's Senate seat, and Jeffords planned to add the remainder of his House papers to an already considerable collection at the University of Vermont. Senator Leahy's personal assistant was interested in the idea, but the senator did not want to make any commitments regarding his papers that early in his career.

Initially, I had planned to spend July through September of 1988 in the Stafford office, spend October through December with Jeffords, and then use the spring semester to complete the appraisal and description of the papers received by the university. This would have been an ideal scenario, for I would have had Senate experience with Stafford, House and campaign experience with Jeffords, and time to bring this experience to fruition in a purely archival setting. Instead, the Jeffords plan fell through because of a problem with funding, and Leahy asked me to work with his staff for the entire spring semester to review his records management/archival program. This second internship gave me a very valuable point of comparison because Stafford's and Leahy's offices were set up quite differently.

Stafford brought me on as a full staff member for six months, and I agreed to spend nine weeks in Washington doing the same kind of things done by Blesse: "to inventory, pack, and ship to the library all inactive records in storage; [and] to familiarize myself with the day-to-day operation of the senator's office, particularly regarding the creation and storage of correspondence and other office records."[8] The last year in a member's term is ideal from a budgetary point of view, because other staff leave and funds may be available to hire an archivist. My status as a full member with a Senate identification card was helpful. It gave me access to committee rooms, committee staff, the Congressional Research Service, and many other offices on Capitol Hill. Negotiations were completed in one visit with a brief exchange of letters, and I began work on July 1, 1988. The amount of time was sufficient to do most of the things I felt were important.

WASHINGTON OFFICE FUNCTIONS AND THEIR RECORDS

Robert T. Stafford was a career politician. Before entering Congress in 1960, he served as Vermont's attorney general, lieutenant governor, and governor. By Vermont standards, he was a moderate Republican, strong on defense, and a fiscal conservative. He served on the House Committee on Armed Services, supported the concept of the all-volunteer army as co-author of *How to End the Draft* (1967), and endorsed the Morse withdrawal plan for Vietnam in 1968 after a second trip to that war-torn country.[9] He also served on the House Ethics Committee, was vice chair of the House Republican Conference, and was on the short list of vice-presidential candidates when Gerald Ford became president. Stafford moved to the Senate following the death of Winston L. Prouty in 1971 and served on the Environment and Public Works Committee, the Labor and Human Resources Committee, and the Committee on Veterans Affairs. He became chair of the Environment Committee and the Subcommittee on Education during the Republican takeover of the Senate in 1980. As a senator, Stafford supported legislation to clean up the air and water, reduce acid rain, prevent global warming, and establish a superfund for toxic wastes. He was also a strong advocate of equal opportunity in education for handicapped and disadvantaged students. Although Stafford was a "good" Republican for most of his career, he fell out with the Reagan administration because of his strong support for environmental regulations and federal aid for education. The papers generated in these years, 1980–1986, while he was a committee chair, are the most voluminous and seem to be the most interesting.

I thought I knew what to expect when I arrived for duty in July 1988, for I had processed a number of congressional collections already. The Stafford papers, like the Aiken and Prouty papers, were really the records of an organization rather than an individual, but for the first time I realized that these papers documented the activities of the staff more than those of the senator. The staff does the "work"; the senator presents the case in committee, on the floor, and to the public. His role is to persuade other senators and to vote.

I read Karen Paul's *Records Management Handbook for United States Senators and Their Repositories*,[10] visited with her at the Senate Historical Office, and met with the two other archivists who were working on Capitol Hill that summer, all to help me to adjust to the complex world of the U.S. Senate.[11] I reported to Stafford's administrative assistant (AA), the most important person in the office next to the senator. He was Stafford's chief political officer, his "eyes and ears," and the "office Republican"—according to Stafford's chief legislative assistant (LA), who styled himself the "office Democrat." It was important to report directly to the AA because he had the most authority on the staff and could facilitate access to files and people. In Senator Leahy's office, I reported to the senator's personal assistant. Although she lacked the power of the AA, she was a strong individual, very close to the senator, and had the senator's full backing in the archival project. She helped me to schedule staff interviews, and she made all of the appointments for me.

In Stafford's office, the AA and the office manager were the only people who backed the archives project from the beginning. I represented the first sign of the end for staff who had an average tenure of 15 years in the office. The AA explained that, once hired, I worked for the senator and that the expectation was "loyalty" and "integrity." Staff were concerned that a stranger with wide access to files would not respect the privacy they guarded so carefully, and that the senator's image might be compromised inadvertently. They needed to get to know me, and this would take a little time.

I kept a low profile in the beginning by concentrating on the 350 feet of records in the attic. This work needed to be done, but at the same time I wanted to take advantage of opportunities to learn how the Senate worked, and more particularly, how the senator worked in it to achieve his goals. I followed Stafford as much as time would permit. I attended hearings, committee meetings, press conferences, and floor sessions; interviewed key staff members on the senator's most important committees; and noted that wherever he went, there was an LA at his side to brief or advise him as needed. The LAs helped to write legislation, and they prepared speeches, briefings, and position papers. Each had extensive files, kept up with issues, and studied the positions of friends and foes. Good work on their part strengthened the senator's hand in committee; he always knew how the vote would go before he entered any committee room. The files of the LAs would be an important adjunct to the senator's.

The workings of the typical congressional office and the associated documentation are clearly discussed in Aronsson and Paul.[12] The functions are divided between administrative and legislative.[13] In the Stafford office, the administrative staff consisted of the AA, who really functioned on both sides of the aisle, office manager, press officer, secretary/case workers (nearly all of the secretaries carried some caseload), and receptionists. The legislative (or professional) staff included three assistants with responsibilities for Stafford's three committees: Environment and Public Works (EPW), Labor and Human Resources (LHR), and the Subcommittee on the Handicapped.[14] Stafford, as a Republican, was in the minority for most of his career, but with seniority he achieved the status of ranking member on EPW and the Education Subcommittee of LHR. The minority staff of EPW (14 persons) and Education (three) reported to him. The minority staff director of the Education Subcommittee functioned as Stafford's LA for education, and therefore all of the records relating to education were interfiled with the official records of the subcommittee.

This blending of responsibilities is very common in Congress, and senators typically move staff from the personal office to the committee payroll at will. This creates much confusion in the records, and archivists must be aware of this if they wish to find full documentation of their member's activities. The best way to discover this is to interview key personal and committee staff and actually look at the records. Stafford's AA considered all of the records in the minority office of the Education Subcommittee to be part of the senator's personal papers, and so they are.[15] The records of EPW, although not as clearly personal, were available on microfilm, and a copy was ordered to supplement the Stafford papers.

Stafford's office, with a high ratio of administrative to legislative staff, maintained a centralized file system. It was obvious that he inherited most of this from his predecessor, Senator Winston L. Prouty, because many of his file series are exactly the same as Prouty's, but quite different from Aiken's or Leahy's. Nine of Stafford's 12 Washington staff served the administrative functions of the office, handling most of the constituent mail, press relations, and casework.

Leahy, on the other hand, has 12 administrative staff and six legislative assistants to cover the three committees he chairs and the four others on which he also serves. Some key committee staff report directly to him, as they did to Stafford. The main difference in the workload of the two senators relates to the fact that, with the Democrats in the majority, Leahy is a committee chair. There is also a difference in personality. Stafford preferred to concentrate on the few issues for which he became known, while Leahy is active in most of the legislation that comes before the Senate.

According to Aronsson, the files of the AA are potentially the most important files produced in a congressional office because of the political nature of the position and, often, close personal relationships.[16] Members and their AAs usually communicate orally, eyeball to eyeball, and do not tend to write much because of the sensitivity of their positions. Stafford's AA had been with the senator since he was lieutenant governor, and the two had adjoining offices. The AA claimed to have no files except for two cartons of political polls on the floor in the corner of his office, and this proved to be an accurate statement. The AA is usually the chief personnel officer, and I did find some files relating to personnel decisions. It was interesting that the AA was responsible for all of the military academy appointment files as well. Next to the senator, this person is probably the best candidate for oral history.

The next single most important person in the Stafford office was the senator's personal secretary because she was the conduit to the senator and because she maintained all of his personal files, including financial disclosure statements, tax returns, appointments, invitations, annotated copies of speeches, photographs, travel records, and memberships. Stafford's secretary maintained the most extensive files in the office, and although most of these became part of the papers, she was the least forthcoming and the most protective member of the staff. Some of these files were transferred directly to the senator's home in Vermont for use in his retirement. We hope that most of them will eventually be added to his papers at the university.

The files of the office manager included filing guides, procedure manuals, and documentation on office expenditures and routine personnel actions. These files were reviewed and selectively weeded. The press officer was responsible for clippings, tapes, position papers, some speeches, and press releases. Duplicates were weeded, but otherwise these files were kept in their entirety. Other administrative staff did not keep separate files but helped to maintain the large central office file. This file included series entitled "Blue Slips" (copies of all letters sent, 35 feet); "Federal Government" (files of contacts with the executive branch, 56 feet); "Committees" (83 feet); "Cases" (51 feet); "General Subjects" (33 feet); "Acknowledgments" (7 feet); "Requests" (20 feet); "Robos" (form letters, 19 feet); and "Vermont Issues" (29 feet). These centralized files were arranged alphabetically by topic for each session of Congress, and they received a preliminary weeding in Washington during the packing process. The "Blue Slips" series had little intrinsic value because it was a duplicate file and because the contents were repetitive. Still, it had some "slice of life" value as a record of every outgoing letter.[17] This file was microfilmed and the originals were destroyed.

Senators have free access to a microfilm service, but it is inadequate to meet demands; there was a 40-day backlog in the summer of 1988. The Microfilm Office used a rotary camera and 35mm roll microfilm. The member's office must do all of the preparation, including removing staples and clips, arranging the papers, and providing targets.[18] Stafford provided a full-time intern to help with the project, but the preparation of 35 feet of onionskin copies still took nearly two months. This was not a profitable use of time, so we abandoned earlier plans to film 17 feet of clippings and the large casework file. Members really need to use microfilm as a records management tool over the long term; it is impossible to do much in a few months.

The large "Federal Government" file included mostly constituent correspondence, particularly requests to support municipal and institutional federal grant projects, agency reports, and other documentation of federal programs. The "Committees" file was similar, although it included correspondence from committee chairs, lobbyists, and others seeking the senator's support, as well as constituent correspondence relating to the work of all of the congressional committees. Most of the publications in these large series were removed and shipped separately to the university for addition to the general library collections. Both series may be further weeded, but we do wish to retain documentation of the ways federal funds are expended in Vermont.

Cases remain sealed, but the intention is to sample them heavily and to retain only the flavor of the senator's casework together with a few "fat files" on more important issues that may have consumed a lot of staff time and effort.[19] "General Subjects" and "Vermont Issues" still need to be reviewed. The former will probably be thinned of subjects that were tangential to the Stafford legislative program, but files on the environment, education, handicapped, and other issues important to the senator will be preserved. The Vermont file will be retained in its entirety. Form letters, "Robos," will be retained because they reflect the senator's positions over time. "Requests" and "Acknowledgments" have been discarded because of their low informational value. There was very strong Vermont content in every series in the centralized files, and I found this was also characteristic of similar files in Senator Leahy's office, although to a slightly lesser degree.

The press officer's files included speeches, news clippings (mostly from Vermont newspapers), press releases, newsletters, radio and television scripts, audiotapes, and videotapes. Duplicates, particularly the overlap with state office files, will be discarded, but for the most part these files will be retained in total. Researchers, particularly students, find press files very useful.

The three legislative assistants considered themselves professional staff. They maintained the working files on legislation that came before the senator's committees. These files included virtual legislative histories of bills. All three LAs maintained large reference files of printed matter, including books, documents, and reports. I considered keeping this material with the collection but have decided that it would be more useful if added to the general library collections. A list of publications removed will be placed with the files of the LAs.

The LAs shipped some files to the senator's attic in the Russell building but retained most files as their own property. They were surprised that I was interested in their files as part of the senator's papers, and it took some convincing before they agreed to relinquish them. It took time to build my credibility. I tagged along with the LAs when they accompanied the senator to committee meetings or hearings and showed an interest in their work. Legislative assistants are often subject specialists, and as they move from job to job, they want to take their files with them. In some cases, they believe the files are too confidential because they document confidential maneuvering. Stafford's AA was surprised that I wanted the files of the LAs and warned that their opinions were not necessarily the same as the senator's. I assured him that these files would be maintained as a separate satellite series and clearly identified as advisory. (Many congressional collections arrive at repositories without the files of the legislative assistants.)

I kept a daily journal to mark progress, prepared regular oral and written reports for the AA, and made recommendations for the disposition of retrospective files based on the guidelines outline in Karen Paul's *Handbook*.[20] I actually copied the section of the handbook that pertained to each staff member and used this as a primer for interviews regarding the person's role in the office and the files produced. This printed authority gave my requests more credence.

THE VERMONT OFFICES

Both senators maintained offices in Vermont as well as in Washington, and there I followed the same procedures for file review and staff interviews. Files in Stafford's state offices differed somewhat from Leahy's. Leahy's Vermont staff do all of the Vermont casework, most of the grants and projects, particularly municipal ones, and serve as the front line in the famous Leahy outreach program. Stafford's state staff did some of these things on a much smaller scale; casework, however, was done by Washington staff. The state staff was very small; it served as an outpost and a campaign base.[21] Staff monitored Vermont issues in detail, collected information on active state politicians, particularly potential opponents from either party, and served the local community as specialists on the federal government. I identified over 25 feet of historical records from Stafford's Rutland office alone, including important papers that document the senator's campaigns for attorney general, lieutenant governor, and governor, all previously thought lost. State office staff act somewhat independently from the main Washington staff, and often there is little accountability in terms of records. Few state office files were deposited with the Prouty and Aiken papers, so we have little idea how these important offices worked for them.

The collection was beginning to take shape. The core would be composed of Stafford's personal files, the central office files, and the press files. These would be flanked by the files of the legislative assistants, including some committee records, and the records from the state offices. The operational integrity of each part of the office would be reflected in the integrity of its files. I would not have been as aware of this model if I had not been a member of the senator's staff.

The Stafford and Leahy offices functioned differently because one was more centralized than the other. All important information was funneled to Stafford through his AA, usually orally. The youngest and newest LA prepared written reports for the senator, but the other staff were more informal. Leahy's office was decentralized and the AA was not a crony, so there was more need for written reports and summary documents. The AA, for instance, holds full staff meetings every week, works with each LA to set written goals and objectives, and prepares a strategic plan for each session—and all of these summary documents are maintained in the files of the AA.

HISTORY MADE AND PRESERVED

The congressional office tends to focus on tomorrow's headline and the next election. From time to time, someone with a historical perspective must remind the staff that history is being made—and recorded in the documents produced in the office. The systematic transfer of records to a federal records center or a repository can promote orderliness. Stafford's records were in better shape than Leahy's because of the centralized office and the larger clerical staff. It was more important for me to spend time with each record producer in Leahy's office to encourage them to list files at the end of each session, box them, and transfer them to storage. Most understood the wisdom of such a practice when it was outlined for them.

There were lost chances to preserve history in both offices. Senator Leahy kept an irregular journal that will be very important, but his secretary dismantled his daily briefing book at the end of each briefing session. I hope I persuaded her to copy the contents before the action documents were distributed to staff. These documents were probably preserved in the files of the senator's assistants, but only in the briefing book were they gathered together. Historians would find it invaluable to know how a senator was briefed each day. An archivist *en scene* can advise staff on these important practices.

I think it is important for each records person in a member's office to actually *see* an archivist, so I made it a point to interview as many of them as I possibly could. These interviews gave me an understanding of the office, the kinds of documentation produced, and the recordkeeping problems. I suggested that the member make it official policy that all records produced by staff on the senator's payroll become part of the senator's papers, and that no records be taken from the office when a staff member leaves unless copies are made. I recommended that committee staff copy the office, within reason, on files that showed the senator's personal involvement, and noted that those committee staff who also serve the LA function were responsible for documenting their activities on both sides of the aisle. I was in the position to stress early and regular microfilming for selected files such as clippings.

The repository gained as well. The more time the archivist spends in the office of the member, the better the archivist will understand the collection. Most of Stafford's papers were in series when they arrived at the university, and this facilitated both processing and use. Less than a year after his retire-ment, the History Department was able to take advantage of the availability of the papers, and of the senator himself, for a course on Stafford. This early use of the material helped to familiarize me with the kinds of documenta-tion needed by graduate and undergraduate students. Clippings, briefing documents, and speech files were heavily used, together with published sources such as the *Congressional Record*, Senate and House documents, and the *Congressional Quarterly.*

Both Aronsson and Paul recommend early contact between the member and the repository for all of the reasons described above. Such contact should result in significant reduction in the volume of records received, particularly if the repository has a well-thought-out collecting policy for congressional papers. Aronsson also suggests cooperative collecting based on a subject approach among institutions, and this may work in special cir-cumstances.[22] Karen Paul embarked on a documentation strategy approach to collecting congressional papers, and on a much-needed national survey on the use of these collections. That survey, case studies like this one, and perhaps other research yet unpublished can all contribute to resolution of the twentieth-century dilemma of the "crescendo of volume" in modern congressional records.

NOTES

1. J. Kevin Graffagnino, *Vermont Historical Resources: The Manuscript Holdings of the Wilbur Collection, University of Vermont* (Burlington, Vt.: Special Collections, Bai-ley/Howe Library, University of Vermont, 1986).

2. Lydia Lucas describes the phenomenal growth ("crescendo of volume") in congressional collections since World War II in "Managing Congressional Papers: A Repository View," *American Archivist* 41 (July 1978): 275–76.

3. L. Rebecca Johnson, *Guide to the Papers of Senator John J. Williams of Delaware* (Newark: University of Delaware Library, 1990), 27.

4. *Congressional Papers Project Report Sponsored by the Dirksen Congressional Center and the National Historical Publications and Records Commission, July 15–November 15, 1985* (Washington, D.C.: NHPRC and Dirksen Congressional Leadership Research Center, 1986). Project director, Frank H. Mackaman.

5. The Society of American Archivists Congressional Papers Roundtable was established in 1986.

6. See Robert E. Blesse, "University of Nevada, Reno Acquires Laxalt Papers," *Sen-ate History* 10 (May 1985): 2.

7. Patricia Aronsson, "Appraisal of Twentieth Century Congressional Collec-tions," in *Archival Choices*, ed. Nancy E. Peace (Lexington, Mass.: D. C. Heath, 1984), 83–84.

8. Blesse, "Laxalt Papers," 2.

9. Robert T. Stafford et al., *How to End the Draft* (Washington, D.C.: National Press, 1967).

10. Karen Dawley Paul, *Records Management Handbook for United States Senators and Their Repositories* (Washington, D.C.: U.S. Senate, 1985). This is the most useful single guide for the appraisal of senatorial papers.

11. Carla Kemp of the University of Florida was helping to close the office of Senator Lawton Chiles (D-FL), and Jane Odom was working on the files of Senator Lloyd M. Bentsen (D-TX).

12. Aronsson describes the functioning of a typical congressional office and its standard record series, "Appraisal," 84–86. Paul arranges record series by function and presents a guide for appraisal, *Records Management Handbook*, 4–21.

13. Richard Baker describes the division between legislative and constituent service staff in "Managing Congressional Papers: A View of the Senate," *American Archivist* 41 (July 1978): 292.

14. Stafford used the same LA for LHR and Veteran Affairs.

15. Official committee files will be weeded from Stafford's personal education files, and these will be sent to the National Archives.

16. Aronsson, "Appraisal," 87.

17. Leahy maintained an automated file (CMS) for constituent mail that included incoming and outgoing correspondence arranged chronologically and indexed by name, subject, and county of origin. Staff could print out summary lists by any of these categories for specified periods of time.

18. The Microfilm Office had one planetary camera, but members had to provide staff.

19. "Fat files" are files with extensive correspondence on a particular issue. The assumption is that larger files are more interesting and important because they have consumed more time and effort on the part of the staff. Frank H. Mackaman makes a good case for the preservation of congressional case files in "Managing Case Files in Congressional Collections: The Hazard of Prophecy," *Midwestern Archivist* 4 (1979): 95–104.

20. Paul, *Records Management Handbook*, 4–22.

21. All of Leahy's campaign files were stored in Washington.

22. Aronsson, "Appraisal," 98–99.

4

Collection Policies at State Archives for Legislators' Papers

Sara Roberson Kuzak

While professional standards and theory exist to guide archivists through basic archival processes, there remain stark differences in overall acquisition practices and collecting policies between similar types of archival institutions. The consequence is uneven documentation of broad subject areas and record types, and this is especially true for the papers of state legislators. A sample survey of collecting policies for legislators' papers at state archives illustrates this point:

Sara Roberson, Master's Candidate, Public History
California State University, Sacramento

Questionnaire: State Archives' Legislators' Records Policies
Please respond by July 15, 2005.

1. Does the State Archives have a Legislative records program?
2. If so, what are the Archives' collection and processing policies for Legislative records?
3. Is this information presented in detail online?

If yes, what is the Web address? If this information is not available on the Web, can you send me a copy vie e-mail or by standard post? (I will reimburse you for postage and photocopies.)

(continued)

Please review the following questions. If this information is not included in a collection management or processing manual, please answer the following questions in as much detail as possible.

1. Are state legislators required to send their files to the State Archives, or is it voluntary?
2. If it is mandated, which State Code and section mandate this transfer?
4. If they are not required to come to the Archives, where do they go?
5. How regularly are these records transferred?
6. What are the most common types and formats of these records? (Examples: files relating to legislation, audio and videotapes, bound volumes, electronic records.)
7. Are there any restrictions on the use of these papers?
8. Does the Archives make these records available to the public before they have been processed?
9. What dictates the order in which the collections are chosen to be processed?
10. What are the processing and accessioning procedures for legislators' collections?
11. What are the common series titles for these collections?
12. What is the most popular series requested by researchers?
13. Are there examples of finding aids for legislators' collections available online?
14. What other types of collections do you receive from the Legislature?

Legislative Committee Records
For the sake of comparison, please answer these questions about legislative committee.

1. Is there a different policy for the records of legislative committees?
2. If yes, which State Code and section mandate this transfer?

Suggestions/Comments

The survey, conducted in July 2005, sought to ascertain whether state archives consider legislators' records to be historically significant, and if so, what is being done to promote their retention, preservation, and accessibility?[1] Does the state archives conduct a state legislators' records program and is it mandatory or voluntary? What types of records are included in the program and what kinds of priorities do they receive?

To collect information about these policies, state archives' Web sites were investigated. Some sites present detailed, comprehensive collection policy statements. Other state archives do not have a Web site of any kind. Most of the states fall somewhere in between the two extremes. However, the vast majority of Web sites make no mention of legislators' records in their collections.

Accordingly, a brief questionnaire was composed to gather more specific and consistent data from state archives. A probing e-mail sent to the Archives & Archivists listserv explained the project and asked archivists from state archives to volunteer to answer the questionnaire. Archivists from the states of Texas, Idaho, Vermont, New York, Massachusetts, and Minnesota responded. This paper summarizes their responses, includes information found on the Internet, and incorporates information from the California State Archives legislators' records program.

CALIFORNIA

The California State Archives was created by the legislature on January 5, 1850, and placed under the secretary of state's office. Its holdings from the state legislature are by far the sources most frequently consulted by researchers due to the fact that "legislative intent" is permissible evidence in court. Attorneys consult legislative bill files to determine how the legislature intended a bill to be interpreted. In 1975, the legislature passed the California Legislative Open Records Act premised on the idea that "access to information concerning the conduct of the people's business by the Legislature is a fundamental and necessary right of every citizen in this state." This was certainly a progressive concept; in later amendments, legislators intentionally defined a legislative record "as records contained in an official committee file" and excluded their own records from disclosure.[2] The Legislative Open Records Act divided California's legislative records into two groups: the public legislative committee records and the private legislator's records, a practice which mirrors the public versus private ownership of congressional committee records and personal papers created by members of Congress. As a result, the California State Archives adopted and implemented two separate methods to process and handle legislative records, one for committees and one for legislators. To maintain consistency in handling the unique private papers of legislators, the state archives produced an acquisition and management policy manual, which details how a legislator's records can be accessioned, restricted, and processed.

Some members of the legislature choose to deposit their papers in the state archives, others donate them to a special collections department of an alma mater, and others simply destroy them. As a result, the California State Archives legislators' papers collection is far from comprehensive.

Archives staff regularly visit the state capitol to brief legislators and their staffs on the benefits and importance of donating their records to the State Archives. As a result of these efforts, the number of legislators' papers collections maintained at the State Archives continues to grow.[3]

After a legislator transfers his or her papers to the California State Archives, they remain restricted for the duration of their term in office and can continue to be restricted until a deed of gift is signed stating that the records can be opened for public use. This provision has reduced some of the concern legislators have about their records being opened to the public at any point in their political career. Once a deed of gift is signed and the papers are opened, the State Archives can then appraise and process them.

In California, the bill files series is the most significant series in a legislator's papers. A bill file is created for every piece of legislation a senator or assembly member introduces to the legislature. Bill files can contain committee and caucus analyses, amendments, governor's letters, correspondence, support and opposition letters from interested parties and constituents, background information on the subject matter of the bill, legislative counsel opinions, notes, and newspaper clippings collected as the bill proceeded through the legislature. Lawyers and legislative intent research companies use bill files on a daily basis.

MINNESOTA

In other states, the legal distinction between private and public records mandates the physical separation of those records and prohibits the state archives from receiving private records. According to archivist Charles Rodgers of the Minnesota Historical Society, Minnesota, like California, legally differentiates between the "official records of the Legislature, and the personal records of state legislators." Official records include "tape recordings . . . minute books, and selected committee records of the Legislature," and Minnesota Statute section 138.17 requires that the records of the state legislature be transferred to the state archives. The Minnesota State Archives, which preserves public government records, is a division of the Minnesota Historical Society, a private nonprofit organization. In addition to the public archives, the Minnesota Historical Society also maintains private manuscript collections. Minnesota legislators can donate their private records to the Minnesota Historical Society for preservation or they may donate them to "a county or local historical society, or other repository." Rodgers also pointed out that the collection and processing of legislators' papers is a low priority for the Historical Society, perhaps the reason legislators choose to send their papers elsewhere.[4]

VERMONT

Though developed individually, the subjective and informal collection policies governing state legislators' records in Vermont and New York have similarities in their logic and implementation. According to Vermont State Archivist Gregory Sanford, Vermont maintains relatively structured collection and records management programs that require legislative committee records, original acts, oaths of office, and legislative counsel records to be sent to the archives for permanent preservation. Once the records are accessioned, the Vermont State Archives processes each collection according to established institutional standards and guidelines. However, as Sanford stated, "there is no formal program for acquiring the records of legislators, though the Archives has very occasionally sought and/or accessioned such records." Vermont's selective accessioning depends on the extent of a legislator's involvement in historical legislative issues. The State Archives also solicits certain legislators to donate their papers if they were associated with a particular committee and their papers might supplement those of the committee. In addition, the Archives seeks to collect the papers of the Vermont legislature's House speakers, because they have the ability to show legislative processes, such as the assignment of bills to committees and the marshalling of support for a particular bill. Sanford believes that concerns about confidential information in a legislator's personal e-mail and constituent correspondence are the primary reasons that legislators do not donate their records to the State Archives.[5]

Still, Vermont has collected a wide range of materials created by legislators. These range from a scrapbook of newspaper clippings compiled by a legislator during the 1930s to a collection of photographs taken by a member from his seat in the House during the 1970s. The majority of legislators' records is in paper form and can include "data on the legislator's special interests, models from other states or organizations, bill drafts, and correspondence." Due to the "idiosyncrasy" of the collections, the Vermont State Archives does not have an established processing procedure for legislators' papers. However, the absence of special procedure has not prohibited the State Archives from processing and describing in an inventory every collection of legislator's papers received thus far.

During the summer of 2005, the Vermont State Archives began to investigate which legislative records are the most useful for determining legislative intent and plan to refine their collecting policies to include records specific to this task. Sanford noted, however, that "the records of individual legislators are outside that primary goal and are not being considered in this survey" because the Vermont Supreme Court does not use them to determine intent.[6] An evaluation of the content and research use of legislators' records and a strict interpretation of institutional mission have led the Vermont State Archives to conclude that the historical and legal value of the papers of their individual legislators is minimal.

NEW YORK

The New York State Archives legislators' records policies are similar to those of Vermont. Archivist Bob McDonnell of the New York State Archives Government Records Services explained that his state selects a legislator's records according to "merit." The State Archives encourages legislators to donate their papers only when that individual has played an important leadership role or when their papers contain extensive information on a particular subject. McDonnell bluntly added, "The State Archives generally does not accept papers of rank-and-file legislators." McDonnell also noted, "we have no specific document that summarizes our acquisition policies for the state legislature."[7] Unfortunately, a lack of written policy is not uncommon in archival institutions, as decisions likely depend on a multitude of variables specific to each collection.

One important variable is the willingness of the creator to transfer his or her records to the State Archives. Even though New York state law allows the State Archives to review inactive legislative committee records and administrative files, the transfer of those records to the Archives is still dependent on the committee's cooperation. As McDonnell noted, the Archives can only "encourage" that transfer. McDonnell explained that these legislative records, which can include transcripts and floor debates, are important for legislative intent researchers. However, McDonnell also stated, "there is no particular researcher demand for papers of individual legislators." In the same paragraph, McDonnell apparently reconsidered and added: "researchers might be interested in papers of a legislator who was involved in drafting or promoting a particular legislative item." As in most states where the State Archives does not solicit legislator's papers, the papers sometimes are donated to historical societies, institutions of higher education, or other repositories. And although McDonnell believes that most records are destroyed or retained privately by the legislator, the fact that some are preserved at a variety of repositories tends to imply that some curators and archivists believe they have historical value. Regardless of this fact, the New York State Archives maintains selective collections of only prominent and highly visible state legislators.[8]

In 2003, the M. E. Grenander Department of Special Collections and Archives at the State University of New York, Albany, determined to expand its 30-year-old public affairs and policy archives to include the personal papers of public servants and individuals who have had a significant impact on New York State politics and government, at the local, state, and national level, and the personal papers of local, state, and national legislators of significance. The New York State Modern Political Archive was established. Its holdings grew significantly when, in 2006, Syracuse University transferred all of its political collections to the Modern Political Archive.[9]

MASSACHUSETTS

Massachusetts operates under a similar selective acquisition policy. In Massachusetts, no legislative records are considered public records. However, according to Martha Clark, curator at the Massachusetts Archives, some legislative committees started sending their records to the Archives several years ago because of a records management initiative and "an acute lack of space in the State House." Since then, many committees have regularly sent their records to the Archives following this "tradition." This informal accessioning of committee records is coupled with a policy of not accepting legislators' papers "unless they provide compelling documentation on a legislative committee." Again, the inherent research value of the materials determines whether legislators' records are accessioned, and the collections are evaluated for how strongly they complement other legislative records.[10]

In 2006, Betsy McGovern, chief of Special Collections, State Library of Massachusetts, announced the development of a brochure for managing the donation of legislators' papers.[11] Entitled *Your Records: Your Legacy: Evaluating, Selecting, and Preparing Your Records for Donation*, the guidelines detail the types of records that should be retained and suggest organizations that may be interested in receiving them, the State Library being one of several. Wondering whether the brochure might generate a response that could overwhelm the institution and its staff, she asked members of the Archives & Archivists listserv for comments regarding possible selection criteria for legislative collections. The ensuing discussion on January 9–10, 2007, revealed a diversity of opinions concerning selective retention of legislators' papers and an absence of widely accepted definitive criteria for selection. There was general agreement among those who participated in the discussion that such selection criteria could include the following factors: length of service, committee service, causes championed, locality represented (rural vs. urban), and the degree to which a collection documents issues and concerns of the state. However, no specific formula was offered.

While appraisal criteria were not the focus of the online discussion, the topic was touched on in remarks by Dean DeBolt, university librarian, Special Collections, University of West Florida, who advocated "aggressive processing" of legislators' collections as a way to cope with a potential overload of donations. As an example, he mentioned that in his view, state-generated documents and reports and newsletters from special interest groups are prime targets for "weeding," unless there is some major compelling reason to retain a particular set. In response, Jennie Levine, curator for historical manuscripts at the University of Maryland, said, "For us, all of those state documents and miscellaneous newsletters from the PTA and Boy Scouts and so on have been extremely helpful in filling out our gaps in our state document holdings. So sometimes we just redistribute things a little bit."[12] Perhaps this variation in specific appraisal values reflects the variations in assessing the values of legislators' collections as a category of documentation.

IDAHO

The Idaho Public Archives and Research Library is in a difficult situation with regard to the records of their state legislators. There is no doubt that state archivist and state historic records coordinator Steven Walker believes strongly in the importance of legislators' records. In fact, Walker is adamant that legislators' records should be preserved at the Idaho Public Archives according to the Idaho Public Records Law (Idaho Code, sections 9-337 through 9-350). However, this statute lacks an enforcement provision to regulate the proper management and transfer of these records to the Archives. As a result, the Idaho Public Archives has received very few legislators' papers. The few collections they do posses primarily consist of files of textual documents relating to legislation. Because of the infrequency of records transfers, there is no special accessioning or processing procedure, and legislators' files are processed in the same manner as other government records through an evaluation during accessioning of condition, format, frequency of requests, and completeness.[13]

TEXAS

In comparison to the informal policies of the state archives described above, Texas has one of the most organized, comprehensive, and explicit plans for legislators' records and therefore will be reviewed in detail. In Texas, legislators' records are public records and must be preserved in an archival repository. According to the Texas State Library and Archives Commission Web site, it has the authority to "take custody of, preserve, and make available for public use state records and other historical resources that document the history and culture of Texas" under Texas Government Code, section 441.006. This legal authority allows the Texas State Library and Archives

Commission to determine that "records produced by the Texas Legislature, particularly the records of individual legislators, committees, and administrative arms" are essential to the understanding of the development of Texas law and government.[14] It is significant to note that, in this survey, Texas is the only state which unquestionably considers legislators' records to be public records and collects them systematically.

The individual records within these general categories can vary greatly from legislature to legislature. However, archivists at the Texas State Library and Archives Commission identify the records that they believe are important. The commission defines important records as the "correspondence, memoranda, committee hearing and background files, legislative bill files, press releases, speeches, subject/research files, news clippings, reports, publications, schedules, legal documents, notes, newsletters, photographic media, and audio, video, and electronic media collected, created, or maintained in the course of conducting public business during the legislators' terms of office." With such a specific list, Texas ensures retention of richer and more complete legislative collections.[15]

The Texas State Library and Archives Commission receives legislative records in a variety of ways. Records from the Texas House of Representatives are regularly scheduled on an approved records retention schedule, which is compiled by the House records management officer. A retention schedule that is properly filled out by the legislator's staff facilitates the transfer of the legal and physical custody of the records to the state Archives. The Texas House of Representatives Records Retention Schedule indicates that a legislator's records must be transferred within three years after the legislator's final term. With such a specific and direct retention schedule, all parties involved are well aware of the state's policy. While the Texas senate did not have an approved retention schedule as of October 2004, it does have a professional records manager who assists the senators, committees, and staff with the transfer of their records.[16]

Legislators often desire to deposit their papers in the place where they were born and grew up or where they attended college. Texas's flexible program accommodates requests by legislators to have their records transferred to a different Texas depository. The Texas State Library and Archives Commission maintains a list of designated regional historical resource depositories at which legislators' records can be deposited, while legal ownership remains with the Texas State Library and Archives Commission. These depositories include private and public Texas universities such as Baylor University, Texas A&M University, and the University of Texas; municipal public libraries; and the libraries at a few select junior colleges. The value of having all legislators' records at one depository is outweighed by the value of having a more equitable distribution of the records across the state, thereby increasing public access and satisfying the desires of legislators.[17]

Texas's program is mainly concerned with obtaining informational value from documents in the form of paper. While they do accept audio and video recordings of committee hearings, Texas policy explicitly states its inability to accept electronic records. They ask that permanently valuable electronic documents be printed onto paper. When this is not feasible, for example with large databases, the creators are required to retain the database as well as the technology required to retrieve the electronic information.[18]

Details of this program are publicized on the official Web site. In fact, when Carolyn Foster, the assistant director for state archives, Archives and Information Services Division of the Texas State Library and Archives Commission, responded to the questionnaire, she immediately referred to the Web site for collection policy questions and then only briefly answered some of the more specific processing questions.[19] By making their policies widely known to the record creators and the general public, they encourage preservation and facilitate research use of the materials. By following through on the institutional mission to "preserve Texas history and culture," and specifically the "development of Texas law and government," the commission has created a model by which all other state archives may be compared.[20]

GENERAL CONCLUSIONS

With only six responses from 50 states and a review of California's program, this survey is not comprehensive; however, it does reveal some general points. Archivists expressed a desire to preserve legislators' records but have been limited in one way or another from achieving their goal. The primary obstacle inhibiting the implementation of legislators' records programs is the legal definition of legislators' records as private records. As a consequence, they are either ineligible for permanent retention at the state archives or they are accepted only as a voluntary donation. In instances where state law mandates that legislators' records be sent to the state archives, a lack of political support prevents the archives from forcing legislators to follow the law. The absence of a strong program in turn leads to a dearth of researcher demand. This causes archivists to place a low priority on the research value of legislators' papers, and thus the cycle is perpetuated. The survey also revealed that "traditions" play a role in how state archives manage legislators' papers, and that the role of such traditions has not necessarily been conducive to the preservation of a complete legislative record. The uncertainty that archivists share with regard to the value of legislators' records was perhaps mirrored by the lack of responses received to the survey. That the existing situation can be much different is demonstrated by the Texas and California examples.

In some states, the lack of academic, legal, or political research interest in state legislators' papers coupled with limited funds and staff forced state archives to refuse these records and refer the donors to other institutions. However, it is also the case that some archivists do not see the importance of preserving these records. Archivists share a generally low regard for the research and educational value of legislators' records. Several archivists mentioned that committee files had importance because of their usefulness in determining legislative intent, yet they did not see this same usefulness in legislators' records. Neither did they comment specifically on the value of legislators' papers for reflecting issues of concern to state citizens. The fact that the quality of files maintained by legislators varies so much seems to have lessened archivists' overall assessment of their research value.

Archivists will always maintain differing opinions about collection development and appraisal policies because they must factor in institutional mission statements, financial support, space requirements, and essential prioritization. Unfortunately, in the case of state legislators' records, it seems to be less a matter of these basic considerations than an overall lack of experience with this resource. This in turn has led to undervaluing them for research and education, and has prevented archivists from systematically seeking to acquire and preserve them. Archivists are urged to survey state legislators' records as an important resource, and to implement formal and structured appraisal and acquisition policies. Only when this happens will a more complete and balanced legislative historical record be preserved.

NOTES

1. This chapter originated as a thesis chapter for a master of arts degree in public history, May 2005, California State University, Sacramento.
2. California, Legislative Open Records Act, Government Code (1975, 1996), sec. 9070-80.
3. Kathryn E. Haley, "The Historical Value of Legislative Records at the California State Archives: The Papers of Senator Patrick Johnston" (master's thesis, California State University, Sacramento, 2004), 23; e-mail from Nancy Zimmelman in possession of author, sent April 12, 2005.
4. Charles Rodgers, Minnesota Historical Society, response to questionnaire, July 2005.
5. Gregory Sanford, Vermont State Archives, response to questionnaire, July 2005.
6. Sanford, response to questionnaire, July 2005.
7. Bob McDonnell, New York State Archives, response to questionnaire, July 2005.
8. McDonnell, response to questionnaire, July 2005.
9. M. E. Grenander Department of Special Collections and Archives, "Collection Development Policy," Active Collections, C.2., Archives of Public Affairs and Policy,

http://library.albany.edu/speccoll/cdp.htm; and Karen Dawley Paul, telephone interview with Brian Keough, curator of manuscripts, New York Modern Political Archive, 25 April 2007.

10. Martha Clark, Massachusetts Archives, response to questionnaire, July 2005.

11. Betsy McGovern, "Collecting the Papers of State Legislators," Archives & Archivists List, www.archivists.org/listservs (9 Jan. 2007).

12. Dean DeBolt and Jennie Levine, Archives & Archivists listserv (9 and 10 Jan. 2007).

13. Steven A. Walker, Idaho Public Archives and Research Library, response to questionnaire, July 2005.

14. Texas State Library and Archives Commission, "The State Archives Answers FAQs for Legislators," www.tsl.state.tx.us/arc/faqforleg/faqindex.html.

15. Texas State Library and Archives Commission, "Legislative Working Files," www.tsl.state.tx.us/arc/faqforleg/workingfiles.html.

16. Texas State Library and Archives Commission, "FAQs for Legislators."

17. Texas State Library and Archives Commission, "FAQs for Legislators."

18. Texas State Library and Archives Commission, "FAQs for Legislators."

19. Carolyn Foster, Texas State Library and Archives Commission, response to questionnaire, July 2005.

20. Texas State Library and Archives Commission, "FAQs for Legislators."

5

A Hint of Scandal:
Problems in Acquiring the
Papers of Herman E. Talmadge

Pam Hackbart-Dean

On May 30, 1994, *Roll Call*, a weekly newspaper for Capitol Hill, boasted an emphatic headline on its front page: "Congress Has Strictest Ethics Rules in World, According to a New CRS Study of 24 Nations." But the ethics of Congress proved less scandalous than the headline for the Thursday edition that same week, which announced in heavy bold type: "Rosty Indicted on 17 Counts." These telling words condemned Representative Dan Rosten-kowski, Democrat of Chicago and chair of the powerful Ways and Means Committee, for his graft charges.[1]

Although junior members of Congress have their allotment of ethical and legal dilemmas, it is the senior members, with the power and contacts of a committee chair or a leadership position, and other highly placed government officials that attract the headlines. And it is the papers of senior members that repositories most vigorously endeavor to collect, because over a lengthy career in Congress or in a high-level appointment, an official amasses papers that document major issues of regional, national, and even international importance—papers that researchers are eager to use.

Hale Boggs, Democrat from Louisiana and formerly a majority leader of the U.S. House of Representatives, characterized Congress as a collection of regular men and women with extraordinary problems.[2] The government of the United States is founded on the belief that any citizen could assume the role of public official. Political leaders are "ordinary people," agreeing to take on the enormous tasks of the government, yet not be corrupted by

Previously published as "A Hint of Scandal: Problems in Acquiring the Papers of U.S. Senator Herman E. Talmadge—A Case Study" in *Provenance: The Journal of the Society of Georgia Archivists* XIII (1995). Reprinted with permission.

Washington politics nor ignore the concerns of their constituents. However, once in office, public officials are placed in the proverbial "glass house." Political leaders are judged ruthlessly for their deficiencies and shortcomings. Congressman William C. Redfield of New York said that the House of Representatives is "probably a fair cross-section of the people, showing us very much as we are and throwing faults and virtues into high relief."[3]

The hint of scandal involving a public figure, whether real or perceived, can overshadow a long and distinguished career. This may involve a person's career that deserves the preservation of his or her papers in a research library. Repository staff must transcend the sensationalism of negative publicity and reassure officials of the long-term significance of their papers, not simply in regard to the official's career but to the study of the American political system.

Lessons can be learned from the experiences of soliciting the papers of a reputedly tarnished individual and funding the processing and housing of these collections, and from donor relations prior to the receipt of the collections for research use. For example, collecting papers is difficult when a senior member of Congress leaves office in disrepute, as in the case of Senator Herman E. Talmadge. The acquisition of his collection, now housed in the Richard B. Russell Library for Political Research and Studies at the University of Georgia, was especially problematic because the Russell Library was not initially involved with the negotiations between the senator and the university. Reaching a gift agreement proved to be a challenging experience for Senator Talmadge and the Russell Library.

It was once said in Georgia that if you were not a Talmadge man, you were a communist.[4] The Talmadge dynasty began in 1926 when Eugene Talmadge, Herman's father, was first elected commissioner of agriculture. Gene Talmadge would later be elected governor of Georgia for an unprecedented four terms. After Eugene Talmadge's death in 1948, Herman Talmadge began his political career—a career that would begin and end in a cloak of controversy with the "two governor conflict" in 1947 and ethics charges in 1978.[5] The Talmadges dominated Georgia politics for over 50 years, until Herman was defeated in 1980.

Herman Talmadge served six years as Georgia's governor and 24 years as a U.S. senator. Talmadge achieved his greatest national prominence through his role on the Senate Select Committee on Presidential Campaign Activities, which investigated the Watergate break-in and ultimately led to the resignation of President Richard M. Nixon and the conviction of three cabinet members on felony charges. Talmadge thought that the Watergate investigation was one of the most important events in the history of the United States because it demonstrated that a republican form of government has a way of correcting the conduct of public officials and alerting others not to make the same mistake.⁶ These sentiments would prove ironic in light of charges made against him a few years later.

At the same time he was gaining national recognition, Talmadge was besieged by a series of personal and political tragedies. In 1975, his son Robert drowned in a swimming accident at Lake Lanier, Georgia. By the fall of 1977, Betty and Herman Talmadge had divorced. Then, in 1978, Talmadge confronted his serious drinking problem. Following an alcohol treatment program at the naval hospital in Long Beach, California, he returned to Washington ready to work. Instead, he was met with accusations of dishonor.

Shortly after returning to Washington in December 1978, Talmadge was notified that the Senate Select Ethics Committee had "substantial credible evidence" that he had violated Senate rules and faced trial-like hearings on these charges.⁷ He was accused of misappropriating office funds and campaign donations for his own personal use.⁸ The case was the first Senate disciplinary proceedings to go to the trial stage since 1967, when the Senate censured Senator Thomas J. Dodd, Democrat from Connecticut. Thirteen years later, the careers of three senators would be shortened by their involvement in the Keating Five case.

By September 1979, the Senate Ethics Committee unanimously recommended that the Senate "denounce" Talmadge for his financial misconduct. He was charged with submitting bogus expense vouchers and diverting campaign funds for personal use through a secret account. The committee rejected a proposal to censure Talmadge. Censure was considered the strongest Senate penalty short of expulsion. The committee stated that Talmadge's conduct "was reprehensible and tended to bring the Senate into dishonor and disrepute."⁹ Yet the committee evaded the question of Talmadge's direct involvement in the financial misconduct. Instead the committee stated that "Talmadge either knew, or should have known, of these improper acts and omissions, and therefore, by the gross neglect of his duty to faithfully and carefully administer the affairs of this office, he is responsible for these acts and omissions."¹⁰

Talmadge proclaimed the committee's action "a personal victory" and said the findings "support my basic contention . . . that I was negligent in the oversight of my office, but that I have committed no intentional wrongdoing."¹¹ By a vote of 81 to 15, with four voting "present," the Senate "denounced" Herman E. Talmadge, and he was required to refund at least $13,000 to the Senate. His administrative assistant, Daniel Minchew, who was a key witness in the Senate investigation, later pled guilty to making false statements to the government. Minchew served time in a federal prison.

Despite the problems surfacing in his fourth Senate term, Talmadge sought reelection in 1980. Many were surprised, especially Talmadge himself, when he was rejected by Georgia voters, Talmadge's only electoral defeat. His 24 years of service in the U.S. Senate had ranked him fifth in seniority among Senate Democrats and seventh overall by the time he left office. Talmadge had gained national recognition during the Watergate investigation and emerged out of the shadows of his controversial father, Eugene Talmadge, and former senior senator from Georgia, Richard B. Russell.

In 1977, a year before the Ethics Committee charges, a $3 million endowment fund was established by the University of Georgia School of Law to honor "the contribution of United States Senator Herman Talmadge and the Talmadge family to the state of Georgia."[12] Several prominent Georgia attorneys had major roles in the fundraising campaign. The endowment was to establish the Talmadge Foundation, encompassing the Dean Rusk Center, the Talmadge Library, a moot courtroom named after Talmadge, and an endowed Talmadge professorial chair in the law school.[13] Another focus of the foundation fund was to increase student scholarship aid in an effort to attract many highly qualified law school applicants.

According to James Dunlap, endowment chair, the fund was established in Talmadge's name "in recognition of his contributions to his state and nation as senator and governor, and the prominent role the Talmadge family has played in the advancement of Georgia, especially in education and economic development."[14] During Talmadge's six years as governor, $275 million worth of new schools and college buildings were constructed. More state money was spent on public schools and colleges than during all previous administrations combined. He continued to support education as a U.S. senator on the Finance Committee by encouraging industrial development in Georgia, which provided additional revenues for public education both at the secondary level and college level.

Talmadge was approached for the fundraising campaign because of his popularity in the state. The University of Georgia law school believed he was a sure way to raise money for them. Although he did not actively solicit money for the law school, he gave his support to the project. Then, during the height of the ethics controversy, it appeared to Talmadge and his supporters that a conscious decision was made by the law school not to proceed with the Talmadge Foundation.[15]

In spite of this apparent decision, Fred Davison, university president, solicited Talmadge's papers in early 1981. The papers, 1,650 boxes or 25 tons of material, arrived at the university later that year and were temporarily stored in the Richard B. Russell Memorial Library. The ultimate disposition of the papers had not been decided; they would either stay at the Russell Library or be placed in a special facility inside the law school. Talmadge had also been approached for his papers by the agriculture school at the university. They, like the law school previously, promised the senator his own library.[16] Neither the law school nor the agriculture school had an archives, nor were they considering developing an archival program for just these papers. The University of Georgia Libraries already had three established special collection departments, which included the Russell Library.

The papers came to the Russell Library initially because Talmadge was very familiar with this particular institution. He was the first chair of the Richard B. Russell Foundation, which established the library in 1974. Senator Russell personally selected Talmadge to be the first chair. Talmadge, according to a former Russell aide, raised over 80 percent of the funds to establish the Russell Foundation.[17] Talmadge attended the dedication of the Russell Library with several of Russell's contemporaries, and he knew of its solid reputation.

Yet it would not be until 1988 that a final decision was made as to where the Talmadge papers would be housed permanently. According to Talmadge's administrative assistant, Rogers Wade, there was no question in Talmadge's mind that if there were no Talmadge Library established in the law school, then the papers were to go to the Russell Library. Although some $2.5 million was raised by the law school project by 1979, the proposed Talmadge Foundation, separate Talmadge Library, and moot courtroom never materialized. Only the Talmadge Chair of Law, established in 1978, exists. It should be noted of the approximate $2.5 million raised by the law school, none was given to the Russell Library to assist in the expense of processing or housing this collection. There is no apparent animosity between Talmadge and the law school, although to this day there is a distinct chill. Talmadge felt used and discarded by the law school, according to his former administrative assistant Wade.[18]

Despite the earlier uncertainty of where the Talmadge papers would ultimately be housed, the Russell Library gladly accepted the official donation of the Talmadge Collection in 1988. The Talmadge Collection fits the mission of the Russell Library, which is to collect the papers of twentieth-century Georgia politicians, elected officials, federal appointees, and political parties and groups. It also complements the Richard B. Russell Collection, the cornerstone collection of the library, in subject matter, date span, and events. Furthermore, these two collections are important because members of the Russell and Talmadge families dominated Georgia politics during the first three-quarters of the twentieth century.

Processing of the Talmadge papers was completed in 1992. In accordance with the Privacy Act of 1974, the only section of the collection that is not available for research use is the case mail. Case mail consists of correspondence from constituents and federal departments or agencies and casework reports. This documents the public official's assistance with constituents and their difficulties related to the federal government. Talmadge has not restricted any section of his papers for research purposes, and no part of his collection has been destroyed. Even sensitive topic files like those on civil rights, Vietnam, Watergate, and transcripts from his ethics trial remain open to the public. The Talmadge Collection consists mainly of official files reflecting the career of the former Georgia governor and U.S. senator. Talmadge himself has been accessible to students and other researchers for interviews on a variety of topics.

A reception honoring Talmadge for the donation of his papers to the Russell Library was held in the spring of 1988. Senator Talmadge was touched by the outpouring of support of old friends and colleagues on that day. Many people from around the state and region attended the reception, much to his delight and surprise. "It was a day that meant more to him [Talmadge] than any other since his defeat in 1980," declared Rogers Wade. "Talmadge is an historian by nature, although he has no understanding of his place in history."[19]

There are numerous other public figures who have left office touched by scandal, and undoubtedly there will be more in the future. Many of these individuals are resentful of their forced retirement from office, whether it is precipitated by the Congress or the electorate. That resentment or resulting distrust of the media and the public can easily impact the acquisition of such collections as well as their subsequent research access.

Acquiring the Talmadge papers was a valuable experience for the staff of the Russell Library. The primary difficulties included not being part of the initial discussions on soliciting these papers and lack of available funding to care for the collection once it was decided where it was to be permanently housed. Being outside the loop hindered the library staff members from making contact with the donor directly. The politics involving three different university areas impeded decisions concerning what was ultimately best for the collection.

An important lesson to follow is to try to participate in the preliminary discussions concerning the acceptance of collections before they are given to one's repository. Today, the Russell Library staff has more leverage to participate in these initial discussions than they did during the period of the Talmadge gift. With over 20 years of successful development, the Russell Library now enjoys a position of strength within the university libraries' administration, and the staff has gained considerable support for the Russell Library's programs and services. The Russell Library, a department within the University of Georgia Libraries, is administratively under the director of libraries.

Equally important is the need for repositories to approach high-ranking public officials at the moment they enter office. By starting a relationship with a public official early in his or her career, a repository ensures a better chance of obtaining that individual's papers. Subsequently, if any problems occur, at least the public official will have given thought to the disposition of his or her papers. In times of crisis, an official's staff may take it upon themselves to make major decisions about the disposition of papers. Fearing damage to a reputation after a lifetime of service, staff aides tend to adopt the attitude: "when in doubt, throw it out."[20] This is a disastrous move for repositories interested in a public official's papers.

Another advantage to working with a public official early in his or her career is the establishment of a trusting relationship with the individual and the staff, and establishing the archivist as someone who is acting in their interest. Organizing their noncurrent records for the reference needs of the office and preserving the history of the accomplishments of the entire staff will validate the importance of these records. In addition, by working with the staff at the beginning, the archivist will be able to document the workflow of the office. This is an important step in understanding the work of an office and will assist in future appraisal and processing decisions. The archivist will also be able to assist with implementing records management, weeding, and storage guidelines. Being able to offer advice on archival and records management should improve the quality of materials saved.[21] This will help prevent hasty decisions from being made in a time of crisis.

A repository should be ready to respond quickly if unfortunate circumstances do arise. When Harrison Williams, the senator from New Jersey, was convicted in the Abscam scandal and left office, he contacted the archivist at Rutgers University to pick up his papers. The archivist was given only 24 hours' notice to collect Williams's papers. Williams has not restricted any of this collection from research, although use has been hindered by lack of funding to process the collection.[22]

The archivist must be prepared for hurt feelings on the part of the donor and for difficulty in raising funds for processing and housing the collection. Although the initial response by researchers may be to study the scandal itself, later they will begin to utilize the entire collection. It is important to obtain these collections and make them available for future use.

While it may be true that bad news tends to get more attention than good, controversy only holds public attention for a very short period of time. It is crucial to emphasize to those public officials affected by disgrace that they should not forget how significant their work has been overall. Since they were elected to hold office by the electorate, every citizen has the right to have access to these papers. It is crucial for the public official to make sure this occurs. "The archivist has a major role to play in guaranteeing that these collections will be as rich and available as possible," asserts Richard Baker, U.S. Senate historian. "The quality of research in the late twentieth-century political history will be determined in large measure by the foresight and initiative of today's archivist."[23] When controversy has touched a public official, archivists must rise above the sensationalism of negative publicity and inform officials of the long-term importance of their papers, not simply in regard to the official's career but to the study of the entire American political system.

NOTES

1. "Collecting Papers of Public Officials," opening remarks at the 58th Annual Meeting of the Society of American Archivists, Indianapolis, Indiana, September 10, 1994.

2. Cokie Roberts, "Why the M.I.A.'s Live On," *New York Times*, September 20, 1991, A19.

3. William C. Redfield, *With Congress and Cabinet* (New York: Doubleday, Page, 1924), 15.

4. Gary Pomerantz, "Herman Talmadge, the 'Late' Senator? He Gets Up at 3:30 in the Morning," *Atlanta Constitution*, December 27, 1992, D11.

5. The "two governor conflict" began in 1946 when Eugene Talmadge was elected governor in the general election. Because he was in failing health, some of his supporters had started a write-in campaign for Herman Talmadge, his son, during the general election. Eugene died in December 1946, before being sworn in as governor. The Georgia General Assembly elected Herman as governor. Outgoing governor Ellis Arnall refused to surrender his office unless it was to the just-elected lieutenant governor, Melvin Thompson. After a period of uncertainty, the Georgia Supreme Court ruled that the constitutional portion under which the General Assembly had elected Herman Talmadge did not apply. The court declared Thompson acting governor until a special election could be held. In September 1947, Talmadge was elected governor. He was reelected in 1950, serving until January 1955.

6. Herman E. Talmadge, *Talmadge: A Political Legacy, a Politician's Life* (Atlanta: Peachtree, 1987), 298.

7. "Senate Ethics Committee Votes for Formal Action in Talmadge Investigation," *Inside Congress*, December 23, 1978, 3493.

8. "Talmadge Opens Own Defense in Ethics Case," *Congressional Quarterly*, May 5, 1979, 828.

9. "Panel Urges Senate 'Denounce' Talmadge," *Congressional Quarterly*, September 15, 1979, 2025.

10. Talmadge, *Talmadge*, 334.

11. Talmadge, *Talmadge*, 334.

12. "Multi-Million Dollar Fund to Honor Talmadge," *Columns/University of Georgia Faculty-Staff News*, October 31, 1977, 1.

13. Rogers Wade, administrative assistant to Herman Talmadge, telephone interview by author, June 1, 1994.

14. "Multi-Million Dollar Fund to Honor Talmadge," 1.

15. Wade, June 1, 1994.

16. Wade, June 1, 1994.

17. Charles Campbell, 1980 campaign manager for Herman Talmadge, interview by author, 26 May 1994.

18. Wade, June 1, 1994.

19. Wade, June 1, 1994.

20. Richard B. Baker, "Managing Congressional Papers: A View of the Senate," *American Archivist* 41 (1978): 295.

21. Susan Goldstein, "Appraising a Retiring Senator's Papers: A View from the Staff of Senator Alan Cranston," *Provenance* 10 (1992): 30–31.

22. Ron Becker, "Beyond Abscam: The Harrison Williams Senatorial Papers," paper delivered at the 58th Annual Meeting of the Society of American Archivists, Indianapolis, Indiana, September 10, 1994.

23. Becker, "Beyond Abscam."

Part II

DOCUMENTING CONGRESS

6

The Documentation of Congress: Summary Report and Recommendations

Karen Dawley Paul

THE PROBLEM

The historical records of the U.S. Congress are the building blocks of legislative histories. They are used to evaluate past legislation and to develop new legislation. Historians and political scientists rely on them to tell the story of the development and intent of public policy and to study the democratic process. When combined with records of the executive and judicial branches, they form the basis of our national history.

Historical records do not simply materialize. They must be identified amidst the vast amounts of material that have little historical or intrinsic value. Documents need to be selected for archival preservation based on an evaluation of their uniqueness as information sources, the usefulness of their format, and their research importance. Once identified, they need to be described, preserved, and made available for research purposes. All of these activities require time, effort, and funds. Over the past decade, congressional collections archivists have become increasingly alarmed about the growing volume of these materials and their lack of richness and consistency. Their overall research usefulness has been seriously questioned.

The effort to make congressional primary source material accessible is further complicated because committee records are "official" and are governed by statute and the internal rules of each body, while the records of members' offices are "private" and depend on the widely varying administrative wishes of each member. Although these are vital and complementary information

Previously published in *The Documentation of Congress: Report of the Congressional Archivists Roundtable Task Force on Congressional Documentation*, S. Pub. 102-20, 1–16.

sources, they are not administered in a uniform manner. In addition, many other important "congressional" materials fall outside either of these two major recordkeeping traditions.

Further complications result from the fact that Congress has grown dramatically over the past half-century. Although the legislative branch now includes five major support agencies, very little has been done to evaluate the records of these agencies and to determine how they supplement the "official" records of Congress.

Another problem stems from the information explosion and the computer and telecommunications revolutions that have conspired to create even larger quantities of records, not fewer, as many originally thought. Locating information of lasting value has become more difficult, and preserving it in a form that will be accessible in the future despite changes in technology poses some tricky problems.

A final major challenge to establishing a strong body of congressional documentation derives from the democratic nature of Congress and its need to interact extensively with the executive and judicial branches and with the legions of interest groups outside of government. The records of these "significant others" have never to our knowledge been systematically evaluated to determine their value in telling the history of Congress and public policy.

As a result, congressional documentation is geographically scattered and administratively fragmented, and its overall strength is difficult to evaluate. Even archivists who work with congressional collections generally have little conception of the scope of available sources and how they fit together. Without this knowledge, archival appraisal has become exceedingly difficult, preventing archivists from serving as truly effective teachers of congressional research methodology and strategy.

With these concerns in mind, the Task Force on Congressional Documentation of the Society of American Archivists' Congressional Archivists Roundtable conducted a study to determine ways to address the effects of documentary fragmentation and loss. The study and its findings are delineated in the full body of the group's report.[1] The principal recommendations are summarized below.

MAJOR AUTHORITIES

Central to this plan for coordinated action is the recognition that three primary authorities are responsible for preserving the records that document the legislative branch:

First, the members and officials of Congress are individually responsible for the on-site management of the information that is collected and maintained in their offices. Each member of Congress determines the archival disposition of his or her personal office records. The secretary of the Senate and clerk of the House are directly responsible for administering the collection of official records for their respective houses and for overseeing their transfer to the National Archives.

Second, the Center for Legislative Archives at the National Archives preserves and provides access to the official records of Congress.

Third, literally hundreds of archival repositories across the country preserve and provide access to the personal papers that are deposited in them by the members.

The analysis and recommendations embodied in this report represent a comprehensive, coordinated approach that recognizes the interests and responsibilities of these three groups. Participation by all three is vital for the successful, cost-effective preservation of the historical records of Congress.

MAJOR FINDINGS

The task force systematically identified and evaluated the status of relevant sources of archival information about Congress. It found:

1. While congressional committees are relatively, although not uniformly, well documented, there is great variation in the documentary quality of individual members' collections. This variation is the result of uneven administration of collections in Washington, lack of planning, and lack of resources at some state repositories. The identification and preservation of records of enduring value in congressional committees and in members' offices need to be strengthened in certain specific areas discussed below.

2. Of the five major congressional support agencies, only one, the Government Accountability Office (formerly known as the General Accounting Office), has a comprehensive, though uneven, records management program. While two agencies, the Office of Technology Assessment and the Government Printing Office, have partial programs, two others, the Congressional Research Service and the Congressional Budget Office, have none. Despite the fact that these agencies provide vital information and services to Congress and play major roles in developing legislation, conducting investigations, and ensuring oversight, there exists no coordinated information retention plan that meets the long-term needs of Congress and that helps to complete the historical record of the legislative branch.

3. Records of the executive and judicial branches that document Congress are either under very good control, as in the instance of the presidential libraries, or are on the way to substantial improvements due to new historical and archival initiatives aimed at improving the preservation of the official records of the courts and the personal papers of judges. Most of these are outside the direct responsibility of the Congress but are nevertheless

within the collection and preservation interests of one or possibly two of the other major authorities, the Center for Legislative Archives or specialized individual repositories in the states.

4. Other sources enjoy varying degrees of archival management and accessibility. They include those of the national, congressional, and individual campaign committees; the political party organizations; and the congressional member organizations and caucuses. To these must be added the significant "outside" groups that interact with Congress in an integral way—the Capitol Hill press corps, the lobbyists, and the "think tanks." All are linked inextricably with the history of legislation, politics, and the progress of a democratic society. Yet they have been largely overlooked by the major congressional archival repositories as important sources for documenting Congress.

5. Individuals who use congressional collections find them to be the most valuable source of information for biographical and public policy studies, but many of the collections are difficult to use. For example, academic researchers seek improvements in access through better indexing, more detailed descriptions, standardization of finding aids, and microfilm publication of important sequences so that scholars may access them through interlibrary loan.

6. Many important collections remain unprocessed due to lack of resources on the part of the archival repository. While many members of Congress assume responsibility for processing their collections while in Washington, D.C., many more members need to add professional archival expertise to their staffs. Given the quantity of material that accumulates in an office, continuous identification and selection of potential archival materials is the only cost-effective way to ensure that information of long-term value will be preserved.

METHODOLOGY

Task force members first established a working definition of the "functions" of Congress and then identified the sources that document each function. The functional definitions are included in the full body of this report, in order to establish a framework for analyses. This approach was chosen deliberately to avoid studying the problem in the traditional way, by concentrating on collections that have already found their way into archives. Instead, the team members began by asking, "What does Congress do and what sources document what Congress does?" The answers revealed a much more complex and detailed picture of congressional information.

The sources identified were examined through an evaluation of specific holdings, through surveys, through interviews with knowledgeable individuals, and by a review of relevant literature. In addition, a survey was conducted during 1991 to determine what records researchers use and which they judge to be most "useful." When the survey results were combined with the results of the documentation study, a detailed and specific action plan emerged.

RECOMMENDATIONS

This report is compiled as a working document to guide the plans and activities of those who share responsibility for and interest in the history of Congress, public policy, and democratic government. To improve the documentation of Congress and the legislative branch, the project members make the following recommendations.

Full discussion of these points may be found in pertinent sections of the complete report.

LEGISLATIVE DOCUMENTATION

The archives of Congress have always been preserved for the purpose of documenting the development of legislation, the oversight of executive agencies, the review of nominations and treaties, and the conduct of impeachment proceedings. The main sources of documentation are committee records and members' papers. Because of the growth in the size and complexity of these collections, congressional staff and archivists need to improve their understanding of what constitutes archival material and to develop the management skills to ensure its preservation. Implementation of the following recommendations will help to create and preserve a more comprehensive, more efficient, and more useful historical record.

1. *Records management programs and guidelines.* Authorities in both houses of Congress, with assistance from the Center for Legislative Archives, should develop strong records management programs through publications and seminars. Publications should include records management and disposition guidelines for members' offices and for congressional committees. A handbook has been produced for senators, but similar guidance does not exist for members of the House. The handbooks currently available for House and Senate committees should be reviewed for thoroughness and updated regularly.

The handbooks should be supplemented by pamphlets or information papers that highlight specific topics such as records ownership and disposition, the appraisal and disposition of electronic records, including information transmitted by electronic mail, the administration of and access to sensitive materials in the office and in the repository, and the care of fragile media. The pamphlets should be designed as handouts for all staff, while the handbooks present in-depth information for office managers and committee chief clerks.

Seminars should cover records management issues in setting up an office and records disposition for offices that are closing. The House and Senate should collaborate to produce joint records management and disposition guidelines for joint committees which at present have none. The Center for Legislative Archives should encourage the transfer of committee records to the archives and should identify gaps in the holdings where additional acquisition efforts must be made.

2. *House archivist.* The House of Representatives should establish a position of professional archivist to oversee the disposition of committee records and to assist members with matters of records management and disposition.

3. *Survey of members.* The Senate and House archivists should conduct a survey of all members of Congress to ascertain which and how many have designated repositories to receive their papers. Such a survey would produce useful information for shaping the congressional records management and archival programs. It could also encourage members to designate a repository earlier, rather than later, in their congressional careers.

4. *Special investigating committees.* Records management guidelines should be provided to staff of special investigating committees of the House and Senate as they are setting up. Many of these staff are new to Congress and are unfamiliar with recordkeeping requirements. Records disposition language should be added to the legislation establishing these committees so that specially hired staff are reminded of each house's rules regarding committee records.

5. *Records of legislative counsels.* The House and Senate archivists should survey the records of the offices of legislative counsel in the House and the Senate to evaluate their records for possible archival retention. Materials from these offices have never been added to Congress's archival holdings. The Center for Legislative Archives should encourage the transfer of these records to the archives.

6. *Documenting members' legislative activities.* Archivists both in Congress and in the members' archival repositories should evaluate ways to improve documentation of members' actual involvement in the legislative process. Most sources detail the input of staff more than that of the members. These archivists should compile examples of effective methods of documentation from congressional or related (presidential, for example) collections and share this information with members' offices that are interested in improving documentation of the member's day-to-day activities.

7. *Other records management initiatives.* Authorities in both houses should explore other possible initiatives to improve overall records management.

These activities might include the provision of archival services or the distribution of guidelines designating specific member operating funds for archival management. They might also include establishing archival fellowships to bring archivists from the home state or district to Washington, D.C., to perform archival work for members who had agreed to donate their papers to an archival institution in the home state.

8. *Coordination with repositories.* Archivists in Congress and the Center for Legislative Archives should work closely with those in members' designated archives to ensure preservation of as complete a documentary record as possible. Achieving this goal will require cooperation in observing each house's rules regarding records ownership. It is recommended that all members' deeds of gift that transfer ownership of their papers to an archives include a phrase specifying that committee records belong to the respective body and may not be transferred out of the legal custody of that body. This approach would support the preservation and retention of records that belong to each body and would help counter the tendency by individual committee staff to send committee records to members' repositories. In cases where committee records become inextricably mixed with members' papers as a result of frequent crossover from one staff to the other, the presence of committee records should be identified and the archivists in Congress notified. Where possible, copies should be made of pertinent files and the originals returned to the Congress.

REPRESENTATION

Members of Congress serve as representatives of the views, goals, and agendas of their constituents. Representation includes voting according to constituent desires, representing points of view in policy matters, assisting constituents with grant applications for government project funds, assisting constituents who have difficulties with the government bureaucracy, and providing information. Such activities result in the accumulation of massive volumes of constituent mail and casework both in the Washington, D.C., and state offices. Office management systems need to address the problems of preserving significant information while disposing of transitory material on a regular basis. The following recommendations are designed to enhance written records management guidelines and to alert office managers about ways to improve management routines.

1. *Establishing and maintaining constituent-related files.* Office managers should establish discrete files for project assistance, casework, issue mail, VIP or substantive mail, and legislative correspondence, in order to facilitate disposition and preservation of the different kinds of information retained in these files. Segregating these files from one another is *the single most important action an office can take* to aid in their disposition.

Effective maintenance of project assistance files should focus on eliminating duplication by consolidating the function either in Washington or
state offices. Routine casework files should be filed separately so that they
can be stored at the Federal Records Center until they are no longer needed
or until the member departs Congress. Offices are encouraged to microfilm
constituent issue mail and discard duplicate copies prior to microfilming.
Only issue mail of substance should be filmed, and the originals discarded.
Offices should regularly dispose of routine requests and avoid filing them
with issue mail.

a. *Guidelines.* The Congressional Archivists Roundtable should develop
guidelines on appraising and sampling casework and issue mail so that
repositories wishing to maintain some casework files or a sampling of issue
mail may do so and still reduce bulk.

b. *Databases.* Office managers should use standard database management
software when they cross-reference and index a variety of textual files maintained within the office, such as constituent correspondence, project assistance information, and various press files. If project work and casework are
not filed separately and instead are interfiled with other records, they should
be identified on computer-based indexes so that separate listings can be created. Systems managers should establish adequate indexing for representation records. It also is recommended that offices establish a methodology for
identifying important issues or correspondents. These records can then be
located through the electronic index and pulled for preservation.

Where the capability exists to produce constituent correspondence indexes on computer output microfilm, it should be used. Standard software
databases containing documents, information files, and index information
should be preserved in electronic format.

c. *Standards.* Office and systems managers should adapt information
management standards, including filing, indexing, and information routing
and disposition routines. They should promote their consistent use by all
staff in both the Washington, D.C., and state offices. A system of quality
control should be implemented to ensure the continued application of the
standards.

2. *Coordinating with the repository.* Repository archivists should establish
communications with the offices of new members early in their House and
Senate careers for the purpose of encouraging good records management
practices. If a member has not selected a repository, a designated archivist
from the state should contact that member to emphasize the importance of
preserving his or her collection and to urge its deposit at some repository in
the state. This contact should be made in cooperation with the House and
Senate historical offices and archivists.

a. *Issue mail.* Archivists and congressional offices must reach mutual
agreements on the need to discard, microfilm, or sample originals of incoming constituent issue letters. This must be done on an office-by-office

basis due to the diversity of types of material that offices define and file as "issue mail."

b. *Statewide efforts.* Archivists should establish guidelines for developing statewide cooperative documentation efforts in order to minimize duplication of information and identify desirable documentation. Within each state, all repositories specializing in congressional documentation should develop a statewide cooperative collections-development guideline. Someone should be designated as the spokesperson for archivists within the state to ensure that all members of the state's congressional delegation are contacted about preserving their papers.

3. *Role of the Congressional Archivists Roundtable.*

a. *Information project.* The Congressional Archivists Roundtable should prepare an information paper on project assistance documentation in federal, state, municipal, and local records. The research paper should assess the relative value of information in the files at different levels of government and evaluate the extent to which information is duplicated among them. This information could be generated as part of a congressional archival information database project modeled on the National Archives' Intergovernmental Records Project.

b. *Guidelines.* The Congressional Archivists Roundtable should work with the museum community to prepare guidelines for members on the disposition of memorabilia and gifts. The guidelines should reflect applicable laws and regulations of the House and Senate, provide guidance on the type of memorabilia that is suitable for transfer to a member's designated archival repository, and contain suggestions for disposing of material not suitable for inclusion with a research collection. Suitability might depend on factors such as whether the object provides valuable information or evidence regarding the member and his or her family, its intrinsic significance, whether it is handcrafted or commercial, and whether it relates to an interest or project of the member. These guidelines would be helpful to members, their staff, and to repositories that receive and preserve collections of members of Congress.

CONGRESSIONAL LEADERSHIP
AND MEMBER ORGANIZATIONS

Sources for studying leadership in Congress are highly valued by historians and political scientists. They include records of individuals elected to leadership positions and those serving as committee and subcommittee chairs and ranking minority committee members. While some congressional leaders have maintained excellent collections, others have not. A major effort should be undertaken to ensure the preservation of materials generated in leadership offices. Since the often hectic atmosphere of such offices provides a less than ideal environment for records preservation, establishing a workable system will require the combined efforts of the leadership, their designated repositories, archivists within Congress, and the Center for Legislative Archives.

1. *Cooperative effort.* All archivists associated with congressional documentation should collaborate to ensure the preservation of leadership records, which are essential for documenting the political and legislative activities of Congress. Archivists in Congress should produce an informational pamphlet discussing preservation of leadership records and highlighting their exceptional historical and research value.

2. *Records ownership evaluation mechanism.* Authorities in the House and Senate should consider establishing an internal mechanism to resolve disputes about the ownership of files of committee chairs, subcommittee chairs, and ranking minority members that are maintained by the committees. The mechanism should permit evaluation of the files to determine whether they belong with the committee archive or the member's papers. Committee staff frequently retain what they deem to be politically sensitive information, either for their own use or for subsequent inclusion with the member's collection. When such material is withdrawn from the committee files, it usually is lost forever. If a method cannot be established to resolve questions and disputes, all research repositories receiving material that is clearly identifiable as committee generated and related to committee business should bring it to the attention of the appropriate authority in the respective house. If feasible, the material should be copied and the original returned to the Congress. If such material is inextricably mixed with a member's personal office records, the archival repository that receives the collection should administer the committee records according to the rules governing access to the official records.

3. *Policy committees and caucuses.* Archivists in both houses should systematically survey the records management practices of policy committees and caucuses. The congressional leadership should be encouraged to institute measures to preserve these records and make them available to scholars. Recently, the Senate Democratic Conference has taken steps to preserve its minutes at the Center for Legislative Archives. Other conferences and caucuses should be encouraged to take similar action.

4. *Congressional member organizations.* Commonly known as policy committees, caucuses, coalitions, informal groups, or ad hoc task forces, these groups help establish legislative priorities and compile and distribute timely information to their memberships. There are over one hundred such groups, including the party policy organizations, legislative service organizations, and caucuses.

a. Archivists in Congress, in cooperation with the Center for Legislative Archives, should systematically survey records and prepare disposition guidelines for congressional member organizations (CMOs). Historically valuable records should be transferred to the Center for Legislative Archives.

b. Repository archivists preparing finding aids to collections of members' papers should identify CMO materials. CMO records in presidential libraries should also be noted in finding aids. This information should be included as part of a national congressional information database.

POLITICAL ACTIVITIES

The records of candidate recruitment and election campaigns, of political activities, of party leadership and congressional party organization are among the most frequently sought and used by scholars. Yet they are among the most difficult to collect and preserve, due to the fluid environment in which they are created, their sensitivity, their long-term usefulness to the members in subsequent campaigns, and the fact that there are no firm rules governing ownership and disposition of these materials. These recommendations are designed to improve documentation in this especially significant area.

1. *Candidate recruitment and campaigns.* Repositories specializing in documenting Congress should collect materials regarding candidate recruitment and campaigns, both of unsuccessful candidates and elected officials. Selection criteria might single out candidates in hotly contested, very interesting, or unique races. Repository archivists need to work closely with members of Congress to ensure the preservation of campaign records, which frequently become scattered in various places in the state and are not part of a regular disposition routine. In addition, fragile media (video and audio tapes of speeches, interviews, advertisements) comprise a significant portion of this material and are in need of proper storage and maintenance.

2. *Noncongressional political organizations.* Repository archivists should identify and evaluate records of organizations such as the Leagues of Women Voters, political consultants, and media consultants for possible inclusion with their congressional collections. While not all records of all such organizations should be preserved, a cooperative statewide or regional plan among repositories could ensure the preservation of representative organizations and add some resources that would fill gaps in the documentary record of the legislative/ political process. Efforts should be made to preserve major advertising sequences and records of endorsement. To assist in this goal, the Congressional Archivists Roundtable should develop a pamphlet describing the materials sought by repositories and use it for solicitation purposes. A list of likely organizations by state or region should be drawn up.

3. *Political party records.* Archivists need to develop positive strategies to overcome such major obstacles to collecting political party records as decentralization, high staff turnover, organization finances, and donor reluctance. Archivists should contact all units of the established parties, as well as temporary political associations while they are active, and encourage them to save their records. Cooperative efforts are needed among repositories to obtain commitments for long-term deposit. The Congressional Archivists Roundtable should prepare a solicitation pamphlet directed at political parties that emphasizes collecting the records of campaign managers.

a. In the 1970s, both of the major political parties' national committees formulated deposit agreements with the National Archives. Under these arrangements access and ownership reside with the committees for 10 years from the date of deposit and then are deeded to the United States. The Congressional Archivists Roundtable should contact each party committee to encourage its respective state and local organizations to deposit their records in appropriate institutions in the states.

b. An interested archival repository should consider compiling a comprehensive guide to the locations of political party records, in order to facilitate their preservation, evaluation, and use. A grant might be obtained to fund such a project.

c. Archivists also need to aggressively solicit the papers of minor parties, ad hoc party groups, interest groups, and PACs. Losing candidates should also be included when their influence and impact appear to warrant documentation, for example, if their influence on mainstream politics can be measured. A survey of literature or of researchers using these sources could help in developing appraisal guidelines.

d. Congressional archivists should investigate the possibility of creating a coordinated national effort at documenting political parties, in order to determine, for example, whether such coordination would make possible systematic preservation of political party collections in selected states, cities, or regions.

ADMINISTRATION AND SUPPORT: INSIDE CONGRESS

Administrative functions within the Congress are generally well documented due to statutory requirements for full public disclosure of congressional operations. The following recommendations are designed to improve archival management and documentation.

1. *Clerk of the House.* Records of the offices of the clerk of the House of Representatives should be surveyed, appraised, and scheduled.

2. *Sergeants at arms.* Records of the sergeant at arms of each house should be surveyed, appraised, and scheduled.

3. *Architect of the Capitol.* A guide to the holdings of the architect of the Capitol should be produced and distributed in order to improve scholarly access to these rich collections. Records within those holdings documenting buildings in Washington other than those of the Congress should be evaluated for transfer to appropriate archival repositories where they would be preserved and made available for research (e.g., Smithsonian Institution buildings to Smithsonian, other records to National Archives). These could be deposited in the appropriate archives, with ownership retained by the architect.

4. *Legislative counsels.* Records of the legislative counsel of each house should be surveyed, appraised, and scheduled.

5. *Capitol police.* Authorities within Congress should ensure that the historical files of the Capitol police are identified and transferred to the Center for Legislative Archives.

CONGRESSIONAL SUPPORT AGENCIES

The Congressional Budget Office, the Congressional Research Service of the Library of Congress, the Government Accountability Office, the Government Printing Office, and the Office of Technology Assessment provide Congress with information and services that are integral to its legislative, oversight, and investigative activities. No integrated archival program exists for these holdings, even though the records of these agencies are as relevant to the establishment of legislative histories, the evaluation of public policy, and the overall history of Congress as are the records of congressional committees and of the members.

GOVERNMENT ACCOUNTABILITY OFFICE

The Government Accountability Office (GAO; formerly the General Accounting Office) is unique among congressional support agencies in having a comprehensive records schedule. While its records program is efficient in terms of *disposing* of materials, it has not adequately provided for the *retention* of historical files and data relating to Congress's long-term information needs.

1. *Survey and appraisal.*

a. A survey and appraisal should be made of the Government Accountability Office's centralized files, the so-called "A" and "B" files, and the retention period changed. Dating from 1921, these files contain a great mass of information of varying historical value. Because the files deal with GAO's work with other federal agencies, they contain much valuable documentation about the history of the federal government and the nation. There are probably no other records in the federal government that document so directly the rights of citizens and the obligations of their government. The GAO records schedule specifies a retention period of only 80 years for these files, which means that in less than a decade, GAO's earliest records will be subject to destruction.

b. These subject files often concern ongoing issues and may contain material spanning a period of 20 years. There are 999,999 A-files and over 244,000 B-files, some of which contain multiple folders. The files should be reviewed file by file, and item by item. This is the only method by which important historical materials may be identified and saved for permanent retention while allowing other material of little value to be destroyed. The selected materials should then be offered to the Center for Legislative Archives. In the meantime, the retention period should be extended pending a full review of the files.

This project may require special funding, since it will be time-consuming and probably of several years' duration. It should be carried out by professional historians and archivists devoted specifically to the task.

2. *GAO Law Library.* Archival materials in the GAO Law Library consisting of orders, circulars, bulletins, and memoranda should be surveyed and evaluated as potential record copy, because a record copy may not exist elsewhere. Consideration should be given to assessing each item in the collection and offering items of historical value to the Center for Legislative Archives, subject to prior discussion with GAO officials. Items of special significance should be evaluated for preservation copying, using either microfilm or other technology.

3. *GAO Comprehensive Records Schedule.* A full review of the GAO Comprehensive Records Schedule should be undertaken for the purpose of identifying additional historical materials that should be kept permanently. The schedule should reflect the information retention needs of the House and Senate, which it currently does not.

4. *Administering GAO records.* The Center for Legislative Archives should administer all GAO historical records in a manner similar to House and Senate records.

CONGRESSIONAL RESEARCH SERVICE, OFFICE OF TECHNOLOGY ASSESSMENT, CONGRESSIONAL BUDGET OFFICE, AND GOVERNMENT PRINTING OFFICE

While the Office of Technology Assessment (OTA) and the Government Printing Office (GPO) have transferred some records to the Center for Legislative Archives, neither has a comprehensive records schedule that governs all of its records. The Congressional Research Service (CRS), despite the importance of its files for documenting the history of legislation and public policy, does not have a comprehensive records schedule nor does CRS participate in the archival program of the Library of Congress. The Congressional Budget Office (CBO) also lacks a records schedule and has never transferred material to the archives. This is a serious omission in Congress's historical records program that should be addressed as soon as possible.

1. *Congressional Research Service.* The administrative and reference materials of CRS constitute a significant source of documentation of the legislative process. Current materials constitute an important resource for members and staff; older and noncurrent records form a major resource for documenting the history of Congress.

a. A comprehensive records survey of CRS holdings should be undertaken either by the staff of CRS or by Library of Congress records management staff, and a schedule should be produced.

b. The CRS schedule should be reviewed and approved by appropriate authorities of Congress to ensure the identification and preservation of records of lasting value to the Congress.

c. A CRS archives should be established.

d. A public access policy for CRS archival material should be drawn up and approved in consultation with appropriate authorities in Congress.

2. *OTA, GPO, CBO.* Records management staff in each agency, with assistance from the Center for Legislative Archives and House and Senate archivists if needed, should conduct a comprehensive survey of OTA, GPO, and CBO records and schedule all archival records, including electronic records. The archival records should be consolidated under the administrative control of the Center for Legislative Archives.

a. The Center for Legislative Archives should ascertain the whereabouts and encourage the preservation and donation of the personal papers of past directors of the OTA, CBO, and GPO.

b. The Center for Legislative Archives should ensure that a record set of all OTA and CBO publications is preserved.

c. The Center for Legislative Archives should evaluate retention of GPO published congressional documents and determine what additional records should become part of a permanent collection at the center. An evaluation of formats (text, electronic) for retention should also be conducted.

3. *All congressional support agencies.*

a. A formal process should be established within the House and Senate (such as a review committee composed of congressional historians, archivists, and relevant committee staff) to ensure that the interests of both bodies are represented in the creation of records disposition schedules for the congressional support agencies.

b. Records management officials within each agency should establish a vital records program.

EXTERNAL RELATIONS: EXECUTIVE BRANCH

The executive branch and the president are important influences in congressional decision making. While presidential libraries and the National Archives administer strong archival programs for these sources, there is a need to identify and describe the materials that relate to Congress, which in some instances are more revealing than parallel information in members' papers or committee records. The existence of this information needs to be better publicized throughout the congressional research community.

1. *Presidential libraries.* Archivists at the presidential libraries should compile resource articles describing the material they have about Congress and the development of legislative programs. This information should be incorporated into a legislative/congressional finding aids database.

2. *Identifying congressional material in departmental and agency records.* Archivists at the Center for Legislative Archives should compile resource articles on significant material concerning Congress that is located in departmental and agency records. Articles could explain the nature and extent of congressional material and evaluate its relevance to traditional legislative history sources. A survey of selected existing National Archives inventories would be a possible first step to identify such material. This survey data could be incorporated into a congressional database of archival sources.

JUDICIAL BRANCH

While most documentation of interaction between the Congress and the judiciary resides in the records of congressional committees and in the personal papers of members of Congress, additional material also exists in official records of the courts, records of bar associations, and in the personal papers of judges. The following recommendations are designed to strengthen existing archival programs and to suggest others.

1. *Congressional–judicial cooperation.* Congressional archivists should encourage and assist the efforts of the National Archives, the Administrative Office of the United States Courts, and the Federal Judicial Center History Office to improve the archival and records management practices of the federal judiciary, so that interactions between the legislative and judicial branches can be better documented. Likewise, the National Archives should work with appropriate authorities to improve documentation of the Supreme Court and preservation of its records, as it has with courts below the Supreme Court.

2. *Personal papers of judges.* Congressional archivists may wish to expand their congressional collections by adding the papers of judges who were associated with particular politicians or political philosophies, who may

have assisted Congress in the development of legislation pertaining to the courts, or who were significant players in statutory interpretation decisions that were overridden by Congress. These archivists should encourage federal judges, especially those serving in leadership positions and those on the Supreme Court, to place their personal papers, including their working papers, in appropriate manuscript repositories.

3. *Identifying congressional materials in judicial records.* The Center for Legislative Archives should prepare resource articles describing material in National Archives judicial holdings that document congressional–judicial relations. This information should be incorporated into a legislative finding aid or database.

THE MEDIA

The relationship between Congress and journalists is as old as Congress. It is the subject of much comment and study. Members' papers contain strong documentation on this topic from the member's point of view. Collections of legislative and political journalists are also considered valuable archival sources, but they have not been systematically identified and collected by congressionally focused archives. The collections of editorial writers, columnists, and cartoonists can be strong documentary additions to the history of Congress and the democratic process. The records of the congressional press galleries also remain outside of archival control.

1. *Media records at the National Archives.* The Center for Legislative Archives should incorporate into a legislative database or finding aid information about journalistic and media sources within the National Archives that document the history of Congress. For example, the C-SPAN videotape recordings of congressional committee hearings are not generally known in legislative research circles. The Center for Legislative Archives should evaluate inclusion of journalistic and media records as part of its collections development policy.

2. *Periodicals.* An interested congressional archivist should identify the major periodical sources of news coverage of Congress and survey them regarding their archival holdings, access policies, and available reference staff. A guide to such holdings could then be compiled. This might be an appropriate project for grant funding.

3. *Press galleries.* Appropriate authorities in each house should systematically contact the governing committee of each press gallery to offer guidance in the use of the Center for Legislative Archives to store their permanent records. Each house should issue guidelines to the press galleries on identifying and preserving permanently valuable files and on gaining access to sensitive records. The permanently valuable records maintained

by press galleries should become part of the permanent historical record of Congress.

4. *Journalists' papers.* Congressional archivists might encourage an interested archival repository to undertake development of a location guide to the papers of individual journalists that have been deposited in archives and manuscript collections. Such a guide would be a useful finding aid for congressional archivists, as well as journalism students, and would be worthy of potential grant funding.

a. The Congressional Archivists Roundtable should consider preparing a biographical list of individual journalists who have covered Congress, together with guidelines for state and local archival repositories to collect, preserve, and make available for research the papers of such journalists. This information could be incorporated into a model congressional collections development statement.

b. Congressional archivists should undertake surveys of the records and papers of those journalists who routinely cover legislative affairs and who also act as legal correspondents. Such collections would be appropriate for accessioning with other congressionally focused materials.

LOBBYING ACTIVITIES

Lobbying has played a critical role in the development of legislation and public policy since the beginning of the United States government. While documentation of lobbying exists primarily in public interest group collections that have found their way to research repositories, archivists have not systematically evaluated lobbying information for its value in documenting the legislative process. To improve documentation of lobbying, the task force recommends the following.

1. *Identification.* Congressional archivists who wish to develop resources on the legislative process should identify lobbyists and lobbying groups that have played a significant role in issue areas that the repository wishes to document. For example, if the repository holds collections of members who were outstanding in promoting national defense, that repository might wish to identify the firms and particular lobbyists associated with the efforts of the member. The Center for Legislative Archives should evaluate inclusion of lobbying records as part of its collections development policy.

2. *Survey.* The repository should survey the records of the sources (firms, individual lobbyists, public interest groups) it has identified and ascertain their status and availability for research. The archivists can then appraise the records for possible accessioning or maintain information for researchers about the whereabouts and availability of privately held collections.

3. *Policy statement.* A model congressional collections policy statement should discuss the records of lobbying groups, lobbyists, and PACs as po-

tential sources for strengthening documentation of the legislative process. Criteria for selecting representative lobbying collections and appraisal criteria should be developed and incorporated into the statement.

4. *Documentation strategy.* The Congressional Archivists Roundtable should debate and evaluate the broader rationale of the existing situation, in which institutions generally keep documentation related to lobbying as part of a larger subject area like civil rights, rather than in a separate category to document the role of lobbying in the legislative process. Is the current procedure enough, or should archivists devise a separate documentation strategy for lobbying?

5. *Solicitation.* Archivists who decide to document the role of lobbying in the political/legislative process need to be aggressive in soliciting the papers of lobbyists and PACs. Lobbying groups should be encouraged either to preserve their archives in-house or to donate materials to an appropriate repository.

POLICY RESEARCH CENTERS

Since their inception in the early twentieth century, public policy research centers have played an increasingly important role in the development of public policy. These nongovernmental, nonprofit public policy organizations are more commonly known as "think tanks." One has only to glance at congressional committee records to discover the extent of their contact with Congress. While a few of the older, traditional think tanks have established archival programs, many of the newer groups have not. To encourage preservation of the records of the more influential policy centers, the task force recommends the following.

1. *Identification.* Because think tanks have an important function in the development of public policy, both in the executive branch and in Congress, archivists interested in the documentation of Congress should identify those think tanks that have played strong roles on the congressional scene. The Center for Legislative Archives should evaluate inclusion of think tank records as part of its collections development policy.

2. *Survey.* When the think tanks have been identified, a systematic survey, building on one conducted in 1987 by Michele Pacifico of the National Archives, should be undertaken to ascertain the status of each institution's archival program and the availability of its holdings for research.

Repositories interested in developing holdings in the congressional area can use information obtained from a systematic survey to identify potential collections. The Center for Legislative Archives may wish to evaluate its interest in this area.

3. *Preservation.* Think tanks active in the legislative area should be encouraged either to preserve their archives in-house or to donate their materials

to an appropriate repository. The institutions should be encouraged to provide whatever support they can to repositories that agree to accept their collections. One type of assistance, for example, might be preliminary processing to lessen the financial burden on the repository.

4. *Policy statement.* A model congressional collections policy statement should include an observation that the records of think tanks are a potential source for strengthening documentation of the legislative process.

5. *Guide.* A guide should be completed giving the locations of public policy center archives and including information regarding public access. This guide should be made available to congressional researchers, especially in the Center for Legislative Archives and at other repositories that specialize in congressional materials. Preparation of such a finding aid would be useful in encouraging notable think tanks to identify and provide for the long-term care of their historical records.

IMPROVING CONGRESSIONAL DOCUMENTATION THROUGH USE OF ORAL HISTORY

Because a great deal of legislative business is conducted orally and is not recorded, congressional archivists need to consider the use of structured interviews to fill out some of the steps in the documentary record. Information is spotty or nonexistent in the areas of conference committee actions, oral exchanges during the last-minute pull and tug of a final controversial or major vote, last-minute legislative bargaining, partisan disagreements and the development of partisan strategies, the investigative process of committees, the conduct of campaigns and recruitment, and the role of political parties. The following recommendations are directed at improving existing congressional oral history programs and suggesting some new ones.

1. *House.* An oral history project patterned after the Senate Historical Office project to interview long-serving Senate committee and administrative staff should be started for the House of Representatives. Guidelines for a model congressional oral history project should be developed and promulgated.

2. *Repositories.* Manuscript repositories holding congressional papers should consider doing oral history interviews with family, staff, and associates of the congressional donors. Questionnaires might be used effectively in instances where a full interview is not possible.

3. *Center for Legislative Archives.* The Center for Legislative Archives should encourage oral history projects to focus on congressional topics in need of amplification and itself conduct selective oral history interviews to fill gaps in the textual records.

4. *Exit interviews.* While most committee investigative records thoroughly document the subject of the investigation, they rarely shed light on the

investigative process itself. Congressional oral history projects could add to the available documentation by doing selected interviews with investigative staff prior to their departure. Exit interviews with selected staff would contribute greatly to the documentary record of congressional investigations and the history of each house.

5. *Candidates and campaigns.* Archival repositories should develop oral history programs to supplement their political history collections. Interviews are essential to the creation of a full documentary record of modern political life but are especially useful for documenting recruitment and an individual's private decision to seek public office. A facile answer, such as "I wanted to serve my state," may actually be the reason that motivated a candidate, but certainly at some point the individual running for Congress had to weigh such other factors as: would I enjoy the office, can I win, and what changes will this make in my life. Under careful questioning, a thoughtful respondent can add a great deal to the historical record, particularly regarding recruitment. Interviews also are useful for documenting the campaign itself, which if hotly contested causes strategies to be frequently adjusted with little record kept of the changes. Besides the candidates and their campaign directors, other potential interviewees include family members, local newspaper editors, political advertisers, and colleagues from prior public service or business/professional backgrounds. Oral history projects should broaden their scope to include such relevant individuals.

Interviews with candidates, campaign managers, and party officials would help to document the inner workings of party organization and its power structure, as well as behind-the-scenes political maneuvering. Projects should begin early in the repository's relationship with the donor and be broadly based, focusing, for example, on "the life and times of congressperson X."

6. *Leadership.* A major oral history project should be developed to document the history of congressional leadership. Much of the art of leadership is not recorded, and archivists must seek other ways to document it. Perhaps one of the emerging "congressional research centers" might wish to undertake or coordinate such a project. Grant money could be a possible source of funding. The Center for Legislative Archives should evaluate doing such a project as part of its effort to document congressional leadership.

7. *Policy committees.* Since textual documentation of policy-oriented CMO floor activities is nonexistent, create a model congressional oral history interview guideline that includes staff of the party policy committees and focuses on their floor support role.

8. *Congressional–judicial relations.* Oral history interviews are valuable for filling gaps in the historical record. The history of legislation and of congressional–judicial relations would be enhanced through such efforts. Several interviews with district, circuit, and Supreme Court judges already

reside in a number of repositories, including the curator's office of the Supreme Court. Funding should be encouraged for oral history projects with federal judges, and repositories holding the papers of judges should consider doing interviews.

9. *Lobbying.* Oral history interviews can capture information about lobbying, and when longtime lobbyists are interviewed, they present a picture of the ways lobbying has changed over time. Guidelines for political/congressional oral history projects should discuss the use of this source.

PHYSICAL PRESERVATION OF NONTEXTUAL SOURCES

Increasingly, archival records reside on nontextual media. Without exception, these new record formats are fragile and are in need of better on-site care. The following recommendations are designed to improve the preservation of nontextual media, which increasingly have been arriving at archival repositories in poor, if not irreparably damaged, condition.

1. *Guidelines.* Both houses should promulgate records management guidelines that emphasize the need to preserve audio and video tapes, films, news releases, and clippings within congressional papers. The guidelines should include information about preservation microfilming of scrapbooks and photocopying of clippings and should discuss the issues of acid-free paper, recycled papers, and the archival implications for a member's collection. Both houses should conduct workshops or seminars on the proper care and handling of photographs, slides, tapes, and films to prevent their inadvertent destruction.

2. *Office storage.* Office managers need to pay greater attention to the preservation of fragile media stored on site. They should institute appropriate filing, labeling, indexing, and storage of photographs, tapes, and other fragile media that accumulate in their offices. To preserve newspaper and *Congressional Record* clippings, which are valuable research sources, office managers should ensure that the material is either photocopied or microfilmed and cross-referenced with relevant press files.

3. *Computerized records.* House and Senate records management guidelines should include recommendations for preserving records maintained in personal computer systems and on centralized systems. Such records should be transferred to paper or ASCII files or should be retained in computer format, as determined in consultation with the House and Senate archivists and the repository archivists.

The Congressional Archivists Roundtable should compile case studies on particular instances of appraisal of congressional electronic records, including electronic mail systems. Specific examples of appraisal decisions would assist archivists confronting congressional computer systems for the first time. The Center for Legislative Archives, in cooperation with the Center for Electronic Records, should identify and preserve valuable electronic records and monitor developments in new automated recordkeeping systems and formats used in Congress.

ACCESS TO CONGRESSIONAL SOURCES

Congressional archival sources are geographically scattered and have not been brought under intellectual control through a common finding aid or database. There is great variation among existing finding aids, both in the use of descriptive terminology and in the level of comprehension of the legislative process among the archivists who prepared them. With certain exceptions, archivists have not consciously set out to create congressional research centers collections built around the theme of documenting Congress. Even the research centers that have established Congress as a major collecting theme infrequently evaluate congressional resources in their full and broad context. The following recommendations are designed to improve the public's access to information about Congress and the legislative branch.

1. *Access to members' collections.* Congressional archivists should encourage members to establish reasonable access guidelines for their collections so that the collections will be available for research at the earliest possible time consistent with personal privacy and national security considerations and limitations set by federal law. The Congressional Archivists Roundtable should study the question of access to collections and make a recommendation for standards that could be widely adopted in congressional donation agreements.

2. *Archival database.* To facilitate access to information about the location and content of congressional source materials, congressional archivists should study the feasibility of developing an inter-institutional archival descriptive project or national congressional archival database. Such a project could be designed to encourage the sharing of information about holdings, appraisal decisions, and reference services. There are already a number of national network structures in place, and the National Archives is creating a computer-based finding aid for its holdings. The next step would be to investigate the creation of a database that would link descriptions of congressional holdings in private archives with the archival collections of Congress. Information about congressional oral histories should be incorporated into the database, together with information about other types of closely related legislative and political sources. The Center for Legislative Archives could act as a clearinghouse for this effort. The Center can also serve as a national reference facility on the study of Congress by creating a collection of finding aids to the legislative holdings of other institutions.

3. *Campaign finance data.* The Center for Legislative Archives should prepare a resource paper detailing and explaining how to access the campaign
spending information that is available to scholars at the National Archives
and the Federal Election Commission. Congressional repositories in the
states should compile guides to state sources of campaign finance, personal
finance, lobbying, and related information. These finding aids should be
available to congressional researchers.

4. *Model policy statement.* The Congressional Archivists Roundtable
should develop a model "collections development policy statement" for
archival institutions that are interested in specializing in congressional/leg-
islative/political research. This model statement would be designed for use
by any repository planning to develop its holdings in this area. The policy
statement should outline a comprehensive development plan to acquire
research collections that supplement each other, in order to create an integrated meaningful body of primary source information about Congress.
Such a statement would assist states in developing statewide cooperative
collecting efforts.

a. The statement should specify that congressional collections should be
donated to a research institution in the member's home state, because that
is where the collection will be of greatest use.

b. The statement should identify as potential areas of interest the collections of party officials, journalists, political parties, and congressional
scholars that are relevant to the goals of the institution. It should include
pertinent (non-Congress) journalistic sources, like the C-SPAN broadcasts
of congressional events that are preserved at the National Archives and at
Purdue University, and the personal papers of local editors and journalists
who focused on Congress.

c. Archivists seeking to build collections strength in the area of the history
of Congress should evaluate the private research collections of academic
and independent scholars who study Congress and who compile hard-to-
obtain information in the course of their research. Archivists should actively
seek these collections, rather than waiting until the individual scholar dies
or retires. This recommendation should appear in a model congressional
collections policy statement.

5. *Cooperative efforts.* Congressional archivists, both those in the states
and those in Washington, D.C., should devise a "cooperative documentation strategy statement." Sister institutions sharing the same interests
should also develop cooperative efforts, such as devising a complementary
appraisal and retention strategy, sharing efforts to contact and form deposit agreements with members of an entire state delegation, deciding on
specialized collecting areas that would result in a more comprehensive and
selective historical record of Congress, or even sharing staff expertise if trips
to Capitol Hill become necessary for records management purposes. The

Center for Legislative Archives, in cooperation with the House and Senate Historical Offices and the Congressional Archivists Roundtable, should develop a collections policy statement that outlines major areas of documentation to be collected by the center.

6. *Creating additional documents.* Individual archival repositories can also create their own documentation that will enhance the usefulness of their congressional collections. A self-contained clipping service, for example, or systematic gathering of local newspaper and ephemeral materials could supplement information about Congress.

7. *Privacy Act guidelines.* The Congressional Archivists Roundtable should produce guidelines on how the Privacy Act affects access to information retained in congressional records. The guidelines should offer appropriate advice regarding access to members' collections.

8. *Outreach activities.* The Congressional Archivists Roundtable should compile and publicize examples of successful archival outreach projects, including exhibits, development of special courses, teaching packets, and other programs designed to promote access to and use of congressional archival information. The Center for Legislative Archives should support efforts by other institutions to disseminate information about and increase the understanding of Congress, as well as engaging in its own outreach activities.

RESOURCE REQUIREMENTS

Many of the recommendations in this report can be implemented without additional funding. This includes all recommendations that are based on better planning, improved communications, and coordination and sharpening of efforts by the three authorities that are responsible for preserving the documentation of Congress. Improving the records management programs within Congress, for example, can be accomplished largely through improved educational efforts directed at existing staff using existing resources. Projects calling on the expertise and time of the Congressional Archivists Roundtable membership can be accomplished by their incorporation into the roundtable's agenda of programs and activities.

Other projects, such as developing oral history projects, appraising the records of the GAO, establishing outreach programs, and developing a congressional archival database probably will require additional funds in most instances where these projects are undertaken. Occasionally, funding is available through state and federal grant sources. Private sources also have been tapped successfully by a number of repositories. A list of prior examples of funding for congressional papers projects is maintained by the Senate Historical Office. The Congressional Archivists Roundtable newsletter also reports instances when its members have obtained funds for congressional archival projects. These reports are featured at the Roundtable's annual meeting. Finally, the Center for Legislative Archives carefully monitors its resource requirements and reports them to the Advisory Committee on the Records of Congress, which was established under authority of Public Law 101-509 (November 5, 1990) to advise Congress and the archivist of the United States on the management and preservation of the records of Congress. (See Advisory Committee on the Records of Congress, *First Report*, December 31, 1991, available from the Center for Legislative Archives.) However, additional funding sources will need to be identified in order to implement fully the documentation strategy. This is particularly true of projects to arrange and describe congressional collections that remain unprocessed, and of those projects to identify and preserve congressional papers where there is no coordinated statewide effort to collect such material.

NOTE

1. Karen Dawley Paul, project director, *The Documentation of Congress: Report of the Congressional Archivists Roundtable Task Force on Congressional Documentation*, S. Pub. 102-20 (Washington, D.C.: U.S. Senate). This report served as the basis for the development of numerous collecting and documentation programs at the Center for Legislative Archives at the National Archives and at a number of congressional archival repositories around the country.

7

Congressional Papers and Committee Records: Private vs. Public Ownership

Karen Dawley Paul

Archivists who acquire papers of members of Congress must determine whether all of the materials being donated are in fact "owned" by the donor and are therefore being transferred lawfully to their repository. By custom and tradition, members of Congress personally own and control the records created and maintained in their own congressional offices, and these records are traditionally donated to a research institution in their home state when they depart Congress. They do not own the records of the congressional committees on which they serve. Committee records are defined by law *and* by House and Senate standing rules to be public records (House and Senate rules and public laws governing the ownership and disposition of committee records are reproduced at the end of this chapter). As such, they remain in Washington, D.C., and become part of the official archival holdings of Congress preserved at the Center for Legislative Archives at the National Archives. This collection dates from 1789 and includes almost 200,000 cubic feet of material and over 20 terabytes of electronic records.

About half of the documentation of Congress resides in the records generated by committees. Committee staff frequently transfer from committee employment to a member's personal office and bring records with them. Committee records sometimes are moved to a member's office when committee chairs and membership changes. Whatever the reason, it is not unusual for committee records to become mixed with members' personal papers despite efforts to ensure that all committee staff are aware of the law. When this unfortunate situation occurs, it will fall to repository staff to identify any "alienated" committee records and return them to Congress.

Ignorance of the law or maintaining positive donor relations is not an acceptable excuse for repositories to retain committee records that either have inadvertently or deliberately been transferred back to the state and out of the custody of the respective body. Members of Congress or former committee staff cannot donate such records to a repository because they do not own them. Repositories cannot legally accession them because they are not being "donated."

When committee staff, either out of loyalty to a particular member or out of personal ignorance of the law, incorporate committee records with those donated by a member, *it is the professional and ethical duty of the receiving archivist to inform both the donor and either the Office of History and Preservation (202-226-5200), if the records belong to the House, or the Senate Archivist (202-224-3351), if they belong to the Senate.* When violations occur, the House and Senate expect to be able to recover the records promptly. Many institutions comply readily by contacting House and Senate authorities when such material is discovered during processing; others have not and have been "caught" when the records have been needed by the committee.

The most efficient way for repositories to address this issue is to follow a very good example set years ago by the Minnesota Historical Society. One of the country's oldest congressional documentation centers, the society has been collecting and preserving the papers of all Minnesota congressional delegations since 1946. The Historical Society includes a standard clause in its congressional deposit agreements or deeds of gift. The clause simply states that as provided by Senate Rules XI and XXVI 10(a) and House Rule VII (for the text of these rules, see the end of this chapter), all committee records are the property of the Senate or House respectively, and if official committee records are found by the Historical Society in the donated papers, the society will notify the donor and the committee records will be returned to the appropriate committee or to the Center for Legislative Archives. The society will also notify the Senate archivist or House archivist as appropriate.

The National Study Commission on the Records and Documents of Federal Officials' *Final Report* (1977) recommended that the "public papers" of the president of the United States and members of Congress should be the property of the United States. While Congress acted to bring presidential papers under public control by the Presidential Records Act of 1978 (44 U.S.C. 2201–2207), it did not provide for public ownership of congressional members' papers. The commission also recommended that Congress develop disposition standards to identify materials of enduring value and facilitate the timely disposal of records that do not merit permanent retention. It also suggested that members should be allowed to select their own archival repository.[1] Both the House and the Senate have implemented these recommendations and developed disposition standards and guidelines to identify material of enduring value. They are shared with repository archivists in the guidance that follows.

PRIVATE OWNERSHIP

Members' Papers: A Working Definition

It is essential that repository archivists have a clear understanding of what constitutes members' papers. Members' papers are defined as: "all records, regardless of physical form and characteristics, that are made or received in connection with an individual's career as a member of Congress, and are preserved either as evidence of the organization, functions, and operations of the office or as information about the individual member or the matters with which he or she dealt." This includes records created and received by a member's personal office staff. It does not include records of committee staff (44 U.S.C. 2118; 2 U.S.C. 72a). In addition, 18 U.S.C. 641 and 2071 provide penalties for destruction or removal of committee records. (For the relevant text of these sections of the U.S. Code, see the excerpts at the end of this chapter.)

In cases where the repository has had no prior contact with the donor and is generally unaware of what is being transferred, a review during accessioning or a closer look during archival processing will reveal the identity and the role of the creator of the files. If a series of files was created by one individual, the archivist can ascertain from the content of the files whether this person was a committee or a personal staff member. Other sources useful for the identification of personal and committee staff include the *Congressional Directory*, *Congressional Staff Directory*, House and Senate *Telephone Directories*, and the House Office of History and Preservation or Senate Historical Office. Further investigation will reveal the functions that the files served, the reason that they were created. While personal staff normally track legislation in broad subject areas, committee staff work on particular legislation referred to the committee. They also review nominations and conduct investigations in a well-defined committee jurisdictional area. Clues such as letterhead, titles, salutations, and the contents of a series as a whole will indicate the source. Information about the jurisdictions and major legislation before committees can be readily found on committee Web sites, through the Library of Congress *Thomas* site, and through printed sources such as Congressional Quarterly's *Guide to Congress*. When repositories have questions about whether *particular* records belong to a committee or a member, the House and Senate archivists should be consulted. Together with the staff at the Center for Legislative Archives, they will be able to determine where gaps exist in the relevant committee files.

The ownership of electronic records is easier to distinguish. When a member departs Congress, the electronic records of the personal office that are determined to be part of the member's permanent archives are forwarded to the designated repository. Committee electronic records always remain on the committee servers until the permanently valuable information is sent to the Center for Legislative Archives. *Copies* of either electronic or textual committee records *may be* incorporated with the members' collection, *provided the committee has authorized the copy to be made and placed elsewhere.* Repositories receiving such material are advised to observe the access restrictions placed on the material by the respective body and committee.

Specifically, the following types of records may comprise members' personal collections. They are listed under the type of activity that caused them to be created: personal and political, legislative work, constituent services, and press/communications.

Personal/Official Records of the Member

This activity entails scheduling the member's meetings and providing the member with information in preparation for the meetings, managing the member's personal mail, maintaining the member's personal files, maintaining biographical information about the member, maintaining financial disclosure and other required reports, and maintaining information about party and caucus matters. These activities are normally performed by individuals holding the job titles of chief of staff, personal secretary, appointment or scheduling secretary, executive secretary, office manager, state director, or executive or special assistant. They may work in Washington, D.C., or state offices.

Typical documentation of these activities includes the following: appointment logs, accepted invitations, biographical files, caucus/political materials, chronological files/staff memos, daily schedules and briefing materials, desk calendars, diaries, e-mail, financial disclosure reports, guest books, members' correspondence, memorabilia, memos of phone conversations, party leadership files, scrapbooks, VIP appointments/judgeships files, and VIP correspondence. Some of these types of documentation will be in electronic format.

Campaign Records

Created by and belonging to the campaign committee, they include polling data, position and strategy materials, research and background files, speeches, and memorabilia. The member typically donates them to a repository along with the congressional papers.

Members' Legislative Staff Records

Legislative activities consist of developing legislative initiatives and policy positions, setting legislative priorities and goals for the year, monitoring legislative issues and tracking them in committees and on the floor, research and writing briefing memoranda, position papers, speeches and other statements, answering legislative mail, scheduling and chairing legislative issue meetings, and maintaining voting, attendance, and legislative activity records and reports. Staff with titles of legislative director, legislative assistant, field representative, legislative secretary, or project director normally perform these duties.

Documentation for these activities can include bill files, briefing books, memos *from* committees, *Congressional Record* inserts, member legislative activity reports, legislative assistant's files, polling data, staff memos, project files, and voting and attendance records. The format can be textual or electronic.

Constituent Service Records

Offices provide a wide range of constituent services that involve processing and monitoring high-priority issue mail, processing high-volume single-issue mail, developing and maintaining prepared text or library items that are used to respond to constituent mail, handling special mailings, generating statistical reports on mail volume and content, serving as ombudsman for constituents asking for assistance with federal agencies, answering correspondence and corresponding with agencies on behalf of constituents, and assisting communities and organizations in the home state in their efforts to secure federal grants or with other projects. Staff with the titles of administrative assistant, executive assistant, special assistant, state director, production manager, correspondence specialist, caseworker, or constituent services representative perform these functions.

Typical files include the administrative assistant's files, casework, grants/projects records, issue mail and indexes, library of mail response forms, staff memos regarding constituent matters, and statistical reports on volume and topics of mail. This documentation can be in textual or electronic format.

Press Relations/Media Activities Records

Press secretaries, assistant press secretaries, and press aides are responsible for communicating effectively with constituents via television, radio, print media, and electronic means. They work closely with the member and legislative assistants to communicate information about issues and the member's positions to local, state, and national news outlets. Press staff provide information for the member's Web site, track journalistic coverage of the member, maintain a photographic record, and maintain or create recordings of interviews and press conferences.

Typical press files include articles, newsletters, newspaper clippings, opinion editorials, optical images, photographs and negatives, press releases, specialized mailings, speeches, and TV, radio, and Web broadcasts. Media can include a variety of textual, tape, and electronic formats.

PUBLIC OWNERSHIP

Committee Records: A Working Definition

Congress, in the Federal Records Act (44 U.S.C. 3301), provided the executive branch with a definition of "records." This statutory definition serves as the basis for defining committee records as all documentary materials, regardless of physical form, made or received and maintained by committees in connection with the transaction of committee legislative, oversight, and executive business. These records document committee work on bills referred to the committee, oversight of government programs within the jurisdiction of the committee, investigations, consideration of nominations and treaties (Senate), and impeachment proceedings. While committee staff may also have purely personal papers in their offices, such items are easy to identify because they *were not prepared for transacting committee business.* (Examples include records relating to campaign activities, papers accumulated before joining the committee, materials resulting from outside pursuits, or records resulting from work performed for a member's office such as constituent casework or state projects.)

Committee Legislative Review Records

Most legislation introduced in Congress is referred to a committee for consideration, but only a small portion actually is selected by the committee for intensive review prior to being reported out of committee. Documentation of this review process is a valuable part of official committee records. Committee legislative files should fully document staff review, research, and analysis of the bills that are given priority during a Congress. At a minimum, all substantive legislation reviewed by a committee should have supporting documentation in the archival records.

This documentation can include staff analytical memos; communications with House and Senate leadership, committee members, agency staff, and interested parties; briefing books prepared for hearings; hearing transcripts and exhibits; substantive drafts of legislation and committee reports; transcripts and minutes of business meetings and "mark-up" meetings, where members amend a measure and determine whether to report it to the respective house; a record of roll-call votes and polling records; audiovisual materials submitted as exhibits; committee press releases, speeches, statements; conference committee minutes, transcripts, and reports; and "side-by-side" comparisons of House and Senate versions of a bill.

Committee Oversight/Investigation Records

Committees also review and study the application and administration of laws that are within the subject matter of the legislative jurisdiction of the committee. Staff analyze, appraise, and evaluate issues and programs, or require a government agency to do so and report to the Congress. Committee oversight is characterized as either legislative or investigative in nature. Legislative oversight involves examining government programs for the purpose of deciding whether new legislation is needed. Investigations are more exploratory, with a view toward uncovering incompetence or wrongdoing in the administration of public policy.

Essential documentation includes the basic types enumerated for legislative review, with the addition of document submissions, subpoenaed documents, depositions, studies, reports, surveys, and questionnaires.

Nominations and Treaty Review (Senate)

Senate committees also review presidential nominations and treaties. Records of this process include the types of documents enumerated for legislative review, with the addition of nominee biographical and financial data files, committee nominee questionnaires, executive reports and substantive drafts, and country subject files.

Official Communications

Committees also receive official communications that are referred from the floor. These include executive communications, petitions and memorials, presidential messages, and reports required by law. This type of document is easily identified because it receives a sequenced number as it is forwarded from the floor to the committee.

PRESERVING PRIVATE AND PUBLIC: IS A SOLUTION POSSIBLE?

A renewed interest in fashioning a more rationalized and orderly policy for preserving the papers of members of Congress has arisen. At meetings of the Association of Centers for the Study of Congress, historians and political scientists have decried the present state of preservation and access to congressional collections.[2] In response to this, the John H. Brademas Center for the Study of Congress at New York University hosted a symposium in October 2005 on the history of the 1974 Presidential Recordings and Materials Preservation Act, its role today, and current policy options and obstacles in archiving the papers of government officials. John Brademas (D-IN, 1959–1981) was responsible for the legislation that resulted in the Presidential Records Act of 1978. In opening remarks at the symposium, he commented that the time has come "to fashion a more rational, orderly public policy for dealing with the papers of senators and congressmen."[3] The Brademas Center's symposium report calls for a congressional discussion of the issues.[4]

Symposium participants recalled that 30 years earlier, the National Study Commission on the Records and Documents of Federal Officials recommended the following:

- "Public papers" of members of Congress should be the property of the United States.
- Congress should develop disposition standards to identify materials of enduring value and facilitate the timely disposal of records that do not merit permanent retention.
- Members should be allowed to select their own archival repository.
- Members should maintain control of access to their papers for a period not to exceed 15 years from the end of their service.
- The Archivist of the United States should assume custody of members' papers that were not donated to a repository.
- Congress should consider providing a "small one-time, Federal grant" to nonfederal repositories receiving congressional papers to encourage adequate treatment of these materials.[5]

For a variety of reasons, the report was not adequately publicized. However, the intervening years have seen much progress in three of the six areas specified by the commission. Both houses have devised records disposition guidelines for their members. Retiring members generally do select a repository for their papers, and access to these collections is spelled out in deeds of gift and deposit agreements that tend to parallel the access rules for the official committee records of each body. A Congressional Papers Roundtable of the Society of American Archivists was established in 1984, and this group has helped to further standardize the appraisal and processing of congressional collections.

Through the 1970s and 1980s, members sometimes were confronted with the fact that a chosen institution "did not want their papers." There was a widely held view that collections were too voluminous, too expensive to maintain, and too underutilized to warrant the expense. But the combined effects of better records management, more publicity, greater use, and better-informed archivists and administrators in the states eventually has created a much more favorable attitude about accessioning these collections.

One additional development has occurred that has great potential for systematizing the preservation of members' papers: the development of centers for the preservation of these papers. The Advisory Committee on the Records of Congress was established in 1990 to advise the leadership on the preservation of the records of Congress. In a 2000 report, the committee addressed the status of preservation of members' papers.[6] The report inspired the Congressional Papers Roundtable to sponsor a forum in 2001 that made specific recommendations about the value of concentrating these collections at institutions that specialize in congressional documentation.[7] The economies of doing so were noted, as well as the fact that it would be an incredible boon for researchers to have sources concentrated in several large research centers rather that scattered about the nation in numerous isolated institutions.

To this end, the Roundtable developed a working definition of public policy research centers, a kind of ideal institutional model for the preservation and use of congressional *and related political papers*. The following checklist was developed for the Roundtable's congressional papers management guidelines.[8]

- Collection policy specifies legislative collections as a particular area of interest.
- Broad collection policy includes ancillary collections of primary sources as a collecting priority; these are expected to supplement a strong core of secondary sources supporting congressional scholarship, politics, public policy, and history.
- Ongoing oral history projects to supplement the documentary record.
- Professional staff with archival training and experience with legislative collections.
- Sufficient staff to process a large legislative collection in an agreed-upon time period.
- Sufficient archival-quality space to store and process a large legislative collection.
- Equipment, expertise, and financial resources to conserve and preserve paper, photographs, film, video and audio recordings, and electronic media typically found in legislative collections.
- Human and financial resources to provide knowledgeable reference assistance to researchers.

- Public programming to excite interest in the study of the repository's legislative collections.
- A distinctive profile within a larger repository organization to highlight the legislative collections.
- Knowledgeable staff with a broad understanding of legislative holdings at other repositories, as well as a professional working relationship with other congressional collections repositories, the House Legislative Resource Center, the Senate Historical Office, and the Center for Legislative Archives, as appropriate.

The Association of Centers for the Study of Congress—institutions that further the study of Congress and also collect congressional documentation and use it to enhance their outreach and scholarly programs—was established in 2004 to foster collaboration among existing centers. Membership has continued to grow each year, and these centers have provided additional impetus to realize the original recommendations of the 1977 National Study Commission, especially in the following areas:

- Developing and refining records management guidance.
- Persuading members to donate collections to research institutions.
- Encouraging the development of research institutions that specialize in congressional documentation.
- Developing standardized access to collections by following each other's examples.

As these centers multiply and begin to add to their store of political documentation, their potential as research and educational entities will grow exponentially.

Efforts to raise awareness of the need to preserve the private and public records of Congress are succeeding. Of the 120 senators who have departed the Senate between 1982 and 2005, only 14 (or 11 percent) have not donated their collections, either because the politicians are still active or they are not ready to donate. No collections have been outright destroyed—something that used to happen more regularly 30 years ago. And there certainly are fewer collections being donated to institutions with inadequate resources to manage them. Representatives also are donating collections more frequently as a result of increased archival consultations both when new members arrive and when members announce retirement. During the 107th Congress, there were 22 consultations for 54 departing members (or 41 percent). For the 108th Congress, there were 16 for 43 departing members, and for the 109th, there were 20 for 36 departing members (or 55 percent).

Currently, House and Senate archivists brief members and staff on records management upon arrival in office. They are told about the importance of their papers and urged to establish office policies and procedures that result in well-organized, accessible collections of records. When members announce retirement, they are advised to hire archival help to prepare the records for donation. They receive a lot of assistance with preparing electronic files for transfer to an archive. In fact, electronic records in congressional offices have to some extent advanced preservation awareness of personal papers as a whole. During the past several years, almost all senators and an increasing number of representatives have hired staff with archival assignments at some point prior to the office closing—a remarkable change.

Despite these improvements, there are continuing challenges to mandate the preservation of private and public records of Congress. There is an intractable problem with ensuring that the official records (records of committees) are sent to the archival collections at the Center for Legislative Archives. Some members continue to regard *everything* as their personal papers. It is difficult to reach an understanding, and it is always an issue that must be explained and negotiated. The current system is an honor system that depends on the honesty and integrity of congressional staff for successful implementation. Political sensitivities and viewpoints, fear and distrust of the system, or destruction of documentation for individualized reasons are just some of the problems that confound adherence to proper procedures.

There continue to be problems with members not choosing the most appropriate (in terms of supporting resources and collecting priorities) repository for their papers. An alma mater always remains attractive, even when the institution does not specialize in maintaining congressional and political archival collections. And there still have been 14 senators in the past 20 years (five of whom served more than a single term) who have not donated anything at all. Despite the fact that there are over 40 centers now established, or on the way to developing fully as such, some members still choose to deposit their collection in an unlikely institution—a place without a graduate school or other immediate researchers, without professional archival staff, without the necessary resources.

Another problematic area in the case of members' papers is ascertaining the quality of material being donated. Do the collections contain the "heart" of such a collection? Guidelines exist, but are they voluntarily being followed? Or are the collections being "sanitized"? (Members' staffs are known to exercise a lot of ad hoc discretion in this regard.) Despite the fact that archivists have developed guidelines, have developed a network of knowledgeable archivists in the states, have learned to better express the need for adequate funding, it cannot be said with certainty that members are donating documentation of consistently high quality. This situation is exacerbated in offices that have not adopted sound management practices for their electronic records.

Does the future hold a preservation policy for the papers of public officials, such as called for by John Brademas? The Brademas Center report significantly recommends that the presidential library system, characterized by its ease of use and centralization of resources and funding opportunities, be used as a model for congressional papers, in terms of how to define them and how to provide access to them. Despite obstacles, the development of a public policy tailored to the special characteristics and history of preserving congressional papers is highly desirable. As the report states, access to these records is "just as important" as access to presidential papers.[9]

To an extent, a policy had evolved in practice. What remained was to put it into writing. This milestone was achieved when the House passed House Concurrent Resolution 307 on March 5, 2008. (The text of the resolution is included at the end of this chapter, along with remarks from Representatives Robert Brady and Vernon Ehlers, who spoke eloquently in its behalf.) The Senate in turn passed it by unanimous consent on June 20. This resolution puts in place the final piece of a puzzle whose design element is the documentation of Congress, specifically the preservation of the papers of its members. With this concurrent resolution, the Congress finally expressed in writing its "policy" regarding the preservation of these materials.

H. Con. Res. 307 states Congress's opinion that the collections of its members are "critical" historical resources, and that members should "take all necessary measures to manage and preserve" them. Further, members should deposit or donate them to a research institution appropriately equipped to care for them, and "to make them available for educational purposes." Over time, as this language is cited in remarks and in written guidance, the resolution will assume the status of a "precedent."

This written "policy" provides congressional archivists, historians, administrative managers, political scientists, and teachers inside and outside the Congress with a persuasive and useful tool for articulating the documentary importance of the materials that result from the members' service, and it underscores the role and responsibility of the members in ensuring their preservation. Service in Congress is a high public trust, and the records of that service are invaluable. H. Con. Res. 307 underscores this importance and affirms their preservation.

To summarize, the history of Congress is documented in official records administered by House and Senate rules. They are sent to the Center for Legislative Archives, where they join other national public records at the National Archives. Significant history is also documented in the personal papers of members of Congress, which, as privately held properties, are preserved at the discretion of the individual member within the framework of H. Con. Res. 307 of the 110th Congress. A definitive history of Congress requires balanced preservation and access to these public and private collections. Archivists who acquire congressional collections of members for their repositories should be prepared to identify alienated committee records as part of the public record and return them to the rightful owner. Congressional collections management practices will become more standardized through implementation of the Congressional Papers Roundtable guidelines available via the Society of American Archivists Web site. What remains to be done is to seek ways to provide more regular funding for congressional collections preservation and access projects. Progress is being made in this area with the establishment of the Association of Centers for the Study of Congress, and one of its goals is securing improved funding. When and if this is realized, the records of Congress truly will have reached parity with records of the executive branch, and our democratic institutions will be strengthened accordingly.

RULES OF THE HOUSE AND SENATE AND RELEVANT STATUTES

Rule VII: Records of the House

1. (a) At the end of each Congress, the chairman of each committee shall transfer to the Clerk any non-current records of such committee, including the subcommittees thereof.

(b) At the end of each Congress, each officer of the House elected under rule II shall transfer to the Clerk any non-current records made or acquired in the course of the duties of such officer.

2. The Clerk shall deliver the records transferred under clause 1, together with any other non-current records of the House, to the Archivist of the United States for preservation at the National Archives and Records Administration. Records so delivered are the permanent property of the House and remain subject to this rule and any order of the House.

Public Availability

3. (a) The Clerk shall authorize the Archivist to make records delivered under clause 2 available for public use, subject to clause 4(b) and any order of the House.

(b)(1) A record shall immediately be made available if it was previously made available for public use by the House or a committee or a subcommittee.

(2) An investigative record that contains personal data relating to a specific living person (the disclosure of which would be an unwarranted invasion of personal privacy), an administrative record relating to personnel, or a record relating to a hearing that was closed under clause 2(g)(2) of rule XI shall be made available if it has been in existence for 50 years.

(3) A record for which a time, schedule, or condition for availability is specified by order of the House shall be made available in accordance with that order. Except as otherwise provided by order of the House, a record of a committee for which a time, schedule, or condition for availability is specified by order of the committee (entered during the Congress in which the record is made or acquired by the committee) shall be made available in accordance with the order of the committee.

(4) A record (other than a record referred to in subparagraph (1), (2), or (3)) shall be made available if it has been in existence for 30 years.

4. (a) A record may not be made available for public use under clause 3 if the Clerk determines that such availability would be detrimental to the public interest or inconsistent with the rights and privileges of the House. The Clerk shall notify in writing the chairman and ranking minority member of the Committee on House Administration of any such determination.

(b) A determination of the Clerk under paragraph (a) is subject to later orders of the House and, in the case of a record of a committee, later orders of the committee.

5. (a) This rule does not supersede rule VIII or clause 11 of rule X and does not authorize the public disclosure of any record if such disclosure is prohibited by law or executive order of the President.

(b) The Committee on House Administration may prescribe guidelines and regulations governing the applicability and implementation of this rule.

(c) A committee may withdraw from the National Archives and Records Administration any record of the committee delivered to the Archivist under this rule. Such a withdrawal shall be on a temporary basis and for official use of the committee.

Definition of Record

6. In this rule the term "record" means any official, permanent record of the House (other than a record of an individual Member, Delegate, or Resident Commissioner), including

(a) with respect to a committee, an official, permanent record of the committee (including any record of a legislative, oversight, or other activity of such committee or a subcommittee thereof); and

(b) with respect to an officer of the House elected under rule II, an official, permanent record made or acquired in the course of the duties of such officer.

Withdrawal of Papers

7. A memorial or other paper presented to the House may not be withdrawn from its files without its leave. If withdrawn certified copies thereof shall be left in the office of the Clerk. When an act passes for the settlement of a claim, the Clerk may transmit to the officer charged with the settlement thereof the papers on file in his office relating to such claim. The Clerk may lend temporarily to an officer or bureau of the executive departments any papers on file in his office relating to any matter pending before such officer or bureau, taking proper receipt therefore.

Senate Standing Rule XI: Papers Withdrawal, Printing, Reading of, and Reference

1. No memorial or other paper presented to the Senate, except original treaties finally acted upon, shall be withdrawn from its files except by order of the Senate.

2. The Secretary of the Senate shall obtain at the close of each Congress all the noncurrent records of the Senate and of each Senate committee and transfer them to the National Archives for preservation, subject to the orders of the Senate.

Senate Standing Rule XXVI: Committee Procedure

10(a) All committee hearings, records, data, charts, and files shall be kept separate and distinct from the congressional office records of the Member serving as chairman of the committee; and such records shall be the property of the Senate and all members of the committee and the Senate shall have access to such records. Each committee is authorized to have printed and bound such testimony and other data presented at hearings held by the committee.

44 U.S.C. section 2118: Records of Congress

The Secretary of the Senate and the Clerk of the House of Representatives, acting jointly, shall obtain at the close of each Congress all the noncurrent records of the Congress and of each congressional committee and transfer them to the National Archives and Records Administration for preservation, subject to the orders of the Senate or the House of Representatives, respectively.

2 U.S.C. section 72a: Committee Staffs

(d) Recordation of Committee Hearings, Data, etc.; Access to Records

All committee hearings, records, data, charts, and files shall be kept separate and distinct from the congressional office records of the Member serving as chairman of the committee; and such records shall be the property of the Congress and all members of the committee and the respective Houses shall have access to such records. Each committee is authorized to have printed and bound such testimony and other data presented at hearings held by the committee.

18 U.S.C. section 641: Public Money, Property, or Records

Whoever embezzles, steals, purloins, or knowingly converts to his use or the use of another, or without authority, sells, conveys or disposes of any record, voucher, money, or thing of value of the United States or of any department or agency thereof, or any property made or being made under contract for the United States or any department or agency thereof; or

Whoever receives, conceals, or retains the same with intent to convert it to his use or gain, knowing it to have been embezzled, stolen, purloined or converted, shall be fined under this title or imprisoned not more than ten years, or both; but if the value of such property does not exceed the sum of $1,000, he shall be fined under this title or imprisoned not more than one year, or both. The word "value" means face, par, or market value, or cost price, either wholesale or retail, whichever is greater.

18 U.S.C. section 2071: Concealment, Removal, or Mutilation Generally

(a) Whoever willfully and unlawfully conceals, removes, mutilates, obliterates, or destroys, or attempts to do so, or with intent to do so takes and carries away any record, proceeding, map, book, paper, document, or other thing, filed or deposited with any clerk or officer of any court of the United States, or in any public office, or with any judicial or public officer of the United States, shall be fined not more than $2,000 or imprisoned not more than three years, or both.

(b) Whoever, having custody of any such record, proceeding, map, book, document, paper, or other thing, willfully and unlawfully conceals, removes, mutilates, obliterates, falsifies, or destroys the same, shall be fined not more than $2,000 or imprisoned not more than three years, or both; and shall forfeit his office and be disqualified from holding any office under the United States. As used in this subsection, the term "office" does not include the office held by any person as a retired officer of the Armed Forces of the United States.

H. Con. Res. 307, 110th Congress

Concurrent Resolution

Whereas Members' Congressional papers (including papers of Delegates and Resident Commissioners to the Congress) serve as indispensable sources for the study of American representative democracy;

Whereas these papers document vital national, regional, and local public policy issues;

Whereas these papers are crucial to the public's understanding of the role of Congress in making the Nation's laws and responding to the needs of its citizens;

Whereas because these papers serve as essential primary sources for the history of Congress, the study of these papers will illuminate the careers of individual Members;

Whereas by custom, these papers are considered the personal property of the Member who receives and creates them, and it is therefore the Member who is responsible to decide on their ultimate disposition; and

Whereas resources are available through the Office of the Clerk of the House of Representatives and the Secretary of the Senate to assist Members with the professional and cost-effective management and preservation of these papers: Now, therefore, be it

Resolved by the House of Representatives (the Senate concurring), That it is the sense of Congress that—

(1) Members' Congressional papers (including papers of Delegates and Resident Commissioners to the Congress) should be properly maintained;

(2) each Member of Congress should take all necessary measures to manage and preserve the Member's own Congressional papers; and

(3) each Member of Congress should be encouraged to arrange for the deposit or donation of the Member's own noncurrent Congressional papers with a research institution that is properly equipped to care for them, and to make these papers available for educational purposes at a time the Member considers appropriate.

Below are the relevant remarks from Representatives Robert Brady (D-PA) and Vernon Ehlers (R-MI) as recorded in the *Congressional Record*, March 5, 2008, H1254.

Expressing Sense of Congress That Members' Congressional Papers Should Be Properly Maintained—(House of Representatives—March 05, 2008)

The SPEAKER pro tempore. Pursuant to the rule, the gentleman from Pennsylvania (Mr. *Brady*) and the gentleman from Michigan (Mr. *Ehlers*) each will control 20 minutes. . . .

Mr. BRADY of Pennsylvania. Mr. Speaker, I yield myself such time as I may consume.

Mr. Speaker, it is very easy for Members to get caught up in the day-to-day responsibilities of their job. In between regular correspondence, speeches, and vote recommendations, Members accumulate a lot of paper. Most will not give consideration to the importance of this paper until the end or middle of their careers.

The papers generated by Members while in office reflect the issues of the day and are of historical benefit to students, scholars, and citizens in understanding the role of the House of Representatives in the Federal Government.

Mr. Speaker, H. Con. Res. 307 is a concurrent resolution that reminds Members of the importance of maintaining and archiving their papers so that future leaders and citizens of history may learn and understand the decisions that we have made. I urge passage of H. Con. Res. 307.

Mr. Speaker, I reserve the balance of my time.

Mr. EHLERS. Mr. Speaker, I yield myself such time as I may consume.

Mr. Speaker, I rise in support of H. Con. Res. 307, which expresses the sense of the Congress that congressional papers should be properly maintained and encourages Members to take all necessary measures to manage and preserve these papers.

This is a very important issue, and one that I am also delinquent on, as I suspect most Members are. At various times I have encouraged my staff to be certain that we take proper care of papers, that we maintain them, and that they are available for archiving once we leave office. But yet, it is a very difficult task to do this on a day-to-day basis and remember to do it.

Let me also bemoan the fact that the executive branch has been subjected to lawsuits on this issue, and the courts have declared they must save every little piece of paper, every message, and they are open to scrutiny and subpoena at any time in the future. The net effect of this is that the White House puts hardly anything down on paper, a practice that was developed in the previous administration as well. That is unfortunate. We should have the freedom to express our thoughts freely and make certain that they are preserved in a fashion that prevents them from being used improperly in future times.

As Members of Congress, we are routinely faced with an abundance of notes, letters, and other papers that cross our desk each day. For each of us, there is a temptation to rid ourselves of today's notes and papers and begin each day anew, free from the scourge of clutter. And I know my office certainly should be more free of clutter. It would be easiest to discard these items along with the rest of the day's castoffs, but as history has shown us, it is often these mundane items that have painted the most accurate and detailed picture of our Nation's history.

These papers and their contents separately may tell us very little about the place and time in which they were created, but they are threads that, when woven together, create the fabric of our democracy.

While congressional papers are the property and responsibility of the Member, the Clerk of the House and the Secretary of the Senate stand ready to assist Members of Congress in the disposition and handling of these materials. I urge all of my colleagues to join me in the effort to retain congressional documents, and in doing so, preserve a piece of history for the sake of our individual and collective posterity.

NOTES

1. National Study Commission on Records and Documents of Federal Officials, *Final Report*, March 31, 1977 (Washington, D.C.: Government Printing Office, 1977), 19–22.

2. For a list of the relevant sessions and speakers, see the Web site of the Association of Centers for the Study of Congress, www.congresscenters.org.

3. Bruce Craig, "Symposium Raises Concerns over Disposition of Congressional Papers," *American Historical Association Perspectives* (January 2006): 23.

4. John Brademas Center, "Preserving and Expanding Access to Public Papers," www.nyu.edu/ofp/brademascenter/events.html.

5. National Study Commission on Records and Documents of Federal Officials, *Final Report*.

6. Advisory Committee on the Records of Congress, *Third Report*, December 31, 2000, S. Pub. 106-52, vii–viii, 1–11.

7. Congressional Papers Forum, Third Report of the Advisory Committee on the Records of Congress, *Proceedings*, August 29, 2001, S. Pub. 107-42.

8. Kimberly Butler, Herb Hartsook, Karen Paul, and Jeff Thomas, "Draft Guidelines for Congressional Papers Repositories," working draft of the Congressional Papers Roundtable, Society of American Archivists, 2004.

9. Brademas Center, "Preserving and Expanding Access to Public Papers."

8

Congressional Papers: Collection Development Policies

Faye Phillips

"Large Number in Congress Calling It Quits," read a headline on January 30, 1994. At that time, 33 members of the House of Representatives had announced their intention not to seek reelection, a record number so early in the year. Moreover, 65 members had voluntarily retired in 1992, and 110 freshmen representatives took office when the 103rd Congress convened in 1993.[1] Each representative who leaves Congress and every new representative or senator who arrives will create office files. Such files and the congressional activities they document are a part of U.S. history.

What becomes of these office files when a representative or senator leaves Congress through election defeat, retirement, or death? The office closes and files are boxed, but where do the records go? Who is responsible for answering these questions and implementing the necessary actions?

The Center for Legislative Archives at the National Archives and Records Administration is responsible for the preservation of the official records of Congress, while representatives, senators, and their staffs are responsible for the management of the information created in their offices. By tradition, members' office files—papers—are considered personal papers. Who is responsible for their care? The office staff and the senator or representative must assume responsibility for establishing a records management plan for the office and for the preservation of historically valuable materials. They also are responsible for locating a proper repository for the housing and care of the papers. The repository is responsible for final

Previously published as "Congressional Papers Collecting Policies" *American Archivist* 58 (summer 1995), 258–69. Reprinted with permission.

appraisal, for arrangement and description, and for making the collection available for research use.

The Library of Congress holds nineteenth-century congressional papers and some from the twentieth century, but most are preserved in archival repositories across the country. Hundreds of libraries, historical societies, and nonprofit agencies throughout the country collect, appraise, arrange, and describe congressional papers and make them available for research. The *Guide to Research Collections of Former United States Senators 1789–1982* lists 350 repositories that have collections of congressional papers representing men and women who have served in the U.S. Senate from 1789 to 1982. The *Guide to Research Collections of Former Members of the United States House of Representatives 1789–1987* lists information from 592 repositories containing historical material on approximately 3,300 former House members. Over 10,000 men and women, however, have served in the U.S. House of Representatives since 1789. Papers not currently in archival repositories must be cared for if and when they are found.[2]

The struggle for repositories and archivists to make the commitment to collect, preserve, and make congressional papers available for research is not a new one. The 1978 Conference on the Research Use and Disposition of Senators' Papers challenged archivists, historians, and congressional staff to study systematically the problems associated with the acquisition, research use, organization, processing, arrangement, description, and size of papers of U.S. senators.[3] In 1985, the Dirksen Congressional Center and the National Historical Publications and Records Commission (NHPRC) sponsored a conference on congressional papers at Harpers Ferry, West Virginia, with the intent of answering these questions. A report issued by the conference participants made recommendations for minimum standards for congressional collections and for repositories collecting them.[4] The minimum recommended standards for repositories include the following:

1. Environmentally and security controlled storage areas.
2. A commitment to bearing the cost of processing, housing, and making the papers available for use on a continued basis.
3. Appropriate collecting policies.
4. Adequate and professional staff.
5. An ability to handle sensitive data and classified information.
6. An ability to do timely processing.
7. Technology to make machine-readable records usable.
8. Complementary collections and research resources and the ability to service the materials.
9. A commitment to participate in national databases.

These minimum standards can, of course, be prioritized in many different ways, but thorough planning necessitates that appropriate collecting policies be the first priority.

A MODEL COLLECTION POLICY

The Documentation of Congress: Report of the Congressional Archivists Round-table Task Force on Congressional Documentation, by project director Karen Dawley Paul, immensely aids the work of archivists of congressional papers and the repositories that collect such papers.[5] The report presents a viable, working documentation strategy for the Congress. Included are definitions, sources and status of documentation, and recommended actions for congressional functions. As part of the documentation strategy, the task force recommends that a model policy statement be written for archival institutions that are interested in specializing in congressional/legislative/political research. In conjunction with the documentation strategy, archivists need to refine repository collection development policies to focus on subject areas such as congressional papers.

Effective policies reflect the objectives and plans of the organization. They are consistent but flexible, so that they can be changed as new needs arise. They can be distinguished from rules and procedures: policies allow for latitude, but rules and procedures remain firm. Finally, they are written. The model established for written collecting policies contains the elements outlined in Example 1.[6]

Example 1.   Model Collection Policy

    I. Statement of purpose of the institution and/or collection
   II. Types of programs supported by the collection
      A. Research
      B. Exhibits
      C. Community outreach
      D. Publications
      E. Others (specify)
  III. Clientele served by the collection
      A. Scholars and professionals
      B. Graduate students
      C. Undergraduates
      D. General Public
      E. Other (specify)

(*continued*)

Example 1. (*continued*)

IV. Priorities and limitations of the collection
    A. Present identified strengths
    B. Present collecting level
    C. Present identified weaknesses
    D. Desired level of collection to meet program needs
    E. Geographical areas collected
    F. Chronological periods collected
    G. Subject areas collected
    H. Languages, other than English, collected
    J. Exclusions
  V. Cooperative agreements affecting the collecting policy
 VI. Resource-sharing policy
VII. Deaccessioning policy
VIII. Procedures enforcing the collecting policy
 IX. Procedures for reviewing the policy and its implementation

The detailed congressional papers collection development policy should be written into the overall policy under Section IV, Priorities and Limitations of the Collection, Subsection G, Subject Areas Collected. A manuscripts repository may be geographically oriented with many strong subject areas; however, to refine the collection development policy, these subject areas need further delineation. An example of such delineation appears in Examples 2 and 3.

Example 2.   Model Congressional Papers Collection Development Policy

To meet its mission more fully, the (name of institution) will collect the personal papers of this state's congressional delegation, except those discussed in the Collecting Policy, Section IV, Priorities and Limitations of the Collection, Subsection J, Exclusions.

Definition: Congressional papers are by tradition considered to be personal papers that may be acquired by universities, historical societies, and libraries. These papers are created in the offices of U.S. senators and members of the House of Representatives by the senator or representative and their staffs. This includes papers from members of all sessions of Congress since 1789.

Parameters: This repository will collect the papers of any elected or appointed senator or representative from the state of XXXX who has served in any Congress since 1789 up to and including the present. The only papers that will not be accepted are covered in Subsection J, Exclusions.

Criteria for Acceptance: All congressional papers (for current members, post-1950s members past, and pre-1950s members past) must meet the following criteria to be accepted by this repository:*

A deed of gift or deposit agreement has been signed.

Only limited and reasonable restrictions are requested.

The files are complete for the congressional period, and pre-congressional papers are included.

The member of Congress served a significant number of years or was involved in events of historical importance that give the papers extensive research value.**

When electronic records system documentation exists along with texts and indexes, those electronic records can be accessed through the repository's computers. Paper back-up systems exist where appropriate for electronic records.

Appropriate files have been microfilmed, and the microfilm is indexed and in good physical working condition.

Nonpaper media items are identified, dated, indexed, and in good physical condition.

The member of Congress and his or her staff and family are willing to assist in oral history projects and in collecting the papers of ancillary persons and organizations.

The components of the papers are well defined and in good order, as well as good physical condition.

The weedable series (series which might be sampled) are easily distinguished.

For sitting members of Congress, their office must have a current working records management plan.

---

*Much of this section is drawn from Frank Mackaman, *Congressional Papers Project Report*, 17–27.

**Cynthia Pease Miller, assistant historian, U.S. House of Representatives, sees a need for archivists to rethink this appraisal guideline. In a letter to the author, dated 23 March 1994, she stated, "More members are coming to Congress at a younger age, and they are leaving at a younger age, especially from the House, to pursue other interests, run for other office, or accept appointment to other office. There are only 48 members of the present House with more than 20 years service (roughly 10 percent) and only 14 of those with 30 years service. If the present retirement/defeat rate continues, when the 104th Congress convenes in January 1995, more than half of the House will have been elected since 1990. This has serious implications for archivists and repositories interested in congressional papers. Foremost, it means there will be fewer personalities, members with long service who may have been identified with certain issues."

Example 3. Model Congressional Papers Collection Development Policy: Ancillary Persons and/or Organizations to Be Collected in Conjunction with Congressional Papers

Definition: Congress is not an isolated organization. Thousands of individuals who are not members of Congress affect who is elected, what bills are presented and passed by Congress, the public's view of Congress, judicial efforts, fundraising, and almost every aspect of what Congress is and does.

Examples: The following are examples of the types of individuals and organizations that are ancillary to Congress:

Unsuccessful candidates in significant elections
State and local politicians and political parties including temporary
    political associations
Educating, nonpartisan political organizations
Media consultants
Political consultants
Special-interest groups
Political action committees (PACs)
Judicial personnel
Media individuals and organizations
Lobbyists and lobbying groups
Public policy research organizations
Congressional scholars
Campaign volunteers

Parameters: This repository will collect the papers of ancillary individuals or organizations that had a significant impact on the constituent services performed by elected or appointed members of Congress from the state of XXXX from 1789 up to the present, or had significant impact on those members' elections, legislative and oversight activities, voting, campaigns, and media perceptions.

Criteria for Acceptance: Papers and records of ancillary individuals or organizations must meet the criteria established for the papers of members of Congress. Organizations currently in operation must have a working records management plan.

Model policies are intended to be used by individual repositories as guidelines for creating their own unique collection development policy. The model congressional papers policy contains elements suggested by *The Documentation of Congress*.

APPRAISING CONGRESSIONAL RECORDKEEPING

Congressional papers can be viewed in three chronological periods: sitting members, past members whose papers bulk in the years after 1950, and past members whose papers bulk in the years before 1950. The nature and makeup of the way work is done in Congress has changed most dramatically since the 1950s, which leads to this appropriate division. Before World War II, Congress was essentially a part-time institution. Since World War II, Congress has become a full-time institution, and congressional staff have increased from about 2,000 to 12,000. *The Documentation of Congress* gives a thorough explanation of how post-1950 Congresses differ from pre-1950s Congresses, citing the following major changes:[7]

A drastic increase in the workload of Congress.
A subsequent increase in size of the legislative branch.
The evolution of committees and subcommittees, and the trend toward greater decision making on the part of subcommittees.
An increase in congressional oversight activity.
A greater reliance on staff.
An increase in the number of informal groups within Congress, which diffuses power.
A proliferation of special-interest groups outside Congress.
The opening of Congress to more thorough public scrutiny.

Most repositories would collect any material found about the earliest senators or representatives from their states if such papers could be located. However, it is important to define this in the collection policy. The policy might include a statement that all materials created by eighteenth- and nineteenth-century members of Congress from the state will be collected regardless of completeness or other conditions.

Another important consideration in the division between pre- and post-1950 congressional papers is the creation and use of automated correspondence systems and computers, the development of local area networks, the use of e-mail systems, and the creation of biographical databases. After the 1980s, e-mail and relational databases began to be used in most Senate offices. For example, Senator Russell B. Long of Louisiana was elected in 1948 and retired in 1986. Not until the late 1960s did the office employ any type of automated correspondence system. The Senate Computer Center's Correspondence Management System was not used in Long's office until 1982. When he retired four years later, all staff members in Long's office had personal computers on their desks. Electronic recordkeeping systems and their management affect what records are created and how archivists deal with them.[8]

Collection development policies, documentation strategies, and appraisal are interdependent. Strategies and policies identify the materials to be collected and contain the conditions the materials must meet to be acquired. Many of these conditions are appraisal decisions, and these conditions should appear in appraisal checklists as well as in criteria for acceptance and minimum standards for collections.

One cannot overemphasize how closely appraisal and acquisition of appropriate materials are bound together. Appraisal is the subject of a substantial body of archival literature, but collection development policies are not. *The Records Management Handbook for United States Senators and Their Archival Repositories* (1991) by Karen Paul, the House of Representatives "Guidelines for Disposition of Members' Papers" (1992) compiled by Cynthia Miller, and *The Documentation of Congress* are necessary aids in appraising congressional papers. Other helpful publications are *Guidelines for Standing and Select Committees in the Preparation, Filing, Archiving, and Disposal of Committee Records* (1990), a Committee on House Administration publication; *A Guide for the Creation, Organization, and Maintenance of Records in Congressional Offices* (revised 1990) by the Library of Congress, Central Services Division; and the *Congressional Handbook*, a GPO publication issued for each Congress.[9]

The Records Management Handbook also assists in the difficult appraisal decisions associated with electronic records. The first edition of the handbook (1985) helps explain some of the older computer systems used in the Senate. Electronic records (machine-readable records) have not eliminated paper files as once predicted. On the contrary, they have made the archivist's job more difficult, for all congressional offices now have electronic records. Electronic records may come to the repositories with a host of problems. The staff creating them may not have used conventional file naming procedures, making it impossible for archivists or researchers to locate needed files. Moreover, staff may have deleted important drafts of documents without making backups, thus creating incomplete records. Because of the proliferation of computers and software, the repository archivist must understand the wide variety of systems used in congressional offices to make the electronic records accessible for researchers in the future. Finally, the best of archival repositories may not have the necessary hardware to read all electronic records.

Other criteria in the collection development policy may or may not be appraisal questions. However, appraisal cannot be completed unless these questions are answered.

Is there a signed deed of gift or deposit agreement? Most repositories are now fully aware of the critical need for legally accurate and current contracts with donors detailing the terms of the gift or of the deposit. The deed protects the rights of the repository, the donors, and the future researchers. The July 1993 issue of the Society of American Archivists newsletter *Archival Outlook* carried a draft joint statement by the American Library Association and the Society of American Archivists, "On Access to Original Materials in Libraries, Archives, and Manuscript Repositories." This statement should be used as a standard for deeds of gift. Sample deeds of gift and deposit agreements for congressional papers can be found in the *Records Management Handbook for United States Senators.* Cynthia Pease Miller, of the Office of the Historian for the House of Representatives, has written a brochure on deeds of gift for members of Congress. A deposit agreement is sometimes the only agreement the repository is able to gain from the donor, but caution is always required. As shown in Ronald L. Becker's recent case study "On Deposit: A Handshake and a Lawsuit," the best of intentions can lead to ownership problems when no deed of gift is signed."[10]

Are any required restrictions limited and reasonable? The question of restrictions may not exactly be an appraisal question, but restrictions or the lack of them will affect acceptance or nonacceptance of the collection. Many archivists will agree with the maxim "No gift is ever free," and restrictions are one of the costs associated with manuscript collections. Members of Congress and their families may request that certain portions of personal materials be closed for a reasonable period of time to safeguard sensitive information, protect living persons, and prevent libel. Archivists may be faced not only with the requirements of the Federal Privacy Act and Freedom of Information Act but, in some cases, with national security classified files that are restricted by statute. Although the personal papers of members of Congress are not governed by these acts, most wish to adhere to the spirit of the laws. Finally, any photocopies of records of congressional committees are governed by House and Senate rules.[11] Original archival committee records are housed in the National Archives.

Is the member of Congress and his or her staff and family willing to assist in oral history projects and in collecting the papers of ancillary persons and organizations? Twentieth-century papers most often have gaps that need to be supplemented by oral history. The verbal nature of Congress is well covered in *The Documentation of Congress*, which recommends that all repositories collecting congressional papers establish oral history projects to enhance the research value of such collections. The Carl Albert

Congressional Research and Studies Center's *Oral History Project: Procedure Manual*, by Daniel J. Linke, is an excellent model for other congressional repositories' oral history programs.[12] The member of Congress or his or her family can also influence the collection of the papers of ancillary persons or organizations.

COLLECTING THE PAPERS OF
ANCILLARY PERSONS AND ORGANIZATIONS

The inclusion of papers of ancillary persons or organizations in the collection development policy for congressional papers was first discussed in *The Documentation of Congress*, which recommends that the consideration of such papers and records be part of the overall documentation strategy and that collecting policies for congressional papers include them. Any ancillary persons and organizations can also be grouped under other subject areas collected by the repository, such as journalism, statewide organizations, minority groups, judiciary, or state politics. But to emphasize their relationships to congressional papers, they should be viewed as part of the congressional papers collection development policy. The various groups included in this section represent the interrelationships and overlapping staffing that Congress and the political parties have with other organizations.

The papers of unsuccessful candidates that document a point of view differing from that of the winner in significant elections should be collected. At the national level, Ross Perot and George Wallace are good examples of such individuals. At the state level, the papers of a defeated candidate for Congress who continues to play a role in state activities and who might run for future office should be collected.

The records of state and local political parties or organizations, including temporary political associations, merit collection. These entities might include state and local Democratic, Republican, and third-party organizations such as Socialist or Libertarian groups. Many congressional membership organizations also have a regional or local focus, such as that of the Northeast-Midwest Legislative Service Organization. In some states, a temporary political association may exist, such as the Louisiana "No Dukes" organization that opposed senatorial and gubernatorial candidate David Duke in the 1980s and 1990s. Just as important are "unofficial" congressional membership organizations (those that do not receive appropriated funds, such as the Democratic Study Group or the House Wednesday Group) that have regional or local interests.[13]

State and local politicians also have influence with Congress, and their papers should be collected.[14] Many states legally require that the records of state and local officials be transferred to the state archives. When that is not the case, local repositories may collect them. Noncongressional political organizations are excellent candidates for regional or statewide cooperative collecting policies.[15] These may include organizations that have as their goal the education of all voters regardless of party or nonparty affiliation. The records of the League of Women Voters, a nonpartisan, political education group, should be collected in all 50 states. Other nonpartisan groups might be similar to the Public Affairs Research Council of Louisiana, whose only purpose is to educate voters. Special-interest groups such as the right-to-life groups, pro-choice groups, World Wildlife Fund, and the Louisiana Coalition Against Racism and Nazism can affect congressional activities as well as influence voters at national, regional, or local levels. They affect voting through mailing campaigns, running their own candidates for office, supporting think tanks and political action committees (PACs), and lobbying. Their officers may be volunteers who hold the organizations' records, which, if not collected quickly, may disappear, since many of these groups are only temporary. Their records are difficult to locate, but their activities are critical to compiling a complete picture of lobbying that affects Congress and voters.

Although it often seems to the public that PACs are an official part of Congress, they are not. These committees are usually large campaign contributors, and they are required to report to the Federal Election Commission. They raise and make donations to campaigns and even pay for advertising for and against candidates. They are attached to business or other special-interest groups. The financial influence they have had since the early 1970s has changed the way campaigns are run and has lessened the candidate's personal influence over campaigns. They can be categorized as corporate, labor, trade, membership, health, "nonconnected" (related to neither the candidate nor his or her party), cooperative, and corporate without stock.[16]

The papers of many consultants also add to the documentation of Congress. Political consultants work for a specific candidate or political party and their job is to get their candidate elected. Media consultants and political consultants change roles frequently. Individuals may also serve as lobbyists or think-tank employees when not working with a candidate.

The papers of judges associated with particular politicians, parties, or philosophies should be collected, as should be the papers of judges who assisted or opposed Congress in the development of legislation relating to the courts.[17] Federal and Supreme Court justices' papers should be acquired at the state or national level as well.

Many media individuals and organizations focus on the functions of Congress and produce ancillary papers and records that repositories should acquire.[18] Individual legislative and political journalists in print, television, and radio can be included, as can political cartoonists. Many repositories already have substantial collections of journalists' papers. Because these collections include all types of journalists, it is helpful to list legislative and political journalists in the collection development policy for congressional papers. Organizations such as the National Press Club advise journalists on appropriate repositories for their papers. Most states have a state journalism association, and large cities may have local ones. These membership organizations' records give an overview of policy concerns of state and local journalists, and they may also include information on lobbying by these organizations.

Film, videotapes, and audiotapes from broadcasting stations offering political coverage or political programs are also valuable to a study of Congress. A repository cannot afford to collect the entirety of records from local television and radio stations, but they could develop an agreement whereby one or two stations send appropriate political coverage to the repository. Cable Satellite Public Affairs Network (C-SPAN) broadcasting is collected at the Purdue University Public Affairs Video Archives, and copies of tapes can be purchased. The Vanderbilt University Television News Archives records, abstracts, and indexes national evening news broadcasts of networks such as ABC, NBC, CBS, and CNN. Copies are available.

The role of media consultants has become increasingly important in political campaigns, and their papers will add to the historical record. Some congressional press secretaries become media consultants after leaving Congress. Media consultants still tend to stay behind the scenes in political activities, which makes their papers harder to collect. Public relations firms and advertising agencies also serve as media consultants.

In addition, the influence of lobbyists and lobbying groups has grown since World War II.[19] Numerous businesses, state officials, organizations, and individuals lobby Congress at one time or another on issues important to them. PACs may fall into this category as well. Lobbying information is contained in the records of many organizations, such as those of the National Rifle Association, the National Association for the Advancement of Colored People, the American Library Association, and the American Association of Retired Persons (AARP). Individual lobbyists who have long careers, or organizations that have lobbied for a number of years, will have the most complete files. Repositories should collect the papers of lobbyists and records of lobbying groups closely associated with issues that concern their state's congressional delegation. For example, Louisiana is economically dependent on the petroleum and chemical industries, and Louisiana repositories will therefore want to collect files from the significant petroleum and chemical industries lobbyists.

Often overlooked are the records of public policy research organizations, or think tanks.[20] These are nongovernmental, nonprofit public policy organizations. Some have been around since the early 1900s, but most have been established only since the 1960s. They may not legally lobby if they are registered as tax exempt. Think tanks can be partisan or nonpartisan, and individuals who have served as lobbyists, organization officers, politicians, consultants, and even congressional scholars move in and out of employment with these groups. Many legislative service organizations in Congress have affiliated private organizations that function as public policy organizations. For example, the Democratic Study Group supports the Democratic Study Center.[21]

University archives or manuscripts departments usually collect the papers of their professors who are congressional scholars, but those who are not affiliated with universities should be collected as well. Historians, political scientists, legal scholars, social scientists, and faculty in mass communications may all study the history, activities, and functions of the U.S. Congress. Most repositories collect the papers of faculty and scholars, but those collecting congressional papers should also seek out the papers of scholars in their state who concentrate on the study of Congress.

Political campaigns have always been run with the help of volunteers. Volunteers work in campaigns and on committees, serve as part of special-interest organizations, and function in many other unpaid capacities related to members of Congress. These volunteers may or may not become designated officials in the organizations for which they work. In collecting ancillary papers to congressional collections, repositories should look for evidence of volunteer activity in the papers of business people, educators, artists, journalists, and members of civic and community organizations, including garden club members.

All repositories operate more effectively with written collection development policies. If such policies are the foundation on which the collection is built, then documentation strategies provide the structural framework. *The Documentation of Congress* serves as the framework for repositories' congressional collections. This model collection development policy for congressional collections is a preliminary road map.

NOTES

1. Karen Hosier, "Large Number in Congress Calling It Quits," *Baton Rouge Sunday Advocate*, January 30, 1994, 1A, 9A.

2. Kathryn Allamong Jacob, ed., *Guide to Research Collections of Former United States Senators 1789–1982*, U.S. Senate Bicentennial Publication No. 1, S. Pub. 97-41 (Washington, D.C.: U.S. Senate, 1983); Cynthia Pease Miller, ed., *A Guide to Research Collections of Former Members of the United States House of Representatives 1789–1987*, H. Doc. 100–171 (Washington, D.C.: U.S. House of Representatives, 1988), ix.

3. J. Stanley Kimmitt and Richard A. Baker, *Conference on the Research Use and Disposition of Senators' Papers Proceedings* (Washington, D.C.: U.S. Senate, 1978), 121.

4. Frank Mackaman, *Congressional Papers Project Report* (Washington, D.C.: National Historical Publications and Records Commission, 1986), 17–27.

5. Karen Dawley Paul, *The Documentation of Congress: Report of the Congressional Archivists Roundtable Task Force on Congressional Documentation*, S. Pub. 102-20 (Washington, D.C.: U.S. Senate, 1992).

6. For a more thorough discussion of elements, see Faye Phillips, "Developing Collecting Policies for Manuscript Collections," *American Archivist* 47 (Winter 1984): 30–42.

7. Paul, *The Documentation of Congress*, 17–21. Such change is so significant that a recent National Heritage Lecture in Washington, D.C., "Changing Congress," addressed the changes in Congress and its membership since World War II. See "Society to Host National Heritage Lecture," *Capitol Dome* 29 (Winter 1994): 1.

8. See Faye Phillips and Mera W. Ford, *The Russell Billiu Long Collection Guide* (Baton Rouge: Special Collections, Louisiana State University Libraries, 1994).

9. For a repository point of view, see Division of Library and Archives, Minnesota Historical Society, "Report of the Congressional Papers Appraisal Committee," 1993. The author is working on appraisal guidelines for congressional papers for the Louisiana and Lower Mississippi Valley Collections. Also very important to this discussion is Patricia Aronsson, "Appraisal of Twentieth-Century Congressional Collections," in *Archival Choices: Managing the Historical Record in an Age of Abundance*, ed. Nancy E. Peace (Lexington, Mass.: D. C. Heath, 1984), 81–104.

10. Ronald L. Becker, "On Deposit: A Handshake and a Lawsuit," *American Archivist* 56 (Spring 1993): 320–28.

11. It is recommended that House committee records have restricted access for 30 years and Senate committee records for 20 years. See Rules XI and XXXVI of the Rules of the House of Representatives, Senate Rules XI and XXVI 10(a), and S. R. 474, 96th Congress.

12. Daniel J. Linke, *Oral History Project: Procedure Manual* (Norman, Okla.: Carl Albert Congressional Research and Studies Center, 1990).

13. See Gary Hoag, "Congressional Member Organizations," in Paul, *The Documentation of Congress*, 69–78.

14. See Paul Chestnut, "Legislative Records," *American Archivist* 48 (Spring 1985): 167–78.

15. See Aronsson, "Appraisal of Twentieth-Century Congressional Collections," 98–100.

16. Paul, *The Documentation of Congress*, 48.

17. See James Cross, "Congress and the Judicial Branch," in Paul, *The Documentation of Congress*, 91–98.

18. See Faye Phillips, "Congress and the Media," in Paul, *The Documentation of Congress*, 99–104.

19. See Sheryl Vogt, "Congress and Lobbyists," in Paul, *The Documentation of Congress*, 105–12.

20. See Karen Paul, "Congress and Think Tanks," in Paul, *The Documentation of Congress*, 109–12.

21. Paul, *The Documentation of Congress*, 71, 159.

9

Oral History as a Documentation Strategy for Political Collections

Jeffrey S. Suchanek

> In 1944, [future Chief Justice Fred M. Vinson] invited me for lunch. He was the economic czar of Roosevelt's last campaign. And that morning I had a conference with Roosevelt. And when Fred and I sat down to dinner I said, "Fred, the President's sick." "Oh," he said, "you've been listening to these damn Republicans." I said, "No. I just left him. And I'll guarantee he didn't know who I was. He didn't know what I was saying. If you go down there, he won't know that I'd been there." We elected a dead man in 1944.[1]

Conducting oral histories, the process of recording spoken memories of individuals, has become increasingly recognized as a worthy method of creating valuable primary resources by scholars and as a unique documentation strategy by political collections archivists. The past 30 years have witnessed a rapid growth in the citation of oral histories by serious scholars in their publications, and by political collections archivists as they attempt to document more fully the lives and careers of politicians who have donated papers to their repositories. Many major political collections repositories, such as the University of South Carolina, University of Wyoming, Mississippi State University, Tulane University, University of Georgia, University of North Texas, University of Connecticut, University of California at Berkeley, and a host of others, now incorporate oral history as part of their political collections documentation strategy. In addition to acquiring personal papers, these institutions actively pursue supplementary sources by interviewing the principals, related individuals, and others who can bear witness to the history being documented through oral recollections. Recognizing shortcomings such as subjectivity, selective recall, and genuine oversight due to the passage of time, a careful oral history documentation program will make an effort to gather broad and varied points of view from multiple participants.

The University of Kentucky established the Louie B. Nunn Center for Oral History in 1973 with funds allocated by Governor Louie B. Nunn to document the lives and careers of U.S. Supreme Court Chief Justice Fred M. Vinson and U.S. Senator Thruston B. Morton. Governor Nunn's interest in oral history can be traced to a speech he delivered to the Glasgow Lions Club on October 25, 1950. "Our county's history is at risk. We can improve this situation by asking our older people about what they remember. If we record what we find out, we will not only learn more of our county history, but we will also leave written information for future generations."[2]

Governor Nunn's support provided the foundation for the University of Kentucky's extensive and internationally recognized collection of over 6,500 oral history interviews. Topics covered in the collection include politics, public policy, and the university's own history. Although many of the interviews within the Nunn Center's Oral History Collection are with ordinary men and women who otherwise would not have a voice in the state and nation's history,[3] the core projects within the collection remain political and public policy oral histories.

In the realm of congressional history, archivists and scholars recognize that the written record comprising a majority of modern political collections does not come close to providing a comprehensive picture of the lives of politicians and the political events that have helped shape recent American history. The very nature of politics in a democratic, representative form of government involves the oral practices of discourse and debate, only a portion of which is reported officially in the *Congressional Record* and committee reports. The majority of documents found in today's political collections lack the detail necessary to determine the motivations behind important congressional votes and other actions. They fail to document fully the genesis of legislation, the behind-the-scenes bargaining, campaign strategies and candidates' styles, personal relationships among congressional colleagues, and the inner workings of congressional committees and offices. If members do not keep diaries, and most do not, oral history provides the best way to capture their views of important events. Interviews with former members of Congress and members of their office staff, congressional colleagues, lobbyists, political opponents, campaign organizers, political supporters, local newspaper editors and reporters, local civic leaders, and family and friends help to fill in the gaps not found in the donated papers. Oral histories put a human face on the individual behind the political career and personalize the documentation found in the voluminous collections of mostly routine papers.

John Sherman Cooper represented Kentucky in the U.S. Senate over three intermittent periods (1946–1949, 1952–1955, 1956–1973), alternating those years with diplomatic service such as delegate (and alternate delegate) to the General Assembly of the United Nations (1949–1951), or ambassador to India and Nepal (1955–1956). Cooper also served as a county and circuit judge prior to his Senate service, and toward the end of his career, as ambassador to the German Democratic Republic (1974–1976). The John Sherman Cooper Collection at the University of Kentucky consists of 998 manuscript document cases, and covers his political career, from his 1928 election to the Kentucky General Assembly, through his Senate service, to his ambassadorships in India and East Germany. The collection includes documents typically found in most modern political collections: official and constituent correspondence, government-generated reports, speeches, press releases, newspaper clippings, photographs, voting records, scrapbooks, audiotapes, and film, as well as the ubiquitous memorabilia. What the collection explicitly lacks is specific evidence indicating why this moderate Republican became one of the most highly revered politicians in a historically Democratic state. To supplement the written materials, the Nunn Center for Oral History initiated the John Sherman Cooper Oral History Project. That project now totals over 100 interviews, and includes over 250 interview hours with Cooper, staff members, political opponents, newspaper publishers and reporters, senatorial colleagues, former Kentucky governors, former state Republican Party leaders, friends, and family members.

The oral history interviews provide information regarding Cooper's personality and public appeal as well as insights into his political philosophy and motivations that cannot be found anywhere else. For example, although he hailed from a border state, the interviews reveal that Cooper became one of the first southern politicians to support civil rights legislation in 1957, and they help illustrate how a county judge could rise in a career to become an international ambassador:

> Well, to me, growing up in southeastern Kentucky, which did not have a large black population, it never did seem to be a problem as you grew up [or] as I grew up, at least. We got along well with all our black citizens. They called them different names then. They called them Negroes and some had worse names for them. They were law-abiding in the county I lived in and church-going. I remember many times I'd stop on my way to the First Baptist Church and go to the Methodist Episcopal Church, [a] black church, because I liked to hear the preaching and the singing. They could always vote in my county. None was ever denied the right to vote.[4]

With his career spanning state, national, and international service, Cooper's oral histories inevitably include personal accounts related to significant historical events. Cooper and his wife, Lorraine, had become close friends with John F. and Jacqueline Kennedy while both Cooper and Kennedy were serving in the Senate in the 1950s. It was Cooper's sad duty to accept President Lyndon Johnson's appointment to the commission investigating Kennedy's death. In one interview, Cooper provided little-known details of service on the Warren Commission to investigate the assassination of President Kennedy.

> Well, I was at home in Somerset, Kentucky, at my brother's house and a telephone call came through and they said it was for me. And [chuckling] the operator said, "There's a man on the phone who says he's the president of the United States; wants to talk to you." [Laughing] "Says to say he's the president of the United States." But it was, and he told me that he was appointing this commission and he wanted to know if I would serve on it. "Well," I said, "if you want me to serve on it, I will." . . . They [the commission's staff] took literally thousands of affidavits, and I think we had about a hundred before the committee including the wife of [Lee Harvey] Oswald twice. We [the commission members] disagreed on one chief item, and that was the question whether the shot that went through John Connolly had also gone through President Kennedy. There were two shots. One hit him some place in the lower neck, the other one blew the top of his head off. . . . Connolly was certain it hadn't. He said, "I know guns. I have rifles. I fire them all the time. When I heard the shot, I looked immediately over my right shoulder," which was the place where Oswald was [shooting], "and then I turned around and I was hit." His testimony was very convincing and . . . it made it more difficult to say that Oswald was the sole assassin because the shots came that close together, and you would have to have been a very good marksman. But we finally wrote into our summary that there had been two views and gave the explanation, and I guess really left it in the air.[5]

Alben W. Barkley's long political career began in 1913 with his election to the U.S. House of Representatives, where he served six terms, after which he was elected to four terms in the U.S. Senate (1926–1949). He returned to the Senate for a brief period before his death (1955–1956), after being elected vice president of the United States in 1948 on the Democratic ticket with President Harry S. Truman. Although Barkley's career led to the position of majority leader in the U.S. Senate and the vice presidency, his political collection is modest in size (150 cubic feet) when compared to those of individuals who served comparable lengths of time or reached such prominent leadership positions. The collection consists mainly of drafts of speeches, constituent correspondence, and scrapbooks. The essence of Barkley's character is distinctly missing. If not for the oral history interviews conducted by Sidney Shalett in 1953 that contributed to Barkley's autobiography *That Reminds Me*,[6] scholars would have difficulty determining his political philosophy and the principles behind his actions. In one interview, Barkley discussed his resignation as majority leader in 1944 in a dispute with President Roosevelt over a tax bill.

Well, I told Mr. Roosevelt that if he vetoed this bill, he would not get any additional revenue at all, and that I thought [the amount in the bill] was better than none. He went on then to say that this was a bill not for the relief of the needy, but for the relief of the greedy. Well, that language offended me very deeply because I had been a loyal supporter of his whole [New Deal] program. And I believed in it. I was not just a "yes man" [or] a "me too" man. I believed in the program because I was a liberal and a progressive long before I ever heard of Franklin D. Roosevelt. I was a liberal under Woodrow Wilson. Even before Wilson was elected I was a liberal, and I became more liberal under Wilson. I got the rudiments and the foundations of my liberal progressivism really at the feet of Woodrow Wilson.[7]

Interviews with colleagues, staff members, opponents, friends, and family often reveal a behind-the-scenes look at a politician's personality and working style. Kentuckian Stanley F. Reed served as solicitor general of the United States from 1935 to 1938, arguing many New Deal cases before the Supreme Court. President Roosevelt appointed Reed to the Supreme Court in 1938; among the key decisions during his 19 years on the Court was *Brown v. Board of Education of Topeka, Kansas*. The Reed Oral History Project contains 22 interviews with his former law clerks, some of which help historians understand how this moderate, Southern Democrat joined the opinion of the Court in ruling for desegregation of public education in the United States. George B. Mickum III, Reed's law clerk at the time of the *Brown* decision in 1954, commented:

I think the notion that is sometimes rampant that Reed's clerks told him what to do is just utter bullshit, utter bullshit; at least not when I was there. . . . I can tell you that it was not an easy case for Reed. I think it's public knowledge that at the commencement of the term he was really in dissent in that case. The fact is I could tell you that when that opinion was read from the bench, he cried.[8]

Albert B. "Happy" Chandler was twice elected governor of Kentucky (1935–1939, 1955–1959) and served in the U.S. Senate from 1939 to 1945. But his collection (over 200 cubic feet) probably garners more attention from researchers looking for information about his tenure as Major League Baseball's commissioner from 1945 to 1951, when the color barrier was broken by Jackie Robinson. Not much official documentation of this historic issue is present in the collection, but the A. B. Chandler Oral History Project, consisting of 199 interviews, serves to fill in the gaps of not only his political career, but also his role and motivation in helping to integrate the great game of the "nation's pastime."

I felt certainly the situation would arise. They were moving in the direction of trying to see that arrangements were made to permit them [African Americans] to play. They had numerous players who were outstanding. Josh Gibson, that

I recall, and Satchel Paige and [Buck] Leonard and some of the others, I knew about them. They were fine. I saw some of them play. But it must be remembered that Commissioner Landis, my predecessor, for 24 years said no to them every time they asked, and that was because the owners didn't want them to play. No question about that. The owners did not want them to play. And, of course, when Landis died, the owners had that in mind. It wasn't that they wanted to be caught with their pants down, and they knew I was a southerner and they knew I was a Confederate, had Confederate leanings, and that was all true. And they thought I'd be the last fellow that would agree to let a black boy play. In January of 1947 at a meeting at the Waldorf Astoria in New York, a club owner's meeting, they voted 15-1 not to let this boy [Jackie Robinson] play. And [Branch] Rickey was then on the verge of bringing him in. So that was supposed to be advice to me and advice to Rickey. Rickey said to me, "Commissioner, I can't do it without your complete support." So we talked it out and I told him then, "I'm going to have to meet my maker some day, and if he asks me why I didn't let this boy play and I say it was because he was black, that might not be a sufficient answer, and I'm wholly unwilling at this stage of my life to say to this fellow, although you have the ability, you can't play in the major leagues because you're black." I said, "You bring him in and we'll make a fight with you," and of course, the rest of it is history.[9]

Sometimes, oral history interviews are the only means to document an individual's contributions. This was the case with Edward F. Prichard Jr., a protégé of Supreme Court Justices Felix Frankfurter and Fred M. Vinson and a former member of President Roosevelt's White House "Brain Trust," who had preserved little written documentation. The Nunn Center conducted over 70 interviews, including 23 interviews with Prichard prior to his death. These interviews led to the publication of Tracy Campbell's monograph *Short of the Glory: The Fall and Redemption of Edward F. Prichard, Jr.*[10] In one interview, Prichard gave a behind-the-scenes glimpse into the Roosevelt White House.

FDR became very upset about leaks that were coming out of the White House. Every president is always upset about leaks. That's just as old as the brass band, you know. And he got upset about it and he called everybody in, including me. He had the whole kit and caboodle in, and he read us the riot act, that he wasn't going to stand for any more leaking, that he wasn't going to have any-more gossiping about things going on there, and if it kept on somebody was going to be in trouble! And he put the fear of God into us. And then he tossed his head back and with that Roosevelt grin he said, "Of course there comes a time occasionally when there should be a leak. Now," he said, "there's a certain matter that I'm going to make a decision on that needs to be leaked." And he looked at me and he said, "Prichard, I guess you're the one that ought to leak it. Won't you tell Drew Pearson about it?" And I said, "Well, Mr. President, I already have."[11]

Florence Cantrill, a suffragist, was the first woman elected from Lexington to the Kentucky General Assembly in 1934. Like Prichard, she left behind few personal papers when she died in 1981, but the four oral history interviews that were conducted with her help document her suffragist activities and political career.

> The year that women got the vote we were going to have a Democratic convention in Louisville. I was demanding that we have an equal number of women delegates to that convention. My feeling was that the way for the women to get influence was to join the parties and work within your party. I was the woman chairman in Fayette County the first time that women did vote and we just had a pretty good organization. On Election Day the men were terribly worried. The Republicans had long lines of their voters, both men and women. I went down to [Democratic] headquarters. They were simply panicky. They said our women were not coming out [to vote], and I said, "Well, our women don't come out until they get dressed in the afternoon." So sure enough, after lunch, they began to come out in great big numbers and the Democrats did carry the county. The men felt better about it. They felt that they hadn't done so badly to give women the vote after that.[12]

Oral history projects at the University of Kentucky are carefully planned to thoroughly and broadly document any given subject. The Louie B. Nunn Center for Oral History prefers to conduct "life history" interviews with politicians and public policy advocates that involve multiple interview sessions over a period of months or even years. This requires a substantial commitment of time and resources by both the oral historian and the institution. Pre-interview research and preparation is necessary in order to conduct meaningful interviews. Whether the interviews are conducted with an analog or digital recorder, the recordings must be transcribed to facilitate access and for preservation purposes. Digitization is not a permanent preservation medium, although it shows more promise than magnetic analog tapes. Preservation "reformatting" of oral histories to printed transcripts is a viable preservation method that will ensure long-term access to the recorded information, and experience has proven that, when given the choice between the audio interview and the verbatim transcript, researchers almost always choose the transcript because time is a researcher's most valuable commodity. Rather than listen to a two-hour interview that may or may not contain relevant information, a researcher can scan through the 60-page transcript of the interview in less than half the time required to listen to the audio recording of the same material. There are several fine published manuals on how to conduct oral history interviews that are readily available, as well as texts and essays about the craft and theory of oral histories. The Oral History Association maintains a Web site that includes a pamphlet series, with useful titles such as *Evaluation Guidelines*, which addresses ethical and legal issues.

Oral history can also be an important development tool for a political collections archive. Over the course of several interviews, personal rapport may be established with the interviewee that inevitably strengthens his or her bonds with the institution, and financial support can be forthcoming. Multiple interview sessions allow the individual to develop a deeper understanding of the institution and its mission. Through the experience of being encouraged to tell their story in their own way, individual participants come to understand that the institution is interested in them as people, not just as celebrity donors. During the last years of his life, former Kentucky Governor Louie B. Nunn recorded over 80 hours of oral history interviews, resulting in one of the most extensive and informative life histories in the entire collection.

Financial support to help facilitate processing the political collection and oral histories can come from the individual or from a network of former supporters. Monies can be used to establish or supplement an existing endowment. Interviewees can also be helpful in soliciting new collections or serving in an advisory capacity for institutional programs related to the oral histories. Before his death in 2004, Governor Nunn chaired the Nunn Center's Endowment Committee and helped secure $250,000 toward the endowment. After his death, his son, Kentucky State Representative Steve Nunn, successfully sought $1 million in additional state funding during the 2005 session of the Kentucky General Assembly to supplement the endowment. He and his sister, Jennie Nunn Penn, continue to work to achieve the $2 million endowment goal. Political archives with an oral history component can derive both short- and long-term benefits, not the least of which is the valuable information that is garnered for the historical record.

Oral history cannot and is not intended to take the place of the written records. Oral history is not instant history. In fact, oral history is not recorded history but recorded memory. And, in the course of conducting interviews for a thematic oral history, the archivist is creating a sort of "shared authority" in collecting new primary sources.[13]

Important sources for public policy researchers always have been, and will remain, written documents such as letters, diaries, press releases, voting records, newspaper articles, and written speeches (whether paper or electronic). Oral histories, however, can provide a blueprint to the documents collection, serving to connect the dots through seemingly fragmented sources. This may become more important as researchers use them to navigate electronic archival collections. Such memories provide added value to the traditional archival sources by providing needed context. With the interviewee serving as tour guide, the personal recollections found in oral histories can almost serve as a road map to reading the impersonal documents found in large collections.

Political collections archivists should build oral history projects into their institutional goals and priorities. Plans for the inclusion of oral history projects in collection development and documentation strategies will ensure that invaluable memories will not be lost to future generations. The process itself can lead to lasting relationships that benefit both donors and archives alike.

NOTES

1. Interview with John Y. Brown, Lexington, Kentucky, March 9, 1976, Fred M. Vinson Oral History Project, Division of Special Collections and Digital Programs, University of Kentucky Libraries.

2. "Nunn Relates History to Lions Club," *Glasgow, Kentucky, Evening Journal*, October 25, 1950, 1.

3. John Van Willigen and Anne Van Willigen, *Food and Everyday Life on Kentucky Family Farms, 1920–1950* (Lexington: University Press of Kentucky, 2006).

4. Interview with John Sherman Cooper, Washington, D.C., May 16, 1981, John Sherman Cooper Oral History Project, Division of Special Collections and Digital Programs, University of Kentucky Libraries.

5. Interview with John Sherman Cooper, Washington, D.C., June 5, 1983, John Sherman Cooper Oral History Project, Division of Special Collections and Digital Programs, University of Kentucky Libraries.

6. Alben W. Barkley, *That Reminds Me* (Garden City, N.Y.: Doubleday, 1954).

7. Interview with Alben W. Barkley, Schroon Lake, New York, July 21, 1953, Alben W. Barkley Oral History Project, Division of Special Collections and Digital Program, University of Kentucky Libraries.

8. Interview with George B. Mickum III, Washington, D.C., March 18, 1981, Stanley F. Reed Oral History Project, Division of Special Collections and Digital Programs, University of Kentucky Libraries.

9. Interview with Albert B. Chandler, Versailles, Kentucky, September 22, 1980, A. B. Chandler Oral History Project, Division of Special Collections and Digital Programs, University of Kentucky Libraries.

10. Tracy Campbell, *Short of the Glory: The Fall and Redemption of Edward F. Prichard, Jr.* (Lexington: University Press of Kentucky, 1998).

11. Interview with Edward F. Prichard Jr., Lexington, Kentucky, July 29, 1982, Edward F. Prichard Jr. Oral History Project, Division of Special Collections and Digital Programs, University of Kentucky Libraries.

12. Interview with Florence Cantrill, Lexington, Kentucky, July 27, 1977, Kentucky History Oral History Project, Division of Special Collections and Digital Programs, University of Kentucky Libraries.

13. Michael Frisch, *A Shared Authority: Essays on the Craft and Meaning of Oral and Public History* (Albany: State University of New York Press, 1990), 5–27.

10

Electronic Record Systems on Capitol Hill: Finding and Obtaining What You Want

Elisabeth Butler and Karen Dawley Paul

While electronic records present many uncertainties for archivists, those who collect the papers of members of Congress can be particularly challenged when they try to identify and select electronic records for preservation. This is partly due to the evolving nature of technology, but it is also because members of Congress do not use one particular type of system, nor do they use systems in exactly the same way for any given time period. For example, the Senate, since 2004, has provided offices with the use of OnBase, an Internet-based document management system. Approximately one dozen offices use it, but they use it for a variety of purposes. When it comes to electronic recordkeeping, there is perhaps less consistency among congressional offices than there is with textual files. Probably no two office records management systems are alike, reflecting both variations in software and the records being managed. This lack of consistency within the Congress is exacerbated by the frequency of staff turnover, particularly among systems administrators, who are in great demand.[1] Repositories that specialize in preserving the documentation of Congress are well advised to work one-on-one with a member's office to identify and preserve the records that they wish to maintain. Repositories that do this will have an opportunity to collect useful and complete information. Repositories that do not have this opportunity will be dependent on the vicissitudes of staff that close the office to select, organize, and transfer pertinent electronic files.

The House and Senate both maintain lists of approved systems from which an individual office makes selections. Offices then utilize the systems to meet their own perceived needs. A description of the general types of systems is provided to guide congressional archivists in the identification and selection of electronic records. Since the bioterrorist attacks on

Congress in 2001 and 2004,[2] the transition to electronic records creation
and retention by staff has greatly accelerated. Because all incoming mail is
irradiated, the retention of digitized files of this material is seen by many
to be safer and more efficient.[3] As a result of this increasing dependence
on electronic records to process work, the Senate saw the first major investigation (regarding Hurricane Katrina) conducted by the Homeland Security and Governmental Affairs Committee in 2005–2006 consist almost
entirely of electronic records. The end of the 109th Congress saw the first
all-electronic collection assembled by a member, that belonging to Senator James Talent (R-MO). The end of the 109th Congress also witnessed
an unprecedented amount of committee electronic files transferred to the
Center for Legislative Archives.[4]

The extent to which congressional staff use electronic records to process
their work is graphically described in the last section of this chapter, which
summarizes an electronic archival project that commenced in 2004 in the
Senate Homeland Security and Governmental Affairs Committee. This project demonstrates the significance of managing and preserving electronic
documents within congressional offices, especially those residing in e-mail
and attachments. It also serves to alert archivists who collect members' papers about the importance of the information contained in them and their
significance as archival sources.

CORRESPONDENCE MANAGEMENT SYSTEMS (CMS)

All members respond to constituent contacts that are made via mail, phone,
fax, and e-mail. Staff rely on correspondence management systems to respond to these contacts and to keep track of what responses were made and
when they were made. These systems generally are used in members' offices
rather than in committees, because it is the member's office that responds to
constituent contacts. Contemporary systems are more elaborate than those
of the 1990s and earlier (as described in Naomi Nelson's chapter in this
volume), but they essentially perform the same type of function that they
always have—that of tracking incoming communications from constituents
together with the responses that were sent in reply. At a member's request, a
copy of the system data (correspondent information and form-letter library
of response paragraphs) is transferred to the repository as a flat file. At the
end of each Congress and again at the member's request, an updated CMS
archiving format document that delineates all of the fields and exports all
the data within the system database is prepared by computer staff. The retiring member may elect to send this document to the repository along with
the CMS data. The receiving repository then must decide whether to transfer
the data to another database for data manipulation purposes.

Archivists should note that, in addition to the current data, congressional offices may also have information generated from obsolete correspondence systems or from the current system that is not available electronically. This might include old library response paragraph items in textual format, issue/topic code lists, copies of incoming correspondence, and various statistical reports. Those who receive CMS data are advised to ascertain whether any of the additional information is available. Other documentation of potential use to a repository includes a description of the office mail handling procedures and information about office procedures for migrating and purging correspondence data. This can be obtained by interviewing the system administrator if it has not been previously compiled in an office operations manual.

Archivists should ascertain from the member's office whether any data other than constituent name, address, and contact history is contained on the CMS system. This could include the member's scheduling information, e-mails, or incoming documents that have been scanned into the system. The presence of this information will vary from office to office and from system to system.

CMS systems can generate various statistical reports, some of which will be of interest to archivists receiving the collection. "Hot topic" reports identifying the 10 most significant topics for specified time periods can be useful for studying the influence of constituent opinion on member's views and also may be useful to perform selective sampling on the mail. Reports generated by specified zip codes can reveal differences of opinion in various geographic areas. If such reports have not been produced regularly by the office, they can be done prior to the office closing, while the software is still available. It is up to the repository archivist to ask for them, and it presents an opportunity to work with the office to define which reports are of interest. It is important to keep in mind that the retiring member must request that the data from this system and from all of the systems be processed and sent to a designated repository. This does not happen automatically. It is equally important that archivists ask for it if they want it.

LEGISLATIVE INFORMATION SYSTEMS

Both the House of Representatives and the Senate have developed in-house legislative information systems to track the development and evolution of legislation. These systems are constantly being enhanced to facilitate the composition and movement of legislation within Congress. The systems generate legislative activities reports that list all measures and amendments sponsored or co-sponsored by a member for each session of Congress. They are produced at the end of a session and on special request. The reports include a subject index to the measures and amendments. Beginning with the 100th Congress, reports are available in printed and/or electronic format. Prior to the 100th Congress, they are available in print only. Archivists should ascertain that these useful reference tools are included with the donation of the member's papers.

LOCAL AREA NETWORKS

All congressional offices maintain their own local area networks. There is wide variation in the type and arrangement of legislative activities information that individual offices maintain on their systems. Each office implements its own policies as to what information is maintained and how it is arranged and filed. Committees are responsible for archiving permanently valuable electronic information residing on their LANs. When a member's office closes and at the request of the member, the systems administrator is responsible for doing a backup of the LAN with appropriate assistance from available in-house technical staff. The member decides whether to transfer the data to a designated repository.

Archivists are advised to work with the member's office to arrange for transfer of the LAN files in a format that they can receive and preserve. The office should provide a printout of the directory for the archives. Generally, the information is maintained in its current software, and directory structures are maintained. File arrangement might be by individual staff person, with folders or a directory structure that is reflective of the staffer's name, or there might be a shared centralized filing system arranged by function or topics. For example, Senator Talent's office developed a knowledge management system using Microsoft SharePoint Portal Server. This system is an intranet-based software package that facilitates team collaboration as well as organization and searching of documents. Functional sections in the Talent knowledge management system included offices (administrative materials), legislative, press, and scheduling. Documents can include briefing memos, memos for the file, remarks, speeches, correspondence, drafts of legislation, notes, schedules, and documents that have been scanned and transferred into the system. While several offices use SharePoint, no two will use it exactly the same way. Archivists acquiring LAN-based system files should ask that the system be documented both for particular SharePoint setup and general description of how the system was used by the office.

Because of the extensive use of computers by legislative staff, most member-designated repositories should be receiving at least some electronic files of LAN material. Indeed, some staff create and retain only electronic files. Of all the types of electronic systems in use, the office LANs undoubtedly contain the most significant information for archival purposes.

LEGISLATIVE DATABASES

Archivists who are receiving a member's papers collection should ascertain whether the member's office has created special databases, what information they contain, and what software was used to create and maintain them. If the database is particularly important, the repository must decide whether to retain it in its current software or to reformat the data to a flat file format for long-term preservation. The repository should obtain a description of the database elements so that the schema can be restored or migrated. Repositories also may wish to receive a version of the database in the software dependent version in order to support any immediate research needs.

MEMBERS' SCHEDULES

It is important for repositories to obtain a full set of the member's schedules for the archival collection. This likely is the only systematic and complete source of chronological documentation for the individual's career. Archivists need to be aware that schedules may reside in word processing, on a correspondence management system, or in Microsoft Outlook Calendar or similar systems. Schedules probably will not reside on paper. If the schedule resides in word processing, it should be processed according to procedures followed for preparing the LAN for transfer to the archival repository. If it resides on the correspondence management system, depending on the particular system and the options it provides, offices may be able to export their schedules directly from the system, or they may need to pay a vendor to convert the schedule information for them. If the schedule resides on Microsoft Outlook, it must be exported to a personal folder file and given a name that includes either the H or S drive, or it can be exported as .PST files (see e-mail discussion below). It can then be transferred to the repository with the other LAN files. Again, archivists should ascertain where this information resides and ask for it.

HOME PAGES

At the end of the 104th, 105th, 106th, and 107th Congresses, the Senate captured snapshots of its public Web sites and transferred them to the Center for Legislative Archives at the National Archives. Beginning with the 108th Congress, the National Archives began to obtain snapshots of all public government Web sites, including congressional sites. There were 52 legislative branch sites captured for the 108th Congress. The first Congress-specific harvest in the fall of 2006 captured 615 Web sites, an estimated

120–160 gigabytes of information. The National Archives captures the congressional sites once per Congress. The archived sites are available on the National Archives home page, where they are documented and clearly labeled as a National Archives historic record, with the date of capture and all external links blocked, so that users do not confuse the historic site with current live sites. If repository archivists wish to obtain more than a once-per-Congress snapshot for a particular member's site, they will need to ask the member's office to preserve more frequent versions.

E-MAIL

Options for preserving staff e-mail include printing out on paper, or exporting to a word processing, PDF, or HTML format, making certain that links to attachments, along with relevant e-mail metadata such as date/time sent and received, are included. Most e-mail systems, including Microsoft Outlook, include this type of capability. In the case of Outlook, a prevalent export method is to use the "PST" format, which represents a comprehensive export of an entire individual mailbox. In any of these methods, the resulting export files can be copied to a specific drive, where they can be retained with other LAN files. This needs to be done on a routine basis by the staff who are receiving and creating it, with assistance from an archivist/records manager who is trained to select and file this information. Repository archivists who will be receiving a member's papers should ascertain what the office policy is regarding e-mail retention of individual staff. Constituent e-mail can be included in the CMS system if the office has chosen to do so. Again, archivists need to ascertain whether this is the case. There are no systems in use that are solely devoted to e-mail management. The selection and preservation of e-mail is covered in greater detail in the following section.

A COMMITTEE ELECTRONIC RECORDS PROJECT

Preserving electronic information is one of the great challenges facing archivists today. Software applications quickly change and become obsolete, making document collection and retrieval difficult and complicated. Congressional offices, like offices everywhere, are in a state of transition as staff work to implement ways to capture and organize their electronic records so that they can be retrieved when needed. The Senate Committee on Homeland Security and Governmental Affairs was forced to confront these challenges earlier than many congressional offices, and its experience provides a useful model for managing electronic documents.

The committee produces a wide range of records of historic value relating to the examination of governmental accountability and efficiency (including E-Government initiatives). It possesses the broadest subpoena powers in the Senate, which means that oversight investigations make up a substantial part of its work. Beginning in 2003, the committee assumed oversight responsibility for the new Department of Homeland Security and over portions of the intelligence community. At the time, the committee had a full-time archivist overseeing records management and processing permanent committee records for transfer to the Center for Legislative Archives.

In 2004, electronic records suddenly became a significant consideration in the committee's archiving procedures as a result of work on a major intelligence community reform bill. There had not been such a large-scale national security reorganization since 1947, when the National Security Act created the Department of Defense. Because this earlier reorganization is thinly documented in the archival records, it became a committee imperative to thoroughly document this government reorganization. Within a matter of weeks, the committee had to put together a series of hearings and draw up and shepherd a bill through Congress. This meant that communications and staff analysis largely would be conducted via electronic means. Indeed, some intelligence community detailed staff stayed for such a short time that they left little or nothing that was not in an electronic form. Staff electronically created and exchanged legislative drafts, memos, and other analytical documents. Seemingly overnight, the majority of documentation about the creation of the Directorate of National Intelligence was electronic. Once this pattern was established, it became set. While staff were aware that they needed to save their records, especially their e-mails, it was difficult for them to do so in a comprehensive or consistent way because of the extreme time pressure.

The committee quickly moved to prevent an imminent loss of information. A policy memo advised staff to file their e-mails into folders and to retain their electronic documents on their H drive on the committee's server. Staff were advised to save memos, correspondence and communications, briefing summaries, and pertinent downloaded reports and research material. Because committee records are transferred to the Center for Legislative Archives at the National Archives, the center's director, deputy director, and an information specialist from the Electronic Records Archives (a multimillion-dollar project of the National Archives to acquire and preserve government electronic records) were invited to a meeting with the committee's archivist, systems administrator, and Senate archivist. The result was the creation of an electronic records "protocol" for the committee to follow.

The protocol governs the style, format, and some specifics of export and transfer methods for the committee's electronic documents that are designated for the archives. The selection and organization of these documents are performed by the committee archivist at the time a staff member departs. Generally, the documents are organized by staff member and by committee functions of hearings, legislation, nominations, oversight, and investigation subfolders. This mirrors the processing of textual records and sets up categories to administer access to the files. Under the resolution governing access to Senate records (S. Res. 474, 96th Congress), most committee records are opened when they are 20 years old. Investigations and nominations records are closed for 50 years because of the sensitivity of the information they contain, unless the committee determines otherwise.

In this particular case, it was decided that the archivist should convert selected documents into Adobe systems PDF format, a widely used export format that will be supported by the Electronic Records Archives, and burn them onto a CD-ROM.[5] The CD-ROM is labeled with the staffer's name, title, party affiliation, Congresses covered by the records, and series title, and is usually placed in its own acid-free archives box, either under its own accession or as part of the staffer's textual collection, if one exists. When the accession is transferred to the Center for Legislative Archives, accompanying documentation identifies the presence of electronic records, and the electronic records are immediately sent to the archive's electronic records specialists, where they are transferred to a long-term storage medium as determined by the archives.

The electronic records protocol proved especially useful for managing the Hurricane Katrina investigation records of 2005–2006, as much of the responsive material received by the committee was electronic. Because all staff needed equal access to these records, the systems administrator created a shared drive to display all the electronic and PDF-scanned versions of federal, state, and local document productions. The drive also included Republicans' and Democrats' strategic shared documents. By the end of the investigation, the collection of responsive records was about 3 GB, enough to fill several CD-ROMs. Because the database was complete and well-organized and the volume of existing textual records was excessive and difficult to use, only the electronic versions were transferred to the Center for Legislative Archives on a portable hard drive. This marked the first time that a Senate committee's records of a major investigation were almost completely electronic.

Many of the records that the committee received from federal and state agencies were e-mails. A review of these communications revealed that many were of permanent record quality. This underscored the importance of managing this form of communication from the point of creation and throughout office use. It is a challenge that many offices find difficult to meet. A 2005 report from the University of Maryland (partially funded by the National Archives) found that many of the 21 federal agencies surveyed (including the Department of Homeland Security) were confused about the proper definition and disposition of e-mails and did not have complete policies governing their retention. This haphazard treatment often results in offices incorrectly storing or even destroying e-mails, leaving federal offices in potential violation of the Freedom of Information Act (FOIA) and other records laws.[6] At the other end of the spectrum, some offices (like the White House) have systems that are designed to save every e-mail, irrespective of value, causing them to potentially transfer thousands to millions of e-mails with indeterminate record status to the National Archives.

Committee e-mails, like so many in the federal offices studied in the University of Maryland's report, are numerous, difficult to capture, and reside in an impermanent native format (as in the case of the Senate Outlook PST files). Committee staff are relied on to save their significant e-mails either by clicking and dragging or Auto Archiving them into their Archives/Personal Folders in Outlook, because the committees do not have a system which automatically captures staff e-mails. E-mails usually end up being stored on an H drive. Many individually saved e-mails had collected on the committee server prior to 2004. These were inaccessible to the archivist. In 2004, the committee obtained software called UniAccess, which converts the individually saved e-mails into a readable format like HTML. UniAccess also maintains the e-mails' complete attachments in their original formats (Microsoft Word, WordPerfect, PowerPoint, etc.), so not just the message but the accompanying material can be read. At this point, the archivist can appraise the e-mails and attachments. The converted e-mails are usually kept in HTML (which the National Archives requested), and the attachments are converted to PDF. Both are burned onto the CD-ROMs, usually into topical "E-mails" folders, along with the processed H drive documents.

Processing e-mails can be time consuming but well worth the effort. It is not necessary to actually read each of the thousands of e-mails that staff accumulate during their tenure. It is sufficient to skim through them to make sure they are readable and relevant. Staff work in sequences according to the legislative issue currently the focus of action. It is possible to identify significant sequences of communications that relate to hearings, nominations being considered, legislation under review, or investigations under way. E-mail attachments also are scanned for relevancy. Many are working documents and drafts that are already present in other saved files. Messages typically are from other congressional staff, contacts in lobbying firms, interest and constituent groups, agency personnel, and think tank experts. These sources frequently are not represented in staff textual records. The documents vividly portray competing influences on legislation, constituents' interests, the rival opinions of various experts and interest groups, and the extensive networks that exist among governmental and private sectors. Most importantly for archivists and future researchers, the e-mails essentially provide a chronology and context both for staff electronic and textual documents. They are an invaluable historical resource.

Besides containing information directly relevant to legislation and nomination issues that are taken up by the committee, the e-mails document the extent of oversight issues that simply die from lack of interest, evidence, or time. These issues that never receive a hearing or get publicized in other ways are particularly revealing of the committee's priorities and mindset at a certain time.

Because electronic records, especially e-mail, provide so much information, they have come to shape committee archival processing procedures. Staff frequently do not adequately organize or label their textual records, because it is more efficient to file and retrieve online. In some cases, the quantity of electronic material exceeds the amount of paper that staff retain for archives. Therefore, in the committee, it has become a higher priority to process the electronic records first. They in fact become a road map that provides the necessary context for the textual records. Much of this appraisal and processing work is accomplished by an archivist/records manager. While chief clerks are designated to oversee the archiving process in committees, the complexities of selecting and preserving electronic records demand greater time and attention than most clerks possess. Electronic archiving must be accomplished on a regular, consistent basis, and it is best done by a dedicated, appropriately trained individual who will meet with all new staff to brief them on their recordkeeping responsibilities and suggest ways to meet them. Staff need to be reminded periodically and even assisted, especially during work on major legislation and investigations. When staff depart, they again need to be assisted and briefed.

Managing and preserving electronic records is a collaborative effort, involving the support of the chief clerks, office managers, staff directors and legislative staff, and the technical assistance of the systems administrators. Committees, like other congressional offices, face enormous challenges in implementing good management and preservation of their electronic resources. The experience of the Senate Committee on Homeland Security and Governmental Affairs demonstrates why this is important and proves that "where there is a will, there is a way." Properly trained staff can utilize software to capture/convert various types of electronic documents to prepare them for submission to the archives. It is possible to establish a workable policy governing their disposition. A successfully implemented policy and procedure will help all congressional offices, whether they be member or committee, conduct major or ongoing projects successfully, preserve institutional memory, and prevent loss of critical information.

NOTES

1. This is nicely illustrated in Emily B. Robison, "Electronic Recordkeeping in the United States Senate: A Case Study at the Louisiana State University Libraries," master of library and information sciences thesis, Louisiana State University, August 1999, 20–36.

2. On October 15, 2001, a letter containing anthrax was opened in Senator Tom Daschle's mailroom in the Hart Senate Office Building. When traces were found in the ventilation system, the building and other congressional office buildings were shut down until they were tested and declared safe. On October 20, anthrax spores were discovered in the Ford House Office Building. The House office buildings were closed for five days. The Russell Office Building reopened on October 24 and the Dirksen Building reopened on October 26. The Hart Building required fumigation by spraying chlorine dioxide throughout the building and did not reopen until January 22, 2002. On February 2, 2004, ricin, a toxic substance, was discovered in Senator William Frist's mailroom in the Dirksen Office Building. The Senate office buildings were tested, the mailroom cleaned, and the buildings reopened on February 5.

3. Irradiation, the process used to sterilize incoming mail to Capitol Hill zip codes by using high dosages of radiation to kill viruses and bacteria, accelerates the aging process of paper, causing it to become dry, brittle, and discolored. It erases magnetic storage media, exposes film, fades color photographs, and creates gases as chemical reactions take place within the irradiated materials. The side effects can be particularly serious for materials wrapped inside plastic shipping envelopes or containers.

4. The total number of committee electronic files transferred during the 108th Congress was eight accessions consisting of 23 CD-ROMs, holding 9,644 files and 749,754,976 bytes (or 749.7 megabytes). During the 109th Congress, 59 accessions consisting of 374 CDs and disks, holding 299,491 files and 72,845,471,510 bytes (or 72.8 gigabytes), were transferred.

5. See Brad Reagan, "The Digital Ice Age," *Popular Mechanics*, December, 2006, www.popularmechanics.com/technology/industry/4201645.html; and Eric Bangeman, "Adobe to Make PDF an Open Standard," Ars Technica 1998–2006, http://arstechnica.com/news.ars/post/20070129-8724.html.

6. University of Maryland, College of Information Studies, *Best Practices in Electronic Records Management: A Survey and Report on Federal Government Agency's Recordkeeping Policy and Practices*, December 19, 2005, www.archives.gov/records-mgmt/initiatives/umd-survey.html.

Part III

APPRAISING POLITICAL COLLECTIONS

11

Appraising Modern Congressional Collections

Patricia Aronsson

Congressional collections of the twentieth century, and now the twenty-first, present archivists with unprecedented challenges.[1] Comprising characteristics of both public records and personal papers, they are difficult to process and are becoming expensive to maintain. Furthermore, dwindling research use raises questions about their value compared to the value of other types of archival collections. These problems, in addition to diminishing staff, space, and financial resources, contribute to the crisis facing archivists who are trying to deal effectively with the collections of recent U.S. senators and representatives.

Congressional collections are hybrids, neither strictly archival nor strictly personal. According to "A Basic Glossary for Archivists, Manuscript Curators, and Records Managers," from the Society of American Archivists (SAA), personal papers are "formed by or around an individual or family," while records represent the "cumulation of a corporate entity."[2] Congressional collections fit both definitions. Most archivists treat the papers of senators or representatives as personal papers, processing them as they would process most manuscript collections. That is, they examine collections at the item level, discard little, and refolder most of the material. Processing such papers with a straight records approach, however, may not be any more appropriate. While an archivist or records manager can easily establish a retention schedule to meet the needs of most same-type, same-size businesses, one schedule is not likely to work for all members of Congress. Each

Previously published as "Appraisal of Twentieth-Century Congressional Collections" in *Archival Choices: Managing the Historical Record in an Age of Abundance*, ed. Nancy E. Peace (Lexington, Mass.: D.C. Health, 1984). Reprinted with permission.

congressional office revolves around a unique personality and the needs of a single state or congressional district. Thus, traditional formulas do not help archivists to make these collections useful.

Congressional collections are more expensive to acquire and maintain than they have ever been. In recent years, the quantity of information accumulated in the personal offices of senators and representatives has increased dramatically. Members of Congress accrue 50–100 cubic feet of papers per year. Their predecessors of 50 years ago accumulated this quantity over a career of 20 years.[3] Several factors contribute to this proliferation of papers. Constituents write their representatives and senators more often and about more issues than they did in the past. Senators and representatives are called on to address a greater variety of legislative issues than ever before, and to accommodate these legislative demands, they employ more staff members than did their colleagues of 20 and more years ago. As staff increases, so does the amount of paper produced. Furthermore, legislative employees have become more specialized to meet the more complicated demands made on senators and representatives. This specialization and the amount of paper produced have increased the time and money needed to evaluate the records and to prepare them for research use. In an effort to avoid being inundated with thousands of boxes of records at one time (when a member retires or is defeated), many repositories send archivists to Washington to arrange for the shipment of small quantities of records periodically throughout the career of the senator or representative. This approach also has drawbacks, however. Annual or biannual trips to Washington, D.C., are expensive and often result in the acquisition of mundane records. Moreover, congressional offices frequently request access to records already sent to the repository. Valuable staff time is expended responding to these requests. Considering that congressional collections occupy enormous amounts of shelf space, the maintenance costs of which increase yearly, and require substantial investments of staff time in acquisitions, processing, and servicing, one begins to understand why the question of their value for historical purposes has become so crucial.

As noted earlier, research use of congressional papers has plummeted in recent years. In 1978, at the Conference of the Research Use and Disposition of Senators' Papers, Robert Warner noted that it would take a researcher 10 years to examine every document in an average-size senate collection.[4] Few scholars are able to devote that much time to a single collection. Additionally, the sheer bulk of these collections makes it difficult for a researcher to locate particular pieces of information. To document their studies of Congress, many scholars have turned to other sources, such as the *Congressional Record*, executive branch documents, published reports and hearings, and other secondary materials. Without doubt, the current condition of most congressional collections discourages research use.

How, then, should archivists approach contemporary congressional collections? It has become apparent that standard archival practices and theories do not accommodate the special problems presented by these collections. Traditionally, in an attempt to maintain what they understand as the integrity of a collection, archivists have retained tremendous quantities of duplicative and historically insignificant information. The concept of provenance discourages archivists from looking at several congressional collections simultaneously and appraising them so that they complement one another. Archivists also often fail to consider how the substantive issues documented in a congressional collection are addressed in other noncongressional collections. Consequently, congressional collections are far larger than they need to be in order to reflect the important issues and activities that they document. Certainly, archivists are bound to respect the integrity of their holdings, but the meaning of integrity must be reevaluated if repositories are going to continue to acquire collections that typically exceed 1,000 cubic feet and contain large quantities of non-unique materials. When archivists employ traditional methods in their handling of congressional collections, no one's needs are adequately met. The repository is burdened with an enormous collection, the preparation of which requires years of a processor's time. Researchers are overwhelmed by the volume and often find it difficult to locate information. The donor is disappointed when he or she learns that the collection will not be available for years and that, even then, it will generate little research interest.

Thus, congressional collections require a new approach, one that addresses the many problems inherent in these collections. Because many of the drawbacks of these collections are a consequence of their size, it follows that the new strategy should focus on ways to shrink these collections. While appraising to winnow the size of collections is not a new archival technique, archivists typically weed out only categories of material that are generally acknowledged to have little historical significance, such as routine housekeeping records, duplicates, and published information.[5]

When appraising congressional collections, archivists should first take into account the fact that several series within a congressional collection are usually duplicated in the collections of all other members of Congress who served during the same time period. All senators and representatives serving simultaneously receive correspondence about the entire spectrum of issues that will come before them on the floor of the House or the Senate. Additionally, to permit them to vote intelligently, all members of Congress must obtain sufficient background information on these issues. Second, archivists should be aware that each of these collections, even though it consists of the records of an office, revolves around a single personality, that of the senator or representative. Finally, archivists should keep in mind that the congressional collection they have acquired is only one of 535 similar collections (the total number of senators and representatives serving at one time). Only by paring down these collections to their unique elements will archivists succeed in making them useful to researchers and manageable for archives.

This appraisal approach requires meticulous background work. Archivists must become as familiar as possible with the U.S. Congress, the individual senator or representative, the member's office, and the issues important to the member's home state. Only by thoroughly understanding the context in which the records are created can archivists be certain of the validity of their appraisal decisions. The ideal time for an archivist to gain these insights is while the senator or representative is still in office. Then the archivist can observe the operation of the congressional office, learn from congressional staff members what issues are of special importance to the member of Congress, and inquire about the value of particular categories of information.

Becoming involved with a congressional collection while it is being created offers the archivist additional benefits. The archivist can work with the congressional office to ensure that it has a viable records management program and can take advantage of the support services offered to senators and representatives. For example, the Senate offers micrographics services free of charge to current senators. Both senators and representatives also have access to automated systems that can facilitate the indexing of certain portions of the collection.

Archivists should be careful, though, not to interfere with the creation of records. The archivist's role in Congress is to observe and understand, not to persuade the office to create or store information in ways that facilitate archival use but do not enhance office use.

Every archivist responsible for congressional collections should learn about Congress firsthand. Such knowledge enables the archivist to identify the unique characteristics of individual collections. Archivists also find it useful to compare their observations with each other. The following descriptions of congressional office activities and assessment of the records created are based on the author's experiences in four congressional offices.

UNDERSTANDING THE CONGRESSIONAL OFFICE

Senate and House offices all engage in the same three activities: meeting constituent needs, representing the home district's interests in Congress, and legislating national policies.

Senators and representatives serve their constituents in a variety of ways. When home-state residents visit Washington, D.C., Senate and House offices cater to their needs. They provide tickets for tours to the White House and other federal buildings as well as to the Senate and House galleries. Some congressional offices even prepare elaborate tour guides for their constituents. Congressional offices are no less responsive to written requests. They send constituents autographed photographs, flags that have flown over the Capitol, items for charity auctions, and birthday greetings. Most congressional offices have one staff person who devotes at least part of every day to filling constituent requests.

Senate and House offices also meet constituent needs through casework, a term that refers to a congressional office's efforts to help an individual solve a specific problem with a federal or state agency. Essentially, the congressional office serves as the liaison between constituent and agency. Most casework involves problems in getting Social Security checks, welfare assistance, veterans' benefits, or travel visas. In a typical case, a constituent writes to his or her senator or representative seeking help with a problem. The office photocopies the letter and sends it to the appropriate federal or state agency, along with a note or "buck slip" asking the agency to please assist this constituent. Some offices ask the agency to respond directly to the constituent, but others prefer to serve as the conduit between the constituent and the agency. In either case, the office writes back to the constituent to say that the senator or representative has intervened on the constituent's behalf and he or she should hear about the resolution of the problem soon. Casework requires a tremendous amount of paperwork and staff time. Most congressional offices employ between two and five people to handle casework. Some senators and representatives view casework as the most effective way they can serve their constituents.

Congressional casework meets an important need, but it is not one of the fundamental responsibilities of members of Congress. Representing the state's or district's interests in the House or Senate is a key responsibility, and most members of Congress fulfill this obligation in one of two ways. The first is for the senator or representative to sponsor or at least vote in favor of legislation that benefits the home state or certain segments of its population. For example, the elected representatives from Connecticut pay particular attention to legislation that could affect the insurance industry. The second way that senators and representatives represent their state's or district's interests is by helping to channel federal dollars into the state. Often, state and local groups write their senators or representative asking for support and assistance in their efforts to obtain federal funds. Most congressional offices write letters endorsing grant applications from home-state applicants. Some offices review applications and offer to help the groups complete the necessary forms. Others arrange meetings between the applicants and the granting agency or work closely with local agencies to develop fundable project proposals. Congressional offices usually employ at least one individual who works full-time helping state and local agencies (and individuals) compete for federal dollars. This same individual often monitors federal legislation that could affect the state and reports this information to the representative or senator.

While most members of Congress devote considerable energy to serving their home states, they also are responsible for legislating national policies. The U.S. Congress considers legislation pertaining to an incredible range of issues: social, domestic, foreign, trade and manufacturing, regulatory. No one member of Congress could ever become an expert in all the subject areas on which he or she must vote. Consequently, senators and representatives employ subject specialists to advise them. The staff of every congressional office includes several people who monitor legislation about to come before the Congress. These staff people prepare background reports and often recommend to their senator or representative how to vote. Legislative staff members attend the numerous hearings held in the Senate and the House, and they assimilate and condense all this information for presentation to their employer. Legislative staff also keep track of how people back home are reacting to particular issues and inform the senator or representative so he or she can take that information into consideration when voting.

By understanding the major congressional activities—meeting constituent needs, representing the home district's interests, and legislating national policies—archivists acquire the necessary framework for evaluating the records. But archivists also must familiarize themselves with those characteristics that make each office unique. Only then are they equipped to effectively appraise congressional records.

The residents of each state and of every congressional district within it demand different services from their elected officials. For example, West Virginia residents seek congressional assistance to ensure that protection against black lung and other mine-safety legislation is enacted. Consequently, the papers of West Virginia's senators and representatives will reflect these special state concerns. Because their constituents care about these issues, representatives elected from this region are more attuned to them than are many of their colleagues, and that sensitivity will be reflected in their papers.

Archivists also must realize that senators and representatives have their own pet interests. The office records probably document these interests as fully as they document those issues of importance to the state. Many members serve on at least one committee that addresses their particular concerns and employ at least one individual who specializes in those subjects. When senators or representatives exhibit a special interest in a subject, their staff members make an extra effort to say abreast of developments in that subject area. In addition, senators and representatives receive a great deal of correspondence regarding their special interests from outside experts as well as from knowledgeable amateurs.

Finally, archivists need to identify the popular causes that surfaced during the senator's or representative's tenure. The files probably contain a tremendous amount of mail on these subjects. If these issues captivated the nation, archivists can be certain that every Senate and House office received identical mail. If a senator or representative is identified with a particular social movement, however, it is reasonable to expect that his or her mail includes more thoughtful and more sophisticated communications on that subject.

ASSESSING CONGRESSIONAL RECORDS

While every congressional office generates and stores unique information, most of it can be categorized easily. However, each office is organized a bit differently, and the location within the files of any specific type of record varies. This diversity makes the suggestion of detailed retention and disposition schedules impractical. Instead, this section presents descriptions of and disposition recommendations for the major categories of information found in most congressional offices. The categories are listed in order of descending research potential.

Administrative Assistant's Files

The administrative assistant is the staff director in the senator's or representative's personal office. Typically, this individual is the senior staff person. His or her responsibilities are diverse and often include monitoring the member's political standing, both locally and nationally, overseeing key legislative issues, and supervising the senator's or representative's staff. The administrative assistant also handles the most sensitive telephone calls and correspondence.

Very often, administrative assistants retain few files. They conduct a lot of their work over the telephone, and because of its sensitive nature, they commit little to paper. The routine responsibilities of the administrative assistant are usually the most fully documented aspects of the job. Other records that often survive include memos between the assistant and the representative or senator, correspondence with the boss's personal friends, personnel files, and legislative research files.

The administrative assistant's files should be preserved in their entirety. This person plays such an important role in the congressional office that his or her activities should be documented as fully as possible. Although a moderate amount of this material may not merit preservation, the end result of weeding the files does not justify the amount of time this task would require, particularly because this series is likely to be the smallest in the entire collection.

Legislative Assistants' Files

Legislative assistants monitor legislation and advise their senator or representative about all legislation pending before the House or Senate. The
number of legislative assistants in Senate and House offices varies from two
to as many as seven per office. Usually, there are fewer legislative assistants
in a House office than in a Senate office. Consequently, legislative assistants
in the House are less specialized than their Senate counterparts. However,
because the issues before Congress are so diverse, every legislative assistant
must be responsible for several unrelated subjects.

Legislative assistants are engaged in a variety of activities: they answer
some of the mail that comes into the office on the topics for which they
are responsible, they monitor all pending legislation in those areas, they
meet with lobbyists and constituents who want to discuss issues, and they
assist the senator or representative on the Senate or House floor and with
all preliminary work for measures the senator or representative sponsors. In
some offices, legislative assistants suggest possible legislative initiatives to
their bosses, and many are acknowledged experts in at least one of the areas
they handle. Legislative assistants comprise the majority of the professional
staff in most congressional offices.

The types of files legislative assistants keep depend on the filing system
their office uses. In an office with centralized files, they keep only their research and pending files at their desks; all their correspondence and memos
are filed in the office's central files. Many legislative assistants working in
offices with centralized filing systems keep a chronological file of their
memos as well as copies of their most important correspondence. In offices
where staff maintain their own files, legislative assistants typically keep at
hand their correspondence and memos, notes of their meetings with lobbyists and other people, notes from the hearings and other committee
meetings they attend, copies of speeches they wrote, and their research
files. Their files usually reflect both their special interests and the interests
of their boss. In most congressional offices, legislative assistants establish
their own filing systems. Many of them organize their files by legislative
bill number, others organize them by subject, and still others arrange their
papers chronologically.

The files of legislative assistants should be kept in their entirety unless the
archivist has sufficient time to process them item by item. This is the only
series that archivists should consider processing at the item or folder level.
These files usually include a great deal of bulky, published material, much
of which can be discarded. Archivists should be cautious in discarding material, however. Some of the publications may not be available from other
sources because they were not distributed widely. Many small organizations
produce publications and reports for lobbying purposes, for example. The
Library of Congress also prepares reports for congressional offices. These

reports are not available elsewhere, and the quality of the work frequently is outstanding. Legislative assistants' files are likely to be the most substantive in a senator's or representative's collection because, unlike the administrative assistant, legislative assistants often keep a paper record of their work. The greatest problems archivists will face with these records is finding them—legislative assistants often take their files with them when they leave the employ of the senator or representative.

Press Files

Press files contain the senator's or representative's speeches, press releases, newsletters, miscellaneous writings, and all the published articles about her or him. Most press files are arranged in chronological order, with each item filed in a separate folder. Press files provide valuable information about the attitudes and opinions of the senator or representative and should be kept in their entirety. Archivists probably should not refolder this material, however, because of the wealth of information found on the folder labels: title of speech or release, place and date of delivery, and sponsoring organization (if a speech). In at least one congressional office where the information was placed on the label, it indicated whether the member received an honorarium. All speeches a senator or representative delivered on the House or Senate floor appear in the *Congressional Record*, which is fully indexed. While some archivists may be inclined to discard loose copies of these speeches, they should remember that juxtaposing them with the member's other speeches can facilitate research use.

Project Files

When senators and representatives work to channel federal money to their home states, the files that document these efforts are usually labeled as projects or grants and projects files. Typically, projects files include the entire dossier on each project with which the senator or representative was involved. The file contains a copy of the original application for funds, the application's supporting documentation, correspondence between the applicant and the congressional office, and correspondence between the congressional office and the funding body.

In many congressional offices, projects personnel are left alone to devise their own filing system. Some projects staff develop elaborate systems that allow them to retrieve information from any of a number of reference points, such as county, funding agency, type of grant or loan, date of application. The archivist must solicit from the projects staff a copy of their file guide. Project files provide important information about the state and should be preserved.

Personal Files

More often than not, the label "personal files" is a misnomer. Few members of Congress keep files of a truly personal nature in their offices. These files are labeled personal because they contain the material that was brought to the attention of the senator or representative. Personal files contain a tremendous amount of information about the senator's or representative's daily activities. Included here are invitations to social and business events, letters between the senator or representative and those VIPs with whom she or he has become friendly or who merit personal responses, and records of the senator's or representative's personal meetings.

This file consists mostly of correspondence, invitations, phone and visitor logs, and the senator's or representative's appointment calendars. In many congressional offices, these records are separated from the other records created in the office. Sometimes the personal secretary keeps these files at his or her desk, and sometimes they are divided among the administrative assistant, the appointments secretary, and the personal secretary. The category "personal files" may include information that has little if any historical value, such as office expense records (the member of Congress is required to personally sign many expense vouchers), invitations that have been rejected, and routine personnel matters.

Invitations require special attention by the archivist because some (those that were accepted) merit preservation while others (those that were rejected) do not. Accepted invitations reveal the activities of an individual member of Congress and also may help a researcher identify categories of social events attended by high-level federal officials. Many archivists and historians argue that rejected invitations are of value, too, because they identify those organizations that a member of Congress did not think were of sufficient importance to warrant her or his support. Most representatives and senators cannot possibly accept all of the invitations they receive, and their reasons for turning down any given invitation would be almost impossible to determine. Researchers who want to study rejected invitations can identify these invitations by going through the computerized indexes of the office's correspondence.

The senator's or representative's personal files are valuable for the insights they provide about the member's activities while an elected official. The personal files reflect the senator's or representative's lifestyle and ways of interacting with cohorts, and they contribute to a researcher's understanding of the senator or representative as a person.

Administrative Files

The office's internal files are known as administrative files. Archivists often overlook these files, which include file keys, support files for the automated records, and staff lists. Almost every congressional office prepares some type of key to its files, but few include this key with records sent to the archives. As the files change and new keys are prepared, some offices destroy the earlier file codes. Without adequate file codes, archivists spend a great deal of time trying to decipher the filing system. When unable to do so, they often rearrange the files into chronological or alphabetical order. Reorganizing records is a time-consuming process and can compromise the integrity of the collection. Instead of waiting until the collection arrives at the repository to see if the file system can be easily understood, the archivist should visit the congressional office as early in the member's career as possible and establish a working relationship with the office manager. The archivist should request that one copy of each successive file code be sent to the repository along with an explanation of the changes in the code.

Archivists also face a serious problem if the office does not preserve its compendium of computerized form letters. The computer tapes, both Senate and House, contain only indexing information; they do not include the texts of the letters. Some congressional offices discard the master copies of their form letters once the language becomes outdated. If they do this, the value of the computer indexes diminishes because the indexes identify form letters solely by their identification numbers. Without the actual texts, researchers will be unable to reconstruct the content of the correspondence. As early as possible, archivists should inquire about the office's policy toward outdated form letters and, if necessary, should persuade the office to retain a permanent master file of such letters.

A list of all former and current staff members is another valuable research tool. With such a list, researchers can determine authorship for every initialed document. If researchers know who wrote a document and the position held by that person in the office, they are better able to reconstruct the hierarchy of decision making in a congressional office. Archivists or researchers can, at any time, generate a staff list by going through the salary reports published by both houses of Congress, but it is easier for congressional offices to prepare such a list because they can engage the help of the administrative officers of Congress. Furthermore, many congressional office managers would find a list of this type useful for various administrative purposes.

Issue Mail

Issue mail presents archivists with some difficult decisions. Citizens from all over the country write to their elected officials about every conceivable topic. While each congressional collection should not have to document the universe of issues concerning the U.S. people, it should reflect those issues that were important to the senator or representative and his staff. Typically, congressional offices pay little attention to letters about issues with which the senator or representative is not especially concerned. The office answers such letters with form responses that either present the member's position on that issue or simply thank the correspondents for sharing their views. On the other hand, letters about the senator's or representative's special interests often provoke an individualized response prepared by the legislative assistant responsible for that subject area. Both these categories of mail are often integrated in the files. While it is relatively simple for archivists to use the computer indexes to separate the two categories, they must first identify what issues fit into which category. To do so, archivists must study the career of the particular senator or representative and talk to her or his staff, bearing in mind, though, that the interests of members of Congress change over time. Archivists should make an effort to identify those issues with which the member used to be involved by talking to long-time staff members as well as to former employees and by looking through the speech and press release files.

Issue mail, because of its volume and repetitiveness, lends itself to sampling. Offices that use automated systems prepare most of their issue mail with the help of a computer. If archivists become involved with a collection while the member of Congress is still in office, they can elicit the help of either the Senate computer center or the vendor used by the House office in preparing the computer programs needed to generate a statistically valid sample. The decision about whether to sample depends on two factors. First, archivists must recognize that, in generating a sample, they are committing the repository to preserving material it would not otherwise retain: a sample of routine correspondence about issues not important to the principal of the collection. Second, the repository must have sufficient space to store this material and sufficient personnel to service it. Once archivists decide to sample, they must determine the purpose of that sample: for example, to document the range of interests expressed by constituents or to show how interest in a particular issue corresponds to geographical region.

Political Files

Information about the senator's or representative's campaigns for reelection as well as information about other home-state political races are included in political files. Federal regulations mandate the separation of personal staff and campaign staffs. Consequently, many congressional offices do not even store campaign records in Washington. Instead, they scatter these files among the campaign manager's home or office, the candidate's home, and the homes of various campaign workers. Archivists will have to hunt for the background information candidates used in formulating their position statements as well as for campaign literature. Archivists should not routinely discard the information a senator or representative retains about someone else's political races; the senator or representative may have viewed this person as a possible future opponent or may have borrowed the person's rhetoric or format of campaign literature.

Whenever possible, political files should be preserved. These files provide useful grist for scholars of various disciplines, but they may contain confidential information. Unless the archivist convinces the donor that the confidentiality of the political files will be respected, this material may well be destroyed before it ever reaches an archives.

Casework Files

Casework files are one of the more voluminous categories of information found in a senator's or representative's office. Although the staff devotes a tremendous amount of time to helping constituents with their personal problems, the historical significance of this category is minimal. Every congressional office handles large quantities of casework, much of it identical to that answered by other congressional offices. Researchers need to know that casework consumed much congressional staff time, but they probably have little use for the actual letters. Some letters are poignant and reveal the agonies people experience, but researchers can more efficiently identify the problems of the U.S. people from other archival records, such as the collections of social welfare agencies. Researchers cannot expect congressional collections to document the whole of the U.S. experience. Because this material is bulky and can be found in other sources, the archivist should consider recommending to the congressional office staff that they schedule casework for periodic destruction. Archivists should be aware, though, that many constituents send members of Congress important original documents, such as birth certificates and military discharge papers, and they should urge the congressional office to return these documents to the constituents as soon after receiving them as possible. Some casework should be preserved. Certain problems are unique to a specific geographical region (such as the problem of black lung disease in West Virginia), and the corresponding casework reflects a special characteristic of that region. Casework also should be preserved when a senator or representative is particularly interested in an issue that generated case mail, such as the refugee problem (immigration casework) or veterans' affairs.

Casework contains little substantive information, but many researchers relish its anecdotal value. To accommodate them, archivists may choose to retain a small sample of the case files. Archivists who decide to keep casework, however, must develop access policies that protect the privacy of the individuals who wrote to their senator or representative for help.

Clippings Files

Clippings from newspapers and other information sources can be found in all congressional offices. Many senators and representatives subscribe to clipping services and most accumulate huge quantities of clippings, often gluing them into oversized scrapbooks. Many congressional offices keep multiple copies of identical articles, one for each time it appeared in a local paper. Staff members often believe that newspaper and magazine articles are the essence of history, and they make special efforts to preserve this material.

An archivist's decision about whether to keep a clippings file should reflect the resources of the repository. Some archives index all the home-state newspapers and would have no need for a senator's or representative's clippings file. Others would view these files as a valuable addition to their resources. An archivist who decides to keep the clippings may want to request that the congressional office have them microfilmed and ship only the film to the archives.

An alternative approach, and one that works well in some congressional offices, is for the office to selectively preserve clippings. Senator Russell Long's press assistant retains one copy of every published article about Senator Long. She keeps only one copy of wire-service stories. After collecting an entire day's clippings, she photocopies them all and puts one photocopy aside for the archives. Additional copies of these articles are distributed to the senator and his staff. Preparing the one archival copy requires very little extra work on her part and satisfies the office's desire to keep all clippings about the senator. The clippings are then filed in one place, in chronological order, and in good physical condition.

Photography Files

Photographs, like clippings, sometimes present more problems than they seem to be worth. Senators and representatives pose for photographs with almost every tour group from their home state, and their offices often keep file copies. Only the most organized offices label these photographs; others simply file them. The photographs' historical value is negligible, particularly when they are not identified. However, even the identified group shots reveal little information.

Some photographs, though, may be historically significant, such as candid shots of the member's official travels, personal photographs, and shots of the senator or representative in action. Such photographs are often difficult to locate, however. Those sent in by friends and admirers may be filed in the office's main filing system. The archivist must decide how much time to spend searching for them, keeping in mind that public officials are accustomed to being photographed and even the most casual shot may be totally contrived. Although photographs found in congressional collections may not be intrinsically valuable, they can enhance exhibits and are useful as illustrations in publications. Archivists must carefully evaluate their repositories' interest in photographs before deciding whether to keep them.

Academy Files

Senators and representatives are offered the opportunity to recommend candidates to all U.S. military academies, and students from all over the state write their elected officials seeking such recommendations. The academy files in a congressional office typically include correspondence with the applicant as well as the applicant's references and academic history. Some members of Congress stay in touch with the candidates they recommend; others do not. Most archivists agree that the files of the rejected applicants offer little information of interest to researchers. There is, though, disagreement about the value of the files of the accepted applicants. Some archivists contend that these files reveal data about political patronage or, because many illustrative U.S. citizens have attended military academies, may contain information about future national leaders. It is doubtful, however, that a researcher would make a special trip to look at Senator X's academy files. Furthermore, these files are not the only source of this information. The academies themselves maintain files on all their students. Unless a congressional office closely follows the careers of the students the member recommended, these files need not be preserved.

Requests Files

Most congressional offices keep a separate file containing all routine requests for items such as photographs or biographical sketches of the senator or representative, flags flown over the Capitol, and tickets for White House tours. These files contain no historically valuable information and can be discarded.

ARCHIVAL THEORY AND PRACTICE

The size and value of modern congressional collections pose serious problems for archives and archivists. Whether their value merits the storage space and staff time their size requires is questionable. Traditional archival practices have led to a dilemma: repositories must either stop acquiring such collections or continue to devote inordinate and growing amounts of space and labor to their care. Strategies that permit archivists to appraise (weed) these collections at some level of detail between that of the collection and the item must be developed. The preceding part of this chapter provided some practical guidelines for embarking on such a strategy. It offered a sufficiently detailed description of congressional offices to permit an interested archivist to develop an appraisal program. It emphasized that an essential part of that program is early and active interaction with a functioning office.

Archivists should be aware, however, that they will encounter special problems when they accept responsibility for the records of a sitting member of Congress. For example, the originating office may require access to the materials that have been sent to the archives. These demands may represent one more burden to an already overworked reference staff. Also, many members of Congress will want to seal from research use those portions of their collections that are sent to the repository while the office is still functioning. The archives will have to devote an enormous amount of stack space to a collection that may be sealed from researchers for several years. Finally, because archivists who join the staff of a member of Congress represent both the donor and the repository, they may face conflicting interests. Occasionally, members of Congress or their staff may urge the archivist to destroy records that they deem embarrassing or too sensitive for inclusion in the archival collection. As the donor's representative, then, the archivist may have to negotiate with the repository for unreasonably harsh restrictions. Without question, the demands placed on a congressional archivist can be trying.

Archivists must recognize that few congressional staff members devote much attention to the future life of the records they create. To ensure the best possible archival collection, though, archivists need the assistance of the staff. When seeking such help, however, they must remain aware that they are treading on shaky ground. While archivists want to guide the shaping of the records so that the files will be useful in the future, they should avoid actually creating records. *Respect des fonds* is not dead: archivists must remember that their needs concerning these records take second place to the use that the office makes of these files. Furthermore, archivists should avoid making staff members overly self-conscious about the records they are creating. An archivist's early involvement with congressional collections can contribute significantly to the final shape of the collection, but these collections must be allowed to develop on their own without too much interference from the archivist.

The active, interventionist, and differentially selective approach to acquiring and appraising congressional collections takes archivists far from some of their most treasured concepts and practices. Maximizing research potential, a value that underlies most archival thinking and practice, is the explicit goal of this approach. Here the dilemma posed by congressional collections becomes clear. From an administrator's perspective, an institution's sparse resources should be allocated to those collections or activities that offer the greatest promise of payoff, in terms of likely use or research value. Collections never acquired offer no research potential. Immense, rich collections that are poorly organized and badly documented are of marginal research value. With a congressional collection, however, its size alone seriously minimizes its research value, regardless of how well organized or described that collection may be. Archivists must consider the ramifications this bulk will have if they apply standard appraisal methods when approaching congressional collections.

If, however, all archivists were to adopt the perspective outlined in this chapter, another serious problem would quickly surface. The net result would be large numbers of atomistic collections that document only individual congressional offices. This possibility poses questions that the archival profession's thinkers need to address. How can other, sizable institutions be properly documented (at least through this congressional lens) if the focus of each collection is the individual occupant of the office? Can the responsibilities of documenting a larger universe be met without overburdening archival repositories and their patrons? If so, how? And what concepts and principles can be called upon to guide archivists in their appraisals of congressional collections?

These questions are heady and cannot be answered easily. Two different but not mutually exclusive approaches might be explored. First, archivists might reconsider the definition of congressional collections. Second, they might think about creating new institutional alliances. Both ideas, along with their implications for usual archival standards and practices, are explored in the remainder of this chapter.

REDEFINING CONGRESSIONAL COLLECTIONS

Archivists need to consider reexamining the definition of congressional collections. The profession has always accepted that the papers of each representative and senator represents an entity, an entire collection. This may be inappropriate. All members of a state's delegation work on the same problems; therefore, their caseloads are similar, the projects for which they intervene may overlap, and quite often they discuss the same state issues. Perhaps archivists should redefine the collection to be the papers of all members of a state's congressional delegation, with the papers of each senator and representative forming a separate subgroup. By pulling together the papers of the entire delegation, archivists could weed out greater quantities from each collection than would otherwise be feasible. Furthermore, the collection of a short-term member of Congress could be greatly enhanced by juxtaposing it with the papers of more experienced colleagues.

Focusing on the delegation rather than the individual permits archivists to critically evaluate whether the papers of every member of Congress need to be preserved. As long as archivists evaluate collections individually and in isolation, they will continue to justify the acquisition of each member's papers, because each collection documents aspects of the congressional experience. But if archivists appraise each collection as if it were part of a larger whole, they may decide that some collections contribute little, if any, new information.

Redefining congressional collections allows archivists increased flexibility in appraisal and opens the door to an efficient way of coping with the mass of papers received from the offices of U.S. senators and representatives. Although this approach seems to wreak havoc with the archival notion of provenance, perhaps archivists interpret that concept too narrowly. Congressional collections have become a new breed of archival material. The old guidelines may no longer apply.

CREATING INSTITUTIONAL ALLIANCES

Archivists also need to think about creating new institutional alliances. Cooperation among archivists within a given region could greatly facilitate the handling of congressional collections. Within a region, each repository might fully document one or more routine congressional activities, such as casework or popular legislative issues. Then other repositories within that region could discard those series with the confidence that researchers could still learn about those aspects of congressional life. No one repository would have to bear the burden of documenting the entire range of activities. For example, one repository in New England could document Social Security casework; another might collect immigration casework; yet another could retain all correspondence regarding balancing the federal budget. Under an arrangement such as this, every repository would be free to appraise, organize, and describe the remaining portions of its congressional collections in whatever manner it desired. Those series that the repository agreed to preserve as its regional obligation, however, would have to be appraised and organized in a manner agreed on by all members of the network. Ideally, this approach would encourage repositories to reduce significantly the size of their congressional collections so that they reflect the essence of the individual senator or representative and his or her office.

This approach to congressional collections is not without problems. It will require archivists to become experts in the activities they contract to document. Researchers will have to travel as much as a few hundred miles if they are interested in studying the entire scope of congressional activities. Archivists will need to develop suitable mechanisms for working cooperatively. And members of Congress might resist the idea that portions of their collections will become part of a network of similar collections. None of these problems, though, is insurmountable.

Researchers already travel around the country in their efforts to document congressional activities. With a regional approach, they would know where to visit to study particular aspects of Congress and, even more important, they could be confident of finding those aspects well documented. Congressional scholars would accrue an additional benefit in that they would be able to fully document the range of congressional activities within each of several regions of the United States.

A less direct but nonetheless important benefit to researchers would be realized if some of the more sophisticated archival repositories would agree once again to collect congressional papers. Recently, several repositories have rejected these collections because of their size and their marginal research value. By working together with other repositories, these institutions could drastically reduce the size of their congressional collections without sacrificing any unique information. Without doubt, researchers are best served when the collections they study are surrounded by complementary materials, both primary and secondary sources. Increasingly, members of Congress donate their papers to small, out-of-the-way repositories. Often, those are the only institutions that will accept the collection. By developing a plan that encourages repositories to keep only portions of a congressional collection, large research centers might once again be willing to collect in this area.

Archivists may be reluctant to embark on a program of cooperative appraisal of congressional collections for several reasons. Traditionally, archives have had difficulty working together. Also, cooperative ventures often require repositories to shoulder additional financial and administrative burdens. A cooperative approach to congressional collections, however, will save each repository shelf space and processing time.[6] After the initial organizing effort, the only additional administrative activity required will be keeping the network's steering or guidance committee active. Cooperative appraisal of congressional collections will, in the long run, free up staff time, shelf space, and administrative dollars, all of which are scarce in most repositories. Finally, because few repositories currently systematically appraise their congressional collections, most of them would derive great benefits by working with other institutions in this endeavor.

One other stumbling block may be that the members of Congress whose papers are to be collected may hesitate to donate their papers to institutions that are involved in a cooperative venture such as the one proposed. Most senators and representatives donate their papers to archives because they want their careers to be well documented and because they want researchers to use their papers. Once they understand the difficulties researchers encounter in using congressional collections that have been processed in the traditional manner, however, it seems likely that most members of Congress will support a cooperative approach.

The archival profession must do a great deal of preliminary work before initiating a regional approach to congressional collections. Many questions must be answered. For example, how should the regions be formed? What should be the criteria for joining this network? Is a professed interest in congressional collections sufficient, or must member institutions be actively involved in soliciting congressional collections? Should the network be limited to repositories that meet certain standards? If so, who should develop these standards and what should they be? How will the network operate? At least in its early stages, the network will need a coordinator. Who will select this individual, and who will fund the position? Should the Society of American Archivists bear any or all of these responsibilities? If not SAA, then who? All of these questions must be addressed before archivists initiate a cooperative approach to congressional collections.

This chapter has offered some guidelines that may help present-day archivists cope with a new era of congressional collections. In addition, it has suggested some new ways to think about these collections. The archival profession must now begin to ask the necessary questions about and to chart the course for the future handling of congressional collections. A new approach is necessary if archivists are to successfully meet the challenges of tomorrow's congressional collections.

NOTES

1. Throughout this chapter, the term congressional collections is used to describe the papers created and accumulated in the offices of members of the U.S. Senate and House of Representatives. Committee records and the records of the administrative offices of Congress are excluded from this discussion because they are defined as federal records and are sent to the National Archives rather than to other types of repositories. For a full discussion of the distinctions between these three categories of congressional information, see Patricia Aronsson, "Congressional Records as Archival Sources," *Government Publications Review* 8A (1981): 295–302.

2. Frank B. Evans et al., "A Basic Glossary for Archivists, Manuscript Curators, and Records Managers," *American Archivist* 37 (July 1974): 149.

3. At the Library of Congress Manuscript Division, the collection of Emanuel Celler, who served in Congress from 1923 to 1973, is approximately 271 feet, while the collection of Edward Brooke, who served in the Senate from 1967 to 1979, exceeds 2,000 feet.

4. *Proceedings of the Conference on the Research Use and Disposition of Senators' Papers,* ed. Richard A. Baker, September 14–15, 1978, Washington, D.C., 172.

5. Theodore R. Schellenberg, *Modern Archives: Principles and Techniques* (Chicago: University of Chicago Press, 1956).

6. Archivists from five repositories in New Hampshire have established an informal network for managing congressional collections. The thrust of their effort is to provide advice to congressional offices.

12

Appraising the Papers of State Legislators

Paul I. Chestnut

Many state archival agencies have done little to appraise and preserve office files created by state legislators, and few private repositories have collected these papers on a systematic or comprehensive basis. Professional literature that could provide guidance, either by example or by prescription, for the disposition of these files is virtually nonexistent. This chapter attempts to take a first step to remedy that situation by identifying the kinds of papers most likely to appear in legislators' files, discussing the conditions of their creation and official use, and suggesting their possible usefulness to a variety of potential researchers.[1] Rather than finding a model or a list of ready-made appraisal decisions, however, readers are asked to consider various alternatives and to draw their own conclusions based on the needs of individual repositories with their own collecting policies and obligations to parent agencies or user constituencies.

Although professional literature on the appraisal of papers of members of Congress and United States senators is still rather scanty,[2] published sources discussing the disposition of files created by state legislators are even more so. Surveys have been made by various archivists, and local studies have been undertaken by repositories in several states,[3] but archivists have as yet derived few conclusions and developed fewer guidelines concerning the acquisition, appraisal, and processing of the papers of state legislators. Variations in the political environment in which state legislators function, the diversity of legislative styles and traditions among the states, differing established modes of conduct and patterns of activity between state houses

Previously published as "Appraising the Papers of State Legislators" in *American Archivist* 48:2 (spring 1985). Reprinted with permission.

and senates, and individual differences among the numerous incumbents elected to legislative office can at the outset thwart attempts to generalize about appropriate archival methods of dealing with these papers. Reluctance to establish guidelines based on so many crucial variables may be understandable, yet the demand increases for assistance with collections that archivists feel they should acquire but do not yet know why they want them or how to handle them once they have arrived.

Since the appraisal process entails analysis leading to the development of collecting policies, evaluation of the merits of a potential acquisition, and selection of papers for retention once that potential acquisition has been received, archivists must establish a three-tiered structure to accommodate the several levels at which appraisal decisions are made. At each level, archivists must take into consideration the context in which the records were created and the extent to which the interrelationship between this context and the contents of the records governs the value of the records for posterity. In the case of state legislators' papers, variations from state to state, between house and senate, and among individual legislators, in addition to the differences created by the advance of time, can undermine generalizations about content value. Nevertheless, certain fundamental questions applicable to conditions in all of the states can be developed and an attempt can be made to understand the legislative process and the role of individual legislators within that process. This chapter points out various factors that constitute the framework in which decisions may be made at each level of the appraisal process by archival administrators establishing or refining collection development policies, by field agents or records managers evaluating potential acquisitions, and by processing staff organizing and describing records added to their repository's holdings.

Administrators developing a collecting policy must first consider the ownership of papers created by legislators acting as governmental officials. Although public records acts in a few states specifically refer to the matter of ownership of the papers of public officials, most statutory references are vague or nonexistent. Disagreement over the ownership of congressional office files has been voiced for a number of years, and archivists seeking specific guidelines on the ownership of the papers of legislative officials can thus far refer to decisions reached perhaps as much by default as by conscious determination.[4] It appears that archivists in most states must continue to operate without statutory legislation or legal precedent defining ownership, and without such specific guidelines, state legislators' office files, like those created by members of Congress, will be considered private papers that can stray from public custody. As private papers, they can be disposed of as their creators or current owners see fit.

Any decision by a state archives to collect legislators' papers, therefore, will be influenced by the archives' policy governing the acquisition of private papers as well as by its state's public records act. Likewise, decisions by manuscript curators at private repositories within each state will be guided by their state's definition of ownership. In those states in which legislators' papers are by tradition or by statute considered private, competition among repositories, public and private, may become a factor in developing individual collecting policies and procedures, and only the power of persuasion, rather than public statutes, will assure the preservation of any of these papers. Moreover, should a collection be acquired by a repository with regional branches or by a consortium of repositories, negotiations must be conducted with the donor to determine whether that collection should be placed in a branch whose holdings are regional in scope or in the central repository in which collections of statewide significance are housed.

Despite a decline in the turnover rate among state legislators elected to office in recent years, fewer incumbents are serving more than 10 years, and the average turnover rate is still a somewhat high 25 percent.[5] As a result, not only does the volume of records generated by state legislators remain intimidating, but the number of legislators creating those records also continues at a high level. Few, if any, states have repositories sufficient in number and size to house all of these files or even those seen as worthy of retention. Consequently, to adjust collection development policies to meet the realities of their local conditions, archival administrators must identify the types of legislators whose records they will seek to acquire. An obvious first choice appears to be those state legislators in leadership positions, such as the speaker of the house, the president of the senate, or in states in which the lieutenant governor serves as the senate's presiding officer, the senator holding the highest elected office in that body. Party leadership in each chamber may also include majority and minority leaders and whips and their assistants.[6]

Other factors also must be considered to assure full documentation. Are these senior delegates the real leaders? Are there factions within each party whose leaders create more substantive records than the titular head of the chamber? Evaluation should be based on questions concerning the role of the legislative leadership at any given point in time. Additional factors, such as the role of a governor in selecting the leadership, may also reflect on the value assigned to papers among files maintained by legislators in formal leadership positions. Chamber and party leaders may serve as focal points within a communications network, but their records may not be the most substantive. Their files may record decisions only, while the working papers or behind-the-scenes communications documenting factors leading to a decision reside in files housed in other offices.

Retaining only the records of the leadership may also skew later perceptions of the legislative process, since the papers of any elite group may not adequately document all levels of a larger social entity. Although equal priority need not be given to the papers of the less influential members of any group, an argument can be made for retaining the papers of the yeoman legislator whose files may not be of any great significance but may represent the majority of the delegates who did their work while never achieving greatness. If a repository seeks evidence about the functioning of the legislature at its basic level, selection from among the masses of seemingly inconsequential delegates can document the average legislative experience as well as provide information about the role and functions of a legislature at specific periods of time.

State legislative files, rather than congressional ones, may more thoroughly document the demographic, geographic, and political factors that influence decisions concerning what topics a repository wishes to include in its collecting policy and what potential donors to approach. A state's legislature is quite often more broadly representative of the general populace than its delegation in Congress. Districts are smaller, terms shorter, demands fewer, and the relationship of state representatives to their constituents more likely to be personal than that of the representatives voters sent to far-off Washington for a full-time job. Race, sex, and religion are valid criteria for selecting representative legislative collections, as well as for evaluating acquisitions from the population at large, and collections may be sought that indicate the strength of blocs formed by advocates of special-interest groups. Furthermore, states with distinct residential patterns and economic bases will have legislators representing urban, suburban, and rural areas and agricultural and industrial districts. Ethnic groups take great pride in electing one of their own to high office, and certain occupational interests strive to have their economic concerns represented as effectively as possible.

However, few state legislatures at present have many black or female members, and to say that one should automatically collect papers of these members may create such an unbalanced collecting policy that the repository would seek fewer collections from a broader cross section of the legislature's membership. On the other hand, the temptation may be to collect too many papers created by representatives who are practicing attorneys when not legislating in the state capital. The legal profession still provides the greatest single bloc of delegates in most state legislatures, and their files are apt to offer greater organization, better analysis of the legal implications of pending legislation, and more substantive material on state and local politics than those of many of their colleagues. An overabundance of these files, however, may not give due weight to the papers of the farmers, real estate and insurance agents, educators, and other occupational groups comprising a state legislature.

Issue-oriented legislators appear to be prime targets for acquisitive archivists. Their papers have the stuff that make a researcher's dreams come true.

Information on interesting and controversial topics of statewide concern is there for graduate students, faculty, journalists, and others to use in formulating or confirming their ideas. And because potential use is a principal criterion at all levels of appraisal, interest in collecting useful documentation is a valid consideration. Yet issues of local as well as statewide concern should also be taken into consideration. The Equal Rights Amendment may be a hot topic in the state's cities, but better roads in rural areas or aid to school construction in rapidly growing suburban districts may rank higher in the hierarchy of concerns of citizens in those districts than protection and affirmation of the rights of women. A comprehensive approach to appraisal, therefore, will include consideration of both local and regional issues, and if archivists are seeking collections to document legislative activity as well as topics of social interest, they will need to be aware of all concerns brought before the legislature.

A related consideration is the scope of a legislator's files. Many representatives view their election primarily as a mandate to serve the interests of their constituents. Others, especially the more politically secure, may see themselves principally as participants in statewide matters and, as such, obligated and entitled to consider proposed legislation from a broader or statewide perspective. Political scientists have frequently categorized legislators as "delegates," "trustees," and "politicos." Delegates are more attuned to local interests and vote the way they perceive their constituents would prefer. Trustees see themselves as officials elected to represent the best interests rather than the preferences of their constituents. Legislators identified as politicos, blending the characteristics of both the delegate and the trustee, are aware of how the political wind blows but also subject their decisions to the dictates of their own consciences and perhaps those of their benefactors and the party leadership as well.[7] If an appraisal archivist or an administrator developing a collecting policy is more interested in collections of local or regional emphasis, papers of the delegate type may contain sufficient documentation. Files created by trustees and politicos may include papers more comprehensive in scope and thus better serve the purposes of a repository with a broader collecting policy. As with all other appraisal considerations, however, papers of all three types should be sought if a balanced collection documenting the legislature as well as local or statewide concerns is desired.

Appraisal decisions should also take into account the fact that politics may so govern the composition of the legislature that elected representatives more nearly represent state or local parties, factions, or machines than they do the citizenry. Handpicked candidates assured of election in districts controlled by one party or faction may owe their success not to the voters but to their mentors, and files in their offices at the capital may consist of little more than perfunctory records of the way they spent their time following orders. A one-party state, however, may experience the development within that party of factions so strong that they amount to separate political entities, and machine-controlled politics can degenerate into warfare among several machines. Because the activities of informal factions and machines and of many state parties are poorly documented, the papers of even the most subservient legislator may still contain information that does not appear in records documenting the legislative process, the way the group in control functioned, and issues before the chamber. Writing off the papers of any dependent is safe only when the papers of the source exercising control exist and are assured of preservation.

Assuming that a repository has first established a collecting policy and then has identified the potential creators of papers likely to conform to that policy, its staff can turn to the third step in the appraisal process: evaluating the papers for preservation. Despite differences in style and emphasis among individual legislators and the legislatures in which they serve, modern legislators in most states are creating files of a fairly similar nature. Files management may still be much needed to increase the efficiency of each legislator's office, not to mention the accuracy and effectiveness of an appraisal decision. But the recent increase in office space, clerical staff, and research assistance has enabled state legislators to manage with some degree of success the volume of paper finding its way to their files. Archivists working at the folder or series level of appraisal may still yearn to delve within a folder to search for the treasured individual item, but few who work with large numbers of legislative papers can afford to indulge in item-level appraisal. Most archivists must find shortcuts not only by background research into the position, influence, and orientation of a legislator within the overall legislative and political system of a particular state. They must also look for consistency in filing systems and for similarity in the types of papers among the records created by the many legislators whose files they must appraise.[8]

Archivists traditionally think first of correspondence when approaching an appraisal decision. Some may still hope to find the uninhibited, reasoned expressions of preferences, demands, instruction, need, or fact so analytical and to the point that they can be quoted, or at least cited in a footnote, by a scholar about to produce the as yet unwritten work on a particular subject. In reality, most correspondence sent to state legislators is more useful in the aggregate than in its individual form. And a large aggregate it has become—so large that few legislators can still maintain a simple correspondence file. Those who do probably need assistance from archivists or records managers to revise their filing systems. Among the several usual series of correspondence, preferably grouped by legislative session rather than over time, are constituent correspondence, subject files, and casework files. And it is here that the bulk of opinion, lobbying, requests for assistance, and political concerns is most likely to be expressed.

Constituent correspondence expressing ideas or preferences, however, indicates the involvement of only some citizens in the legislative process. Writing letters tends to be the means adopted more by literate, urban voters to express their views. Other urban dwellers grouse to their neighbors, express themselves only in their vote, or feel so insecure about their inability to express themselves that they do not send written communications to their representatives. Furthermore, citizens in smaller communities are more accustomed to interpersonal relationships and hold their views for the expected opportunity to express themselves on their own turf when the delegate next returns home.[9]

The value of constituent correspondence is further limited by the growth in recent years of letter-writing campaigns undertaken by organized and ad hoc groups attempting to persuade a delegate of the importance and righteousness of their causes and to impress their elected representatives with the number of voters who seek or demand support in the debate and voting on relevant bills. Issue-oriented mail stimulated by sources who are usually easily identified by a legislator is considered by its proponents and by those historians capable of reducing bulk to technological manageability to be of great value in determining the ideas and influence of a large proportion of the citizenry. Political scientists, however, question its role in determining the votes of its recipients. Most state legislators are aware of the organized groups in their districts and already know how Catholics, Baptists, farmers, bankers, welfare recipients, veterans, teachers, industrial laborers, and other blocs may feel on issues related to their special concerns. They do not need bags of mail to tell them how to vote, and the form letter they send in response to such letter-writing campaigns is quite often little more than an acknowledgment sent because constituent correspondence traditionally calls for a letter in return.[10]

Constituent correspondence takes other forms as well. "Crayon mail" may come from children just learning the ABCs of their political system, but it can also come from residents of institutions in which writing implements with sharp points are forbidden.[11] Correspondence may also come from residents of other districts who are writing anybody and everybody to solicit votes on their pet projects, and it may consist in great number of simple requests for flags, pictures, autographs, commendation for friends or family on a special occasion, or some similar personal matter of little consequence to historians or political scientists but in its mass of great impact on a legislator's relationships with his electors. What appears to be inconsequential to posterity seeking greater informational content, therefore, may in fact document the nuts and bolts of the legislative experience, and appraisers once again need to refer to the criteria of their collecting policies to keep their priorities in order.

Casework files, or correspondence related to constituents' requests for assistance, further illustrate the appraiser's dilemma concerning the scope and level of documentation under evaluation. Random sampling and more detailed selection schemes have been proposed for casework correspondence in congressional collections. Thus far, however, there seem to be no similar proposals for dealing with state legislative files, and although none will be developed here, various factors will be noted that may assist in establishing guidelines for appraisal that at the same time may serve as criteria for a sampling or selection scheme.

To an even greater degree than their counterparts in Congress, many state legislators view casework as their reason for being. Though the process of enacting legislation usually ranks first in polls of state legislators asked to list their functions in order of importance, service to constituents is also generally rated high.[12] Some legislators go so far as to see this activity as their principal function and thrive on assisting folk back home in prodding overly slow bureaucracies and slicing through a morass of rules and regulations, even though those very bureaucracies and their rules and regulations resulted from legislation the legislators themselves at first supported. Whether advocacy as a primary role for legislators can be traced to a sincere desire to serve constituents or to a shrewd political sense detecting that voters may express their gratitude in the voting booth, it has nevertheless become an increasingly time-consuming and files-creating activity of all legislators. Any effort to reduce the bulk of casework files, therefore, should take into account the fact that reduction of the aggregate can mislead a researcher by distorting the record of the interaction and priorities of legislative activities. Any reduction should be thoroughly documented in a finding aid or among the repository's files related to the affected collection.

Since casework files generally document the interaction of the legislative and executive branches of government, they can provide revealing information on the relationship of the two branches. The same political party does not always control both branches in each state, and in many states with strong two-party systems, party turnover may occur fairly frequently. The extent to which members of the small minority parties in single-party states intrude into the activities of another branch may vary from the pattern of interaction among members of the majority party in those states. In addition, states with split leadership may experience yet another pattern of interaction as competition for votes increases the intensity of attempts to take credit for services to the voters.[13]

Appraisal considerations based on party affiliations may be complicated by the recent efforts of many legislators to exercise their investigative prerogatives and thereby restore balance to the tripartite form of government that all state constitutions mandate. Since most states have experienced the growth of executive and judicial power that has dominated modern political developments, their legislatures have been drastically altered in composition and influence by the expansion of executive leadership and court-ordered reapportionment. Their fiscal control has been reduced by strong executive budget proposals as well as by judicial mandate to provide funds for the services and obligations to which the legislators committed their states.[14] A resurgence of legislative power has begun, however, and one of the ways in which this power is being exerted is the development of oversight of the executive branch to evaluate the success of programs and policies enacted in statutory legislation and funded with revenue due the state because of legislative action. Oversight generally entails program and performance evaluation by committees of legislators or by legislative staff, and in some of the larger states it is now an accepted function of the legislative system. In other states in which such activity is less well organized and has little funding or staff assistance, it is undertaken principally to maintain the fiscal accountability of administrative agencies in the executive branch. In a few states, active oversight is simply the province of committed, inquisitive, and perhaps meddlesome legislators checking to see how well a job required by the legislature is being done.

Whatever the degree of organized oversight activity, however, it has become a crucial response to the modern legislature's exercise of its constitutional authority to participate in the process of governing its state. At its most basic level, oversight is undertaken in response to citizens' requests for assistance in dealing with the bureaucracy controlled and administered by the executive branch. Such requests prompt a legislator to inquire about policies and procedures, to seek information concerning the reasons why certain functions may not have been carried out, to identify problems caused by ineffective administrators and idle bureaucrats, or even to uncover corruption in state government. At the same time, a legislator may learn that the problems about which he or she inquired were caused by insufficient funding to hire adequate agency staff to assist constituents promptly, or that certain legislation was so vague as to confuse personnel authorized to implement it. Had not a citizen written to seek assistance, a legislator may not have engaged in the correspondence that brought important information to his or her attention concerning the executive branch. If casework files are routinely discounted as marginal in value, much of the documentation related to executive–legislative interaction may be lost.[15]

Casework files also help to redress the imbalance noted as occurring in issue-oriented correspondence. Whereas constituent correspondence may express only the concerns of a more elite segment of the populace, casework files tend to represent the needs of the less well-connected citizens. A state senator in Montana has categorized constituent mail as the "I want," "I don't want," "I believe," and "Please help me" expressions of citizens' contacts with their legislators. The "I want" and "I don't want" writers are those who would be directly affected by proposed legislation and are letting their representative know how they feel about changes in working conditions, funding, regulations, and the like. Correspondents beginning their letters with "I believe" are the most numerous and are expressing their views on the issues their church, patriotic organization, union, friends, family, or quite possibly their individual consciences prompted them to address. The "Please help me" writers, however, are those seeking the assistance or intervention of their legislators. Their files indicate the personal needs of people who seldom express themselves in other forms of documentation available to researchers, and they contain information on a legislator's efforts to represent people without influence and representation elsewhere.[16]

Intervention may also be undertaken in behalf of local officials asking for help or influence in dealing with agencies and commissions based in the capital, and records related to their cases may have research value for local history in addition to insights into the interaction of political factors in the legislative and executive branches.[17] Although issues of confidentiality may enter into evaluation of any form of casework correspondence, efforts to appraise these files may find a record of considerable value to social, demographic, racial, and ethnic studies as well as to an analysis of the functioning of all branches of state government.

A third series of files may consist of a subject file. Correspondence and other papers related to a specific issue or topic may be segregated by subject to improve access to constituent opinion, background material, and other records on a topic before the legislature. Although correspondence in this file may be subject to the considerations noted above in the discussion of constituent correspondence, a subject arrangement can be of great assistance to an archivist in that most relevant documentation considered by a legislator or staff concerning an issue is placed together, so that its common subject matter is contained in a single series, thereby eliminating the need to evaluate several series on the basis of interrelated informational content. On the other hand, the failure to file by format or function may greatly reduce an archivist's opportunity to appraise on the basis of evidence on how the office actually functioned.

A series of files arranged according to bill title or number may include merely copies of draft legislation. If no research file has been created, a bill file may also include printed matter, memoranda, research notes, and information compiled by legislators or their administrative or research assistants, the staff of a committee, a central research agency, the state library, or any other agency or interested party submitting data and analysis related to a specific piece of pending legislation. Much of this material may be duplicated elsewhere in committee files and the files of other legislators, and it is doubtful that the printed matter is unique. If not duplicated, however, papers in bill and research files can contain data and recommendations that are valuable for future use by scholars studying a variety of topics. Even if duplicated, certain of these files may indicate how and why a specific legislator sponsored a bill and how hard he or she fought for it with colleagues in the chamber.

The existence of committee files of any great depth and breadth depends on a number of factors. In a fairly institutionalized legislature with strong committees supported by paid staff, committees create their own files and provide for their maintenance by the committee staff. Files maintained in an individual legislator's office are apt to duplicate records kept by the committee and thus may be of little value. Even if committee files are kept by the committee leadership rather than by staff in offices assigned to the committee, files maintained by individual members are unlikely to contain extensive information not duplicated elsewhere. An uncooperative committee leader who fails to preserve his or her papers, however, may force an archivist to place greater value on files created by other legislators who offer their papers for preservation. Consultation with archivists at other repositories can lead to a cooperative approach to the determination of who saves what among the files of committee members serving during the same legislative sessions.

Practices related to party caucuses vary from state to state. In some states, the caucus meets regularly throughout the session and provides a forum for debate to determine the party stance on a particular issue. In other states, it meets only to elect the leadership in each chamber and upon call thereafter. Strong leadership may convene a caucus to instruct members how to vote, whereas less entrenched or less managerial leadership may use the caucus to reach a consensus or a compromise. A few states have caucus staff or staff assigned to the leadership who devote much of their attention to preparing for caucus meetings.[18] In approximately half the states, the caucus, however regular and organized its meetings, is generally seen as an off-the-record gathering at which candid remarks by the leadership or the members can be made without concern for coverage by the media, intervention by the executive branch, or scrutiny by the citizenry.[19] Few records are created by most caucuses, and should any appear in the files of individual legislators, they may be real finds or merely routine agendas and copies of draft bills circulated to all members to place in the briefcases they bring to the caucus meeting. If records are maintained by caucus staff or by its leadership, the files of party members may contain little documentation unavailable in expanded form elsewhere.

Files of a more personal nature are created to maintain a legislator's schedule, to retain a copy of a speech, to keep clippings and photographs related to various activities, to keep press releases, and to document campaign efforts.

Vanity files of clippings and press releases offer biographical information that is usually duplicated or recorded in greater depth in other sources, whereas photographs must be appraised on the basis of content and format generally used in evaluating any photographic series. Speeches, however, represent many politicians' most public associations with their constituents, and the increasing number of audiovisual records of speeches, interviews, and other public appearances offers the researcher an especially rich source. Content analysis and user accessibility must be considered during appraisal of these as of any other records, but the existence of audiovisual material has expanded the opportunity to document the legislative experience.

Campaign files are often eagerly sought by archivists striving to provide researchers with sources for local history. Quite often, material for eye-catching exhibits will turn up in such files as well. Correspondence, circularized literature, lists of contributors and campaign volunteers, schedules, and other associated records reveal the activities of both the candidate and her or his local supporters and should be retained at least in a representative sample. Questions can be raised concerning the validity of maintaining such papers with the records of a legislator's official functions, but the presence of these papers in legislative office files may indicate the extent to which elected officials see their campaigns as the first stage or continuing links in their legislative careers.

Since potential research use is an important criterion in appraisal decisions at the administrative level in developing collecting policies and at the level of folder or series evaluation, the appraisal process must include an analysis of research trends and the type of constituency the repository serves. Historians appear to continue to be interested in political and social studies that depend on documentation of voting patterns and groups based on religious, social, or ethnic similarities, such as the role of women in society, economic and demographic trends, and other movements or issues identified with population masses in specific regions or socioeconomic classes. Biographical studies have declined in interest, and the general historical treatment of great events and grand schemes is often the magnum opus many hope to write but few now undertake.

Research interest in political science, sociology, and other social sciences has for some time been concentrated in the compilation of empirical data to document behavioral activity. Methodological development and the procedures for collecting accurate and representative samples comprise much of the research effort, and the principal goal is to amass adequate data to reveal how the subject of research behaved at a given point in time or responded to certain stimuli. Few historians and fewer social scientists are studying institutional development or seeking motives undocumented by empirical data. They seldom ask why individuals and collective entities acted and felt as they did, and it appears that efforts begun in the nineteenth century to apply scientific research methods to social studies have reached their culmination in current social research aided by the modern technology needed to amass and organize the raw data of human activity. Analysis and commentary have become secondary concerns, and the objectivity of data compilation and dissemination is the most popular game in town.

Although any generalization of research trends is subject to legitimate criticism based on exceptions to the rule, one can nevertheless note that many archival reading rooms are increasingly visited by researchers seeking masses of data to compile, organize, and compare. Constituent correspondence and casework files of legislators are used not to identify individuals who wrote but to collect numbers in order to document how many citizens expressed an idea, what that idea was, and how various types of legislators responded to identifiable stimuli. In such a context, not only do the masses of correspondence and casework files take on added importance in the aggregate but so do the masses of legislators whose aggregate collections provide *more* data than the files of any one of them.

If any contemporary scholars should be interested in documenting activities of legislators rather than of their constituents, it is quite likely that those researchers will be more interested in legislators as participants in the legislative process than as individual politicians. They want to be able to determine how legislators functioned as a collective entity and will seek access to records of legislators as component parts of a larger whole. The more collections, the better. State archival agencies collecting legislative records may take a similar view. Administrators of repositories housing the evidence of how state agencies and institutions functioned may see records of state legislators as complementing the records of committees and legislative agencies and staff by providing additional information on the operations and policies of the legislative branch. Although much current legislative research appears to be confined to the official records of the legislature, the existence of the files of recent members would enable researchers to find additional sources for the study of the legislative process and the place of the legislative branch in state government.

Legislative intent is yet another area of research that has proved quite popular at some state archives. Journalists, attorneys, citizen watchdog organizations, business representatives, and others seek to determine what an act really intended to enforce or require. Research may be undertaken by legislators and their staff to try to understand the implications of legislation passed in previous sessions of the legislature.[20] Regulations impinging on the rights and obligations of a particular group need to be understood by that group if they are to be implemented, supported, or evaluated, and legislative intent has become an area of study attracting visits to archival reading rooms by researchers who may not fit the scholarly mold but demand and deserve adequate service.

Justice Robert H. Jackson of the U.S. Supreme Court once remarked that
the use of state legislative records to determine legislative intent amounts
to abandoning analysis of a statute in favor of psychoanalysis of the legislative body enacting that statue.[21] Despite the late justice's reservations,
however, the intended meaning of legislation has become an important legal consideration, and papers of legislators are being sought to supplement
committee files and printed sources related to a specific piece of legislation.
The wording of a bill may be modified during a committee's deliberations
and mark-up sessions during which compromises may be incorporated
into revised wording drafted by, or at least acceptable to, a majority of the
committee. Further revision may be done by the leadership or by amendments once a bill reaches the floor of either or both of the chambers. With
so many cooks preparing the broth, the end result is quite often acceptable,
but far from the intended one. It may also be so equivocally worded that
the sponsor's intent in introducing the bill, the committee's intent in passing it to the floor, and the majority's intent in enacting it are obscured by a
lack of clarity and precision.[22]

Efforts to determine intent in the state of Washington now comprise a
large proportion of the total usage of the public archives of that state, perhaps the most active repository in collecting legislative records and papers
of legislators. Use by legislators and their staff represents a substantial percentage of the requests for these records, and archivists in Washington have
found that such service to their budget-making friends in the legislative
branch is both professionally satisfying and administratively shrewd.[23]

Even large repositories with comprehensive collecting policies cannot
accommodate vast collections of state legislators whose high turnover rate
increases the likelihood of a large number of collections available for acquisition. Plans for reappraisal at a later date, cooperative collecting programs
among repositories, and building legislative support by the development
of effective, though at times somewhat pragmatic, collecting policies may
provide much-needed assistance, but appraisal from the collecting policy
level to the series level must incorporate some representational scheme
whereby illustrative units of the whole can be retained while the repetitive
mass is reduced to manageable size.[24] Even though they may fully document their appraisal decisions and describe discarded records, archivists
turning to sampling and selection methods either to identify collections for
acquisition or to apply within a collection may be accused by researchers
of failing to recognize current research trends and the needs of the research
community. More realistically, and in defense of archivists struggling to
balance user needs with such practical considerations as space and staff, it
appears that sampling and selection are legitimate areas of appraisal, but
ones needing continued and greatly intensified study. The older among us,
trained as historians, librarians, or social scientists in the more traditional

approaches to research, need to consult with colleagues having more recent training and with historians and social scientists whose familiarity with sampling techniques and data compilation can help us to appraise more adequately records of the numerous legislators whose files we seek but cannot fully accommodate.

NOTES

1. This chapter was originally written as a product of the author's participation in the 1983 Research Seminar on Modern Historical Documentation held at the Bentley Historical Library, University of Michigan, and funded by the Andrew W. Mellon Foundation. The author gratefully acknowledges the assistance, encouragement, and suggestions of the other Mellon Fellows Frank Boles, Leonard Rapport, JoAnne Yates, and Julia Young, as well as Bentley Library staff members Francis X. Blouin Jr. and William K. Wallach. He also wishes to thank the Virginia State Library for granting him a leave of absence to participate in the seminar.

2. A recently published essay has done much to fill this void, and its comments on coordinating collecting policies and considering individual congressional offices as part of the larger whole consisting of the entire state delegation ought to generate productive discussion of the appraisal of congressional files. See Patricia Aronsson, "Appraisal of Twentieth-Century Congressional Collections," in *Archival Choices: Managing the Historical Record in An Age of Abundance*, ed. Nancy E. Peace (Lexington, Mass.: D. C. Heath, 1984).

3. See, for example, the results of a survey conducted in 1981 by Sidney F. McAlpin for the National Association of State Archives and Records Administrators on file in the Washington State Archives, Olympia, and "Accessioning the Papers of Public Officials: An Examination of the Laws and Practices of the States," 28–29, an unpublished report prepared by F. Gerald Ham in 1976 for the National Study Commission on Records and Documents of Federal Officials. The unpublished "Report on the Status of Legislative Records" (1979) compiled by the Archives and Field Services Staff of the State Historical Society of Wisconsin is an important first effort to deal with the collection and appraisal of the papers of state legislators.

4. William Leuchtenberg's comments in *Proceedings, Conference on the Research Use and Disposition of Senators' Papers*, ed. Richard A. Baker (Washington, D.C., 1978), reflect the view that even though the papers of U.S. senators should be considered public records, they should remain at the disposal of the senator creating them. See especially 17–22 for Leuchtenberg's justification for what appears to be a somewhat contradictory resolution of this problem.

5. Alan Rosenthal, *Legislative Life: People, Process, and Performance in the States* (New York: Harper and Row, 1981), 135–9; and Kwang S. Shin and John S. Jackson III, "Membership Turnover in U.S. State Legislatures, 1931–1976," *Legislative Studies Quarterly* 4 (February 1979): 100.

6. Rosenthal, *Legislative Life*, 150–80. See also Malcolm E. Jewell and Samuel C. Patterson, *The Legislative Process in the United States*, 3rd ed. (New York: Random House, 1977), 119–50.

7. Rosenthal, *Legislative Life*, 95–96; Jewell and Patterson, *The Legislative Process*, 360–1.

8. An interesting proposal for files management of legislators' papers is recommended in Mary R. Patton, "An Appraisal Proposal for the Political Papers of Wisconsin State Legislators" (unpublished paper, 1978), 11–13.

9. Jewell and Patterson, *Legislative Process*, 307–8.

10. Rosenthal, *Legislative Life*, 98.

11. Jewell and Patterson, *Legislative Process*, 307–8.

12. Rosenthal, *Legislative Life*, 314–5.

13. Rosenthal, *Legislative Life*, 316, 335; Jewell and Patterson, *Legislative Process*, 445.

14. Thad L. Beyle, "The Governor as Chief Legislator," *State Government* 51 (Winter 1978): 2–10; and Barbara B. Knight, "The States and Reapportionment: One Man, One Vote Reevaluated," *State Government* 49 (Summer 1976): 156–9.

15. Richard C. Elling, "The Utility of State Legislative Casework as a Means of Oversight," *Legislative Studies Quarterly* 4 (August 1979): 354–6, 374; Alan Rosenthal, "Legislative Behavior and Legislative Oversight," *Legislative Studies Quarterly* 6 (February 1981): 115–31; and Keith E. Hamm and Rory D. Robertson, "Factors Influencing the Adoption of New Methods of Legislative Oversight in the U.S. States," *Legislative Studies Quarterly* 6 (February 1981): 133.

16. Rosenthal, *Legislative Life*, 103–4.

17. Glenn Abney and Thomas A. Henderson, "Representation of Local Officials by U.S. State Legislators," *Legislative Studies Quarterly* 4 (February 1979): 63–77.

18. Rosenthal, *Legislative Life*, 169–70; Jewell and Patterson, *Legislative Process*, 159–61.

19. *Legislative Openness: A Special Report on Press and Public Access to Information and Activities in State Legislatures* (Kansas City, Mo.: Citizens Conference on State Legislatures, 1974), 97.

20. Rosenthal, *Legislative Life*, 335.

21. Jewell and Patterson, *Legislative Process*, 423.

22. National Legislative Conference, *Summary of Proceedings of the Fifteenth Annual Meeting of the National Legislative Conference. Part II: Legislative Service Workshop Sessions* (Chicago: Council of State Governments, 1962), 50.

23. Unpublished remarks made by Sidney F. McAlpin at session of the Mellon Seminar on the Appraisal of Modern Documentation, University of Michigan, May 27, 1983.

24. For useful experimental attempts at sampling, see Lydia Lucas, "Managing Congressional Papers: A Repository View," *American Archivist* 41 (July 1978): 275–80; and Eleanor McKay, "Random Sampling Techniques: A Method of Reducing Large Homogeneous Series of Congressional Papers," *American Archivist* 41 (July 1978): 281–9.

13

Appraisal of Congressional Records at the Minnesota Historical Society

Mark A. Greene

The papers of U.S. senators and representatives are fundamental sources for local and national history. However, their tremendous bulk and complexity make such collections increasingly difficult for repositories to appraise and administer. The Minnesota Historical Society, which has one of the largest collections of congressional papers in the nation, assembled an internal committee to tighten its appraisal criteria. Drawing from two decades of mostly abstract articles and books on congressional records appraisal, the society created a concrete records disposition list. This list has been invaluable in communicating with congressional staffs (improving the content and reducing the size of accessions) and promises to deliver substantial space reductions through reappraisal.

"Because the documentation of Congress . . . directly reveals the will of the people as expressed through their elected representatives, it is especially crucial to preserve evidence and information about the legislative process and make it accessible to the public."[1] That Congress should be documented is surely indisputable. The hard question is how to document Congress and—perhaps hardest of all—how much documentation is necessary. Both these hard questions have been discussed on and off in the archival literature for many years. But little has been published that attempts to connect the theory of appraising congressional papers to the reality of a repository with an aggressive and broad collecting mandate. This chapter is a case study of how one such repository, the Minnesota Historical Society, converted theory into practice.

Previously published as "Appraisal of Congressional Records at the Minnesota Historical Society: A Case Study" in *Archival Issues* 19:1 (1994), 31–44. Reprinted with permission.

THE HISTORY OF COLLECTING CONGRESSIONAL PAPERS
AT THE MINNESOTA HISTORICAL SOCIETY

The Minnesota Historical Society's interest in documenting public affairs has a long history, beginning with its organization in 1849 by individuals who were themselves active participants in politics and government. For more than a century before this emphasis was defined in a Public Affairs Center (1967), they and their successors on the society's governing board, the staff, the state legislature, and the public at large collaborated in bringing together a rich store of information. Among its holdings are the papers of many of the state's representatives and nearly all of its senators. These collections have brought the society prestige, research use, strong documentation of individuals and issues throughout Minnesota, and (not unimportantly) relationships with politically powerful elected officials.

The breadth and depth of the society's holdings of congressional papers places it in a unique position nationally as the single largest repository of such material outside the federal government. To date, these collections total nearly 6,200 cubic feet (this does not include the vice-presidential portions of the papers of Walter Mondale and Hubert Humphrey), or approximately 16 percent of the society's total manuscript collection. A full 95 percent of this volume documents congressional activity since World War II—82 percent (5,000 cubic feet) since 1960 alone. These figures do not include ancillary public affairs collections such as the papers of the state's governors, the papers of appointed officials such as U.S. ambassadors Max Kampelman and Eugenie Anderson, the records of the state's major (and several minor) political parties, and the records of organizations such as the League of Women Voters and the Citizens League. The Minnesota Historical Society serves, moreover, as the archives for the state of Minnesota. Decades before the "documentation strategy" called for in *The Documentation of Congress*, the society recognized the essential interrelationship of the state's many layers and kinds of political documentation.[2]

The society's collecting of congressional papers has taken place within the context of certain important assumptions and principles. As Roger Davidson argued in 1991, to understand Congress, or the reasons for documenting it, "one must first recognize its duality. One Congress is the lawmaking institution, the Congress of the textbooks. The second Congress is the representative assemblage of . . . men and women of diverse backgrounds . . . and personal and political beliefs. Their electoral fortunes depend . . . not upon what Congress produces collectively, but how well they individually cultivate the support and goodwill of voters . . . miles from the Nation's Capitol."[3] Hence the importance of documenting Congress and its members has both a national and a local/personal component. On the one hand, the records of Congress are essential for understanding the nation's political history; on the other hand, "all politics is local" and each individual senator and representative (shaped by his or her own background and beliefs) represents and shapes state or district concerns. The personal papers of individual congresspeople are one key component to documenting this duality.

Moreover, the society has implicitly made a commitment to document its congressional delegation, not simply to document individual congresspeople. Unlike many other repositories of congressional papers in other states, it has embraced the idea that the group of individuals representing the state in Washington is more than the sum of its parts. These collections are important both as pieces of a national collection documenting Congress as a whole, and as resources for more local study: the lives and attitudes of individual elected officials; the interaction (political and personal) of the state delegation; the local (district, state, and regional) issues and concerns which formed the crucible of national action. In the past, however, the commitment to the delegation existed side by side with a desire to comprehensively and exhaustively document each congressperson individually. Implicit in this approach was a belief that all functions of every congressional office must be documented, and an unwillingness to make difficult (and possibly unpopular) appraisal choices. Short of financial receipts and award plaques, every record generated by every congressional office was sought and retained. By contrast, only a small portion of the records created by a business or other organization are accepted.

THE NEED FOR APPRAISAL GUIDELINES
FOR CONGRESSIONAL PAPERS

Historians and other users of congressional papers have admitted (often against their will) that the size of modern congressional collections—and especially the ever diminishing ratio between content and quantity—make them difficult and frustrating to use; at the same time, many researchers are becoming increasingly adept at using the wide range of other sources that document Congress in less bulky form. In the words of one scholar, "Congressional collections are far larger than they need to be in order to reflect the important issues and activities that they document," and "only by paring down these collections to their unique elements will archivists succeed in making them useful to researchers and manageable for archives."[4] To be blunt, however, making congressional collections manageable for archives is an even stronger imperative than making them useful to researchers. Unless archivists can develop appraisal guidelines to significantly reduce the size of congressional collections, overall documentation of Congress will suffer because fewer collections will be preserved. "Because of the growth in the size and complexity of these collections, congressional staff and archivists need to improve their understanding of what constitutes archival material and to develop the management skills to ensure its preservation."[5]

It was, ironically, the Minnesota Historical Society's construction of a $74 million building in 1991–1992 that focused attention on appraisal issues. While the new building (called the History Center) contained about 50 percent more archival storage space than our previous facility, our past rate of acquisitions would fill this space in less than half the time it took us to outgrow our previous building. Simply put, the society does not (and will not) have the resources to acquire, arrange, and store congressional papers at the rate it has done in the last decades. In 1991, therefore, we assembled an interdivisional committee to review our past collecting and issue appraisal guidelines. These guidelines, once approved by the society's director and executive council, would govern future collecting and also guide reappraisal efforts. The committee represented the Acquisitions and Curatorial, Reference, Research, Processing, and State Archives departments. The acquisitions staff is charged with negotiating with donors as well as making appraisal decisions; the reference and research staffs represent both the general public and academic users of our collections; the processing staff organizes and describes the collections; the state archives staff represents neutral but interested observers.[6]

Several previous studies, discussions, and recommendations existed on which to build our appraisal guidelines, but none offered an adoptable blueprint.[7] The most specific set of appraisal recommendations to date has been Karen Dawley Paul's *Records Management Handbook for United States Senators and Their Repositories*. Paul's handbook was indispensable in identifying and defining records series, but in several instances her retention guidelines give disproportionate weight to the individual senator rather than to documenting the office, the delegation, or the institution.[8] The less formal House of Representatives retention guidelines are more realistic about space constraints and researcher interest. However, the House handbook does not (cannot) modify the appraisal of representatives' records in light of parallel records kept by senators from the same state.[9] Moreover, our discussions were informed by conversations with and reports by archival colleagues at the Senate Historical Office, the House Historical Office, the State Historical Society of Wisconsin, the University of Delaware, and the University of South Carolina.[10] Finally, and in many instances most importantly, the guidelines have benefited from conversations with the staffs of several members of the Minnesota congressional delegation.

We quickly found that on many appraisal issues, consensus does not exist and cannot exist, because of the multifaceted character of the institutions and groups of individuals involved in or concerned with documenting Congress. Individuals include historians, who use the papers, and the congresspeople themselves, who create the material. Institutions range from the House and Senate historians' offices, to congressional research centers (such as the Dirksen Center in Illinois), to university special collections (many of which hold the papers of only one or two congresspeople), to state historical societies, and even to county historical societies. Each of these groups of individuals and repositories has a distinct purpose or mission, and a distinct perspective on appraisal. On the other hand, some consensus does exist, although as one archivist remarked, even where agreement exists on appraisal standards, there is often an unwillingness or inability to actually apply them. Thus the guidelines presented here will not be relevant to all other repositories; however, the size and depth of the Minnesota Historical Society's collections, along with the concentrated study afforded by its internal deliberations, may prove useful to other archives which collect congressional papers.

GOALS OF SOCIETY:
CONGRESSIONAL PAPERS APPRAISAL GUIDELINES

The central goal of these guidelines is to balance the Minnesota Historical Society's resources against the increasing bulk of congressional collections, and to define the most stringent appraisal criteria possible consistent with preserving collections which serve the long-term historical objectives of historians and other researchers. To accomplish this, the guidelines specifically rely on the society's accomplishments in documenting the state's entire congressional delegation. Because much redundancy and duplication exists among members of the delegation in terms of the issues and projects dealt with,[11] as well as with the constituents helped or heard from, the guidelines seek to reduce this overlap by treating the collections of senators differently from the collections of representatives. As Frank Mackaman has argued, by choosing to more thoroughly document the activities of senators, a repository has the assurance of receiving materials documenting concerns of importance from all corners of the state.[12] The papers of representatives, therefore, can be reduced further (especially such series as constituent correspondence) and focused to provide better documentation of those activities unique to the particular legislator and his or her district. Also, the guidelines make serious use of the assessment of records—especially constituent correspondence and case files—provided by congressional staff.

The guidelines also have as a goal improved communication between the society and the Minnesota congressional delegation, by enabling society staff to explain from the beginning which series they wish to preserve and why. And the guidelines must reflect a realistic assessment of the needs/demands of the congresspeople themselves and the needs of their offices. While the society does not preserve congressional collections principally as biographical icons to the elected official, part of what motivates politicians to donate their papers is the desire to have their personal accomplishments preserved for posterity. The proposed guidelines ensure that those portions of a congressperson's papers most likely to reflect his or her personality and accomplishments—speech files, clippings files, files of bills authored—will be retained. Fortunately, these series are also generally considered useful by researchers, so their preservation benefits not only the society's relationship with its donors but also the historical record.

EXPLANATION OF APPRAISAL OF SPECIFIC SERIES

Much of what appears in the guidelines will engender no controversy. Our approach to a few specific series, however, is more radical than what passes for conventional wisdom.

Invitations

These files consist of letters (and supporting documentation) requesting the member to appear at a function or give a speech. They are not only bulky but also redundant. The principal information contained in them relates to where the congressperson was at a particular time and what he or she was doing, and this information is available in much more condensed form in the schedule files. It should be noted, too, that invitation files are among the least used, according to a recent user survey.[13] Only if the speech files were integrated into the accepted invitations files would they be considered for retention. Here the society's guidelines are stricter than those in the Senate Handbook but mirror those in the House recommendations.

Academy Files

These files pertain to requests for the congressperson's assistance by constituents seeking nominations to service academies. Virtual unanimity exists in the archival world that these bulky files do not have long-term historical value. Moreover, the contents of the files raise serious questions concerning third-party privacy rights, and access to them prior to the death of the supplicants probably violates federal privacy legislation.[14] Summary lists, if any are compiled by the congressional office, will be maintained, as well as memos and form letters that illustrate the office's policy in responding to academy applications or queries.

Routine Requests

These files contain requests from constituents for such things as flags flown over the Capitol, tours of the Capitol, and copies of congressional publications. No one in the historical or archival community recommends retention of even a sample of these bulky records. The fact that these requests must be dealt with by the congressperson's staff is documented in the office manuals and other administrative records that will be retained.

Issue Mail

Mail sent by constituents expressing opinions on issues before Congress receives moderate research use. However, several factors mitigate against the wisdom of retaining the huge bulk represented by this series of records. First, even the most dedicated historians admit that no one can or wants to read all the letters received on a specific issue; most scholars use this series to find quotable examples. Second, neither historians nor the congressional offices themselves rely on issue mail as an indication of the strength of popular opinion on a specific issue: district and statewide polls, not mail or phone calls, are how offices judge voter opinion. As the chief of staff of one of Minnesota's congressmen noted, while their mail ran 60–40 against gun control, polls in their district consistently showed 70 percent voter approval of gun control. In addition, he added, "most of the letters we receive are inane, and so are most of the responses we send out." One Senate office stopped microfilming or preserving issue mail five years ago and relies instead on summaries and analyses as well as polling data. Furthermore, the system used to film and index this mail often makes it impossible to find letters either by topic or by constituent name (once the film is separated from the congressional services facilities). If a random sample of randomly microfilmed issue mail of the Senate offices is preserved, a selection of letters on most issues of importance to Minnesota will be available for illustrative purposes. Summaries and analyses of issue mail, when created by any congressional office, would be preserved.

Case Files

These files consist of requests for assistance from constituents: for example, seeking an increase in a military pension or some other federal benefit. Conversations with the House and Senate historians' offices, and the staffs of two Minnesota congressional delegates, indicates a growing realization that these files pose a privacy concern that has not heretofore been recognized. Most of the material in these case files is protected by federal privacy legislation. At least three of Minnesota's congressional offices have expressed reluctance even to donate these records; others (and the Senate

Historical Office) have indicated that any case files accepted and retained by a repository will have to be sealed for 75 years from date of closing. A staff member of one of the congressional historical offices was blunt about the fact that "those [case] files aren't worth the papers they're printed on" in terms of long-term historical value. Indeed, the Veterans Affairs Committee of the Senate schedules its casework files for destruction after 10 years, a reflection both of privacy concerns and of appraisal of research potential. The Senate and House Historical Office documentation group reported at the Society of American Archivists (SAA) in 1991 that "projects and casework files are duplicated in many places [e.g., executive agency files], use was complicated by privacy laws," and in any event researchers made virtually no use of these files.

The one element of longer-term historical value that may inhere in case files is a pattern of public interaction (mostly regarding problems) with the federal government that in turn reflects aspects of public policy, especially as it may concern current events or governmental policy or philosophy (e.g., draft issues during Vietnam, shifts in immigration policy). In most instances, however, the responsibility for preserving evidence of the interaction of government and individual citizens should fall on the National Archives. To attempt this through the papers of congresspeople ensures nothing if not inconsistency and redundancy; most cases are not geographically specific (veteran's benefits case files are the same in California as in Minnesota). The appraisal guidelines for the Minnesota Historical Society permit, where feasible, the sampling of case files which (a) illustrate the "personal" aspects of governmental policy and (b) relate specifically to Minnesota. For example, one of our representative's district office kept the "agriculture and economic development" case files separate, and these were sampled to give a picture of the impact that the farm crisis and wetlands legislation had on southwestern Minnesota farmers. In addition, summary lists and statistical reports regarding casework would be retained for all offices. This appraisal approach mirrors that are now suggested by the House Historical Office. Given the extraordinary bulk of these records, their low research rate, and the fact that personal case files will be inaccessible for nearly a century after creation, broader retention strategies are not defensible.

Plaques and Memorabilia

Elected officials receive astounding numbers of plaques, certificates, buttons, hats, jackets, pins, medallions, trophies, shovels (from groundbreakings), and other expressions of gratitude and esteem from constituents, lobbyists, and others. A member who serves for a decade or more may acquire dozens and dozens of cubic feet of such material. These rarely represent significant accomplishments, and most are documentable in some other way (through the appointment calendar, for instance). Some repositories whose collections focus on a single congressperson preserve virtually all of this material, and some even item catalog it. Undoubtedly an element of local color exists in much of the material, but our committee—in consultation with our Museum Collections department—concluded that such value was minimal compared to the bulk, preservation problems, and huge resources necessary to provide reasonable access to such material.

Other Files

By reducing the amount of time and storage space the society spends dealing with series such as case files and constituent correspondence, the acquisition staff will be in a better position to focus energy on the files of administrative and legislative assistants, and on electronic records in the congressional offices—records of indisputable long-term historical value but which have heretofore been acquired only sporadically if at all. Congressional staff tend to view their files as personal, and to overcome this tendency the historical society must take pains to highlight these records and speak specifically to the respective staff members. Electronic records in congressional offices, as in so many other places, are rapidly evolving, and efforts to both understand these systems and to appraise the data contained in them should take precedence over arrangements for the sampling, shipping, and acquisitioning of hundreds of cubic feet of case and issue files. Other series the acquisition staff will be seeking to highlight with congressional staffs are those dealing with the member's party activities and his or her involvement with congressional membership organizations.

PROPOSED APPRAISAL POLICY, BY SERIES

Key:
S and D—Selection and Disposition; series probably needs to be appraised folder by folder.
Retain—Probably will be retained intact, except for duplicates or if inspection suggests that value is minimal.
Dispose—Normally will not be retained (and should not be sent to Society), unless inspection or information from the congressional office indicates value sufficient to warrant S and D or sampling.

Personal Political Papers
Appointment books	Retain
Biographical files	Retain
Campaign committee records	S and D

Chronological file	S and D
(correspondence control file)	
Congressional membership organizations	Retain
Control file	S and D
(correspondence control file, alphabetical)	
Correspondence with other members, White House,	Retain
other dignitaries	
Correspondence with family, friends, colleagues	S and D
Daily schedules	Retain
Desk calendars	Dispose
Diaries or personal journals	Retain
Financial disclosure reports	Retain
Invitations (accepted and rejected), unless interfiled	Dispose
with appearance files	
Job recommendations/patronage	
VIP appointments, judgeships	S and D
All others	Dispose
Memorabilia, plaques, etc.	Dispose
Party leadership files	S and D
Political party files (state and national)	S and D
Polling data	Retain
Scrapbooks or clippings notebooks (only articles	Retain
about the member and only if well organized,	
identified, and in good physical condition)	
Telephone conversations:	
Summary reports	Retain
Message slips	Dispose
Logs	S and D
Trip file	
Investigative/policy related trips	S and D
Speeches, routine appearances, campaign stops	Discard
VIP correspondence (photocopies ok)	Retain

Legislative Records

Agency/department files	S and D
(correspondence and supporting material filed	
by executive department or agency; often relate	
to case files)	
Bill files	
Bills authored/co-authored by the congressperson	Retain
All others	Dispose
Briefing books	Retain

Committee and Subcommittee Files

    (NB: official committee and subcommittee
    records are property of the Senate or House)

Correspondence and memos	S and D
Lists, calendars/agendas, background, minutes, reports	S and D
(those reflecting substantive activity by the	
member should be retained)	

Congressional Record

Items inserted into the *Record* by the congressperson	Retain
Bound sets of the *Record*	Dispose
Legislative assistants' files	S and D
Legislative subject files	S and D
Other staff project files	S and D
Publications of state and federal agencies	Dispose
Voting attendance records	Retain

Constituent Service Records

Administrative assistant's files	S and D
Case files	
If filed by type	S and D
If not filed by type and not microfilmed	Dispose
If microfilmed	S and D
Casework reports and indexes	Retain
Congrats/condolences/greetings	Dispose
(incoming letters acknowledging members'	
election victory, expressing sympathy for	
illness; outgoing letters acknowledging	
valedictorians at district high schools,	
100-year-old constituents, etc.)	
Grants and projects	S and D
(federal grants to state or district organizations)	
Grants and projects reports and indexes	Retain
Issue mail	
Senators: if filmed and indexed	S and D
Senators: if not filmed	Sample if feasible
Representatives	Dispose
Issue mail master library or library of form paragraphs	Retain
(prewritten letters or paragraphs used to answer	
issue mail)	
Issue mail indexes and reports	Retain

Letters from school children
   Senators, if not filmed   S and D
   Representatives   Dispose
Military academy appointment files   Dispose, except
                                         for summary
                                       lists

Petitions — Dispose
Reference files — Dispose
   (clippings and publications used for
   background research)
Requests for material (flags, passes, etc.) — Dispose

Press Relations/Media Activities Records
Constituent mailings — Retain
Editorials written by the congressperson — Retain
Newsletters, updates, and other mailings
   to constituents — Retain
Newspaper clippings (background) — Dispose
Photographs, slides, negatives
   Identified events and activities — S and D
   Unidentified — Dispose
   Duplicates — Dispose
Press mailing lists — Dispose
Press releases — Retain
Speeches, drafts — Retain final
TV and radio files (audio and video tapes, transcripts;
   may include campaign spots and interviews) — S and D

Office Administration Records
Office administrator's files — S and D
Office operations and procedures
Operations manuals — Retain
Staff directives — S and D
Staff meeting minutes — Retain
Records management manual — Retain
Form letters, master library and cumulated indexes — Retain
Personnel
Personnel manuals — Retain
Annual lists of staff members — Retain
Applications — Dispose
Personnel files — Dispose
Security clearances — Dispose

Office equipment (inventories, purchase orders, etc.)   Dispose
Office funds: payroll, accounts; vouchers   Dispose

Travel
  Expenses, vouchers, etc.   Dispose
  Itineraries and trip reports   S and D

POLICY ON FIRST-TERM REPRESENTATIVES

Members of the U.S. House of Representatives who serve only one term are usually less historically important than those who serve several terms. Therefore, normally it will be society policy not to seek donor contracts with representatives until after their first reelection. In the case of a representative who is defeated after one term, the acquisition staff will contact his or her office after the election and request donation of a very limited number of series: mass mailings to constituents, biographical files, VIP correspondence, speech files, press releases, well-organized newspaper clippings, and in some instances selected campaign files.

FOLLOW-UP

As a courtesy to our colleagues in the SAA Congressional Papers Roundtable, these guidelines were circulated to them in the fall of 1993. The Minnesota Historical Society's acquisitions staff has also given the retention schedule to the administrative assistants of all of our senators and representatives. The response from the Hill has been very encouraging, with closing offices expressing great pleasure in having a clear set of guidelines to help them as they begin packing. The schedules have, of course, engendered questions, which has enabled us to speak in more detail to the staffs. One Senate office, while not quarreling with our assessment of plaques and memorabilia, did express frustration that we had not come up with alternative disposition. The only instance in which an office has questioned our appraisal guidelines has been to express doubt that even microfilm of case files should be preserved because of privacy concerns.

At the Minnesota Historical Society, the papers of congresspeople would comprise fully one-third of the manuscript collection if not for the anomaly of the massive records of the Great Northern and Northern Pacific railroads.[15] If one adds to this the vice-presidential papers of Hubert Humphrey and Walter Mondale, and the papers of state senators and representatives, and of governors, then close to half the (nonrailroad) manuscript collections are composed of the papers of elected officials. Without disputing the importance of these people to the history of Minnesota, it is

surely debatable whether their importance is equivalent to the space and
other resources they have traditionally occupied in the repository. As one
of our committee members asked: "Do we really need 116 feet of material
to document Congressman Tom Hagedorn's 8 years in office when we keep
110 feet for nearly 70 years of the St. Paul Area United Way?"[16] For the
society to have the ability to aggressively document communities of color,
major Minnesota industries, women's groups, and all the other aspects of
Minnesota history it wishes to see adequately represented in the manuscript
collections, it is necessary to revise the traditional "take anything" approach
to congressional papers.

Too often in the discussions of documentation strategy, the implicit
assumption is made that there is an objective answer to the question "What
is an adequate record of X?" To document Congress (or an individual congressperson, or even a state's delegation) "adequately" can mean: (a) if this
is all we are worried about documenting, what functions and what level
of detail should we preserve?; or (b) if this is one of many things we want
to document as part of a larger whole, what is the minimum necessary to
do that job? The appraisal criteria developed at the Minnesota Historical
Society sits somewhere between maximum possible and minimum necessary. Committee members advocating for researchers argued for preserving
more, while other members (including the author of this article) argued for
preserving less. But the guidelines are a serious attempt to grapple with the
realities of limited space, important collections, and competing priorities.

NOTES

1. Karen Dawley Paul, *The Documentation of Congress: Report of the Congressional Archivists Roundtable Task Force on Congressional Documentation*, S. Pub. 102-20 (Washington, D.C.: U.S. Senate, 1992), iii.

2. *The Documentation of Congress*, iii–16.

3. Roger H. Davidson, "The Study of Congress," *Understanding Congress: Research Perspectives*, ed. Roger H. Davidson and Richard C. Sachs (Washington, D.C.: Government Printing Office, 1991), 10–11.

4. Patricia Aronsson, "Appraisal of Twentieth-Century Congressional Collec-tions," *Archival Choices*, ed. Nancy Peace (Lexington, Mass.: Lexington Books, 1984), 82–83.

5. *The Documentation of Congress*, 3.

6. The committee consisted of James Fogerty, acquisitions and curatorial (chair); Todd Daniels-Howell, acquisitions and curatorial; Mark Greene, acquisitions and curatorial; Dallas Lindgren, reference; Lydia Lucas, processing; Kathy Marquis, ref-erence; Dennis Meissner, processing; Deborah Miller, research and publications; Duane Swanson, state archives.

7. In addition to those already cited, see Richard A. Baker, ed., *Proceedings of the Conference on Research Use and Disposition of Senators' Papers* (Washington, D.C.: U.S.

Senate, 1978); Frank Mackaman, ed., *Congressional Papers Project Report* (Washington, D.C.: National Publications and Records Commission, 1986); Todd J. Daniels-Howell, "Appraisal of Congressional Papers," unpublished paper presented at the May 1991 Midwest Archives Conference; Eleanor McKay, "Random Sampling Techniques: A Method of Reducing Large, Homogeneous Series in Congressional Papers," *American Archivist* 41 (July 1978), 281–8; Lydia Lucas, "Managing Congressional Papers: A Repository View," *American Archivist* 41 (July 1978), 275–80.

8. Karen Dawley Paul, *Records Management Handbook for United States Senators and Their Repositories* (Washington, D.C.: U.S. Senate, 1991). For example, despite their extreme bulk and high degree of repetitiveness, clippings, photographs/slides/negatives, and TV and radio files are designated by the *Handbook* as permanent records. A thoughtful selection or sample of these materials will, to my mind, serve the needs of virtually all researchers. Also, the *Handbook* designates party leadership files as permanent, even though for most senators, these files will contain mostly circular memos and reports better preserved in the papers of the Senate leaders themselves.

9. "Recommended Disposition: Papers of Members of U.S. House of Representatives," (1993) unpublished handout available from the Office of the Historian, U.S. House of Representatives.

10. We benefited in particular from discussions with, or papers by, Richard Pifer (State Historical Society of Wisconsin), Herb Hartsook (University of South Carolina), Rebecca Johnson (University of Delaware), Karen Dawley Paul (Senate Historian's Office), Cynthia Pease Miller (Office of the House Historian).

11. Aronsson, "Appraisal of Twentieth-Century Congressional Collections," 83.

12. Mackaman, *Congressional Papers Project Report*, 158.

13. *The Documentation of Congress*, 138.

14. *The Documentation of Congress*, 42.

15. The manuscript collection as a whole is 37,000 cubic feet. Of the whole, the railroad records are fully 15,000 cubic feet, and therefore greatly skew most analyses of the Minnesota Historical Society collections.

16. Daniels-Howell, "Appraisal of Congressional Papers," 7.

14

Appraisal of the
John J. Williams Papers

L. Rebecca Johnson Melvin

Traditionally, appraisal decisions for a congressional collection have been made after the arrival of the collection at a repository. In this case, the collection was the papers of Senator John J. Williams of Delaware. Williams represented Delaware in the U.S. Senate from 1947 until 1970, and he was known as "the Conscience of the Senate" for his honest pursuit of integrity in government while serving on both the Finance and Foreign Relations committees. Processing the Williams papers was a dedicated two-year project. A project archivist was hired in 1988, and shortly afterwards, a technician assistant. The project archivist made all of the appraisal decisions, and the technician followed guidelines to assist with sampling selected files. Processing was done in a year and a half. A finding aid, summary guide, and exhibition were completed by the end of the project in September 1990.

From the outset, appraisal was an obvious issue for this collection. It was clear that its final size was a concern for the Special Collections department, with its limited space, and the University of Delaware had deliberately obtained in the deed of gift from the Williams family the right to dispose of the collection according to archival principles. Records of the original extent of the filing series from a survey of the collection and press releases about the collection's arrival at the university set the original bulk at 600 linear feet. The appraisal summary in table 14.1 provides a series outline for the collection, with ratios of original extent to retained extent (in linear feet) for each series. (The initials "ERL" indicate Senator Williams's executive secretary, who was with him throughout his Senate career.)

Previously published as "Appraisal of Senator John Williams's Papers" in *Provenance: The Journal of the Society of Georgia Archivists* x:1–2 (1992). Reprinted with permission.

Table 14.1.   Papers of Senator John J. Williams of Delaware, 1947–1970

Appraisal Summary	Original		Retained
	(in linear feet)		
I. Legislative Staff/Office Files			
A. JJW:ERL subject files	35	:	11
B. Committee files	6.5	:	6.5
C. Projects/investigations			
1. Bureau of Internal Revenue	14	:	14
2. Bobby Baker	9	:	9
3. Medicare	1.5	:	1.5
D. Legislative reference material	3.5	:	3.5
E. Bills of legislation	16	:	8.25
F. *Congressional Record* office index	40	:	2.5
G. Voting records	4	:	4
II. Constituent Correspondence and Cases			
A. Executive correspondence	60	:	25
B. Legislative correspondence	120	:	43
C. Congratulations (received and sent)	5	:	1
D. Academy recommendations	7	:	.3
E. Correspondence master file	80	:	0
III. Administrative and Personal Office Files			
A. Miscellaneous office files	46	:	3
B. Datebooks	1.5	:	1.5
C. Appointments correspondence	1.5	:	.5
D. Invitations	17.5	:	.75
IV. Personal			
A. Campaigns	1.5	:	1.25
B. Speeches	11	:	6
C. Scrapbooks			
D. Biographical information			
E. Periodicals			
F. Cartoons			
G. Citations and awards			
H. Photographs			
I. Audiovisual			
J. Books			
	480.5	:	142.55
			30%

The total of 480.5 linear feet recorded as the original extent in the appraisal summary does not include the senator's library of bound *Congressional Record* volumes and other government publications, crates of framed photographs and memorabilia, or scrapbooks. Not quite a "20-percenter," in the end closer to 30 percent of the original files from the collection were preserved.[1]

It might be valuable to review a few obvious things about appraisal and congressional collections. Congressional collections of the twentieth century and now the twenty-first are classic examples of the bulk records which beg "archival choices." In 1983, Richard Berner wrote, "a body of appraisal theory is perhaps the most pressing need in the archival field today."[2] Patricia Aronsson's seminal 1984 chapter in *Archival Choices* still provides important guidelines for appraisal of congressional collections.[3] She emphasizes the dual nature of such material as both public records and private papers, and the need to weigh the sameness of the record types that appear in all congressional collections against the uniqueness of the collections as they reflect the individual office holder and the state or district represented.

Karen Dawley Paul's *Records Management Handbook for United States Senators and Their Archival Repositories* details the kinds of records found in senate offices and suggests retention schedules.[4] These guidelines are just as useful to archivists at repositories and are helpful in answering the question of what is unique about the particular senator's collection. Paul's *Handbook* and the report of the Task Force on the Documentation of Congress emphasize the need to make appraisal decisions with a broader understanding of the scope of sources available to support congressional research.[5]

In processing the Williams papers, a dull impression hovered in the background: there were 99 other senators who served with Williams at any given time, and there were conceivably 99 collections that paralleled Williams's papers. The evidential value of the collection in documenting the functions of his senatorial office was probably fairly well covered in similar collections around the country. But this was the first twentieth-century congressional collection at the University of Delaware, and the evidential value of the papers as a source for students to research a senatorial office was not overlooked. Evidential value drove the arrangement scheme for the collection, with four subgroups reflecting functions of Williams's office: legislative, investigative, and committee work; the representative work for constituents; administrative details; and personal papers.

Appraisal decisions became more interesting when considering the informational value of the collection. Aronsson's advice is consistent with any informational guidelines: what does the collection tell us about the individual senator and his or her interests, the issues of the home state, the issues of the times, and the achievements of Congress during the senator's terms?[6]

Then there are the basic appraisal guidelines Nancy Peace summarized in "Deciding What to Save," which appeared in *Archival Choices*: importance, uniqueness, usability, reliability, completeness, comparability, cost of preservation, and density.[7] Several of these are clearly subjective factors. With this acknowledgment of the inevitable subjectivity of some of the decisions to come, and after conscientiously contacting colleagues and exploring appraisal decisions for other congressional collections, it was time to plunge into the processing of the Williams papers.

The luxury of having time dedicated to item-level processing as done with the Williams papers is one that comes infrequently. As summarized in table 14.2, "Outline of Series with Appraisal Notes," there were broad appraisal guidelines for the papers and different appraisal methods for the various series in the collection. There were those wonderfully straightforward discards: duplicates, carbons, envelopes, interim correspondence, and secondary printed sources such as government publications. These are obvious, but worth mentioning in a review of what was discarded from the collection because their bulk was considerable.

The standard office filing procedure in Senator Williams's office was to assemble related correspondence in this manner: incoming letter stapled to accompanying envelope; carbon of interim response stapled to that (interim means "thank you for your letter, a response is forthcoming"); attached carbons of outgoing and incoming follow-up correspondence to appropriate individual or agency; final answer from agency; carbon of outgoing answer to original letter; any related clippings, reports, or attachments. Each bundle of correspondence was a colorful cluster of stationery, yellow and white carbons, and an average of five staples and a paper clip or two. Much of this was discarded—all that was needed was the original correspondence, evidence of the office's action, and the final answer.

Other guidelines were applied generally to the correspondence, especially the constituent correspondence. With the luxury of processing at the item level, it was possible to look for things to save: prominent correspondents, first-name-basis correspondents, and regular correspondents. Also saved was correspondence representing views of corporate bodies such as civic, trade, labor, and fraternal organizations; ethnic and religious groups; and special-interest lobbies. The geographical range of constituents was considered before making appraisal decisions. Was the issue important to Delawareans or to the nation as a whole? Senator Williams's papers were unusual in the volume of correspondence he received from Americans nationwide. Another factor considered was retaining the proportion of respondents by sex when the issue was gender related. For example, a large number of women wrote to the Senator to protest the coloring of margarine in the early 1950s, and the appraised files had to represent fairly the original proportion of his correspondents on this issue. And, of course, it was important to save more of the material documenting issues specific to Delaware.

Sometimes the appearance of a letter was enough to warrant its retention. Lengthy replies from the senator, as opposed to noncommittal responses

Table 14.2.   Papers of Senator John J. Williams of Delaware, 1947–1970

Outline of Series with Appraisal Notes

I. Legislative Staff/Office Files—this is the key subgroup, and most of the material in these flies was saved. General appraisal guidelines were used to remove duplicates, carbons, interim correspondence, envelopes, secondary sources such as government reports and hearings, etc.

A. JJW:ERL subject files—this series was the main office reference file maintained by "ERL," Senator Williams's executive secretary throughout his entire Senate career. It is arranged topically under department and agency names. This structure parallels the department and agency arrangement of the executive correspondence and legislative correspondence series. Chief discards from this series were voluminous reports and financial charts, many used for reference and many reprinted at Williams's request in the *Congressional Record*. 30 lin. ft. reduced to 11 lin. ft. An additional 5 lin. ft. of ERL's stenographer's notebooks were completely discarded.

B. Committee files—this series pulled together scattered files of Senator Williams's committee work. The files are not very complete even though almost everything found was saved. They include 1.5 lin. ft. of hearing transcripts for the Committee to Investigate the National Defense. 3.5. lin. ft.

C. Projects/investigations—these files are expected to be the primary research interest of the collection, so the entire contents of files were retained.
   1. Bureau of Internal Revenue—14 lin. ft.
   2. Bobby Baker—9 lin. ft.
   3. Medicare—1.5 lin. ft.

D. Legislative reference material—these files included material supporting preparation of legislation but also contained information of an investigative nature about Senator Williams's colleagues. All 3.5 lin. ft. retained.

E. Bills of legislation—this series was mainly an office reference file of duplicate bills, but some folders did include supporting documentation of legislative work. The series was extensively weeded of duplicate bills. 16 lin. ft. reduced to 8.25 lin. ft.

F. *Congressional Record* office index—only the office index was saved. Originally, this series included the full paper issues of the *Congressional Record* containing Senator Williams's comments in the Senate. The tearsheets from these speeches are available in the speech file, and there is a complete set of the *Congressional Record* available elsewhere in the library. 38 lin. ft. reduced to .5 lin. ft.

G. Voting records—this useful voting analysis was retained in its entirety. 4 lin. ft.

II. Constituent Correspondence and Cases—this subgroup contains series of material generated in response to constituent concerns. The bulk and repetitiveness of the file contents called for heavy sampling and appraisal.

A. Executive correspondence—this series contains correspondence and reference material from executive departments and agencies, initiated by Senator Williams's office on behalf of constituent concerns. This series also reflects casework. The structure of this series parallels the JJW:ERL series and the legislative correspondence series: it is arranged by executive department and agency subseries, with further topical subseries. Within each subseries is a miscellaneous subseries which received the heaviest appraisal. Some groups of files such as passport and visa application cases within the State Department were completely discarded. 60 lin. ft. reduced to 25 lin. ft.

(continued)

Table 14.2. (*continued*)

B. Legislative correspondence—this series contains constituent correspondence on general or legislative issues. It parallels the executive correspondence and the JJW:ERL files, with arrangement by department or agency and subseries issues. Each subseries contains a miscellaneous group which received heavy appraisal. This series also contained many "robo" or "dura" letters, form letters sent in response to voluminous mail received about a single issue. Approximately 20–25% of robo correspondence was saved with the office robo; a sheet of paper was inserted in each folder documenting the original volume of the correspondence. 120 lin. ft. reduced to 43 lin. ft.

C. Congratulations (received and sent)—this series was correspondence both received and sent by the Senator. Appraisal was pretty casual because of the overall insignificance of the files. Letters of congratulation saved included many to and from colleagues, and typical constituent congratulations were from election years or in response to the senator's stand on certain issues. 5 lin. ft. reduced to 1 lin. ft.

D. Academy recommendations—original files contained a general information folder for each military academy and then folders for each individual applicant arranged alphabetically by year. The folders were marked with a "check" or an "x" indicating whether the applicant gained Senator Williams's recommendation. We were able to do a quick tally of how many individuals sought nominations to which academies each year, and how many of them were recommended. We saved the general information file for each academy and a few files that demonstrated either the typical paperwork for such recommendations or the maintained files of a few service members with successful careers. 7 lin. ft. reduced to .3 lin. ft.

E. Correspondence master file—this comprised yellow carbons of all correspondence sent to constituents, arranged alphabetically and chronologically. Because the constituent correspondence was so heavily appraised, this was not saved. 80 lin. ft. completely discarded.

III. Administrative and Personal Office Files—this subgroup of office files documents general staff duties as well as the personal schedule of Senator Williams. Most office duties were deemed of little permanent value.

A. Miscellaneous office files—this series contains administrative details and personal office management information as well as miscellaneous requests from constituents for publications, tours, and other courtesies. All specific information about Williams was saved. Only samples of the miscellaneous office details and request files were saved with each file, including a statement of the original volume of each subseries. 46 lin. ft. reduced to 3 lin. ft.

B. Datebooks—all saved. 1.5 lin. ft.

C. Appointment correspondence—this series is arranged chronologically and includes requests from constituents for appointments. A sample was taken from each year. 1.5 lin. ft. reduced to .5 lin. ft.

D. Invitations—this series is arranged chronologically and includes invitations both accepted and declined. This series was appraised by sampling invitations from random months at 5-year intervals. Special files for the Delmarva Chicken Festival and "Dinner with Ike" and as many accepted invitations as noticed within the random months were saved. Williams generally accepted invitations to Delaware fraternal organizations, church groups, and Republican Party functions. 17.5 lin. ft. reduced to .75 lin. ft.

IV. Personal—this subgroup of material documents Senator Williams's personal activities and thus most was saved. For example, 1.5 lin. ft. of campaign materials was reduced to 1.25 lin. ft. and 11 lin. ft. of other materials was reduced to 6 lin. ft.

of "thank you for your opinion," generally contained details of his stand on a particular issue. Letters from some constituents were lengthy and, at a glance, appeared to represent an educated point of view. Some handwriting and spelling were quick clues that an author was elderly or uneducated, and it was interesting to have these represented as well. Return addresses were used to identify economically depressed areas (such as Appalachia) or other notable regions. A few things were saved for purely serendipitous reasons: correspondence on interesting letterhead or postcards, a few token pieces of crank mail, and for aesthetic appeal or to demonstrate the subjectivity of appraisal, letters written in green ink.

Different appraisal methods were used for various series in the collection. There were simple discards for the topically specific files, such as the JJW:ERL subject files. These files typically included correspondence, office memos and notes, and background materials. There were instances where retention of representative files documented routine functions of the senator's office. In these cases, a single representative file or several files at random chronological intervals were selected and the others were discarded, with the original extent of the files recorded. For example, only three files from the original requests for agricultural yearbooks found in the series "Miscellaneous Office Files" were saved. The first folder of the appraised files includes a sheet with the statement, "These three folders are representative sample files from five linear feet of requests for agricultural yearbooks in the original office files spanning the dates 1947–1970." This was also done for other routine files, such as arrangements for school group tours.

In some cases, totally random samples of unimportant files were saved to document their substantial but insignificant existence. A small file of unanswered mail in the miscellaneous office files was preserved because there was originally so much of it. The folder retained included this statement: "Sample of correspondence received but unanswered by Senator Williams's office for various reasons: insufficient address, no reply requested, illegible, or incoherent contents. Original files included almost three linear feet of unanswered mail, including four linear inches of unintelligible mail from a character known as 'D.M.'"

Small amounts of some series were saved merely to document the senator's handling of certain types of requests or cases. In the case of academy recommendations, purely subjective criteria were used, and the few "fat" files from each of the academies were pulled. As it turned out, these "fat" files represented individuals who gained the senator's recommendation, had successful military careers, and kept in touch with the senator. A general file was retained for each academy, and a summary list was compiled of the number of applicants recommended and not recommended by Williams. An explanation of this appraisal process was included with the series description.

Issue mail in this collection was primarily in the legislative correspondence and executive correspondence series. In some cases, indiscriminate samples of material in generic topical files were selected. These files addressed a wide range of concerns, often within an agency's jurisdiction, and often not requiring any significant action or comment from the senator. An example of such files to be sampled were those under "Executive Correspondence—Post Office—Mail Delivery Service."

In general, a quantitative sample of constituent correspondence from voluminous single-issue files was saved. Files often contained a single copy of the robo or dura (form letter) response sent by the office and all constituent mail, sometimes including petitions. About 20–25 percent of this type of correspondence was saved. If a subject was deemed to have significant research potential, such as, for example, mail concerning the censure of Senator Joseph McCarthy, a greater portion of the correspondence was saved. The sample was sometimes taken by random selection, sometimes by closer inspection of groups of items, and sometimes by actually counting off two or three letters from every group of 10. Petitions were noted by saving the first page with text and one page of signatures. A close approximation of the number of signers was then penciled onto the petition. The original volume of mail was documented on a reference sheet added to the file. A measure of one inch being equivalent to 80–100 pieces of correspondence was used (thickness of paper, length of letters, and presence of postcards were considered). For example, the file "Legislative Correspondence—Executive Office—Nominations—Haynsworth—Robo to Supporters—1969" includes the statement "October–November 1969 robo sent in response to ca. 1,150 pieces of general correspondence. Samples follow."

More of a qualitative sample of constituent correspondence from lengthy issue-focused files was saved. These files usually contained individual replies, rather than robos, from the senator's office. A combination of random and subjective criteria was used to select approximately 30–50 percent of the material for retention. For example, one-third of the file contents were saved from the "Legislative Correspondence—Agriculture—Humane Slaughter" file, a popular cause in Delaware between 1957 and 1962.

Each agency or topical subdivision in the executive correspondence and legislative correspondence series included "miscellaneous" files. These contained a wide variety of issues within a subject or jurisdiction over many years, and most correspondence received individual responses from Senator Williams's office. A fair-to-moderate-sized portion of material, evenly selected from the files, was saved. For example, the 14 files of "Legislative Correspondence—Agriculture—Miscellaneous" were reduced from an original extent of two linear feet to 10 linear inches.

There were several key series retained in their entirety. Other than simple discards such as envelopes or duplicates, the original extent of those series remained. Only one series, the "Correspondence Master File," was entirely discarded.

It is important to note that the appraisal decisions were duly recorded for this collection. There is an explanation about appraisal following the scope and content note in the finding aid, there are appropriate explanations in the series descriptions, and in many cases, reference sheets explaining appraisal for specific files were added to individual file folders. These explanations were readily provided for the researchers, because in many ways (space savings for the repository aside), the decisions were made for the researcher. Enough can be enough, and it seemed wise to let the researcher know what was chosen to document Senator Williams's career.

NOTES

1. The "20-percenter" sobriquet for twentieth-century congressional collections is used by Thomas Powers, Bentley Historical Library, University of Michigan.

2. Richard C. Berner, *Archival Theory and Practice in the United States: A Historical Analysis* (Seattle: University of Washington Press, 1983), 7.

3. Patricia Aronsson, "Appraisal of Twentieth-Century Congressional Collections," in *Archival Choices*, ed. Nancy E. Peace (Lexington, Mass.: Lexington Books, 1984), 81–104.

4. Karen Dawley Paul, *Records Management Handbook for United States Senators and Their Archival Repositories* (Washington, D.C.: U.S. Senate, 1992).

5. Karen Dawley Paul, *The Documentation of Congress: Report of the Congressional Archivists Roundtable Task Force on Congressional Documentation*, S. Pub. 102-20 (Washington, D.C.: U.S. Senate, 1992).

6. Aronsson, "Appraisal of Twentieth-Century Congressional Collections."

7. Nancy E. Peace, "Deciding What to Save: Fifty Years of Theory and Practice," in Peace, *Archival Choices*, 1–18.

15

Campaign Buttons in a Black Box: Appraisal Standards for Strom Thurmond Memorabilia

James Edward Cross

"Archives as attics" is certainly one of the more unsavory depictions of their professional milieu that archivists try to dispel from the public imagination. The vision of dusty spaces containing yellowed letters with objects and boxes randomly stacked does not encourage people to visit and use the materials imagined to be moldering there. Archival "attics," however, do exist, and they frequently hold the hats, plaques, T-shirts, buttons, bumper stickers, occasional shovels, and other artifactual outcasts of retired politicians.[1] Such material frequently is donated to an institution along with a collection of political papers. Appraising these diverse objects is foreign to many archivists because they believe that the objects belong in museums, not archives. Indeed, numerous repositories either simply refuse to accept memorabilia outright, or they assert the right to return it to the donor or to dispose of it in some other way by inserting a provision for this in the transfer agreement. Even if they do accept the material, it may be squirreled away in the stacks, only to appear from time to time in exhibits.

This is a short-sighted attitude. As archival material undoubtedly has artifactual value, so too do artifacts have informational value. As one proponent of a greater role for artifacts in archives writes, "Individuals and organizations express themselves not just through the written and spoken word, but also through their interactions with their material world. The things that people throw away, the things they choose to keep, the gifts they give, the things they treasure—all of this material residue documents lives in ways that support, complement, extend, and expand the written documentary record."[2] Not every repository will be able to effectively preserve and make use of artifacts in research and outreach; however, the decision whether to include artifacts in the repository's holdings or not, and what to retain if one decides to do so, should be made based on a logical and well-thought-out plan, not on prejudice.

The Special Collections Unit of the Clemson University Libraries did not share the prevailing archival opinion with regard to its rich collection of Senator Strom Thurmond's political memorabilia and decided to develop a systematic way to ascertain what would be useful to retain as part of the collection.[3] Such a project would also help with future accessions (and eventual closing of the office) by providing the archivist with a logical rationale for refusing unneeded memorabilia before it was sent to the repository. At over 100 cubic feet, the Thurmond memorabilia afforded the perfect opportunity to test an appraisal framework based on a model familiar to archivists—the Boles-Young "Black Box."[4]

The archivist, working with the unit's museum-trained exhibits curator, created a preliminary checklist based on various types of uses that objects might have. Since Senator Thurmond was a national figure, a native of South Carolina, and a graduate of Clemson, memorabilia could be useful for interpreting these relationships, as well as various aspects of American, South Carolina, and Clemson University history. The memorabilia came from a wide variety of sources, so it was likely that there would be items related to some of Clemson's other (nonpolitical) documentation interests as well. The evaluation also weighed the intrinsic value of objects.[5]

The collection had been donated with an accompanying set of object description worksheets that had been filled out by a number of different people over the years. Consequently, the amount of detail per object varied greatly, making an examination of each item doubly necessary. As the objects were evaluated, they were placed on one of three lists: those that met the retention criteria, those that clearly did not, and those that partially met the criteria. Objects in the "maybe" category were reexamined after the entire collection was surveyed to determine their final status.

Archives staff conducted the survey from September 1992 to June 1993, spending approximately five hours per month on the task. As each item was inventoried, it was recorded in a database that included the object's name and number, which of the three lists it was on, a short description, and its location. Table 15.1 shows a sample page of the database. Besides serving as a location register, the database helped staff to identify appraisal trends and to spot misnumbered and unnumbered items and possible missing objects.

Staff used the Boles-Young Black Box archival appraisal model to frame their evaluation and justify their opinions. With some modification, the model proved very useful for evaluating the artifacts. An outline of the modified model is provided as table 15.2.

The Boles-Young appraisal model looks at the value of information, the cost of retention, and the implications of the selection decision as a basis

Table 15.1. Sample of Database

List #	Obj. #	Object Name	Description	Box #
1	T347	paperknife	Bennettsville Rotary Club	31
1	T348	shuttle	Graniteville Mill	33
3	T349	paperknife	Andrews AFB	31
3	T350	paperweight	replica key to Ft. Worth	31
1	T351	paperweight	Santee Cooper	31
3	T352	medallion	DC Mardi Gras	31
1	T353	button	Thurmond	31
1	T354	nametag	S.T. / SC	31
1	T355	plaque	Republican Party Puerto Rico	31
3	T356	paperweight	silver dollar in Lucite	31
3	T357	button	"Soy Republicano" Puerto Rico	31
1	T358	button	"Soy Republic" Puerto Rico	31
1	T359	wire	re: McColl, SC grant	31
1	T360 A, B	plate	Puerto Rico	31
1	T361 A, B	plaque on stand	Oriental	31
3	T362	bowl	copper	33
3	T363	hardhat	MaCalloy Plant, Charleston	33
1	T364 mis #ed	bowl	rice	33
1	T365 A, B	cast	feet in plaster	33
1	T366	flag	American	33

Key: 1 = Keep, 2 = Review, 3 = Discard

for evaluation. These concepts, as well as those of the creator's position in the organization, the role of the person's activities in the organization, and how closely the function of the object relates to those activities, were all useful in determining whether the object documents aspects of the person's life that were not adequately portrayed in the written records. For example, the archivist and curator concluded that campaign memorabilia effectively serves to document the public relations and outreach activities of the campaign as well as the personal style of the candidate.

The "subject content" of the objects in relationship to the topics of interest to the repository was another variable in the Boles-Young model that applied to objects as well as documents. If the object documents a topic of significance to the repository and is of the relevant time span to the topic, it has potential value to the repository. Clemson's interest in textile history, for example, gave value to certain textiles in the collection.

Completeness, in the case of artifacts, relates less to the ability of a single object to document a topic than its ability to do so in relationship to other objects. Is the object part of a collection—of baseball cards, state fair posters, or stamps, for example? Credibility relates to the authenticity of the item—is it a fake, a reproduction, or so heavily restored that all of the significant historical information has been lost?

Table 15.2. Modified "Black Box" Appraisal Model for Memorabilia

Value of Information
Functional characteristics
Position in organization
Original purpose
Activities
Content analysis
  Significance of topic
  Time span
  Completeness
  Credibility
Relationship to other artifacts
  Physical qualities
    Scarcity
  Intellectual qualities
    Duplication collection
    Duplication repository
    Duplication extra repository
Use
  User interest
    Administrative value
    Legal value
    Current clientele
    Potential clientele
  Use limitations
    Understandability history
    Material
    Construction design
    Function
  Use restrictions

Status as numinous objects ("objects that are collected for their association, real or imagined, with some person, place, or event endowed with special sociocultural magic")

Costs of Retention
Acquisition
Purchase
Transfer
Processing/registration
  Level of expertise
  Cost of supplies
  Quantity of work
Conservation/preservation
  Level of expertise
  Cost of supplies
  Quantity of work
Storage
  Quantity
  Type

Exhibition
  Space
  Type
  Cost of supplies
Reference
  Object retrieval
  Quantity of work
  Information retrieval
    Level of expertise
    Cost of supplies

Implications of Selection
External relations
  Agreement
    Source
    Other parties
  Authority/influence
    Source
    Other parties
Internal policies and practices
  Value of information
  Costs of retention

How does the artifact relate to other artifacts in the repository? Scarcity in a comparative context is certainly a useful consideration, since the object may be the only one in the collection to document a topic. However, duplication at the collection, repository, or extra-repository level must be viewed differently than it is for archival material. A certain amount of duplication is necessary for material culture studies in order to develop taxonomies and typologies.

To consider duplication adequately, staff turned to Craig Gilborn's taxonomy of the ubiquitous Coca-Cola bottle to illustrate one methodology used in material culture studies. Using a set of diagnostic attributes, Gilborn identified several subtypes and variants of the bottle, constructed a chronology of the types using frequency analysis, and then explored possible reasons for their stylistic evolution.[6] Similar studies have been done for such disparate items as New England tombstones and log cabins, providing new insight on historical questions. For example, the cabin study showed that the construction method used was "not a New World adaptation to environment, nor . . . a Scandinavian introduction; rather, it was introduced by the Pennsylvania Germans and carried by them and by the Scotch-Irish in all directions from southeastern Pennsylvania."[7] There is also a practical side to duplication of objects—some museums keep duplicates to trade or sell. (There is certainly a market for political memorabilia.)

Use is another important consideration for objects as well as documents. Some artifacts, such as patent models, have legal and administrative value to the organization. Of greater significance are the current and potential users of the object. Wilcomb E. Washburn in the April 1964 issue of the *American Archivist* pointed out that "the written word is the Johnny-come-lately of scholarship. The greater part of the history of mankind is 'written' in the tools with which man worked and in the objects he constructed."[8] He argues for the close relationship between the manuscript and the "manu-fact" in historical study. Can the items in the collection be used for material culture studies that describe, evaluate, analyze, and interpret the object in relation to other objects, selected aspects of the artifact's culture, and the values of the present culture? Are they likely to be used in this way? What about the organization's use of its own artifacts, such as the object's use in past, current, or future exhibits?

Of equal importance to user interest are any limitations on use. These may take the form of restrictions imposed by the donor, similar to those found with archival material. Most of the restrictions on use, however, will stem from the object itself. Is there enough information on the history of the object to determine when and where it was made, for whom and why, its provenance, and changes in condition and function? Can the material the object is made of be determined? Does the condition of the item allow someone to determine how it was manufactured, the workmanship involved, and the way the parts are organized to bring about the object's function? By the same token, can the design of the object, its structure, form, style, ornament, and iconography be ascertained? Finally, can one determine the function of the object, both its intended use and the unintended roles it plays in its culture (including utility, delight, and communication)?

A factor that complicates the use of the Boles-Young model when applying it to some of the items in a collection of political memorabilia is their status as association or numinous objects and the controversy that surrounds such objects in museum collections. One definition of numinous objects describes them as "objects we collect and preserve not for what they may reveal to us as material documents, or for any visible aesthetic quality, but for their association, real or imagined, with some person, place, or event endowed with special socio-cultural magic."[9] A good example of this is found in the tuxedo, walking stick, and pair of slippers exhibited by the Louisiana Historical Association Confederate Museum. These items are not shown because they provide information on the clothing styles of mid-nineteenth-century America, but because they were once owned by Jefferson Davis.

Defining the controversy that surrounds such objects is simple. Do they belong as part of museum collections or not? Do they have any value? The controversy itself is anything but simple. G. Ellis Burcaw, a noted museologist, writes that "Relics, curiosities, personal memorabilia, glorification of specific individuals or specific families . . . do not belong in a public museum."[10] Rachel P. Maines and James J. Glynn, on the other hand, point out that elitism characterizes the perception and interpretation of such objects by many museum professionals. They state that while numinous objects may pose a challenge to traditional models of historical objectivity, it is important to respect the belief invested in such objects and to document their role in historical myth-making. Both feel that museums that exhibit objects with perceived emotional content have a responsibility to do so in the same spirit of historical rigor that should characterize all exhibitions. In the case of numinous objects, the museum must interpret not only the attributed association, if this is documented, but the layers of social meaning imposed on the object by successive generations with different agendas for the past.[11] The Clemson staff sided with Manes and Glynn when they evaluated the items in the Strom Thurmond collection.

The Boles-Young cost model includes the expenses of acquiring, processing, preserving, storing, exhibiting, and providing reference service. This is directly applicable to object evaluation. The cost to acquire an item, either by transfer or by purchase, will include such factors as shipping and insurance costs. Costs for processing an item will center mainly on its registration, description, and rehousing. What level of expertise is needed to properly register an item? Can most of this work be done by student/volunteer labor, or does it require a professional to do all of the tasks needed? How much will supplies cost to rehouse an item? What will be the costs of describing an object, whether one uses catalog cards or a computer database? To what level will descriptive standards and controlled vocabularies, if any, be applied, and by whom? Finally, how much work needs to be done to process the material? Preservation costs may directly affect those of processing. Since most archivists are not trained to deal with three-dimensional objects, most, if not all, of the conservation or preservation work beyond rehousing and proper storage would need to be done by a professional conservator.

Preservation affects storage costs, since such necessities as climate control and security must be factored into the overall cost. Not only must the cost of storing the quantity of material be considered, but also the cost of storing different types of items—paintings require different storage than, say, botanical specimens. Related to storage are exhibition costs. How much space and what different types of exhibit spaces are needed to exhibit the materials? And how much will the supplies needed to exhibit an item (such as supports, matting, framing, etc.) cost? There also are costs to physically retrieve the item when requested and to guide researchers in using the item for research. Information about an item may be readily available through a computer database that is searchable by the researcher, but professional guidance may be necessary to help a researcher do a material culture study using the item.

Determining costs can be problematic; there is little museum literature on the subject.[12] In 1983, one authority estimated that the "annual cost to heat, clean, and guard the space in which museum objects are stored was $25 per square foot."[13] Studies in 1988 and 1989 estimated annual costs that varied from $30 per square foot to $60 per square foot.[14] One university museum calculated that its annual storage cost was $50 per object.[15]

There may also be diplomatic or policy ramifications to factor into the decision to retain or not to retain an item. This is probably the area most familiar to archivists, since memorabilia will often become part of the holdings of a repository because of the need to please (or avoid offending) a donor and not because the archivists have thoroughly appraised the objects. Then there is the effect an appraisal decision may have on the internal policies of the repository. Such a decision may alter established policies relating to informational value (collection development) or budget.

The Clemson staff identified 935 objects for deaccessioning out of a total of 2,209. Manipulation of the database revealed appraisal patterns by object class (buttons, pens, and T-shirts, for example). The patterns that emerged from the object-related appraisal decisions were then incorporated into the original criteria. The final guidelines are shown in table 15.3.

These guidelines represent values important to Clemson's collecting goals; they are not meant to be universally applied. They are descriptive, not prescriptive. Just as with the appraisal of archival material, so too the appraisal of memorabilia is affected by the mission of the institution, its policies, and its physical circumstances. A large manuscript repository on a university campus with an American Studies program and ample exhibition and storage space will likely make appraisal decisions that are different from those of a small college archives with limited space and no public service function. Collection development policies play a crucial role in the appraisal of archival material, and they play no less of a role in artifactual appraisal. In fact, political documentation repositories would do well to adopt a development policy for artifacts, since they are such an indigenous part of political collections. Hopefully, the Clemson guidelines will inspire others to clean out their archival attics and make better use of our artifactual heritage.

Table 15.3. Thurmond Memorabilia Retention Guidelines

The purpose of Special Collections is to "help the University Libraries fulfill its educational, research, and public service missions by collecting and providing access to unique research collections." Through the University Archives, Special Collections also "serves as Clemson's institutional memory."

In addition, the policy governing the selection of topics for exhibits in the R. M. Cooper Library and the Strom Thurmond Institute Building is based upon three primary criteria: "relating to the instructional and research functions of the University, disseminating educational information to the Clemson community, and having potential interest to the campus community."

Keeping these criteria firmly in mind, the following general categories will be used to determine if an item should be retained as part of the memorabilia collection:

1. Representative of Senator Thurmond's career and/or personal life (so-called "numinous objects");
2. Significant for the understanding or interpretation of Clemson University, South Carolina, or United States history;
3. Relevant to the major collecting fields of Special Collections (agricultural, business, political, textile history);
4. Unique within the Unit's object collection (to weed out unnecessary duplicates— more than are required for exhibit or study);
5. Intrinsically valuable.

The following supplemental criteria have been used for certain classes of objects:

awards: Retain ALL, except those awarded to Senator on annual or biannual basis for a number of years; in those cases, retain one per decade (or other appropriate period of time).
[*Rationale*: Document honors received by Senator; indicates his areas of interest and measures (to some extent) his success in addressing those issues. Most of the items in this category should be named awards regularly given out by an organization.]

badges: Retain political convention badges.
[*Rationale*: As basis for collection of political memorabilia to document South Carolina and United States political history.]

Retain those for important regional/national political groups (e.g., Southern Governors' Conference).
[*Rationale*: As basis for collection of political memorabilia to document South Carolina and United States political history, and to show the Senator's active involvement in such groups.]

Retain those from meetings of important national organizations the Senator is a member of (e.g., American Legion, VFW).
[*Rationale*: To not only document the Senator's membership in such organizations, but to show his active involvement in such organizations as well.]

(continued)

Table 15.3. (*continued*)

buttons:	Retain political campaign buttons (both Thurmond's own and presidential campaigns). [*Rationale*: As basis for collection of political memorabilia to document South Carolina and United States political history.] Retain a representative sample of "message" buttons (e.g., "Free Kuwait")—criteria: (1) importance of message/event; (2) level of Senator's involvement. [*Rationale*: To document important historical events the Senator was a part of or that took place during his career.]
caps, gowns, hoods:	Retain ALL academic caps, gowns, and hoods. [*Rationale*: See awards, above. Also, while hoods, caps, and gowns may look similar, they are given by different institutions in different subject areas, so each is subtly unique in design and color. Multiple examples give flexibility in display.]
hats:	Retain representative sample of local events (festivals, anniversaries, etc.) and "message" hats—criteria: (1) importance of message/event; (2) level of Senator's involvement; (3) whether event is already adequately reflected in collection by other memorabilia (retain if event is not adequately represented); (4) suitability for "ensemble" display; (5) aesthetics. [*Rationale*: For local events, to document the types of gatherings the Senator would attend in the state to "keep in touch" with his constituents. For "message" caps, see buttons, above. Also for flexibility in display.] Retain those from organizations Senator belongs to. [*Rationale*: To document Senator's membership in such organizations; flexibility in display.]
cards:	Retain one card from each organization Senator belongs to. [*Rationale*: To document Senator's membership in such organizations; flexibility in display.]
cuff links:	Retain one set of presidential cuff links from each president and from any organization Senator belongs to not already represented by hats, pins, etc. [*Rationale*: To document presidents the Senator has served under, and because of interest that people have in presidential items; to document Senator's membership in such organizations; flexibility in display.]
drawings, prints:	Retain those of Senator. [*Rationale*: For illustrative purposes.] Retain limited editions (e.g., "#10 of 100"). [*Rationale*: Intrinsic and aesthetic value.]

envelopes:	Retain ALL *commemorative.* [*Rationale*: See stamps, below.]
	Retain ALL *first day covers.* [*Rationale*: See stamps, below.]
hardhats:	Retain those with Senator's name on them which reflect a major construction project in state or construction of a building named after the Senator. [*Rationale*: Documents an honor received (name on building, etc.) and Senator's role in bringing business or government construction projects to state.]
medal; medallion:	Retain those that function as awards. [*Rationale*: See awards, above.]
pens:	For pens used to sign legislation, retain a representative sample from each presidential administration—criteria: (1) importance of legislation; (2) level of Senator's involvement, i.e., was he chairman of the committee that oversaw bill, or was he the sponsor or a co-sponsor; (3) level of Senator's interest in subject of bill; (4) whether there is a copy of the legislation in "certificate" form already in the collection (if so, retain). [*Rationale*: Documents one of a legislator's major functions—the passage of legislation.]
pins; pins, lapel:	Retain those that function as awards or are given as part of an award (e.g., "40 Years' Service"). [*Rationale*: See awards, above.]
	Retain from organizations Senator belongs to. [*Rationale*: To document Senator's membership in such organizations; flexibility in display.]
	Retain representative sample of South Carolina pins (local organizations, etc.) and "message" pins (e.g., POW-MIA)—criteria: (1) importance of message/event; (2) level of Senator's involvement or interest; (3) whether event is already adequately reflected in collection by other memorabilia (retain if event is not adequately represented); (4) suitability for "ensemble" display; (5) aesthetics. [*Rationale*: See caps, hats above.]
plates, platters, trays:	Retain all silver. [*Rationale*: Some function as awards, or to document an event; mainly intrinsic value.]
shovels:	Retain those which reflect a major construction project in state or construction of a building named after the Senator. [*Rationale*: See hardhats, above.]

(*continued*)

Table 15.3. (*continued*)

stamp albums:	Retain ALL. [*Rationale*: May document events that Senator was involved in, such as ship launchings; can be used for several types of exhibits beyond those just for Thurmond (e.g., Olympic stamps when Olympics come to Atlanta in 1996); aesthetically pleasing; have intrinsic value; basis for good U.S. philatelic collection.]
tie bars; tie clasps:	Retain one set of presidential tie bars or clasps from each president. [*Rationale*: See cuff links, above.]
T-shirts:	Retain representative sample of local events (festivals, anniversaries, etc.) and "message" shirts—criteria: (1) importance of message/event; (2) level of Senator's involvement; (3) whether event is already adequately reflected in collection by other memorabilia (retain if event is not adequately represented); (4) suitability for "ensemble" display; (5) aesthetics. [*Rationale*: See hats above.]

The ability to maintain or conserve an object properly (which includes cost, size, and storage considerations) will also be used as retention criteria, but only after the criteria above have been considered.

NOTES

1. This chapter was originally prepared as a paper for the session "The Appraisal of Memorabilia and Museum Objects or 'What Do I Do with This Rusty Samovar?'" held at the annual meeting of the Society of American Archivists, New Orleans, September 1993.

2. Jill Robin Severn, "Adventures in the Third Dimension: Re-envisioning the Place of Artifacts in Archives," paper presented at the annual meeting of the Society of American Archivists, Washington, D.C., August 2001.

3. Strom Thurmond (1902–2003) served as a South Carolina state senator (1934–1938), circuit court judge (1938–1946), governor of South Carolina (1947–1951), and U.S. senator (1954–2002). He also served as president pro tempore of the Senate (1981–1987).

4. The model is described in Frank Boles and Julia Marks Young, "Exploring the Black Box: The Appraisal of University Administrative Records," *American Archivist* 48, no. 2 (1985): 121–40.

5. As defined in Richard Pearce-Moses, *A Glossary of Archival and Records Terminology* (Chicago: Society of American Archivists, 2005), 217, intrinsic value means "that the usefulness or significance of an item is derived from its physical or associational qualities, inherent in its original format generally independent of its content, that are integral to its material nature and would be lost in reproduction. . . . [Intrinsic value] may be based on an item's direct relationship to a significant person, activity, event, organization, or place."

6. Craig Gilborn, "Pop Pedagogy: Looking at the Coke Bottle," in *Material Culture Studies in America*, ed. Thomas J. Schlereth (Nashville, Tenn.: Association for State and Local History, 1982), 249.

7. Fred Kniffen and Henry Glassie, "Building in Wood in the Eastern United States: A Time-Place Perspective," in Schlereth, *Material Culture Studies in America*, 183–91.

8. Wilcomb E. Washburn, "Manuscripts and Manufacts," *American Archivist* 27, no. 2 (1964): 247.

9. Rachel P. Maines and James J. Glynn, "Numinous Objects," *Public Historian* 15, no. 1 (1993): 10.

10. G. Ellis Burcaw, *Introduction to Museum Work*, 2nd ed., revised and expanded (Nashville, Tenn.: Association for State and Local History, 1983), 180.

11. Maines and Glynn, "Numinous Objects," 17.

12. "But while many acknowledge, in *general* terms, the high cost of maintaining artworks in storage, little is known about its magnitude." Ann Stone, "Treasures in the Basement? An Analysis of Collection Utilization in Art Museums" (dissertation, RAND Graduate School, 2002), www.rand.org.

13. Stephen E. Weil, "Deaccession Practices in American Museums," *Museum News* 65, no. 3 (1987): 45.

14. Stone, " Treasures in the Basement," 9–10.

15. Kent State University Museum, "Donations" page, 2001, http://dept.kent .edu/museum/pr/donations.html.

16

Adventures in the Third Dimension: Reenvisioning the Place of Artifacts in Archives

Jill Robin Severn

Fernand Braudel wrote, "The mere smell of cooking can evoke a whole civilization."[1] Hyperbole perhaps, yet it underscores the significant role that other means of communication besides written words play in the construction of identity and culture. Individuals and organizations express themselves not just through the written and spoken word, but also through representations from their material world. The things people throw away, the things they choose to keep, the gifts they give, the things they treasure—all of this material residue documents lives in ways that support, complement, extend, and expand the written documentary record.

The collection of Senator Richard B. Russell offers an excellent example of this dynamic and integral relationship between material culture and documentary sources.[2] Senator Russell, in his attitudes about civil rights, foreign policy, and internal affairs, was a profoundly conservative man. His credo, "Look to the past as a means of weighing the future," expresses this outlook unequivocally.[3] His material life—his collections of things—also expresses this perspective. Russell was nothing if not a conserver, a gatherer of bright shiny objects and hoarder of the flotsam and jetsam of life—a man who *liked* his stuff. He squirreled away hotel keys, wallets, old medicine, and tobacco labels in much the same way he collected facts and figures in his head. He saved everything from the finer points of parliamentary procedure and the latest baseball statistics to condoms left over from his trip abroad in 1927 and balls of leftover package twine. Some things he stored in his memory, and some he stored in shoe boxes.[4] The arc of his efforts as a politician to conserve a world that was familiar and unchanging matched the arc of his efforts to save the material constituents of his life. In the end, it proved easier for Russell to preserve his material world than it was to preserve his political and social world.[5]

Historians of course know this Russell—the conservative southern politician—through the extensive written and spoken sources that survive him. Yet often these sources are not so ample or trustworthy, and many people and events do not leave any written record at all. Even when the written record is ample and creditable, the material culture record often provides access to aspects of an individual or an organization that words do not reach. So often, people never verbalize or record their personal tastes, habits, interests, and sense of self because they are so entwined with their daily lives that they do not think about them enough to note them. Senator Russell, for example, was a lifelong smoker, beginning as a child and stopping only when he succumbed to emphysema and lung cancer, but most photographs do not reveal this habit, nor do his writings consistently discuss it. The habit was so integral to him that Russell and his associates rarely referred to it in correspondence until the mid 1950s, when his first major bout with respiratory illness led him to quit smoking.[6] On the other hand, Russell's material record does reveal his enduring attachment to tobacco. Tobacco advertisements on the reverse of the baseball cards that Russell fervently collected as a kid remind one that his smoking habit began in childhood. Similarly, one of his other boyhood collections, a notebook of tobacco labels, also confirms Russell's early use of tobacco. The prodigious number of ashtrays in Russell's collection testifies as well to the lifelong habit.[7]

Only when Russell became seriously ill, first in the mid 1950s, again in 1965 when he was absent from the Senate for four months due to complications of emphysema, and finally in 1968 and 1969 when he became seriously ill with lung cancer, did his documentary record reflect his enduring and disastrous attachment to tobacco. Letters apologizing for delays in responding to correspondence, declined invitations, medical reports, and finally an autopsy report ticked off his losing battle to regain his health.[8] Vicks Vapor Rub tubes and myriad medicine bottles, which Russell carefully saved, reveal a man consumed with his illness to the point of hypochondria.[9] Together these material and documentary records offer a sad culmination of Senator Russell's life that is richer than what each offers individually. People do not create artifacts and texts in isolation from each other, and together these products of human activity have much to tell archivists and their researchers.

In many archival repositories, however, artifacts exist at the very margins—literally and figuratively. Often archivists discount, disdain, and worst of all, ignore these materials. Typically, they do not process artifacts as part of the collections from which they originated. Artifacts appear in catchall series obscurely titled "separated materials" mixed in among other problematic materials like videotapes, and sometimes even photographs.

Often artifacts do not appear in finding aids at all. One archivist explained this absence as a preservation decision: "I could not tell people about the objects in our collections because then people would want to look at them."[10] Many archivists refuse to accept artifacts with collections, preferring to direct donors to send these objects to a museum even though this means splitting the collection and ignoring the great attachment donors often have for significant mementoes from their lives.

The paucity of archival literature specifically related to understanding and presenting artifacts as records is significant. With a few exceptions, most notably the work of Gloria Meraz and Hugh Taylor,[11] archival scholarship has ignored artifacts except to mention them in passing as preservation problems and exhibition possibilities. In its listings, the Society of American Archivists (SAA) publications catalog includes books on audiovisual materials, electronic records, architectural plans, TV newsfilm, and slides but offers no works focused on artifacts or memorabilia.[12] Similarly, the Academy of Certified Archivists, the chief certifying body in the archival profession, does not include any work in its bibliography of archival literature that treats artifacts in a substantial way.[13] Artifacts are mentioned obliquely in *A Glossary for Archivists, Manuscript Curators, and Records Managers*, where the authors equate intrinsic value with artifactual value.[14] The 2005 edition of *A Glossary of Archival and Records Terminology* does provide definitions for realia and artifacts that address the function of three-dimensional objects within archival collections as well as their potential status as records, but the other manuals in the SAA's Archival Fundamentals Series do not offer significant discussion of artifacts in archives.[15]

Artifacts are not worth the trouble, it seems. Archivists may accept artifacts merely to satisfy a donor's wishes or to acquire an interesting item for display. Certainly, artifacts *can* be troublesome. They are often difficult to preserve. Many need special enclosures and nonstandard storage shelving, and they usually take up significant storage space. Often, they are fragile, or they may have significant monetary value, which makes them security risks. With limited staff and financial resources, many archivists argue that they must concentrate energy on the *real* records of the archives, the written (and spoken) records. Implicit in their thinking is an assumption that records belong in archives, while artifacts belong in museums—and by corollary, that artifacts lack qualities that would imbue them with sufficient "recordness."

Gloria Meraz, whose 1997 article "Cultural Evidence: On Common Ground Between Archivists and Museologists," eloquently traces the inextricable relationship between artifact and record, and the barriers which prevent archivists and museum curators from recognizing this relationship as well as the demand from the public to surmount these barriers. She points out that "as the public becomes increasingly conversant with the potential offered by electronic access, people will demand that cultural institutions provide more compatible services."[16] Meraz proposes collaboration between archives and museums to address this demand. However, she does not propose integrating artifacts and records within archives. The holistic cultural world she imagines, where archivists and museum curators cooperate, includes "exhibits, information about holdings, and educational programs for staff and researchers."[17] This model is a reasonable approach to begin to achieve change, but collaboration can never fully accomplish the integrated use of records and artifacts she proposes. As long as archivists expect to learn about artifacts from curators and curators expect to learn about records from archivists, neither profession will recognize each other's functions as their own. Archivists do not need collaborators to recognize the "recordness" of the artifacts in collections. Nor do they need to have more exhibits as a means of integrating artifacts into collections.

Clearly, there are challenges associated with making artifacts more accessible to researchers. However, artifacts, like other nonpaper materials that often get short shrift in an archival setting, have tremendous potential to illuminate the individual or organization that collected them as well as the broader culture that created, used, and derived meaning from them. Some archivists wrongly assume that artifacts are somehow not fully records because they were *collected* rather than *made*, as they would be if written, spoken, or typed. But the individual who amasses a collection of items *creates meaning* for an artifact by imbuing it with context and juxtaposing it with other artifacts and records that form the framework of his or her material life. Gloria Meraz expresses this value of artifacts and textual records: "As primary materials, they are tools that serve as original participants in events. Where the tool is physical, the tool creates the activity. Where the tool is textual, the activity creates the tool. And history is both a product of initiating an activity and weighing the evidence left from that event. Archives and artifacts are necessary for a complete historical narrative."[18]

This chapter endeavors to move three-dimensional objects away from the conceptual and physical margins of archival collections, to vary the terrain in what is often a very flat archival landscape. In general, archivists have little knowledge and experience with mining the research potential of artifacts. Without a grasp on the ways in which artifacts can be understood—or, in the parlance of material culture study, "read"—archivists cannot make effective and informed decisions about appraisal, arrangement, description, and ultimately access. Archivists miss a chance to educate users about a vital class of records, and they miss opportunities to connect with a broader array of scholars who are unaware of the material culture hidden on repository shelves. So how does one *read* objects?

The answers to this question are myriad. Like most academic disciplines, material culture study is by no means homogenous in its approach. Indeed, there is significant debate within the field on the appropriate place of the object in modes of interpretation such as historical monographs and exhibits.[19] Although such conflicts should not dissuade us from learning about and applying techniques employed by material culture scholars, they should encourage us to do so with care and consideration. As material culture scholar Kenneth Ames has argued, a balance of approaches seems most reasonable: "not all historic tales or all historic moments or all historic issues are equally accessible through material culture."[20] Still, material culture often provides the only direct avenue into the lives of ordinary people, often illiterate, and for whom personal belongings serve as the only record of their existence. In this sense, "material culture is in fact the most democratic form of historical evidence," according to Moore.[21]

Moreover, just as we may read and reread texts in multiple ways, we may also understand objects as polysemantic. A grand plantation house that illuminates the material wealth and taste of its owners also may illuminate the artisanship and culture of the slaves who built the edifice as well as the power relationships between master and slave. As cultural critic Susan Pearce explains, "The meanings of an object lie both in the object itself, with all the historical and structuralist/functionalist ways in which this meaning is constituted, and equally in the process which the viewer carries out in relation to the object . . . it is the convergence of object and viewer which brings the meaningful object into existence. . . . The object is inexhaustible, but it is the inexhaustibility which forces the viewer to his decisions. The viewing process is selective, and the potential object is richer than any of its realizations."[22]

The field of material culture study has marked a trail for archivists to follow as they begin to explore the possibilities of this material world and has left guideposts for the journey, many of which will seem familiar to archivists. Building on Pearce's important work *Museums, Objects, and Collections*, material culture scholar Kevin Moore proposes the following set of descriptive questions as a practical method for considering and presenting material culture in more meaningful ways:

- *Description*: What is the object for? Why does it look like this? What are some variations? What is the decoration? What is the condition/age of the object? What are its aesthetics?
- *Identification*: What is the typology? How does this object fit in with other items with similar appearance or function?
- *Construction*: How was the object made? What technology was employed? What information is there about the maker's approach? How are the materials for construction considered by the culture in which it was constructed and used (a common everyday item or a fine piece for special occasions)?

- *History*: Who owned and made meaning of this artifact? How has the object been transferred across time and space? What did it mean to the person who owned it?
- *Location*: How does the object relate to other objects that were collected or used in association with it (artifact constellations)? What would the landscape look like in which this object rested in its lifetime (juxtaposition)?
- *Distribution*: Where is this type of object found? How common is it? What sort of distribution patterns exists for ownership of objects like it? Who owned this type of object through time?
- *Significance*: What meaning did users attach to the object over time? How did different contexts of ownership affect the object's meaning?
- *Interpretation*: What meanings can one draw from this object?[23]

Various modes of interpretation are commonly applied to objects. One should use these modes creatively and intelligently as a technique of analysis to spark lateral thinking. For the archivist, this will chiefly inform appraisal decisions and reference services.

APPRAISAL

Outfitted with these tools borrowed from material culture study, archivists can begin to reexamine their collections—both artifactual and textual—and their policies and practices. The logical place to begin this process is with appraisal, or more accurately, *reappraisal*. Evaluating the place of artifacts in a repository's collection policy will yield dividends that outweigh the time expenditure. If an archival repository does not make its policy explicit on acquiring artifacts as part of its general collecting policy, then there is the great likelihood that the repository has been obliged to accept artifacts that often have little evidential and informational value. As Gerald Ham explains, "Many archivists feel inadequate and mystified when attempting to appraise these records. This feeling has led some of them either to accept uncritically . . . or uncritically reject . . . [these special format records]."[24] But there is nothing mysterious about appraising special format records such as artifacts. Many archivists have demonstrated this ably in their own work. The same standards that are applied to textual records can measure the value of nontextual records, with a few caveats.

First, it is vital to consider the artifact on its own terms, using the tools of material culture study to answer the questions that form the basis of appraisal. Second, just like electronic records, sound recordings, film, or video, artifacts often have special preservation and access issues associated with them. Therefore, archivists must pay particular attention to questions of stability and surrogacy. Is the medium stable in its current form? Can an appropriate and effective surrogate replace or buttress the item if it becomes too unstable to provide access to or to retain?[25] Third, avoid applying intrinsic value as simply a measure of exhibit worthiness. Valuing an item because of its age, content, usage, beauty, or circumstances surrounding creation, when applied to artifacts, often means "good for exhibits" and supplants a more careful appraisal of the artifact's real merit in terms of documenting the creator/collector or its potential as a record of broader thematic phenomena. As with the insulting stereotype of the "dumb blonde," artifacts only valued as exhibit items are valued for only a small portion of their full records potential.[26]

With these guidelines in place, an archivist might begin the process of reintegrating artifacts into his or her repository by reevaluating artifacts already present in collections. If these objects do not meet the retention criteria, then archivists should consider deaccessioning them. This is a time-consuming process in an already busy work schedule, and donor agreements and donor relations may preclude such reappraisal, but the process offers an opportunity to separate the wheat from the chaff, and a chance to gain space and control over an increasingly significant portion of holdings in many archives.

ARRANGEMENT

In the process of arrangement, or rearrangement, archivists have another opportunity to reconsider the location of artifacts in their holdings. A good question to ask of an arrangement scheme in this context is: Are the functional relationships between records including artifacts expressed? Too often, an archival repository will arrange traditional records by functional areas and arrange special records such as artifacts by form, with little additional subdivision. So even if buttons, bumper stickers, and even bandwagons are created clearly in the context of a campaign activity and belong logically with a campaign or political series, often they are removed from this original functional context and arranged by form as a series of memorabilia along with unrelated items such as desk sets, plaques, and ceremonial shovels.

Another problem that tends to lead archivists astray when it comes to maintaining artifacts' relationships with similar records is that donors often do not or cannot make this relationship clear. Often donors display artifacts in a home or office away from traditional records, even though they accumulated the two classes of material as part of the same activities or events. The donor may understand these original connections but may lack an understanding of the importance of maintaining these relationships in the archival

setting. Donors who are not the creator of the collection may have little
understanding of the original connections that may have existed between artifacts and records. Archivists can address this lack of contextual information
by interviewing the donors about an object's original use and by evaluating
the object in light of the tools provided by material culture study.

DESCRIPTION

Just as many scholars have pointed out that archival collections contain
hidden groups such as ethnic, cultural, and economic minorities—women,
African Americans, or the poor—these collections also contain hidden
groups based on format.[27] Addressing this issue for catalogers, author
Robert Freeborn asserts that there are several reasons for this inattention
or concealment of three-dimensional objects in the cataloger's queue. Freeborn views the problem catalogers have with three-dimensional objects
as synonymous with the problems identified by cataloger Lynn Howarth
for cataloging audiovisual materials: "AV materials have suffered from the
three D's: (1) They're 'different' from standard print materials; (2) Because
of this difference, they're difficult to catalog; and (3) They 'divert' cataloging
time and resources."[28] According to Freeborn, these problems lead cataloging departments to choose from two options when dealing with three-
dimensional objects: "Either they put them aside in the hopes that someone else will deal with them, or give them minimum-level processing in
order to get them on the shelves and off their desks."[29]

Freeborn encourages catalogers to embrace the challenges associated with
cataloging three-dimensional materials, and he provides detailed examples
of his own efforts to catalog these items, accompanied by his rationale for
decision making. He also provides references for a useful body of literature
related to handling these classes of materials, most notably works by Helen
Olson, who has published extensively in this area.[30]

Similarly, Diane Beattie provides approaches for archivists to address
this inaccessibility of three-dimensional objects. She recommends that
archivists revise the traditional provenance-based view of subject access to
include function/occupation and type of material in addition to topic and
name.[31] By making form and genre explicit in subject access while nesting
all types of records in their appropriate provenance-based order, archivists
facilitate scholars' efforts to locate materials in a variety of ways. As Helena
Zinkham, Patricia Cloud, and Hope Mayo explain, "type of material offers
prima facie evidence of intellectual content and nature."[32] To extend their
observation, artifacts need to be identified by genre as well as by form in
order to function fully as records. Practically, this means that finding aids
need to mention artifacts in series and subseries descriptions, and access

points need to reflect both the intellectual content through use of topical subject terms and the physical form of records through genre terms. Choosing a cataloging scheme that applies consistently to all types of records prevents segregation of classes of records from each other in incompatible databases. Similarly, adopting a structured vocabulary for your diverse collections, such as the Art and Architecture Thesaurus or the Revised Nomenclature for Museum Cataloging, will allow for clear and consistent access to your collections regardless of format.

Several descriptive tools provide significant opportunities for integrating artifacts into archival collections. The Cooperative Online Resource Catalog (CORC) system, used by the Online Computer Library Center (OCLC) for cataloging Web resource material based on the Dublin Core Metadata Element Set, enables neophyte catalogers to create basic catalog records and link them to digital images or objects.[33] For archives with resources to create digital surrogates for their artifacts, CORC offers a relatively simple scheme for making these objects accessible to a wider audience without exposing them to overuse and theft. Similarly, Encoded Archival Description (EAD) provides another opportunity to make significant records, including artifacts, more visible to patrons.[34] EAD provides the ability to link an image into the structure of a finding aid. This allows patrons to see a document, hear an excerpt from a sound recording, see a clip from a film, and look at an artifact within the context of its place in the organization scheme of the collection.

The burgeoning number of digital libraries and commercial ventures provide ever expanding opportunities to organize and present a wide array of formats in archival and museum collections without the typical barriers and with rich description and context. Patrons browsing online digital collections or commercial search engines like Google obtain search results that include film clips, images, and sound files along with standard textual materials.[35] This holistic presentation of cultural materials on the Internet has reshaped patrons' experiences with these materials, and it has raised their expectations for access to all cultural materials.

REFERENCE AND OUTREACH

Of course, access is not limited to the realm of the Internet. Patrons still obtain much of their knowledge about collections and strategies for effective searching through direct interaction with reference staff. Opportunities to educate and inform patrons and potential patrons about special records like artifacts can happen in a variety of locations and contexts. In the repository, archivists can develop formal classes where students can learn techniques for understanding and using objects as primary source material for their projects. Less formally, archivists can build ready-reference collections of texts that support material culture study by example or by theoretical framework. At the very least, archivists can mention artifacts along with more "traditional" paper records when interviewing patrons about their research needs. Various outreach tools such as exhibits and publications can also serve to advertise the presence and possibilities of artifacts in archival collections.

At every turn of the archival process, there are opportunities for archivists to reconsider how they handle three-dimensional objects. From appraisal to arrangement, description, reference, and outreach, the archivist can change practices to incorporate these special records into the body of more traditional paper records more effectively. By doing so, archivists will expand the documentary record and researchers' understanding and appreciation of what constitutes primary evidence.

Traditionally, museums have been the locus for developing this awareness, but often the thematic approach they adopt for exhibits emphasizes narrative interpretations over critical awareness of objects and their potential meanings. Also, exhibits rarely offer opportunities for in-depth learning, in part because they tend to attract more casual visitors who expect to be entertained as well as educated. Archival repositories are already a setting in which sustained research is a primary activity. Patrons come there to find evidence for papers, reports, legal briefs, documentary films, and books— and increasingly, they come to find personal histories through genealogical research. Providing an expanded documentary record that includes artifacts and other special records is a natural extension of what archives do best.

Many archives already make this effort. Historical societies, which typically embrace both museum and archival functions and have artifacts and paper records, are at the forefront of efforts to provide patrons with a less fragmented cultural record. Sometimes the smallest and least formal cultural repositories are most successful. The small historical society or heritage center can do an excellent job in making the whole realm of cultural materials available, although sometimes by problematic means.[36] Archival repositories that do not fit within these examples ought to reconsider the place of the artifact in their holdings. By doing so, they offer their current patrons a broader, more richly detailed view of their cultural world, and they leave a cultural legacy for future generations whose sum is much greater than its parts.

NOTES

1. Quoted in *Material Life in America, 1600–1860*, ed. Robert Blair St. George (Boston: Northeastern University Press, 1988), v. See also Fernand Braudel, *Capi-*

talism and Material Life 1400–1800, trans. Miriam Kochan (New York: Harper and Row, 1975), 32, 66, 113, 139, 235–36, 243, 441.

2. The Richard B. Russell Collection is the cornerstone collection of the Richard B. Russell Library for Political Research and Studies, University of Georgia Libraries, Athens, Georgia.

3. Senator Richard B. Russell, Speech, Bicentennial Midway Church and Society, Midway, Georgia, April 24, 1954, Speeches by Russell 1933–1969, Speech and Media Series, Russell Collection.

4. These artifacts are part of the Richard B. Russell Museum Objects, Russell Collection. Russell Library archivists discovered Senator Russell's baseball card collection in several cigar boxes in a closet of his family home. According to biographer Gilbert Fite, "Russell's friends claimed that he knew more information on football and baseball players than most people would want to know." Similarly, Fite recounts Russell's reputation for committing minute details to memory: "When Senator Stennis first arrived in the Senate, he approached Alben Barkley, the floor leader, and got a copy of the formal Senate rules. But Barkley hastily explained that this book did not contain everything a senator should know. Where could he get a book on the precedents and practices not spelled out in writing here, Stennis asked. 'You cannot get a book,' Barkley replied. 'The rest of them are in Senator Russell's head.'" Gilbert Fite, *Richard B. Russell Jr., Senator from Georgia* (Chapel Hill: University of North Carolina Press, 1991), 202, 496.

5. Biographer Gilbert Fite offers an eloquent summation on this dissonance between Russell and the changing world around him. Fite, *Richard B. Russell,* 494–502.

6. Richard B. Russell to Harry Thornton, May 22, 1959, Dictation Series, Russell Collection. See also Fite, *Richard B. Russell,* 482–4.

7. These artifacts are part of the Richard B. Russell Museum Objects, Russell Collection.

8. Russell's illness history is described in the following oral histories in the Russell Collection: Dr. Andre Ognibene, April 29, 1971; Dr. Rufus J. Pearson, April 27, 1971; Robert Zurek, M.D., April 29, 1971; Major Susanne Phillips, Army Nurse Corps, April 29, 1971. For Russell's own handling of his illness, see: Memoranda, Appointment Books, and Mail Desk Diaries, Intra-Office Communications Series, Russell Collection, and also Illness, Personal Series, Russell Collection. See also Fite, *Richard B. Russell,* 456–93.

9. These artifacts are part of the Richard B. Russell Museum Objects, Russell Collection.

10. From a conversation with an anonymous archivist.

11. See Gloria Meraz, "Cultural Evidence: On Common Ground Between Archivists and Museologists," *Provenance, Journal of the Society of Georgia Archivists* 15 (1997): 1–26. See also Hugh Taylor, "Documents as Artifacts in the Context of Museums and Material Culture," *Archivaria* 40 (Fall 1995): 8–20.

12. "Society of American Archivists Publications Catalog," Society of American Archivists, www.archivists.org.

13. "The Academy of Certified Archivists Handbook," Academy of Certified Archivists, www.certifiedarchivists.org.

14. Lewis J. Bellardo and Lynn Lady Bellardo, *A Glossary for Archivists, Manuscript Curators, and Records: Managers*, Archival Fundamentals Series (Chicago: Society of American Archivists, 1992), 4, 19.

15. Richard Pearce-Moses, *A Glossary of Archival and Records Terminology*, Archival Fundamentals Series (Chicago: Society of American Archivists, 2005), www.archivists.org.

16. Meraz, "Cultural Evidence," 14, 20.

17. Meraz, "Cultural Evidence," 24.

18. Meraz, "Cultural Evidence," 11.

19. Kevin Moore, *Museums and Popular Culture* (London: University of Leicester, 1997), 32–72.

20. Kenneth Ames, "Finding Common Threads: An Afterword," in *Ideas and Images: Developing Interpretive History Exhibits*, ed. Kenneth Ames, Barbara Franco, and L. Thomas Frye (Nashville, Tenn.: American Association for State and Local History, 1992), 313–24, and quoted in Moore, *Museums and Popular Culture*, 39.

21. Moore, *Museums and Popular Culture*, 40.

22. Susan M. Pearce, *Museums, Objects, and Collections* (Washington, D.C.: Smithsonian Press, 1992), 217, 219, and quoted in Moore, *Museums and Popular Culture*, 68–69.

23. Moore, *Museums and Popular Culture*, 54–72.

24. F. Gerald Ham, *Selecting and Appraising Archives and Manuscripts*, (Chicago: Society of American Archivists, 1993), 61.

25. Ham, *Selecting and Appraising Archives and Manuscripts*, 62.

26. See Shauna McRanor's evaluation of the appraisal criterion, intrinsic value, particularly her discussion of exhibit worthiness as a component of this criterion. Shauna McRanor, "A Critical Analysis of Intrinsic Value," *American Archivist* 59 (Fall 1996): 407–8.

27. Diane Beattie, "Retrieving the Irretrievable: Providing Access to 'Hidden Groups' in Archives," in *Reference Services for Archives and Manuscripts*, ed. Laura B. Cohen (Binghamton: Haworth Press, 1997), 83.

28. Robert Freeborn, "Cataloging the Weird: Further Examples for the 3-D Perplexed," *Journal of Academic Media Librarianship* 6, no. 2 (1999): 1–8, available from http://wings.buffalo.edu. See also L. C. Howarth, "Where Have All the Wallflowers Gone? Or AV Cataloguing Meets Virtual Reality," keynote speech delivered at the biennial conference of the Online Audiovisual Cataloger, Charlotte, N.C., November 4–7, 1998; partial text of speech available from http://ublib.buffalo.edu.

29. Freeborn, "Cataloging the Weird," 1.

30. Freeborn, "Cataloging the Weird," 6–8.

31. Beattie, "Retrieving the Irretrievable," 88.

32. Helena Zinkham, Patricia D. Cloud, and Hope Mayo, "Providing Access by Form of Material, Genre, and Physical Characteristics: Benefits and Techniques," *American Archivist* 52 (Summer 1989): 303, and quoted in Beattie, "Retrieving the Irretrievable," 89.

33. "OCLC (2001) Web-based Metadata Creation for Describing Electronic Resources: OCLC Cooperative Online Resource Catalog (CORC)," OCLC, available from www.oclc.org.

34. "Encoded Archival Description (EAD) Official Web Site," Network Development and MARC Standards Office, Library of Congress, www.loc.gov.

35. For a current international list of Digital Library Initiatives, see "Digital Libraries: Resources and Projects, Electronic Collections," International Federation of Library Associations and Institutions, www.ifla.org. For some excellent examples of digital initiatives with rich and varied content with strong search features, see Center for History and New Media, Georgia Mason University, chnm.gmu.edu; Library of Congress, especially American Memory Project, www.loc.gov; and the Digital Library of Georgia, http://dlg.galileo.usg.edu.

36. By "problematic means," I refer to situations where an institution does not apply appropriate preservation standards to an item's length of display or does not make an artifact's context and potential meanings clear to viewers.

17

Taking a Byte out of the Senate: Reconsidering the Research Use of Correspondence and Casework Files

Naomi L. Nelson

In the mid-1970s, a sustained discussion about the management of modern congressional collections first emerged in archival literature.[1] Much of the debate over congressional collections during the intervening 20 years concerned the appropriate disposition of the voluminous constituent correspondence and casework files. Most archivists agreed that the casework and constituent correspondence records created and filed under the old paper-based system were bulky, hard to use, and of little research value.[2]

In the summer of 1976, James K. Benson presented two papers to the Minnesota Historical Society assessing the potential research uses for constituent mail.[3] He identified three possible areas of focus: the content of the mail, the people who wrote, and the impact of the mail on the political decision making. He also identified several potential barriers to research use of these records. These barriers included the large volume of the records, the organization of the records, the inconsistency with which information about the constituents appears in the letters, the difficulty of categorizing letter content, and the time needed to estimate total quantities of mail on a given topic.[4] The congresspeople Benson included in his study all used the paper-based filing systems in use in Congress prior to the introduction of automated correspondence management systems.

In 1978, the Senate began to automate the handling of constituent correspondence, and several archivists and records creators expressed hope that automating (or "computerizing") mail processing would solve many of the

Previously published as "Taking a Byte out of the Senate: Reconsidering the Use of Casework and Correspondence Files" in *Provenance: The Journal of the Society of Georgia Archivists* xv (1997). Reprinted with permission.

processing and access problems posed by the voluminous mail and casework files. According to F. Gerald Ham, "These records possess great advantages for our users. The information they contain can be rearranged, aggregated, compared, and subjected to statistical tests without the laborious tasks of sample selection, data collection, coding, and data entry."[5] Margery Sly sagely predicted that "some archivists will be lucky and will be able to use computerization to their advantage; others will be faced with an unholy mess."[6]

Repositories receiving senatorial papers must now evaluate whether the constituent correspondence and casework records created and organized through the use of these early correspondence management systems are easier to access than records created under the paper-based systems and whether automation might offer any benefits to the archivist and researcher. Senator Sam Nunn served from 1972 to 1996, and his papers, now at Emory University (Atlanta, Georgia), provide an example of the types of benefits and challenges offered by correspondence management systems. The Senate has provided repositories with uniform electronic databases of coded information about constituents and their interests that should appeal to researchers interested in quantitative analysis. The systematization and standardization offered by these files, however, are a mirage. Senate staffers adapted the systems to individual office needs, and the data contain errors and irregularities. Constituent correspondence and casework files continue to be bulky and difficult to use.

CORRESPONDENCE MANAGEMENT
SYSTEMS COME TO CAPITOL HILL

The handling of U.S. senators' constituent correspondence[7] did not change appreciably with the adoption of automation.[8] Staff members answered letters using paragraphs preapproved by the senator and filed the original letter and a copy of the response for later reference. Indexes provided access to the filed correspondence through key access points, usually including constituent name, subject of the letter, and date of the letter. Staff members also compiled lists of constituent names and addresses for follow-up letters, newsletters, and future mailings and generated reports tracking hot topics, mail volume, and other useful derivative information.[9]

In the mid-1970s, Congress embraced automated, word-processing systems as the answer to the increasing volume of constituent inquiries. Senate facilities were unable to handle the mountains of constituent mail and the stored addressograph plates.[10] During a hearing before the Senate subcommittee that oversaw computer services in the Senate, Senator Alan Cranston estimated that in 1979 his office alone received from 10,000 to 15,000 letters per week.[11] Members sought a faster way to send high-quality responses to constituents and a more cost-effective way to keep constituents apprised of member activities. They also wanted to reduce staff time spent on producing, filing, and retrieving correspondence and to institute more managerial control over the mail process.

The constituent mail function was automated first by using increasingly more complex correspondence management systems. Word processing combined technologically more advanced office equipment with a systematic approach to office workflow in order to increase the quality and volume of correspondence produced.[12] Building on the systematization and standardization provided by word processing, correspondence management systems offered sophisticated word processing; the capability of inserting selected, approved paragraphs; personalized salutations and closings; personalized text; the ability to create targeted mailing lists; correspondence records; mail count on issues; automatic filing; and correspondence tracking.

Starting in the early 1970s, the Senate Computer Center developed the first database systems—the Automated Indexing System (AIS) and the Senate Mail File (SMF). They designed AIS to store the basic identification information about a document (name or subject, date, staffer, city, document number, etc.) and then to provide lists of the correspondence sorted by any of those fields. The goal was to end the time-consuming practice of maintaining carbon-copy cross-reference files and to facilitate faster filing and retrieval time.[13] The correspondence was filed by a system-generated document number. Name and topic indexes to the senator's correspondence were generated periodically from the AIS so that the staff could locate a letter by name or topic (see figure 17.1).[14]

The SMF was a centralized database of correspondent names and addresses that could be used to create labels or for follow-up mailings. Initially, staff manually typed the information about constituents and correspondence into these databases, but with the Senate's adoption of the Correspondence Mail System (CMS) in 1978, they could download information in batch files from the CMS system to the AIS and SMF.[15]

The centralized constituent mail system was designed to file information and maintain mailing lists in accordance with Senate rules. Like the AIS, it produced indexes. In addition, it included a topic listing that allowed for easier cross-reference for letters with multiple topics. CMS could produce reports to help office managers summarize the opinions expressed in incoming mail and to assess the efficiency and effectiveness of office staff in responding to mail. It cost more per letter, but the additional capabilities it offered were supposed to compensate for this extra expense. By-products from the system included management reporting, casework management, high-speed production printing, mailing list maintenance, and indexing and filing of correspondence. These additional capabilities became a part of the offices' correspondence function.[16] In the late 1980s, CMS was up-

Figure 17.1. Name index (generated by CMS)

09-25-81	INDEX FILE FOR SENATOR X		NAME REPORT	DOCUMENT #	MICROFILM #
	CRUMLEY, HARRY B., MR.	REQUEST TOURS	09-22-81 WASHINGTON DC	1264062007	
	343 JENIFER STREET PORTLAND, OR 97201				
	MJM WHITE HOUSE TOUR				
	JOHNSTON, JENNY, MRS.	ISSUE ENVIRONMENT INTERIOR	09-21-81 WATER NATIONAL PARKS	1263101001	
	1802 NORTH 24TH STREET SPRINGFIELD, VA 22100				
	ADT ITEMS: 3, 11, 5				
	MULLIGAN, BART, MR. AND MRS.	CASE CONST INITIAL	09-24-81 CONTACTED AGENCY	1266100002	
	492 COPELY LANE BORDENTOWN, VA 22102				
	GPS ITEMS: 1, 47, 6				
	RUTHERFORD, EILIS, MS.	ISSUE INTERIOR	09-21-81 NATIONAL PARKS	1263101002	
	APARTMENT 499 230 KEY ROAD ARLINGTON, VA 22101				
	ADA ITEMS: 1, 20, 0, 7				

graded and renamed the Constituent Services System (CSS). In 1991, the Senate Mail System (SMS) was developed to replace CSS, SMF, and AIS with a single database.[17]

In 1994, the Senate Computer Center decided to stop supporting SMS and began the process of moving all the Senate offices still using SMS to stand-alone correspondence management systems developed by outside vendors. These systems were designed for local area networks (LANs) and located in the senators' District of Columbia offices. The transition to the new systems was completed in 1996. Approved systems included InterAmerica's CapitolCorrespond, Intelligent Solutions Inc.'s Quorum, and Electronic Data Systems' Quick Response. Because these new systems resided in the senators' offices, they gave both more control and more responsibility to senators and their staffs. Individual office staffs designed and generated their own reports, and those senators interested in having a mail file for mass mailings had to maintain it in house.

When a senator left office, the Senate Computer Center sent a copy of selected data fields from the correspondence management systems to his or her designated repository (see figures 17.2 and 17.3). Since the center created the files using proprietary software that the repositories could afford neither to purchase nor to maintain, they sent data in a flat ASCII format that could be accessed using other software. Prior to 1996, they transferred files using seven-inch magnetic reels, nine-inch magnetic reels, or data tape cartridges. Beginning in 1996, they sent the files on CD-ROMs.

Figure 17.2.   Record layout for Correspondence Management System files sent to repositories by Senate Computer Center in 1996

Field	Length	Position	Type
1. Name (last, first middle, prefix, suffix) (Ex. Public, John Q., Mr., Jr.)	39	1–39	char
2. Title	30	40–69	char
3. Organization	30	70–99	char
4. Address line 1	30	100–129	char
5. Address line 2	30	130–159	char
6. City	30	160–189	char
7. State code	2	190–191	char
8. Zip code	10	192–201	char
9. Correspondence type	50	202–251	char
10. Correspondence topic	50	252–301	char
11. Correspondence subtopic	50	302–351	char
12. Letter date	6	352–357	yymmdd
13. Staffer initials	4	358–361	char
14. Document number	10	362–371	char
15. Comments	100	372–471	char

Figure 17.3. Records from Senator Nunn's CapitolCorrespond files (without name and street address fields)

City	State	Zipcode	Document Type	Topic	Subtopic	Date	Staff	Doc. No.	Item Paragraphs
STONE MOUNTAIN	GA	30088	MILITARY AFFAIRS	VETERANS	BENEFITS	920203	WNS	2031293005	ITEMS: 0,CBS.PRM
CRAWFORD	GA	30630	ISSUE	JUDICIARY	GUN CONTROL	940304	MMS	4062296246	ITEMS: 460
WARRENTON	GA	30828	ISSUE	SOCIAL SECURITY	NOTCH	920515	NLU	2135293095	ITEMS: 509
AUBURN	AL	36830	ISSUE	D	HEALTH COSTS	940706	MAT	4186295100	ITEMS: 413
AUBURN	AL	36830	ISSUE	HEALTH	NATIONAL HEALTHCARE	940706	MAT	4186295100	ITEMS: 413
AUBURN	AL	36830	ISSUE	HEALTH	NATIONAL HEALTHCARE	940706	MAT	4186294584	ITEMS: 413
AUBURN	AL	36830	ISSUE	D	HEALTH COSTS	940706	MAT	4186294584	ITEMS: 413
DULUTH	GA	30136	ISSUE	BUDGET	DEFICIT	930520	NLU	3139295711	ITEMS: 101
DULUTH	GA	30136	ISSUE	TAX	REFORM	930520	NLU	3139295711	ITEMS: 101
CALHOUN	GA	30701	ISSUE	TAX	EXCISE	930709	NLU	3189293294	ITEMS: 152
DUNWOODY	GA	30350	MILITARY AFFAIRS	FOREIGN POLICY	CHINA	920326	WNS	2085293025	ITEMS: 1018
DUNWOODY	GA	30350	MILITARY AFFAIRS	TRADE	CHINA	920326	WNS	2085293025	ITEMS: 1018
MONROE	GA	30655	ISSUE	HEALTH	ABORTION	930914	MAT	3256293563	ITEMS: 0,HYDE.PRM
MONROE	GA	30655	ISSUE	HEALTH	FAMILY PLANNING	930914	MAT	3256293563	ITEMS: 0,HYDE.PRM
ALBANY	GA	31707	ISSUE	COMMUNICATIONS	CABLE	921022	NLU	2295054885	ITEMS: 886
DUNWOODY	GA	30350	ISSUE	COMMUNICATIONS	CABLE	921022	NLU	2295053184	ITEMS: 886
COVINGTON	GA	30209	ISSUE	D	HEALTH COSTS	940623	MAT	4173294608	ITEMS: 413
COVINGTON	GA	30209	ISSUE	HEALTH	NATIONAL HEALTHCARE	940623	MAT	4173294608	ITEMS: 413
WASHINGTON	DC	20006	ISSUE	TRANSPORTATION	AIRLINES	920428	MJW	2203052113	
WASHINGTON	DC	20515	INVITATIONS	MEETINGS	DECLINED	930115	AN	3364092017	
NORCROSS	GA	30071	ISSUE	FINANCE	BANKING	921204	NLU	2338293003	ITEMS: 0,LTV.PRM

Electronic files stored on seven- and nine-inch reels require the use of a mainframe, and even files stored on data cartridges and CD-ROMs require large amounts of storage space and specialized software. Understandably, repositories have not been anxious for researchers to use these files and have not worked to make them accessible by researchers. A few repositories, like the Richard B. Russell Library at the University of Georgia and Special Collections at Emory University, have worked with information technology experts and political scientists at their institutions to examine some of the data they have received and to explore possible research applications.[18] To date, however, no researcher has studied data from Senate correspondence management systems. In the case of the Nunn papers, use of the correspondence files has been limited to requests by Senator Nunn for information about particular correspondents.

BARRIERS TO RESEARCH REVISITED

Volume is the most cited barrier to research use of constituent correspondence.[19] The adoption of automated correspondence management systems by Congress, other federal agencies, and lobbying organizations made it easier to send mail and contributed to a further increase in the volume of mail handled by Senate offices, making this problem more acute.[20] The amount of mail generated by Congress increased significantly beginning in the mid-1960s. Volume peaked in the late 1980s, averaging 700 million pieces per year from 1984 to 1989. In 1990, Congress responded to pressure to curb the use of franked mail by imposing new restrictions that reduced the volume of mail sent.[21] Constituent correspondence, however, continues to constitute up to one-third of the volume of members' papers.

The automated correspondence management systems ended the need for carbon-copy cross-reference files. Unfortunately, the topically filed master file has been replaced by correspondence filed by system-generated document number. This number is virtually meaningless to the researcher.[22] In many cases, routine mail (namely, flag requests) and casework are interfiled with issue mail, making it difficult to weed the mail prior to accessioning.

Automated correspondence management systems, however, have allowed Senate staffers to avoid the problems of volume and file order by enabling them to retrieve information from the computer rather than from the correspondence itself. Nunn's staff usually wanted to find letters through personal name or subject and were therefore dependent on the computer system to match the information they had about a constituent or letter with the document number under which it was filed. When they located the online entry for the letter, however, they often found that the information they wanted was recorded in the computer file (see figure

17.3), and that they therefore did not need to retrieve the actual letter.[23] When the letter was processed, the key information from the constituent letter and the senator's reply was captured in the online database. The correspondence itself was filed, more or less accurately, by document number and rarely referred to again.

From Nunn's staff's point of view, the correspondence system records were the most important records concerning constituent correspondence. They demonstrated this by requesting that three years of data from the old Senate Mail System (or SMS) be migrated to the new CapitolCorrespond system when they converted in 1994, so that they would continue to have the previous three years' correspondence history online. The paper indexes to the correspondence were also available, but the speed of access and the clarity with which the system presented information about the correspondence could not be replicated using the paper records under the current filing system.

Paul Chestnut has argued that "most correspondence sent to state legislators is more useful in the aggregate than in its individual form," and Benson's studies demonstrate that the same is true for congressional collections.[24] If researchers are indeed more interested in quantitative studies of constituent mail, the correspondence data files sent to the repositories should encourage their research, because much of the data collection has been done for them. Like the Senate staffers, these researchers will be able to bypass working with the actual correspondence. Researchers looking for particular letters or for anecdotes, however, may find these files more frustrating.[25] It is often much easier to find a record for a specific piece of correspondence than to find the correspondence itself. A researcher looking for sample letters on a particular topic, for example, might have to request many boxes or reels of microfilm, because the letters are filed according to a system-generated number rather than according to topic. Letters on the same topic often received identical replies, and these letters might be grouped or batched together when filed. Each group would then be filed under a system-generated number. In Senator Nunn's office, letters that were part of groups were filed separately from other constituent mail, and letters were arranged in no particular order within a given group. Some of the groups contain over 10,000 letters, and locating a particular letter in such a group takes time and luck.

In addition, data entry errors have resulted in numerous entries in the correspondence management systems with misspelled names, topics, and addresses.[26] File clerks filing the letters by name or topic might catch the error and file the letter under the correct name or topic. Computer-generated indexes, however, will sort the records as entered, leaving the researcher to scan through the entire index to be sure that the desired record was not accidentally entered with an "!" or a "Z" in front of the last name.[27] On the other hand, researchers can use software programs to search for "strings" or groups of characters, letting the computer do the work of scanning the index for the desired term. The online index can also be sorted by address or subtopic rather than name or topic, giving the researcher another way of narrowing the number of entries to scan for the desired correspondence.[28]

Many archivists recommend that constituent mail and casework be sampled, asserting that the volume of mail can be reduced without damaging whatever research value there may be in such files. Other archivists warn, however, that sampling may not sufficiently reflect interactions with constituents and the senator's legislative focus.[29] Accessioning correspondence management systems files will allow repositories to retain a considerable amount of information about the constituent correspondence without retaining all of the actual letters. Researchers will be able to estimate the total volume of mail received and to compare the characteristics of the mail that was retained to the mail that was destroyed.

While researchers may be able to avoid the mountains of paper files by using the information contained in the correspondence management system files, the size of the electronic files raises other problems. The size of the files received by a repository will vary, based on the congressperson's length of service and his or her policies concerning constituent correspondence. Senator Nunn's file for the older CMS (1978–1994) contained 2,320,000 records and took up almost 1.1 GB. His largest files from the newer CapitolCorrespond system (1994–1996) took up a comparatively small 289 MB.[30] Using these files requires a considerable commitment of file storage space and software designed to handle large databases.[31] Both repositories and researchers may be discouraged from working with these files because of their size. Repositories planning to offer access to correspondence management system files should break them down into small files that can be more easily accessed.[32] Doing so will require the use of servers or mainframes that can retrieve a data set from its current storage format and then provide the space needed to manipulate it.[33] Researchers can combine these smaller files to make larger data sets if they so desire. The difficulties caused by the size of the files, however, may be short lived, as advances in technology promise more powerful computers that make processing large databases easier in the future.

Reports, indexes, and lists generated by the correspondence management systems serve as useful summaries of the constituent mail files. The reports helped the senator's staff to interpret constituent opinions expressed in the mail received by their office. When the Senate used the centrally controlled CMS, reports and indexes were generated automatically, and staffers had to make a special request to have a duplicate copy run later if the first report was mislaid. The reports and indexes that were important to the office therefore were filed fairly carefully. The systems implemented after 1993, however, resided on local area networks within Senate offices. The staff generated reports as needed, and they may not have kept them, as another could be generated on demand.[34] Accessioning the correspondence management system files would allow researchers to generate their own reports and to recreate reports the office may have lost or decided not to generate themselves. Researchers using reports and indexes generated by the systems, however, must be cautioned that the data on which the reports are based contain many irregularities. The reports and indexes do represent the information on the mail available to the senators and their staff, but this information may not accurately reflect the amount or content of the mail itself. Depending on a researcher's interests, what the senator knew about the mail he or she received may be more important than the actual content of the mail.

Those repositories choosing not to provide researchers access to the correspondence management system files should work with the senators' staff members before they leave office to determine which information was important to them and to make sure that reports have been generated to capture that information. For example, these could be reports listing mail volume per month or per year, lists of the most popular topics per month, or indexes to correspondence on issues important to the senators. The repository might also want to contact potential researchers to determine what kinds of information they might be interested in seeing. Researchers using any of the reports generated or retained should be shown printouts of data from the system so they can see the kinds of irregularities that exist in the data from which the reports are drawn.[35]

The organization of the files forms another barrier to research. When Benson took a representative sample from the paper-based Minnesota constituent mail, he discovered three problems. First, though the congresspeople all seemed to have some rough, topical organization for their mail, their systems were different enough to make uniform sampling difficult.[36] Second, the topic categories used were too general to be useful for researchers. For example, a researcher looking for letters on open housing legislation would have to oversample the folders on civil rights in order to get a sufficient number of letters for the study.[37] Third, many constituents covered several topics in their letters, but a letter most likely would be filed under only one of them. Benson's sample, therefore, would not be drawn from the total number of letters on that topic, as some of those letters would be filed elsewhere under another topic discussed in the letter.[38] In addition, for quantitative analysis, the topics covered by the constituent's letter must be put in rigorously defined categories. Given the wandering, unfocused nature of much of the correspondence, such categorization was time consuming.[39]

Automation provides some solutions to these problems and presents other problems in a slightly different guise. The Senate Computer Center standardized the correspondence management computer files sent to repositories. The format changed slightly in 1996 after Senate Archivist Karen Paul solicited input from the repositories; however, in general, the same information has been transferred to the repositories over the years. Thus comparisons between the mail received by different senators should be possible. A uniform format, however, can mask differences in the way the staff used the system. System documentation indicates only what the system was designed to do. It does not document the ways in which a senator's staffers worked within the system to record things not anticipated by the system designers. For example, Senator Nunn's Atlanta office overrode the system-assigned document number so that all mail related to a particular case would have the same document number. Lydia Lucas expressed a concern in 1978 that adopting standardized filing systems and means of "computerizing" congressional records would "submerge the individuality of the senator."[40] The danger, however, seems to be not that individual senators will do things differently but that archivists and researchers will not recognize what they have done differently.[41]

Many of the difficulties that Benson had with topic categories were merely transferred to the new systems. Although the correspondence management systems did allow staffers to assign multiple topics and subtopics to correspondence records, there was no control on the terms entered. Topics remained broad and continued to reflect the interests and needs of the individual offices, making comparisons between different offices difficult. Perhaps more significantly, topics could be added at will or accidentally misspelled. Misspellings and unauthorized terms make it difficult to retrieve comprehensive listings of correspondence on a specific topic.

Automation provides two possible solutions to these problems. First, a list of all topics can be generated and any misspellings or unauthorized terms corrected in a copy of the file. Second, researchers can take advantage of the information used to generate the reply letter to locate more accurately letters of interest and to categorize individual letters. In order to create a reply, the correspondence management system needed the codes for the item paragraphs that would make up the reply letter. These codes are listed in a field in the file sent to the repositories. An index for the item paragraphs can be generated from the correspondence management system (see figure 17.4), and the text of the approved paragraphs and their codes can be found in the library of approved items, often located in the Systems Administrator files. Many paragraphs were written to respond to particular kinds of letters: for example, supporting the 1991 Persian Gulf War, opposing a milk tax, or opposing daylight savings time. The item paragraph codes were used to

Figure 17.4. Index to item paragraphs (generated by CMS)

OFFICE: SENATOR SMYTHE **ABSTRACT REPORT** **R02**

Date of Listing: SEP-18-81

Topic	Subtopic	Item #	Synopsis	Updated
Close		4	disagree on issue	JAN-07-80
Close		5	Thank you again: keep in touch	JAN-07-80
Close		6	Thank you again	JAN-07-80
Close		7	good to hear from you: keep informed of activities	JAN-07-80
Close		9	call on me, look forward to hearing from you	JAN-07-80
Intro		1	f. i. subj of ltr: Thanks for letter, happy to know views	JAN-07-80
Intro		2	f. i. date of ltr: Thanks for bring matter to attention	JAN-07-80
Intro		3	f. i. date of ltr: Thanks for letter	JAN-07-80
Intro		8	f. i. publication name: thanks for publication	JAN-07-80
agriculture	dairy	11	dried milk to compete w/ fresh, anti	SEP-05-81
energy	public utilities	13	f. i. county - adverse impact elec. serv. in counties	SEP-17-80
environment	solid waste	16	aprec. learning concern about solid waste managment	JAN-07-80
environment	solid waste	17	newspaper disposal	JAN-11-81
housing	rent control	22	support local rent control. I agree completely	JAN-11-81
interior	national parks	20	Green Valley strip mining	JAN-07-80
interior	national parks	47	ban strip mining and protect wildlife sanctuaries	SEP-17-80
public activities	congrats from senator	18	short - naturalization	SEP-16-80
public activities	congrats from senator	19	short, f. i. occasion - for example, 75th birthday	SEP-16-80
taxes	marriage penalty	17	encl - single and married tax differences	SEP-17-81
wildlife	animal abuse	14	soring of horses	JAN-11-81
wildlife	animal abuse	44	inhumane treatment of animals	MAR-14-81

generate a report listing the most frequently cited constituent concerns or positions. Researchers can use these codes to design the rigorous content categories needed for quantitative analysis. In effect, the senator's staff has already coded each letter for content.[42]

One of Benson's goals in sampling the Minnesota issue mail was to estimate the total quantity of mail received on a specific topic. The correspondence management files should allow a researcher to determine more easily the quantity of mail received on a given topic without having to sample. Researchers, however, will have to take time to carefully examine the data file for irregularities and will need to consult memos and other records concerning correspondence files to determine whether there has been any duplication or data loss. For example, some correspondence management systems allowed staffers to make copies of entries and then assign them different topics/subtopics. When Senator Nunn's office changed its subtopic for Desert Storm from "Middle East" to "Iraq-Kuwait," for example, the staff created a duplicate entry for all records related to the Persian Gulf War and entered under "Middle East" to the new topic, "Iraq-Kuwait." These records, therefore, appeared twice in the database. In another case, shortly after the change to the CapitolCorrespond system, several hundred new records were deleted when data-entry operators accidentally pressed the wrong key. Information about these kinds of data irregularities can only be obtained from the staff members who worked with the correspondence management systems. The greatest amount of irregularity usually occurs during transitions from one system to another.[43]

Benson also pointed to the need for research into who writes to their congresspeople. The greatest problem he identified in this area, aside from the volume of the mail, was that vital information was frequently not present in the letters themselves, including age, race, and occupation.[44] This information is also unlikely to appear in the computer database. Benson suggested that researchers might be able to find additional information about constituents in local directories.[45] The ability to create reports listing constituents by name or by address might make such work easier. Files that have the title data (Mr., Mrs., Dr., Ms., etc.) in a separate field may allow researchers to categorize constituents further. Data entry errors will make any study of constituents difficult, however. Senator Nunn's data files contain numerous examples of misspelled first and last names and incorrect zip codes and state designations in the address fields.

Both the 1978 Conference on the Research Use and Disposition of Senators' Papers and the 1986 *Congressional Papers Project Report* written after the conference on congressional papers sponsored by the Dirksen Congressional Center and the National Historical Publications and Records Commission emphasized that donor restrictions pose perhaps the greatest barrier to research use of congressional collections.[46] Constituent correspondence is generally given long restriction periods to respect constituent privacy. It is a simple matter, however, to create a copy of the constituent management system files without the name and street address fields (see figure 17.3). The resulting file protects individual constituent confidentiality while allowing researchers access to aggregate data about the correspondence. Repositories that plan to offer access to the correspondence management system data files should try to open these files to researchers as early as possible. Computer files that are open and used are much more likely to be refreshed and migrated to new storage formats and are therefore more likely to be preserved in a usable format.

CONCLUSIONS

Automated constituent correspondence systems records are well suited for aggregate, quantitative research. The correspondence management systems records provided in electronic form by the Senate Computer Center are an important access tool, a source of significant information, and the only index to senatorial constituent correspondence. They can be used as a finding aid for the correspondence records and to sample or weed those files. Unlike the correspondence itself, they can be purged of confidential information easily and, therefore, more quickly opened for research. Perhaps most significantly, the Senate staffers have already coded demographic and topical information into the computer files, providing a database that can be readily adapted for use with statistical database software.

Correspondence management systems records, however, promise more than they can deliver. Misspellings, missing data, missing records, and duplicate records combine to undermine the reliability of the data files as both indices and data sets. The repository must be familiar with how the senator's staff used the system in order to help the researcher correctly interpret the files. The size of the computer files themselves make them difficult to manipulate and search, and using the data may require skills that most archivists currently do not possess. The correspondence management files that serve as an index are separate from the correspondence, and the correspondence is extremely difficult to access without that index. The key to the item paragraph codes that provide more precise subject access are also in a separate file.

Repositories planning to provide access to correspondence management files must commit time and resources to working with the Senate staff to document the systems and how they were used, to reformatting the data into smaller files, and to migrating and refreshing the data to keep the information accessible as technology changes. These are significant commitments, considering the problems posed by the data and the lack of interest researchers have shown in constituent correspondence in general. Unfortunately, although correspondence management systems provide some advantages to users interested in data manipulation and quantitative analysis, the data contained in them constitute, as archivist Margery Sly feared, "an unholy mess."

NOTES

1. Looking back from the perspective of 1994, Senate Historian Richard A. Baker identified several factors leading to an increased public awareness of the disposition of the papers of public officials in the 1970s. The unexpected death of influential Senator Richard B. Russell in 1971 resulted in the very visible transfer of 45 tons of records in three tractor trailers to the University of Georgia. Richard Nixon's resignation after Watergate and the legal battle over the ownership of the secret recordings made in the Oval Office led to a debate over which papers created by elected officials should be considered private records and which should be considered public records. And between 1976 and 1980, 53 senators left office (through resignation or election defeat), the greatest turnover in Senate history. When the dust cleared, congressional papers remained private records, and increasing numbers of repositories faced the challenge of accessioning the huge collections. See Richard A. Baker, "Congressional Papers: The Legacy of Richard Russell and Richard Nixon," *Proceedings of the Congressional Papers Conference Held in Portland, Maine, 16–17 September 1994*, ed. Gregory P. Gallant and William E. Brown, Jr. (Waterville, Me.: Atkins, 1995), 15–21.

2. Almost every speaker at the 1978 Conference on the Research Use and Disposition of Senators' Papers addressed the research value of constituent mail, with many concluding that such files were problematic at best and of little use to the social scientist or historian. Lydia Lucas, however, argued that "the way in which a member defines and expresses his relationship to his constituency, and the way his papers reflect this relationship, also shape their most unique and enduring values"; and Frank Mackaman pointed out that constituent correspondence and casework documented a kind of political participation by non-elite members of society. J. Stanley Kimmitt and Richard A. Baker, eds., *Proceedings of the Conference on the Use and Disposition of Senators' Papers, Washington, DC, September 14–15, 1978* (Washington, D.C.: Government Printing Office, 1979); Lydia Lucas, "Managing Congressional Papers: A Repository View," *American Archivist* 41 (July 1978): 280; and Frank Mackaman, remarks during Archivists Panel in *Proceedings of the Conference on the Use and Disposition of Senators' Papers*, 68–69.

3. James K. Benson, "Political Research on Constituent Mail: A Report on Problems and Prospects," paper prepared for the Minnesota Historical Society, summer 1976; and Benson, "Letters to Congressmen as Sources for Research: A Report on the Constituent Correspondence of Congressman Clark MacGregor," paper prepared for the Minnesota Historical Society, summer 1976.

4. Benson, "Political Research on Constituent Mail," 7–8, 10–11, 15.

5. F. Gerald Ham, "Archival Choices: Managing the Historical Record in an Age of Abundance," *American Archivist* 47 (Winter 1984): 19.

6. Margery Sly, "Access to Congressional Case Files: Survey of Practices, Implications for Use," paper presented at the annual meeting of the Society of American Archivists, August 30, 1986, 20.

7. For the purposes of this discussion, *constituent mail* and *constituent correspondence* will be defined as including all kinds of correspondence between a member of Congress and his or her constituents. These will include letters on legislative issues, requests for flags and other routine matters, requesting that the senator intercede on the constituent's behalf with a federal agency, thank-you letters, and mass mailings. Letters on legislative issues will be referred to as *issue mail*, and letters requesting intervention on the constituent's behalf with a federal agency will be termed *casework*. In the Senate, the correspondence management system index provided to the repositories upon the senator's retirement includes all mail indexed on the system, regardless of type.

8. For an interesting assessment of the impact of computer applications on Congress, see Stephen E. Frantzich, "The Implications of Congressional Computerization," *Bulletin of the American Society for Information Science* 13 (February/March 1987): 13–14.

9. See Senate Committee on Rules and Administration, Subcommittee on Computer Services, *Report on Computer Services to the Committee on Rules and Administration*, 95th Cong., 1st sess., 1977, Committee Print, 9.

10. Stephen E. Frantzich, *Congressional Applications of Information Technology* (Washington, D.C.: Office of Technology Assessment, 1985), 22.

11. Senate Committee on Appropriations, Subcommittee on the Legislative Branch, *Oversight on Computer Services in the Legislative Branch: Hearing Before a Subcommittee of the Committee on Appropriations, Special Oversight Hearing Legislative Branch*, 96th Cong., 1st sess., 1979, Committee Print, 14.

12. General Accounting Office, *Federal Productivity Suffers Because Word Processing Not Well Managed: Report to the Congress*, prepared by the Comptroller General of the United States (Washington, D.C.: General Accounting Office, 1979), 1.

13. *Report on Computer Services to the Committee on Rules and Administration*, 11.

14. Karen Dawley Paul, *Records Management Handbook for United States Senators and Their Repositories* (Washington, D.C.: Government Printing Office, 1992), 50.

15. Paul, *Records Management Handbook*, 50.

16. General Accounting Office, *The Senate Should Explore Other Word Processing Alternatives* (1980), 6, 10–11. Eight-eight percent of the offices using CMS reported that they found the CMS management reports useful. Offices that did not use CMS generated the workload and hot topic reports manually. In contrast, only 25 offices used the casework feature, and some senators complained that the system included features that they did not want to use.

17. Paul, *Records Management Handbook*, 51.

18. For a summary of the work done at the University of Georgia and Emory University, see Todd Kosmerick, "Congressional Papers Roundtable Minutes, 1998 Annual Meeting, Orlando, September 4, 1998," *Congressional Papers Roundtable Newsletter*, November 2, 1988.

19. See Lucas, "Managing Congressional Papers," 280; Eleanor McKay, "Random Sampling Techniques: A Method of Reducing Large, Homogenous Series in Congressional Papers," *American Archivist* 41 (July 1978): 284; Ham, "Archival Choices," 18; and Patricia Aronsson, "Appraisal of Twentieth-Century Congressional Collections," in *Archival Choices: Managing the Historical Record in an Age of Abundance*, ed. Nancy E. Peace (Lexington, Mass.: Lexington Books, 1984), 97. Frank Mackaman,

on the other hand, argued that it is the nature of a collection and its arrangement and description, and not its volume, that discouraged use. See Mackaman, Archivists Panel in *Proceedings*, 68–69.

20. See Paul Chestnut, "Appraising the Papers of State Legislators," *American Archivist* 48 (Spring 1985): 165, for a discussion of rising mail volume at the state level.

21. American Enterprise Institute, *Vital Statistics on Congress 1997–1998*, ed. Norman J. Ornstein, Thomas E. Mann, and Michael J. Malbin (Washington, D.C.: Congressional Quarterly, 1998), 159; and David Burnham, "Congress's Computer Subsidy: Federally Financed Computers, Franking Privileges, and Public Funds for Direct-Mail Experts Have Given an Edge to Members of Congress Seeking Re-election," *New York Times Magazine*, November 2, 1980, 97.

22. Document numbers are generally chronological by date and order of reply.

23. Staff members were typically searching for the date on which a constituent had previously written to the senator, which opening paragraph had been used in previous responses, the constituent's address, and the topics on which the constituent had previously written.

24. Chestnut, "Papers of State Legislators," 164. See Benson, "Political Research on Constituent Mail" and "Letters to Congressmen as Sources for Research."

25. Patricia Aronsson has pointed out that many researchers appreciate the "anecdotal value" of casework. Aronsson, "Appraisal of Twentieth-Century Congressional Collections," 93.

26. There are several examples of misspelled words in figure 17.3.

27. For example, in a subset of Senator Nunn's 1990–1991 correspondence management system records, the document type "case" was misspelled in 22 different ways, including "CAS3E," "CO," and "DCAS."

28. Statistical software packages such as SPSS (Statistical Package for Social Sciences) and SAS (Statistical Analysis System) can be used to sort and search large databases.

29. McKay, "Random Sampling Techniques," 281. Aronsson, "Appraisal of Twentieth-Century Congressional Collections," 92–93; and Mark Greene, "Appraisal of Congressional Records at the Minnesota Historical Society: A Case Study," *Archival Issues* 19, no. 1 (1994): 35–36.

30. Senator Nunn directed his staff to answer every letter, postcard, name on a petition, and most phone calls with a letter. He was in office for 24 years, the senior senator from Georgia from 1981 to 1996, and chair of the Armed Services Committee from 1987 to 1994. Senator Nunn had a higher volume of mail answered and indexed than most other senators because of the leadership positions he held and his policies on answering constituent mail.

31. Faye Phillips discusses these difficulties in *Congressional Papers Management: Collecting, Appraising, Arranging, and Describing Documentation of United States Senators, Representatives, Related Individuals, and Organizations* (Jefferson, N.C.: McFarland, 1996), 178.

32. For example, Emory University will break down Senator Nunn's correspondence management system files by year.

33. For a brief summary of Beth Bensman's description of the Russell Library's attempts to work with such large files, see Kosmerick, "Congressional Papers Roundtable Minutes."[distributed through e-mail 2 November 1998].

34. For example, the CMS automatically generates a weekly "hot topic" report listing the most frequently used item paragraphs. Senator Nunn's office maintained a file of these reports. The CapitolCorrespond system that they adopted in 1994 did not automatically generate this report, and the office staff only produced it sporadically.

35. The name and topic indexes generated by the CMS provide this kind of information. The systems implemented after 1994 may not automatically generate such indexes, and in such cases the repository should request that an index to a small portion of the correspondence be generated.

36. Benson, "Political Research on Constituent Mail," 9, 10–11.

37. Benson, "Political Research on Constituent Mail," 8.

38. Historian Richard Lowitt also found this to be true in his research using Senator George W. Norris's papers. His research, however, was not quantitative in nature, and he believed he found important information by browsing through the correspondence and reading documents not directly related to the topic that he was researching. Richard Lowitt, remarks during Historians Panel in *Proceedings of the Conference on the Use and Disposition of Senators' Papers*, 47.

39. Benson, "Political Research on Constituent Mail," 11.

40. Lucas, remarks during Archivists Panel in *Proceedings of the Conference on the Research Use and Disposition of Senator's Papers*, 73.

41. For an expanded discussion of the need for archivists to work closely with congressional offices to document electronic records, see Phillips, *Congressional Papers Management*, 177–80.

42. Some letters, of course, were not answered using the preapproved item paragraphs. In Nunn's office, these letters answered with customized text were known as "perms." In the correspondence management system file, instead of listing the item paragraph code, the staffer would enter the file name for the newly created language (that is, SPACE.PRM or IRAQ.PRM). "Perms" that were used to answer several letters were made into item paragraphs and assigned an item code. Letters that were not created using the correspondence management system, but were indexed in the system, were known as "handtypes" and might not have any item codes associated with them. Letters indexed but not answered were known as "no reply necessary" or "NRN" letters. Sometimes "NRN" was entered in the item code field. See figure 17.3 for examples.

43. Many archivists have recommended that repositories work closely with congressional staff members to ensure that the transfer of records is complete and orderly and to allow the archivist to become familiar with the way that the office functioned. See Paul, *Records Management Handbook*, 129; Connell Gallagher, "A Repository Archivist on Capitol Hill," *Midwestern Archivist* 16, no. 1 (1991): 49–58; and Faye Phillips, "Harpers Ferry Revisited: The Role of Congressional Staff Archivists in Implementing the Congressional Papers Project Report," *Provenance* 6 (Spring 1988): 26–44.

44. Benson, "Political Research on Constituent Mail," 11.

45. Benson, "Political Research on Constituent Mail," 14.

Part IV

ARRANGING AND DESCRIBING
POLITICAL COLLECTIONS

18

Processing Political Collections

Greta Reisel Browning and Mary McKay

Processing a collection of political papers can be a great challenge. The experience can also be educational, daunting, entertaining, frustrating, but ultimately rewarding. Whether novice or veteran archivist, it matters not—confronting a 2,000-plus linear-foot collection of papers, artifacts, photographs, audiovisual materials, and microform, and over 1 terabyte of structured and unstructured digital material, is overwhelming. This chapter offers practical advice, guidance, and reassurance to those intrepid individuals who are wrangling with their first political collection.

Modern political collections are a microcosm of contemporary record-keeping practices, encompassing a variety of obsolete, current, and even cutting-edge media and formats. They cover a world of subject areas. By applying the best methods of accessioning, surveying, and inventorying and following the tips shared in this chapter, archivists will be able to process such collections efficiently and with confidence.

BEFORE YOU BEGIN

As with any special format or subject collection, take time to review professional literature, examine descriptions for similar, already processed collections, and consult peers who have worked with the same type of material. Fortunately, there is a strong professional network of congressional archivists both within the U.S. Congress and in archival repositories who are eager to share their expertise. They can be reached through the Congressional Papers Roundtable (CPR) of the Society of American Archivists (SAA), the U.S. House of Representatives Office of History and Preservation, and the

U.S. Senate Historical Office. Luckily, one does not have to be a member of SAA to participate in the CPR, which offers:

- A listserv for communicating with a group of committed, informed, and supportive professionals who work with congressional collections on a regular basis.
- Internet resources, hosted on the SAA Web site, which provide access to several online sources, including congressional papers management guidelines, bibliographies relating to congressional collections, biographical and historical information about Congress, and links to archival repositories with similar collections.
- A semiannual newsletter, also available on the CPR Web pages, which provides news about current issues relevant to congressional collections, updates from other archives about new collections, and processing "war stories."
- A forum for discussing any issue related to managing congressional collections through annual meetings at the SAA conferences.
- The opportunity to share your own professional expertise developed in processing political collections.

Next, learn about the legislative process. Understanding "how" and "why" the records came into existence, what purpose they served, and the nomenclature that describes the process is essential for successful arrangement and description. For example: What distinguishes "personal" papers of members of Congress from the official records of Congress? What is the function of a congressional administrative assistant versus a legislative assistant, and what types of files are associated with the two different staff positions? Understanding these basics is essential for effective processing, and the chapters in this book are designed to provide you with this background.

Two other significant organizations provide online resources: the Association of Centers for the Study of Congress (ACSC) and the Center for Legislative Archives (CLA). The ACSC (www.congresscenters.org) is a network of centers that specialize in the preservation of congressional collections and in promoting the study of Congress. Its members are at the forefront of those who practice good congressional collections management. The Center for Legislative Archives at the National Archives and Records Administration (NARA) is the archival home for the official records of Congress. To promote broad access to congressional collections, CLA hosts "Congressional Collections at Archival Institutions," a Web site with links to online collection descriptions at congressional collections around the country (www.archives.gov/legislative/repository-collections/).

CONFRONTING THE BEAST: GAINING PHYSICAL AND INTELLECTUAL CONTROL OVER THE COLLECTION

Political collections vary in size and condition based on a variety of factors: for example, the elected or appointed positions held by the creator of the collection and the specific committees on which the individual served; which materials were retained or discarded before reaching the archival repository; length of time served; whether the officeholder's tenure was pre- or post-conversion to electronic recordkeeping, and the degree to which electronic records have been managed. No two collections will be exactly alike.

A donor file is particularly useful for managing political collections because of the typically long period of time which can elapse between initial discussions with the donor and actual deposit of the materials. Staff turnover can be frequent in congressional offices, and it becomes essential to keep a good record of contacts, discussions, and agreements. Some repositories take advantage of new open-source software such as Archivists' Toolkit or Archon for administrative management of their collections.[1] Others use proprietary databases such as PastPerfect or Microsoft Access. Regardless of which system you use, a working file becomes an informational lifeline about the collection and should contain the following:

1. *All communications with the donor or the donor's staff,* including letters, phone messages, and e-mails about arrangements to transfer the collection, or documentation of agreements between the repository and the donor. All requests for materials made by the donor or donor's staff—and whether the material was or was not found—should be documented in this file.

2. *A deed of gift,* which is a legal agreement "establishing conditions governing the transfer of title to documents and specifying any restrictions on access and use."[2] Deeds of gift for political collections sometimes take a while to negotiate, especially if the donor is still in public life. More frequently a deposit agreement or letter of understanding will be in place for a period of time, usually until collections can be opened for research.

3. *A container inventory,* either provided by the donor's office or created at the archival repository, which will provide an overview of the collection and establish preliminary physical control of the material that is transferred. The inventory is especially helpful if some parts of the collection are stored off site. Inventories created by political offices vary in level of detail—anything from a box-title list to a folder listing for each box—and should therefore be checked for accuracy and completeness. The inventory will become an essential tool in

making appraisal plans, developing an arrangement scheme, and determining access.

4. *Accession records,* which document each accrual to the collection.

5. *Staff rosters,* maintained by offices for administrative purposes, which will have ongoing use for processing archivists. Such lists—including staff names, dates of employment, and legislative issue areas or duties—are useful for identifying files and for arranging materials according to dates or subject specialties. When boxes and folders contain staff identification, the archivist can quickly learn more about the materials while minimizing extra background research. If the donor's office did not provide a list, or one is not easily located in the collection, it can be compiled from published sources. Information about congressional staff can be found in the *Congressional Staff Directory, Annual Report of the Secretary of the Senate,* and *Annual Statement of the Expenditures from the Contingent Fund of the Two Houses of Congress* (House, Office of the Clerk), the last two being part of the U.S. Congressional Serial Set. Frequently, state and local politicians do not have staff, and this may be reflected by the relatively smaller volume of their papers.

6. *Biographical information,* which will provide context for the papers. The creator's professional timeline—as well as a list of committee assignments, a summary of his or her major accomplishments, or other useful notes—should be compiled before creating a processing plan. Brief biographies of members of Congress are in the *Biographical Directory of the United States Congress.*[3] State governments often have official registers that provide information about state officials. For donors who are still in office, the official's Web site may also provide information. Beginning in 2004, the Web sites of members of Congress were captured once every two years by the National Archives and the archived sites are available at www.archives.gov/records-mgmt/policy/web-harvest-snapshot.html. Many politicians publish memoirs or policy books during or immediately following their terms in office. Such works provide information for the collection's description and serve as guideposts to significant topics in the papers. The collection itself may contain newspaper clipping files or scrapbooks that illuminate the person's career, issues championed, and public policy issues of significance. Basic information can be found on the Political Graveyard Web site (http://politicalgraveyard.com) and in any number of secondary biographical and historical sources.

7. *Processing records,* which track actions taken with the collection and may be complex or simple. These include basic accession statistics and facts (accession control number, amount of material, restrictions, etc.), collection overview (type of material, arrangement, major subjects, etc.), and a list of processing tasks with a record of dates

completed and initials of the person who completed them. A processing record can also be used to track sensitive information discovered
during processing. An example of a processing record is available in
Faye Phillips's *Congressional Papers Management*.[4]

8. *Files documenting other special actions*, such as appraisal reports, conservation treatments, or submission of materials for declassification.
When any processing activity becomes complex or generates correspondence along with other administrative documentation, it is
prudent to keep this information with the centrally located donor and
working files.

ACCESSIONING

An accession number or code is "assigned to uniquely identify a group of
records or materials acquired by a repository and used to link the materials to associated records," such as details of date and volume received.[5]
While some collections can arrive at a repository in their entirety at one
time, others can accrue in multiple shipments over time, especially if the
donor has a long career in public life. Using the same accession number for
multiple deliveries, and adding the date of arrival or some other indicator
such as a letter to the accession number on each box, is a good way to avoid
potential confusion caused by assigning a new accession number to each
new shipment. In addition, members' staff frequently request items from
"their" boxes by referencing the shipment date, so keep track of the dates
of individual shipments.

Provide a basic overview of the collection's contents. For example, are the
materials solely congressional? Or do they include state legislative papers
from 40 years ago, or perhaps nonofficial gubernatorial papers, such as
campaign materials from an earlier decade? Maybe family materials are included. This information will serve for immediate reference purposes until
a lengthier press release is composed and the final collection description is
completed.

Take care to note the varied formats of materials found in the collection.
Electronic records should *immediately* be reviewed and checked for accessibility. If problems are discovered, the possibility of obtaining a correc-
tion is directly related to how quickly assistance is sought from the House
and Senate archivists or office systems administrator. Generally, the media
used to transfer the records to the repository are not suitable for long-term
storage, and the data should be transferred to a digital asset management
system or dedicated server. The documents may or may not be in a nonpro-
prietary open-source format. Some formats are more at risk for obsolescence
than others, and recommendations for their preservation should be made

during the accessioning process. If possible, use genre terms from an accepted authority list, such as the Art & Architecture Thesaurus Online.[6] A standardized glossary of legislative subject terms is available at http://thomas.loc.gov/liv/livtoc.html. These standardized vocabulary terms will be used in later cataloging or description records.

SURVEYING AND PREPARING THE INVENTORY

When surveying a political collection for the first time, make special note regarding the completeness of series. This can be of help with creating a processing plan. For example, for the papers of Senator Daniel Patrick Moynihan (D-NY), the Library of Congress Manuscripts Division processing staff first attacked the constituent correspondence series, because it was the most complete series and provided an overview of the most significant topics in the collection over time. Karen Dawley Paul's chapter in part II of this book provides concise descriptions of different types of materials produced in senatorial offices. These functional categories often drive the basic arrangement strategy for a collection.

If a comprehensive container inventory—including folder-title listing by box number—comes with the collection, one need only compare the lists with the contents, note discrepancies, and co-opt the office's lists as the preliminary finding aid for the collection. If an archivist is working with the donor prior to or during the closing of the office, it is a good opportunity to request that an inventory be compiled. Members are advised to have such inventories prepared prior to departure, and this in now becoming commonplace.

If an inventory is not provided, the archivist will need to create one, weighing available resources to determine the level of detail necessary. At minimum, the following information should be recorded: who (whose papers), what (what are the topics/titles of folders or boxes), when (year dates), where created (district or Washington office), and any outstanding preservation concerns. Table 18.1 shows a sample inventory that was provided courtesy of the Richard B. Russell Library for Political Research and Studies at the University of Georgia.

As time-consuming as they are to create, inventories are helpful for the following reasons:

- From a legal standpoint, for insurance purposes, and to administer access provisions, it is advisable to have a listing of all materials transferred to the archives.
- Staff time will be saved and stress minimized when the inevitable request comes from the donor for materials already transferred, or thought to have been transferred.

Table 18.1.   Folder Listing: William Armstrong Smith Papers, Preliminary Inventory List

Accession Number	Box Number	Description of Contents/ Arrangement	Years Covered	Size of Container	Preservation Notes
2001/28	1	—Political —Speech Material, 1972 Session —Campaign, 1972 —Senate & House members, Ga. Legislature —Legislative, 1970 —E-Reg Committee, 1973 —Campaign, 1968 —General Ga. Senate materials (loose), 1968–1973 —ERA Committee	1968–1973	1 lin.ft.	All materials appear to be in good condition requiring general preservation care.

- Container lists facilitate physical and intellectual rearrangements, allowing the archivist to match major categories with standard series, arranging the boxes intellectually on paper and on the shelves accordingly.
- Obvious gaps or missing materials can be identified (e.g., campaign materials or speeches).
- Excess materials with no research value (e.g., office stationery and supplies) can be identified and disposed of, observing any disposition clause in the deed of gift.
- Electronic records can be processed, and preservation needs can be addressed.
- If the collection sits in a processing queue, an inventory will make it easier for staff to quickly become familiar with the contents if there suddenly is a need to do so.

INTERPRETING INFORMATION ON THE TRANSFER CASES

Because so many congressional collections are transferred in cubic-foot-sized record-center cartons that have been stored either in locker space or at the Washington National Records Center, it is wise to read any "clues" about contents that may have been recorded on these boxes. Items to look for include:

- *Names written on the exterior of a box*, which are often those of staff members who created the files. Using a staff roster and the position descriptions in Paul's *Records Management Handbook*, one may be able to deduce the box contents and verify with a spot check. For example, the *Congressional Directory* identifies Penelope Hamilton as a legislative assistant in Representative Tilly's office covering the topics of defense, veterans, and energy and commerce. Thus, one can surmise that the "Hamilton" box of files may include background research and memos about legislation and issues, related committee work, and letters from constituents about these topics. A quick check will verify this.

- *Subjects/committees*, such as "Education and Labor, Defense, Agriculture," which indicate the subjects or committees to which the materials relate. It is important to distinguish files created by staff for the member's office from those created by the congressional committee staff. Official committee files are property of either the U.S. House or Senate and are destined for preservation with other official records at NARA. Files maintained by the office are the personal property of the member. See chapter 7 in this volume on how to identify them.
- *Activities*, such as "press, legislative, or administrative." These large categories are potential series, as they each represent major functions and activities of an office.
- *Type of material*, such as "issue mail, letters to constituents, calendars, invitations, or budgets." These may also become major series.
- *Location*, which may indicate that the materials originated in the Washington, D.C., office or a district/state office. Files from Washington are often research files or issue mail. District offices frequently process casework. Other location information (and corresponding accession numbers) may indicate that the boxes were temporarily stored in NARA's Suitland site or regional branches closer to the congressmember's home state.
- *Congress*, such as 98th Congress, 2nd Session; 104th Congress. A Congress refers to a date range of two years. The Office of the Clerk, U.S. House of Representatives, maintains a very useful online listing of congressional dates as well as profiles of House leadership for each Congress.[7]
- *Dates*, indicating the date range of the box contents.

PROCESSING

Processing is the actual work of "arrangement, description, and housing of archival materials for storage and use by patrons."[8] This section focuses on identification of record types and arrangement of series typical of political collections, and it includes a brief discussion of applying minimal processing methods.

Successful processing depends on interpreting the materials within a larger particular context. According to archival theorist T. R. Schellenberg, the arrangement of the materials "should proceed from an understanding of the whole group or collection; it should not be separated on a piecemeal basis."[9] This is especially true for political papers because a member's collection represents only a part of the legislative story; the other major part resides in committee records.

Being familiar with the officeholder's career and understanding the functions of the office help define the collection as a whole. It is important to know what activities are performed, who performs them, and what types of materials result from these activities. It is equally important to be informed about major regional and national issues that developed during the official's time in office, as well as issues of personal significance to the legislator. These will likely figure prominently in the collection and will ultimately be of interest to researchers. Secondary sources can be consulted, but it also is advisable to consult with historians and political scientists to ascertain their research interests. Establishing this kind of contextual knowledge early on in the course of processing will help to rationalize arrangement schemes and provide essential information for writing useful narrative scope notes.

Using the accession inventory to create a processing plan can be especially helpful for managing a large political collection. The plan should identify the major series and their date ranges, indicate to what level the collection or individual series will be processed, and outline preservation goals. This plan can be altered and revised as new information comes to light, and it serves as an important map or blueprint to creating a logically processed collection. The plan also serves as a management tool, making it easy to identify routine processing tasks or "simple" series that can be delegated to support staff or student assistants.

Typical Series and Arrangements

Large political collections exhibit many of the characteristics normally associated with records management schemes for organizations rather than the more idiosyncratic characteristics of manuscript collections and personal papers. As Patricia Aronsson observes, "Congressional collections are hybrids, neither strictly archival nor strictly personal," and therein lies the conundrum and resulting challenge when processing these collections.[10] In the rare, "best-case" scenario when the materials arrive at the archival repository in good order and decent condition, it is possible that very little item-level work will be necessary for a collection to be "processed" and opened for use.

Subgroups and Series by Function

As noted above, there are major activities of members of Congress that vary little and often drive an arrangement scheme by function. These typical functional subgroups or series (depending on collection size and arrangement complexity) include the following:[11]

Personal/Official
Political
Legislative
Constituent Service
Press Relations/Media Activities
Office Administration
Campaign

Not all aspects of a member's activities will be documented in the papers, because much work is conducted verbally. It is important to identify series that are represented and, if possible, try to track down any materials obviously missing. These six functional series may be extrapolated to apply to state and local political papers.

Subgroups or Series by Position Held or Stage in Career

If the official has served in various offices (such as state representative, governor, or federal office), it is logical to assign separate subgroups in the collection for each office. For example, Senator Herman E. Talmadge's papers at the Richard B. Russell Library for Political Research and Studies at the University of Georgia is divided into three subgroups: pre-gubernatorial, gubernatorial, and senatorial. Series begin anew within each subgroup.

Series or Subseries by Topic

Another useful way to sort large political collections is to look for existing topical series that represent major projects or special events. Materials with strong research value that already exist as a discrete group should be identified and kept as such. The "Watergate" and "Civil Rights" series in the Talmadge papers are examples of this type of arrangement. Special investigations, hearings, and other oversight projects often generate these large quantities of materials, which may be handled as topical series, or topical subseries under series in a functional arrangement scheme.

Arrangement Schemes Within Series

Arrangements within subgroups or series should follow as much as possible the original office filing systems. Constituent correspondence and casework normally are centralized systems with either chronological or numerical filing sequences, while legislative staffs normally retain their own files arranged by subject.[12] Ideally, by the time the archival repository receives the collection, the office staff will have had an opportunity to document the types of filing systems that were used. When working with the hastily packed files of a defeated politician, however, it is quite possible to discover that the original order was not maintained. It is then time to decide whether to restore original order, create a new order, or simply use the file listings to put the series in order "on paper" by creating a searchable list. Select examples of typical arrangements within series are as follows:

By Staff Member

Staff ownership arrangement is typical of files maintained by legislative directors, administrative assistants, legislative assistants, or staff assistants, and it is almost always the case with their electronic files. If these files are not expressly identified by the individual's name, it may be possible to group files together by identifying the same handwriting on file folders, similar folder labeling styles, or repetitive filing schemes. Legislative assistants usually maintain their own files, but these materials can also be "inherited" and have multiple "owners." In this instance, files should be left with the last owner, and the series description can explain the file lineage. When working with staff preparing to transfer files from an office, it might be necessary to remind them that all documents created in a politician's office are ultimately the property of the official, regardless of who is the real originator of the work.[13] It is not false flattery to convey to staff members the significance, as documented in their files, of their own contributions to their representative's or senator's legacy.

Staff position titles can also be used as subseries headings (see figure 18.1). Titles and duties vary from office to office, and the archivist can describe the job duties in the finding aid if the scope of duties is not apparent from job title alone. If it is not clear whose files are whose, you may want to consider another arrangement option.

By Congress or Chronological Divisions

Congressional offices handle legislation and other activities in sequential periods by congressional session, and they often identify their materials with such labels as "104th Congress," or more specifically, "94th Congress, 2nd Session." A congress is a two-year period in which the U.S. Congress has the same membership, beginning with the 1st Congress, held 1789–1791. A session is "the period during which Congress assembles and carries on its regular business. By the Constitution, Congress has

Figure 18.1.   Examples of arrangement by staff member, reflecting office assignments

I. Legislative
  A. Legislative Directors' Files
    1. Karen Jones, 1984–1989
      a. Committees and Assignments & Legislative Research
      b. Legislative Mail
    2. Kathy Elliot-Green, 1989–1999
      a. Committees and Assignments
      b. Legislative Research
      c. Legislative Mail
      d. Speeches
  B. Legislative Assistants' Files
    1. Julie Acker (Labor)
    2. Penelope Hamilton (Education)
    3. Ricky Lambert (Medicaid, Medicare)
    4. Christopher Smith (Transportation)
    5. Kelly Stokes (Environment)

two regular sessions; however, the President may call Congress into special session."[14] Files may be ordered by Congress within a staff member's filing system or in other scenarios, such as a central filing system (see figure 18.2). Researchers unfamiliar with using congressional collections may need an explanation of this filing system; those familiar with it will appreciate that the original order has been maintained. It should also be noted that it is not unusual for files, especially staff files, to span more than one Congress, as legislation frequently takes years to pass and certain policy issues are ongoing concerns.

Figure 18.2.   Example of functional series arrangement, subseries by Congress, with topical sub-subseries (or folders)

I. Legislative
  A. 103rd Congress
    Agriculture
    Armed Forces
    Banking
    Defense
  B. 102nd Congress
    Agriculture
    Armed Forces
    Banking
    Defense

By Function or Format

Some series are typically grouped by functional format, including committee records, speech files, legislative research, voting records, and media files. These series may fall under subgroups reflecting broader office functions, such as "Legislative" or "Public Relations" (see figures 18.3 and 18.4). Shared office functions may also result in creation of certain file series by formats, such as schedules, research files, constituent mail, and press releases. Media, with preservation and access issues, may be segregated in a series by format, simply for collection management reasons.

Of course, any combination of the above arrangements is likely to be found in a large collection from an official who has served for many years (see figure 18.5).

Electronic Records

Electronic records processing will focus mainly on documents and e-mail transferred from office servers.[15] These electronic records and e-mails

Figure 18.3.   Example of arranging file types by function

```
 I. Legislative
    A. Committees
       1. Energy and Commerce
          Bills (file type)
          Hearings (file type)
          Research (file type)
       2. Public Works and Transportation
    B. Voting Records (file type)
```

Figure 18.4.   Example of series arrangement by functional format

```
 I. Legislative
    A. Committee files (unofficial) (functional format)
       1. Energy and Commerce
       2. Public Works and Transportation
    B. Legislative Research files (functional format)
       1. Agriculture
       2. Defense
       3. Industry
       4. Interior
    C. Voting Records (functional format)
```

Figure 18.5. Example of combination arrangement (by function > staff > file type > Congress)

I. Legislative
   A. Legislative Directors' Files
      1. Karen Jones
         a. Committees and Assignments & Legislative Research
            98th Congress
            99th Congress
         b. Legislative Mail
            98th Congress
            99th Congress
      2. Kathy Elliot-Green
         a. Committees and Assignments
         b. National Commission on AIDS
            100th Congress
            101st Congress
            102nd Congress
         c. National Commission to Prevent Infant Mortality
            100th Congress
            101st Congress

originally resided on staff and shared drives. The files may be structured or unstructured, depending on the degree to which the office implemented documents management. The arrangement of individual staff files will vary from staff person to staff person. Most processing will focus on staff drive documents and e-mails which can be processed in a manner similar to corresponding paper records, into Congresses and series, and folders (see figure 18.6). They can be described together with corresponding textual files when there are some, or as a separate series. E-mails should be taken out of the native format and converted to an acceptable permanent format such as PDF or a current common format. Their processing depends on the circumstances in which they were saved. If the individual created archive folders for e-mails with the title of the hearings, bills, or issues, the e-mails can be retained in their own folders and grouped with the electronic documents of the corresponding series. If the e-mails were not filed into folders and labeled, they can be moved into a "general e-mails" category or can be grouped into broad subject categories.

If there are too many attachments to review individually, one good strategy is to survey them to identify documents not represented elsewhere in the collection. One way to do this is to first process staff paper and electronic documents to see what exists, and then work on the e-mails.

Figure 18.6. Example of series arrangement for electronic documents and e-mails, using folders and subfolders

> 108th Congress: Files of Jane Smith, Legislative Assistant
>
> I. Legislative
>   A. Health Reform
>   1. E-mails
>   2. Statements
>   B. National Intelligence Reform Act, S. 2845
>   1. Amendments
>   2. Charts
>   3. Conference
>   4. E-mails (July to December 2004)
>   5. Markup
>   6. Memos
>   7. Research
>   C. Veterans Care
>   1. E-mails
>   2. Statements

FULL VERSUS MINIMAL PROCESSING

Mark Greene and Dennis Meissner's study "More Product, Less Process" has engendered a great deal of discussion within the archival community about current archival practices as they relate to processing large, modern collections.[16] It is a fact that congressional collections, for instance, are becoming larger, not smaller, and the growth of backlogs at repositories seems to be growing at a corollary rate. Greene and Meissner's study and conclusions are interesting, relevant, and appropriate to consider for those working with modern congressional collections. It may provide a modicum of comfort to realize that not all collections, or even all series within a single collection, need to be processed to the same level.

In some ways, the Greene-Meissner argument is not revolutionary. Many archivists were using "minimal processing techniques" before the study was published, but they called such work something else: full accessioning. Political papers archivists, for example, have long used box transfer lists and in-house container lists for access to unprocessed congressional collections. A combination of full and minimal processing and selective preservation is in fact practiced by the Center for Legislative Archives, which preserves the records of House and Senate committees. Arguably, Greene and Meissner's most welcome contribution may be in freeing archivists from the guilt that accompanied deviation from traditional full processing practices. For congressional archivists, the article's recommendations also raise the visibility of overhead and resources associated with processing congressional collections, which can be used in leveraging support from administrators and donors.

Some aspects inherent to political collections require the processing archivist to exercise judgment. For example, the presence of sensitive and confidential information is difficult to determine when minimal processing is implemented. Social Security numbers, health information, tax information, classified document status, and other confidential information may be present in likely (or unlikely) places. Archivists ought to be aware of potentially violating third-party rights in providing access to these materials. One way to deal with this problem is to identify the series that are most likely to contain them and spend more time reviewing them. Another approach is to address the issue when researchers request access to the collection by having them sign a statement wherein they agree specifically not to cite confidential information found in the collection.

Generally, three major considerations guide decisions about processing priorities:

1. *Research value.* Because political collections can be so voluminous, research value should be a primary factor in determining priorities for processing individual series. Research value can be ascertained through conversations with the donor and staff, examination of the collection inventory, and from advice obtained from historians and political scientists. Legislative materials (daily briefing material, legislative mail, nonofficial committee files, legislative assistants' files, and project files) are examples of materials that typically have high research value in congressional collections.
2. *Critical preservation needs.* If research value is the same for all materials across a particular collection, the archivist may choose to process the most fragile materials with greater detail to protective housing, allowing the sturdier, newer materials to be minimally processed. Electronic records—ironically the most fragile media of all—need to be reviewed immediately for accessibility and transferred from the original media used (for moving it to the repository) to more permanent storage, such as a digital asset management system. These records also need to be reviewed for content and arrangement, usually an item-level process, if they have not been screened for privacy and confidentiality, and adequately documented prior to donation.
3. *Arrangement needs.* If a collection or series is already in good order and materials are in good condition with no looming preservation con-

cerns, the material is a viable candidate for minimal-level processing and access to the material can be expedited.

A number of archives and manuscript repositories have started to experiment with variations in processing levels and are beginning to report back to the archival community. Tom Hyry, in "More for Less in Archives," explains how the Manuscripts and Archives Department at Yale University implemented Meissner and Greene's approach, and he describes the principles the department applied when following "minimum standards" of processing.[17] The Northwest Archives Processing Initiative, a project funded by the National Historical Publications and Records Commission (NHPRC) to investigate the use of Meissner and Greene's recommendations in processing collections at eight institutions in the Pacific Northwest, maintained a blog during the project to document their experience.[18] Much can be learned from the experiences of others in new processing endeavors.

SPECIAL CHALLENGES

Overall collection size, variety of formats, and the presence of confidential and sensitive materials interfiled in various series represent some of the special processing challenges of political papers. Some of the more interesting campaign records can be difficult to track down because they are not integral parts of a political collection but are the property of the campaign committee. Following are some suggestions to help meet these challenges.

Handling Volume

The sheer size (measured either in feet or bytes) of modern political collections can overwhelm both archival staff and researchers. Mark Greene describes the experience of using congressional collections from the researcher's perspective: "Historians and other users of congressional papers have admitted (often against their will) that the size of modern congressional collections—and especially the ever diminishing ratio between content and quantity—make them difficult and frustrating to use."[19] Frustration relating to volume, however, is not limited to the end user. Linda Whitaker, archivist in charge of processing the personal and political papers of Senator Barry M. Goldwater, succinctly states, "No one talks enough about gaining physical control. Without it, intellectual control is impossible."[20]

It is therefore advisable, and even desirable, to reduce the size of a political collection through sound methods of appraisal and sampling. Greene's "Appraisal of Congressional Records" and Rebecca Johnson Melvin's case study of appraising the papers of Senator John Williams (both of which are reproduced in this volume), as well as Paul's *Records Management Handbook*, recommend specific retention, sampling, and discard actions for record types commonly found in congressional collections. Appraisal can occur at different stages of the collection's life cycle, from pre-transfer to reevaluation after years of use (or nonuse) at the repository. Sampling of constituent mail is always in order and may also be applied to casework when a representative example of that record type is retained.

Nonpaper Formats

Political collections often include photographs, audiovisual materials, memorabilia, and increasing quantities of electronic records on various media types. It is preferable to wait until the processing stage to work on these materials, because separating anything during accessioning can destroy contextual information. Exceptions include materials with known or anticipated high research value (e.g., photographs of VIPs or video recordings of notable events) and those that are at risk of obsolescence (e.g., analog and digital media).

Electronic Records

Electronic records need to be processed upon arrival at the repository. Repositories that receive material maintained within document management systems may decide to replicate the system in order to preserve the material. New Mexico State University archivist Stephen Hussman originally decided to replicate through a cross-platform transfer to a dedicated server the 2 terabytes of Sharepoint system files donated by Senator Pete Domenici.[21] However, this proved impractical and the files were forwarded as folders and attachments. Stephen Van Buren described his experience with the papers of former Senate Majority Leader Thomas Daschle at South Dakota State University, one of the first repositories to receive substantial electronic records:

> The Daschle Collection came to us with a very large digital component, in a number of formats. These included 200+ DVDs, c. 100 CDs, c. 125 3.5" Floppies, and one 300 GB External Hard Drive. The total size of the initial back-up was a little over a Terabyte (1.12 TB). In terms of digital objects, this comes to a register count of 58,905 files and 12,622 folders. This number is misleading because there are some large files (even by our standards—600+ MB) that contain several thousand objects in a digital asset management format. The computer equipment chosen to start on this part of the collection included a stand-alone desktop PC with Microsoft Office Suite 2007. The software was part of the standard licensing for the university; other options were (and are) available as needed. Final decisions on software are still pending, as we run

into file number and size limitations. The PC has a dual-core processor, an 80 GB operating hard drive, and a 160 GB storage hard drive. The main storage is an external 2 Terabyte RAID. We have 400+ analog tapes—Cassette, VHS and Beta—to migrate to a digital format, so this capacity storage is most likely going to be cutting it close. This computer set-up is a couple of "generations" old now, and should be replaced with a faster computer with considerably more internal memory—1 Terabyte internal RAID would work nicely.

The drawbacks to the setup as we started were (a) figuring out how to run the large files through the narrow pipeline the PC offered, and (b) once they were backed up, working on them. In the beginning, it was difficult to convince folks on the receiving end of these records that the size was going to be that much of an issue; the computer that we got to do the work was pretty big, compared to the normal set-up in faculty offices. The files have since been broken down to content, subject and format groups, and copies of these are split between dedicated workstations so the overall file size is no longer that great an issue. It is still important to make sure the different workstations can interconnect as new stations are added, or old ones replaced. It doesn't work well to have a new firewire card in the computer with the RAID storage when trying to transfer data to a laptop or other workstation without one. Half an hour before my new staff started this morning, I wound up transferring large files on DVDs and a flash drive—much like trying to fill a coffee cup with a teaspoon.[22]

The Technology Best Practices Taskforce of the Society of American Archivists has compiled information about sites, handbooks, articles, case studies, and other sources designed to facilitate the management of electronic records and assets.[23] Both House and Senate archivists can share best practices currently being used for archiving electronic records of committees with the Center for Legislative Archives. The preservation of digital and digitized archival assets is an evolving science and will continue to present the greatest challenge for archival repositories specializing in political collections.

Photographs

Political collections frequently include black-and-white and color prints, negatives, slides, and framed and oversize prints (many of which are often inscribed). Offices maintain extensive image files in electronic format. Each repository will need to determine the most appropriate level of preservation, arrangement, and description to give these materials, based on staff time, expertise, and budget. An excellent source for specifics regarding optimum environmental storage conditions and best housing practices is Mary Lynn Ritzenthaler and Diane Vogt-O'Connor's *Photographs: Archival Care and Management*. Another valuable resource is the SAA's Visual Materials Section listserv.[24]

Besides photographs of the famous, political collections contain a discrete group of photographic "grip and grins" with constituents and colleagues, a series that may number in the hundreds or thousands of images. Identifying the subjects is time consuming and the research value may not warrant the effort. Sometimes volunteers or students willingly take on such projects using office visitor logs and schedules to identify individuals and groups and controlled vocabulary lists to provide access. Broad groupings, identified by topic or subject and then by decade, may also provide adequate access to images. A simple descriptive example is "Campaign, 1984."

Audiovisual Materials

Audiovisual materials are common to most political collections—news clips, radio spots, speeches, interviews, press conferences, public service announcements—and usually comprise the Press/Media series of a collection. Notable exceptions are campaign commercials, which form part of the records of the campaign committee. The most typical problems associated with them is lack of identification and obsolete formats. Consider the following while making decisions regarding preservation: Are the materials unique or can they be found elsewhere (e.g., a local or national news station)? What is the cost of preserving, migrating, and providing access to these materials, and do all three steps need to be undertaken? Appraise the materials for content, if possible, before deciding that all should uniformly be migrated or preserved. When resources are limited, only the unique or most historically valuable media materials should be reformatted to provide preservation and use copies. More information about reformatting and preservation of audiovisual materials is available through the Association of Moving Image Archivists (AMIA) and Association for Recorded Sound Collections (ARSC).[25]

Memorabilia

Most political offices are replete with framed images, plaques, and memorabilia, and such material can prove challenging for archivists to appraise and manage. Memorabilia can be documented with on-site photography or at least be inventoried by type before removal in order to facilitate disposition and appraisal. Another option for plaques is to photocopy the front of each and retain only the most valuable. For suggestions about appraisal of memorabilia, see the chapters by James Edward Cross and Jill Robin Severn in this volume.

Confidential Materials

Political collections are replete with personal and confidential information. Sometimes classified information is discovered. Casework files—

which document intervention with federal offices on behalf of constituents—regularly contain personal information. Politicians frequently site casework as particularly satisfying and consider it an important part of their duties, though they often decline to transfer those records with the rest of their papers.[26] When casework is included in a congressional collection, the deed of gift or deposit agreement should clearly spell out the restrictions that govern access to such material. It is imperative that processing archivists be able to identify such material so that it remains restricted until such time as it can be released. For guidelines on how to handle sensitive and classified information, refer to Paul's *Records Management Handbook* and her chapter in part II of this volume.

CAMPAIGN FILES

While campaign records are viewed as a significant part of a political collection, it is important to remember that they are not part of the "official" personal papers of a member of Congress. Federal campaign laws require clear separation of funds and activities, so campaign records technically belong to the candidate's campaign committee. It therefore may be necessary to seek them out before they are scattered after an election. The evolution of campaigning, from stump speeches to Internet blogs, can be traced in the files of political campaigns. Campaign speeches document local and national issues. Political consultants hired by the candidates create significant issue briefs, voter analysis reports, and campaign polls. Campaign records can include a bit of everything: colorful campaign ephemera, speeches, strategy files, memorabilia, mailers, polls, and audiovisual materials. However, the biggest challenge may be acquiring the campaign records as a comprehensive collection. This should be done as soon as possible after an election, especially from those who lose. For incumbents, it is advisable to communicate your desire to receive the material prior to the campaign. The material contained within the files is well worth the effort to pursue it, for it will provide rich documentation of the election issues, the history of campaigning in its time, and what makes a winning strategy.

CONCLUSION

Daunting as they can be, contemporary political papers collections season archivists by providing experience with a spectrum of archival management issues. Bringing archival control to a large, complex congressional collection is a significant professional accomplishment. Voluminous and complex in arrangement, replete with sensitive and sometimes classified information, and more recently, full of electronic records from varying systems—these collections can be challenging to administer and expensive to process. By consulting with other congressional papers archivists, becoming knowledgeable about the legislative process and the history of Congress, reviewing pertinent archival literature, and comparing finding aids for collections from the same period, political papers archivists can prepare for the task. This chapter reviews several arrangement strategies, record types, and relevant processing issues to help the archivist successfully work with political papers. The goal is to help expedite access for a growing number of political scientists, historians, and scholars who are eager and ready to use these fascinating collections.

NOTES

1. Archivists' Toolkit Project, "The Archivists' Toolkit," http://archiviststoolkit .org; University of Illinois, "Archon: The Simple Archival Information System," www.archon.org.

2. Richard Pearce-Moses, *A Glossary of Archival and Records Terminology* (Chicago: Society of American Archivists, 2005), see the entry "Deed of Gift." Also available online at www.archivists.org/glossary/index.asp.

3. "Biographical Directory of the United States Congress, 1774–Present," http:// bioguide.congress.gov/biosearch/biosearch.asp.

4. Faye Phillips, *Congressional Papers Management* (Jefferson, NC: McFarland, 1996).

5. Pearce-Moses, *Glossary*, "Accession Number."

6. Art & Architecture Thesaurus Online, www.getty.edu/research/conducting_ research/vocabularies/aat/.

7. U.S. House of Representatives, Office of the Clerk, "House History," http:// clerk.house.gov/art_history/house_history/index.html.

8. Pearce-Moses, *Glossary*, "Processing."

9. T. R. Schellenberg, "Archival Principles of Arrangement," in *A Modern Archives Reader: Basic Readings on Archival Theory and Practice*, ed. Maygene F. Daniels and Timothy Walch (Washington, D.C.: National Archives and Records Service, 1984), 149.

10. Patricia Aronsson, "Appraisal of Twentieth-Century Congressional Collections," in *Archival Choices: Managing the Historical Record in an Age of Abundance*, ed. Nancy E. Peace (Lexington, Mass.: Lexington Books, 1984), 81.

11. Karen Dawley Paul, *Records Management Handbook for United States Senators and Their Archival Repositories*, S. Pub. 109-19 (Washington, D.C.: Government Printing Office, 2006), inside front cover, 7–8.

12. Central filing systems are discussed in Phillips, *Congressional Papers Management*.

13. Paul, *Records Management Handbook*, 7.

14. "Kids in the House," Office of the Clerk, U.S. House of Representatives, http://clerkkids.house.gov.

15. This advice is supplied by Elisabeth Butler, archivist of the U.S. Senate Homeland Security and Governmental Affairs Committee, who has been processing electronic records successfully for four years. E-mail to Karen Dawley Paul, August 14, 2008.

16. Numerous articles and publications document the large size of modern congressional collections. See Greene and Meissner's notes (10) for the major articles discussing the growing size of collections in Mark A. Greene and Dennis Meissner, "More Product, Less Process: Revamping Traditional Archival Processing," *American Archivist* 68, no. 2 (2005): 211. As far back as 1978, Lydia Lucas noted, "It has by now become a truism that modern congressional collections are massive." See Lydia Lucas, "Managing Congressional Papers: A Repository View," *American Archivist* 41, no. 3 (1978): 276. Lucas provides sound advice for managing and evaluating large collections and offers feasible options for addressing collection size today, 30 years later.

17. Tom Hyry, "More for Less in Archives, *Annotation* 33, no. 2 (2007), www.archives.gov/nhprc/annotation.

18. "Northwest Archives Processing Initiative: A Rasmuson Library Archives Blog," http://library.uaf.edu/blogs/nwapi/.

19. Mark Greene, "Appraisal of Congressional Records," *Archival Issues* 19, no. 1 (1994): 33.

20. Linda Whitaker, "Progress Notes, Report #1," Arizona Historical Foundation, www.ahfweb.org/collections/goldwaterprogress.htm.

21. Stephen Hussman, e-mail to Karen Dawley Paul, December 4, 2008.

22. Stephen Van Buren, e-mail to Karen Dawley Paul, November 26, 2008.

23. "Managing Electronic Records and Assets: A Bibliography," www.aechivists.org/saagroups/bptf/mera-digcoll.asp.

24. Mary Lynn Ritzenthaler and Diane Vogt-O'Connor, *Photographs: Archival Care and Management* (Chicago: Society of American Archivists, 2006). Information about the Visual Materials listserv (VisualMat) can be found on SAA's Web site, www.archivists.org.

25. Association of Moving Image Archivists, www.amianet.org; Association for Recorded Sound Collections, www.arsc-audio.org.

26. One longtime member of the U.S. Senate remarked the following about casework: "Nothing satisfies me more than to be able to help cut through the red tape and take care of the problem. . . . Suffice it to say that service in the U.S. Senate has many dimensions and one of the more significant is serving as an 'ombudsman' for people who are dealing with the federal government." From the Re-elect Senator Mark Hatfield Committee, 1984, Campaign Series, Mark O. Hatfield Papers, Archives and Special Collections, Willamette University, Salem, Oregon.

19

Describing Congressional Papers Collections: A Progression of Access Tools

L. Rebecca Johnson Melvin and Karyl Winn

As a specific archival record type, congressional collections lend themselves to model descriptive practices across an array of traditional and emerging access tools, from old-fashioned summary guides to current standards of Encoded Archival Description (EAD). It is a priority of the Advisory Committee on the Records of Congress to improve access to congressional information and documentation, including advocating better management and preservation of personal papers of members of Congress.[1] Because congressional collections are so geographically dispersed, these diverse access tools—especially those available online with useful details about the collection contents—assume a greater significance in helping distant users plan effective research strategies. Recent congressional historians have called for both online access and greater descriptive detail of collection contents.[2] These ideals are appreciated by archivists who wish to provide best access to their institutional sources. But in fact, the ideals prove difficult to realize, given the practicalities of applying in-depth attention to what may be but one collection of many in an institution's processing backlog, which grows incrementally as it absorbs records of modern times and personal papers of contemporary lives.

But congressional collections afford archivists varied descriptive practices and access tools with which to satisfy congressional historians and other interested parties. As typically large, hierarchically complex archival collections, the compound series structure in congressional papers is subject to creative decisions about "granularity of description" in choosing the level of information desired for the type of material being described, the type of tool being used, and the audience being targeted.

Congressional collections also lend themselves to critical consideration of the integral relationship between arrangement decisions and description tools, and to management decisions about application of the scaled-back processing model proposed by Mark Greene and Dennis Meissner. Both Greene and Meissner had considerable experience with processing congressional collections at the Minnesota Historical Society.[3] And there are several references to congressional collections in their groundbreaking article "More Product, Less Process."[4] It is useful to be aware of varied institutional processing models and existing exemplary access tools when making decisions about levels of description for congressional collections.

There is a full progression of access tools to use in managing congressional collections that may be matched to select audiences, from in-house or behind-the-scenes users to the public. Preliminary box/container lists help congressional staff prepare records for transfer. On the receiving end, these lists, with additional administrative details, expand into accession records to establish repository control. One application of the Greene-Meissner goal of more rapid access to collection descriptions is simply to advance these in-house accession records for public viewing, pending fuller descriptions that may be completed with more thorough collection processing. Outside users include the traditional scholarly researchers, the repository's institutional staff and administrators, and donors and their political peers, all of whom are interested in different levels of information about the collection.

Archival description is an abstracting process whereby narrative and inventorying information is derived from the collection itself. Put simply, archival description aims to tell what is in a collection and where to find it. Both pieces of information may be provided in greater or lesser detail. Using traditional printed publications or more innovative electronic delivery of the information, archivists can create multiple description/access tools to suit varied audiences. The level of description may be tailored to needs of the different users: the scholar may be interested in rich scope notes that highlight research potential of selected series, or the institution may be more interested in "splash" Web pages to profile and promote institutional research strengths across several collections, as at the Arizona Historical Foundation (see figure 19.1).

The level of narrative detail also may correspond to specificity of locational information found with the tool; that is, a collection-level description from an online catalog will provide some sort of call number for a collection, or a detailed finding aid may present item- or folder-level description with exact box and folder number required for physical retrieval of relevant sources.

Access tools may be considered in a progression that reflects managerial stages: accession lists, finding aids for processed collections, collection-level abstracts for online catalogs or institutional subject guides, summary guides for promotion, brochures for publicity, exhibitions for outreach, and reporting at the national level. These access tools are described in the sections that follow, with finding aids covered in greater detail at the end of the chapter.

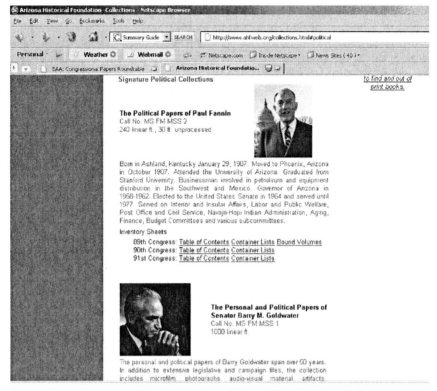

Figure 19.1. Signature political collections, Arizona Historical Foundation

ACCESSION LISTS

From the earliest stages of transfer and survey, preliminary container lists emerge as important description and access tools. If the repository is lucky, it has developed a working relationship with the member of Congress to plan for a collection transfer and inherited a printed box contents list from staff in the congressional office for all materials being shipped to the repository. Even luckier is the repository that receives an electronic version of that list.[5] That box list may have been prepared when papers were sent to storage or by office staff just before the papers are shipped to the repository. The repository archivist should encourage congressional office staff to create such lists and also ask for an opportunity to participate in inventorying files still in staff offices. The opportunity to gather information about staff members' areas of responsibility and the records they create and manage is invaluable. Even lacking a listing of each file in a record-center carton, an archivist can plan processing much more intelligently from a general notion of box content. In the unlucky situation of having no packing lists from the office, a repository should construct a simple one from its own cursory box review, or from building on box labels which are sometimes marked by office staff who lacked time to prepare a list as well.

A general overview of the papers, written shortly after the collection reaches the repository, together with an outline of subgroups, series, and subseries, can shape future processing. A survey of the preliminary box contents lists will help the archivist gain intellectual control over the collection with this series outline, develop a processing plan, and make "easy" appraisal decisions (such as quick disposal of duplicate press releases, excess publications, or some administrative files).[6] The survey stage will also be the point at which to apply the Greene-Meissner "less process" decisions to selected series in the processing plan. For example, a speech series may be deemed "high research value," warranting item-level listing for specific retrieval of topically or chronologically relevant information. On the other hand, subject clipping files may be considered "medium value." They are worth keeping but only merit upper-level description and minimal arrangement and preservation to suit expected "browsing" use for background on a legislative issue.

BUILDING FROM THE CHIEF SOURCE OF INFORMATION

The primary archival description tool, the finding aid, is the fundamental and chief source of information from which all other collection description is derived.[7] The well-planned series outline from the survey stage will expand "downward" with more detail to become the fully developed finding aid, which supplies standard descriptive elements at all levels. Since the mid-1980s, the dual influences of bibliographic descriptive standards and library automation have driven advances in archival description toward consistency in use of core elements and delivery of the description information.[8] The basic elements are the following: locational information, title, date span, extent, and scope note (with authoritative forms of names, places, subjects). Used consistently, these core elements may also be presented "upward" across the array of access tools, from folder-level entries to series-level summaries to collection-level records, as with these sample entries from the Thomas R. Carper congressional papers at the University of Delaware Library:

Sample folder-level entries:
Series I.C.2. Issue Files—Amtrak, 1988–1992

Box 28   F35   Amtrak Safety, Training, and Employee Morale, 1991
               F36   City of Wilmington Acquisition of Amtrak Property, 1992

Sample series note:
Series I.C.2. Issue Files—Amtrak, 1988–1992 (.75 linear ft.)
Box 28
Contents: Correspondence, memoranda, meeting notes, floor statements, testimonies, news clippings, and reports.

Arrangement: Alphabetically by topic and chronologically within. Most file contents were maintained in reverse chronological order and this placement has been retained.

Description: The majority of the Amtrak files deal with conflicts between upper management and railroad worker unions over the four year period of 1988–1992. Major matters in the disputes involved wages, health and welfare issues, and possible changes to work environment regulations. Due to Wilmington's position as a major repair yard and travel station along the "northeast corridor" for railroad travel and movement of goods, Congressman Carper maintained a strong interest in resolutions benefiting both Amtrak and labor. As a result, the files contain a significant body of literature pertaining to this topic, and deal with it on the local, state, and national levels. . . .

Table 19.1.   Sample Collection-Level MARC Record for Delaware's Online Catalog

Format	\<Archive/MSS\> | Internet Resource | Mixed Material
Author	Carper, Thomas R., 1947–
Title	Thomas R. Carper congressional papers, 1979–1993, (bulk dates 1982–1992).
Descr.	84 linear ft. and oversize material.
Arrangement	Organized into three subgroups: I. Official work files, 1983–1992. II. Administrative files, 1979–1992. III. Personal files, 1982–1992.
Location	Special Collections | MSS 399
URL	http://www.lib.udel.edu/ud/spec/findaids/carper/index.htm
Lim. Use	The collection is open for research.
Abstract	Congressional papers of Thomas R. Carper from five terms in U.S. House of Representatives. Includes personal files, committee work, issue files, regional issue files, constituent correspondence, trips, voting records, publications, office administration, communications, campaign records, 1982–1992, photographs, audio-visual materials, and ephemera.
Biog./Hist. Note	U.S. Representative from Delaware, 1983–1992. Born in Beckley, West Virginia, 1947. Graduated from Ohio State University in 1968 with a bachelor of arts in economics. Served as a flight officer in the U.S. Navy, 1968–1973. Attended the University of Delaware earning a master's degree in business administration in 1975. Elected state treasurer in 1976, re-elected in 1978 and 1980. In 1982, elected to Delaware's lone seat in the U.S. House of Representatives. While serving in the House, he worked on transportation, banking, financial, and environmental issues, among others. After five terms, Carper was elected governor of Delaware in 1992.
Per.Sub.	Carper, Thomas R., 1947–
Cor.Sub.	United States. Congress. House—History—Sources. United States Congress. House—Biography.
Subject	Delaware—Politics and government—1951– United States—Politics and government—1945–1989—Sources.

Perhaps more than other archival collections, congressional papers are described via a wider range of access tools, especially those abstracted at the upper levels of description. There are three main reasons for this. The contemporary (mid-twentieth-century and later) collections are large and complex, and the layered access tools support much needed navigation through the sources. But institutions that invest resources in acquiring and processing these collections are interested in touting them as assets, hence a need for promotion and publicity beyond basic reference services provided through these tools. Finally, donors and their political peers live public lives with a tolerance—if not expectation—of media coverage; donors often expect a published guide or public exhibition featuring the archival collection as testament to their public service and political career.

Within the finding aid, there are summary series outlines, expanded series outlines, and series scope notes that serve repository staff and scholars who need to navigate a collection to discover its research strengths. The summary series outline acts as a table of contents and provides a logical overview of the collection. Figure 19.2 shows the outline from the Silvio O. Conte congressional papers at the University of Massachusetts Amherst.

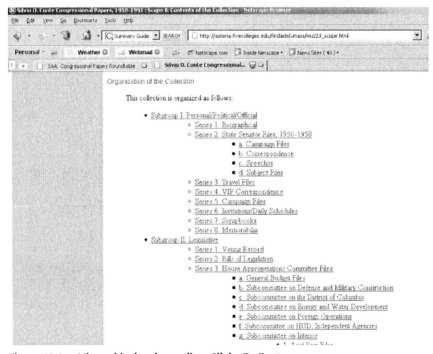

Figure 19.2.   Hierarchical series outline, Silvio O. Conte papers.

The expanded summary series outline adds details such as date span, extent, and brief scope notes that will allow the researcher to assess how much material is available and what use it might be for their information needs. The following series notes are from the expanded series outline of the William S. Cohen papers at the University of Maine:

---

1. Private Papers, 1956–1996, 33.5 cu. ft. boxes
The bulk of Cohen's private papers consist of records related to writing, Cohen's major avocation. Drafts of his poetry and manuscripts from the nine books he has written are included here, and they attest to Cohen's avid interest in writing poetry, fiction, and accounts of his own experience in Congress. The papers also document several aspects of Cohen's life and career before he entered the U.S. Congress in 1973. They include his yearbooks from Bowdoin College, where he received his A.B. cum laude in Latin in 1962, correspondence with his colleagues in the American Trial Lawyer Association, and material related to the JFK Institute of Politics where Cohen was a fellow in 1972.

2. U.S. House of Representatives Papers, 1972–1980, 211.5 cu. ft. boxes
This record group consists of the files that were created by Cohen and his staff in the course of Cohen's duties as a member of the U.S. House of Representatives from 1973 to 1979. They document the five major functional areas of a congressional office: a) personal/political/official, b) legislative, c) constituent services, d) press/media activities, and e) office administration. Each of these five functional areas contains records which form a series.

The series scope notes appear just before the box list and supply greater information, as with this description for voting records in the Silvio Conte papers, allowing the researcher to understand in more depth what may be found in this part of the collection:

SUBGROUP II: LEGISLATIVE
Series 1: Voting Record, 1959–1991, 2 boxes, 2.5 linear ft.
The Voting Record contains printed summaries of Conte's votes in Congress. In addition to the record supplied each member by the House Clerk, this series also includes vote analyses supplied by special interest organizations such as the Americans for Democratic Action (ADA), Brotherhood of Railroad Trainmen, and the Farmer's Union. From the 86th to 89th Congresses there are charts comparing Conte's vote with the votes of House and Senate leadership and the GOP; and from the 87th to 91st Congresses there are useful summaries that provide a synopsis of the bill's intent and the rationale for Conte's vote.

Beginning with the 99th and continuing through to the 102nd Congress, the more voluminous clerk-produced "Legislative Activity Guides" replace the smaller Roll Calls. To supplement these guides there are "Legi-Slate" reports for the 98th and 99th Congresses. These reports were obtained for members by the Congressional Research Service using a commercial online database and are simply a compilation of all votes by the congressman for that particular session, with a short explanation of the bill.

Box 30   SOC's Voting Record 1959–1966
86th–89th Congresses, Votes Charted by Issue (2 folders) 1959–1966
86th–91st Congresses, Attendance Record 1959–1970
86th Congress 1st and 2nd Session 1959–1960
87th Congress (4 folders)

Within the finding aid, the level of detail will expand, as needed, to provide inventory-like information below the series level, either at the box/folder or even item level, or perhaps only at the box or box range level, as suggested by Greene-Meissner.

SUMMARY GUIDES

Abstracted "upward," external to the finding aid, the summary series outline, expanded series outline, and series scope notes are typically the backbone of published summary guides, which formally describe the collection as a significant institutional resource. It is a common practice, for example, for member directors of the Association of Research Libraries to distribute these publications to their peers and others, announcing completion of a big project and the availability of a new congressional collection as a major scholarly resource.

In an academic setting, the published guide prompts institutional administrators to heed the library/repository's accomplishment in providing access to a new resource, and it draws them into a partnership in promoting the collection. In spite of Internet access to a full version of the finding aid, the published summary guide, a bona fide work in print, holds its own place as a physical object that can concretely publicize the collection. Features of the published guide are an expanded biographical narrative, an extended scope and content note for the collection, and ample use of photographs, documents, and other intriguing illustrations such as political cartoons. In this way, the summary guide immensely appeals to the donor and his or her family. They, and the donor's political peers, will sense that the repository has written "a book" with an appreciation of what the congressperson's public service was all about. Additionally, the published guide, once distributed, becomes a "real book," cataloged with its own bibliographic description to increase subject access to the congressional collection.

Now available in a Web version, *The Frank Church Papers: A Summary Guide* was first published in 1988 with an introduction by the president

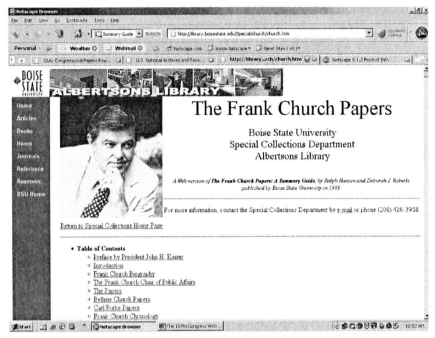

Figure 19.3.   Online version of the Frank Church Papers: A Summary Guide

of Boise State University (see figure 19.3). Though the Web version now reaches an unlimited audience, the print version is still a fine vehicle for publicizing the collection and Boise State's support for it.

SUBJECT GUIDES

Equally important to institutions are collecting profiles and subject guides that highlight congressional resources. The Association of Centers for the Study of Congress, established in 2003, advocates concentrated congressional collections such as those in the Baylor Collections of Political Materials in Texas highlighted in figure 19.4. The University of Delaware Library highlights its congressional papers collections by including them in a broad subject guide for sources related to political and government (see figure 19.5).

EXHIBITIONS

Exhibitions serve much the same purpose as subject guides, though with greater interpretive license than the straightforward objectivity that should

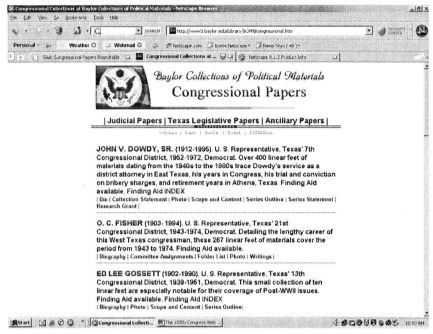

Figure 19.4. Congressional collections focus, Baylor University

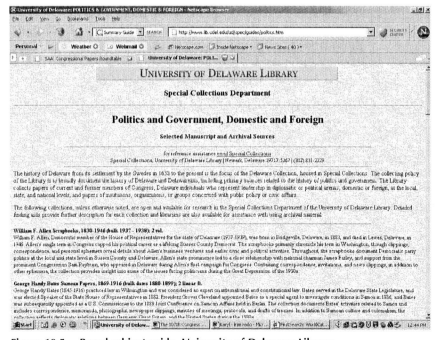

Figure 19.5. Broad subject guide, University of Delaware Library

be the goal of the collection description in the published guides and finding aids. Public exhibitions, especially those with catalogs, again reflect institutional commitments and recognition of the congressional collection as an important resource and asset. Audiences for exhibits include donors and their families, the scholarly community, the general public (especially the constituency represented by the member), and even the professional peers in archives, libraries, and museums who are interested in how these collections are described and promoted. The challenges, as for all archival exhibitions, will be to balance the textual appeal with the visual appeal of the items on display, and to balance the self-evidence of the exhibited items with descriptive text in the accompanying labels.

The age of the Internet provides not only distant but also enduring access to online exhibitions. Whether derived from a gallery exhibition or "born digital," online exhibitions, digital collections, or illustrated finding aids are all significant access tools that help researchers discover a collection via the World Wide Web. The University of Arizona Library mounted one of the earliest congressional papers exhibits on the Web, using first photographs and later documents to introduce the Morris Udall papers (see figure 19.6).

Levels of description, again, are important in planning online delivery and selecting automation systems, but availability of such online collection

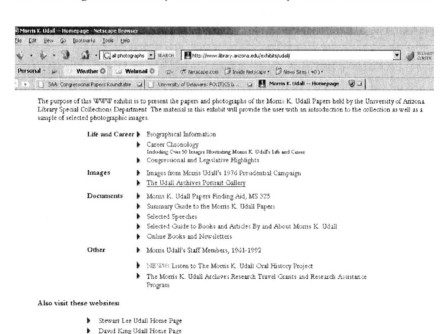

Figure 19.6. Online access to digitized content and collection description, Morris Udall papers, University of Arizona Library

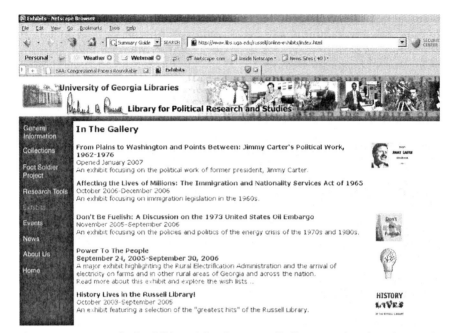

Figure 19.7.   Record of exhibits, Richard B. Russell Library, University of Georgia Libraries

information should not be underestimated for the impression it may make on donors that the institution is "up to date" and using latest technologies to promote a collection. The Richard B. Russell Library at the University of Georgia Libraries makes a strong outreach statement through online information about the record of exhibits shown in its gallery (see figure 19.7).

BRIEF NOTES AND NEWS

Ironically, one of the most traditional, brief, and comparatively economical access tools is the old-fashioned trifold brochure. Cost-effective and easily distributed, a brochure typically includes a short biographical profile and career statement, highlights of the collection, good (preferably professional) graphic design with well-chosen illustrations, and most importantly, institutional contact information. Related to brochures are bookmarks and postcards, which may be considered minimalist access tools. Often produced to promote exhibitions, lectures, or other outreach programs, the bookmarks and postcards still provide limited descriptive information such as collection title and date span, along with institutional contact information.

Such abbreviated tools may have an online version, too, in collection "splash pages" such as the one shown in figure 19.8 for the George J. Mitch-

Figure 19.8.   Collection "splash page," Bowdoin College

ell papers at Bowdoin College, briefly noting events, exhibits, or availability on the Web. Whether in print or digitally presented, these bookmarks, post-cards, and brochures will be most effective when their announcements and information are featured through expert graphic design.

Archivists should not forget another traditional access tool: the time-hon-ored institutional press release that announces the availability of a major new collection and completion of a processing project. Published summary guides are by no means routine, in which case notice of completed projects can be spread by distributing press releases to professional publications and newsletters, such as *C&RL News*, the *Congressional Papers Roundtable Newsletter* and *Manuscripts Repositories Section Newsletter* (both of the Society of American Archivists), electronic listservs, and other news outlets. (See figure 19.9.)

REPORTING AT THE NATIONAL LEVEL

The standards in archival description were driven by the introduction of Archives, Personal Papers, and Manuscripts (APPM) to generate machine-readable cataloging records using information derived from finding aids. The goal was to contribute collection-level records for archives, integrating

« Return to News Article

Traveling Exhibit Highlights Cohen in Congress

July 20, 2006
Contact: Paige Lilly, (207) 581-2665 / paige.lilly@umit.maine.edu

ORONO -- With the mid-term elections only months away, critics of Congress seem to be everywhere. But how well do they (or we) understand how Congress really works?

A new exhibit from the William S. Cohen Papers at the Raymond H. Fogler Library seeks to shed light on how Congress is designed to work and what politicians actually do on a day to day basis in Washington.

Titled "Cohen, Congress and Controversy: Rediscovering civics in the archives," the six-panel exhibit uses facsimiles of photographs, handwritten notes, speeches and campaign memorabilia from the former congressman's political papers to bring the legislative branch into focus. Topics include Bill Cohen's successful 1972 bid for Maine's second congressional district seat; the powers of Congress granted by the Constitution; the busy life of a senator, using Cohen's book about his first year there; and the oversight role of Congress, illustrated with documents from the Watergate and Iran-Contra investigations.

The freestanding exhibit includes interactive panels designed to appeal to young children.

"The Cohen Papers are open for research," says Fogler Library Dean Joyce Rumery. "This traveling exhibit invites people all across Maine to glimpse the richness of the collection."

Secretary Cohen donated his political papers, 1,500 boxes of documents and photographs, to Fogler Library at the University of Maine in 1996. He added a selection of Department of Defense material on 16 compact disks in 2001. The University of Maine is also home to the William S. Cohen Center for International Policy and Commerce.

The exhibit will travel to venues along the route of Cohen's 1972 campaign walk from the New Hampshire border to Fort Kent. The first venue is the Bethel Historical Society, beginning July 25. The exhibit moves to the Wilton Free Public Library in early September and the Lewiston Public Library in late October.

Figure 19.9. Press release, University of Maine

these descriptions with those for print and other source material in online public access catalogs (OPACs). Such automated schemes enabled collection-level reporting practices to move from the printed National Union Catalog of Manuscript Collections (NUCMC) volumes to national bibliographic databases such as the Online Computer Library Center (OCLC) and the Research Libraries Information Network (RLIN).

As with other topically significant primary sources, congressional collections also have been described through published guides with national coverage of repository holdings: *Guide to Research Collections of Former United States Senators* (first published in 1983) and *Guide to Research Collections of Former Members of the U.S. House of Representatives* (1988). As the House and the Senate have built online reference sources, they have moved important print sources to their Web sites, notably the *Biographical Directory of the United States Congress*. The *Biographical Directory* includes locational information for primary source material, which is derived from the old printed guides to the numerous research collections of congressional papers scattered around the country. The results of a query about resources for Senator John Williams, for example, included citations to several small caches in addition to reporting the primary location for his personal papers at the University of Delaware Library (see figure 19.10).

In 1995, a relatively early date in the history of Internet sources, a Congressional Papers Roundtable project established Congressional Collections at Archival Repositories, a Web site hosted by the University of Delaware Library, to serve as a subject gateway to libraries and archives with any level

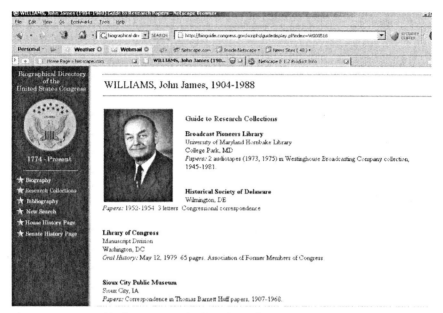

Figure 19.10.   Archival resources via the *Biographical Directory of the United States Congress*

of online information about congressional collections. Seeking greater national visibility, the site was moved and enhanced at the Center for Legislative Archives (CLA) at the National Archives and Records Administration (NARA) in 2003.[9] (See figure 19.11.)

Lacking a true national union catalog for archival collection descriptions, which might be searched by "congressional collections" as a genre/record type (with advanced Boolean search terms), there is still need for this subject-focused guide to archival repositories with congressional collections.[10] There is potential for even more growth and sophisticated searching in this direction. One possibility would be to continue building collection data as collected for the guides and the CLA site, and to contribute it to the popular and useful online *Biographical Directory of the United States Congress*. The authoritative biographical entries from the *Biographical Directory* would support an exemplary Encoded Archival Context (EAC) application, providing links to EAD records for research collections around the country, such as the EAD record for the Silvio Conte Papers from the University of Massachusetts, Amherst, available from the Five Colleges consortial database (see figure 19.12).

A sophisticated central search engine could then exploit a rich data bank providing access to dispersed archival sources. Lacking an opportunity to develop this feature through the *Biographical Directory*, another possibility would be to seek funding for a separate national subject database for

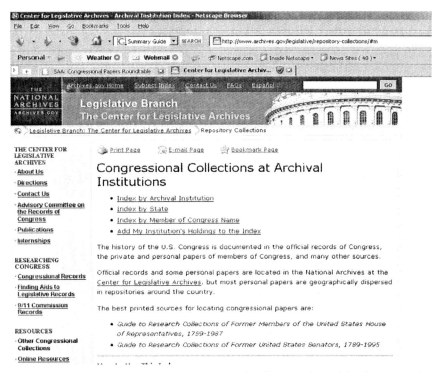

Figure 19.11. Online gateway to congressional collections hosted by the Center for Legislative Archives

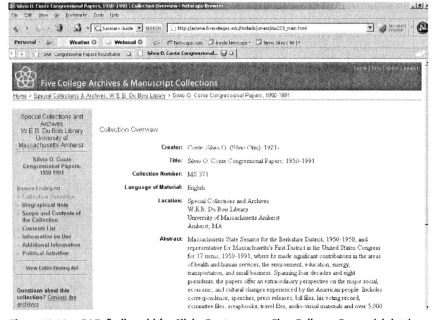

Figure 19.12. EAD finding aid for Silvio Conte papers, Five Colleges Consortial database

congressional collections.[11] In both cases, national standards for EAC and EAD should be used, allowing collection-level records with authoritative context to connect to expanded finding aid descriptions (when available).

THE DETAILED FINDING AID

A finding aid is a road map to the content of papers and records. In such political papers as those from twentieth-century (and later) members of Congress, the finding aid is an essential tool for navigating large collections. Both repository staff and researchers rely on the tool to find and access relevant content. In the case of staff, the search may be in the course of reference service or it may occur much earlier, as described above, during the accessioning and preparation for processing of the papers. As the survey stage and processing plan develops, the finding aid will mature from a preliminary box list to a more structured access tool, flexing in detail in accord with practices advised by Greene and Meissner. The finding aid discussed here suits congressional papers, relating description practices to identification and arrangement trends for congressional records that have evolved since the mid-1980s.[12]

The detailed finding aid will evolve from the archivist's work at the repository in arranging the papers or records. Its complexity and "granularity of description" will depend on how fully the materials are processed. The archivist may take the trouble to clarify and expand file folder headings in some series. Legislative issue files, for example, may be labeled during processing with fuller phrases than the cryptic titles used by the office staff who were more familiar with immediate contents and context for files in the series. Bill numbers also may be added to folder headings during processing. Such indications of content help reference staff and users assess whether a folder is relevant. If it is not, the box need not be subjected to unnecessary handling, and the researcher need not waste precious research time. To the benefit of institutions, which now commonly resort to off-site storage of large archival collections, unnecessary retrieval of irrelevant boxes is especially beneficial.

On the other hand, browsing and serendipity will always be a part of archival research. Some folders will consist of miscellaneous content, such as "Incoming Letters—A," within a similarly general correspondence series. Impossible to amplify, such a heading stands as is and will not merit more time or trouble to identify and describe contents, other than a general scope note about the nature of correspondence applied at the series level. So also may be treated a file titled "Newsletters, 1962." Other realities, such as limited funds for processing, may result in cursory box ranges for record types grouped in series such as "Box 75–79: Audio tapes, ca. 1979–1988" or "Box 62–74: News clippings, 1978–1988." Pending closer identification and appraisal review, such description will work for a minimal access level, as with the general control provided for photographs in the Morris Udall finding aid, as shown in figure 19.13.

Well-written narrative sections of the finding aid, particularly the scope and content notes at multiple layers, will compensate for such generic listings. The introductory biographical note also has an important role. It need not devote great detail to parts of the official's life not documented or only marginally documented in the papers; for example, the person's early life may not be represented in the collection at all. Besides a career summary, the biographical note should emphasize events and positions for existing papers in the collection, providing context to help the user from overlooking these materials. Political material for an aborted campaign, for example, may make more sense to the user if the biography mentions the campaign issues and lists opponents' names. Service on committees and other bodies should note

Morris K. Udall -- A Lifetime of Service
to Arizona and the United States
MORRIS K. UDALL FINDING AID

Photographs, 1956-1990

Boxes 735-746 (12 boxes)

Arranged chronologically or by topic.

Contains black and white, and some color, photographs, contact sheets, transparencies, and negatives. Most photographs are unidentified and undated and were sorted into chronological order. The bulk relate to MKU's activities as a congressman and document bill signings, political campaigns, trips, speeches, openings, and meetings. Subjects of the pictures include John F. Kennedy, Lyndon Johnson, Richard Nixon, members of the Arizona congressional delegation, and Arizona citizens. There are some photographs of the Udall family members.

Box 735 Udall Photographs

Family Photographs-*1900-1990*

- 1 1900-1920
- 2 1930
- 3 1940
- 4 Family Photograph Album, ca. 1942
- 5 1950
- 6 1960
- 7 1970
- 8-9 1980
- 10 Photographs 1987, St. John's
- 11 Mo and Norma's Wedding, Washington DC, 1990

Figure 19.13.   General description and control in the Photographs series, Morris Udall papers, University of Arizona Library

the person's role, if significant, and describe legislation, investigations, or other issues reflected in the papers. Congressional collections are as much, if not more, about a member's public service and work in Congress. In many cases, there is very little about personal experiences and relationships to be found in these collections. Consequently, the biographical note may be closer in form to an introductory historical note, describing important social, cultural, and political events that transpired during the member's terms in office, in the context of what may be found in the collection. Supplementary appendices, such as names of key staff members with their areas of responsibility, the member's committee assignments, names of congressional and party leaders during the member's terms, congressional session dates, and so forth, may be very useful reference aids for staff and researchers alike.

The introductory scope and content note will present, up front, the core description elements for the collection: title, date span (with bulk dates), and total size of the collection. The first paragraph of the scope and content note presents a perennial challenge to the archivist: it should be a succinctly written abstract that may be extracted and carried forward for use in other access tools, such as the 520 field in a collection-level MARC record, or the summary scope "blurb" that will appear in a press release. The introductory paragraph in a scope note should establish the nature of the collection and its research strengths: it should state who, what, where, why, and when, as well as what type of material and how much is available for anyone to explore. It is a professional accomplishment to construct such a tight descriptive statement in the first paragraph of the scope note, but a well-crafted few sentences will migrate successfully across several access tools.

Though EAD prompts a specific arrangement statement elsewhere in the finding aid, identification of the major subgroups and series in the collection immediately after the first paragraph will establish the "road map" role of this narrative section. Stating the structure of the papers may be superfluous to the inventory in a short finding aid, but such elaboration can be immensely helpful in a long one, which is routinely the case for congressional collections. It is the discussion of content, however, which should provide background not readily apparent in listings "further down" in the inventory.

The size and complex arrangement of congressional collections supports the usefulness of scope and content notes at multiple layers, from the introductory narrative down to scope notes available at the series level. The series structure outlined in the introduction will include highlights and research strengths, substantial groups of material, and may also indicate missing materials the user might have expected to find in the collection.

Though office technology and changes in administrative infrastructure have enormously affected the records management practices in congressional offices since the mid-1980s, the functions and services of the member in office still drive the identification, arrangement, and description of the papers.

Congressional papers produced since the late 1980s may not be organized as neatly as they were in times before the use of personal computers by staff assistants, when offices had larger staffs, and when central filing systems were observed. Archival processors establishing minimal control may use box lists as found, often a jumble of unclear folder titles under a subject heading. Much of the documentation on the congressional office's operations may consist of the same or similar materials as that produced decades ago. What functions the files represent, however, may be hard to recognize simply from the box lists. If the boxed-up staff assistant files emerge as a series (more by provenance relating to the individual staffer than by functions shared with other staff members), this situation calls for more definition and explanation at the series level in the finding aid. The contributions of congressional staff members are remarkable and significant in the public record of any member of Congress, and the processing archivist needs to make appropriate arrangement and description decisions to preserve the context of the staff members' working files within the greater context of the member's papers.

In spite of dispersed functions and responsibilities across paper and electronic files generated by multiple staff members, the five major record types by activities in congressional offices remain these: legislative; constituent services; press relations/media activities; office administration; and personal/political/official records. These functional activities often drive the arrangement and description schemes in congressional collections at the subgroup and series level.[13] (See figure 19.14.)

Legislative Records

Legislation is a major functional category. It may consist of one or several series or subseries. Listing these components and describing what each includes is imperative. "Bill files" usually consist of bills and resolutions sponsored or co-sponsored by the member, but such related information as correspondence, articles, drafts, related bills, and press releases may be included. Briefing books put together for floor activity, committee hearings, or other legislative discussions are especially significant and useful to researchers as they document full stories about the topical issues addressed in the legislation. The nature of these supporting documents and the completeness of the files should be described in order to give the researcher a sense of their value. Often in loosely organized papers, legislative files appear as aides' files, under their personal names, or as subject or issue files. Giving examples of key legislative measures and their content is highly advised. If annotated, as files used during deliberations in Congress may be, this should be noted. When legislation is organized by an aide's name, the

MORRIS K. UDALL PAPERS (MS 325)
ARRANGEMENT

Subgroup 1. Personal Files (Boxes 1-91)

Series 1. Biographical Files (Boxes 1-4)
Series 2. Appointment Books, Daily Schedules, and Guest Books (Boxes 5-6)
Series 3. Personal Correspondence (Boxes 7-12)
Series 4. Campaign Files
    Series 4.0 General and House of Representatives (Boxes 13-36)
    Series 4.1 Udall 76 Presidential Nomination (Boxes 37-77)
    Series 4.2 House Leadership (Boxes 78-79)
Series 5. Invitations Accepted and Trips (Boxes 80-87)
Series 6. Publications By and About Morris K. Udall (Boxes 88-91)

Subgroup 2. Legislative Files (Boxes 92-517)

Series 1. Legislative Correspondence (Boxes 92-157)
Series 2. Bill Files (Boxes 158-162)
Series 3. Legislative Assistant Files (Boxes 163-238)
Series 4. Committee Files
    Series 4.0 Committee Files (Boxes 239-326)
    Series 4.1 Chairman's Special Project Files (Boxes 327-470)
Series 5. Voting and Attendance Records (Boxes 471-474)
Series 6. Staff Project Files
    Series 6.0 Central Arizona Project (Boxes 475-492)
    Series 6.1 Public Land Review Commission (Boxes 493-508)

Figure 19.14. Hierarchical subgroup and series outline, Morris Udall papers, University of Arizona Library

scope of his or her responsibility should be described and discussed, especially noting how it changed over time. Other record types that may appear as legislative subseries include voting and attendance records and polling data, all of which should be described for scope of extent and content.

Separate from legislative files may be subject series about a wide variety of issues. Distinguishing the nature of material (secondary reference, position briefs, memoranda, etc.) in this kind of series from other subject files will save time for the researcher.

Committee-related files often occur independently of other series. The archivist should describe the nature of the material in these files, carefully distinguishing what remains in the member's papers from the official committee records maintained by committee staff, which by statute are transferred with the records of Congress to the Center for Legislative Archives at NARA. The extent of each should be stated, and any overlap between subcommittee materials and other series should be explained. If files have been extracted from more general series to form a "Committee" subgroup, that action also should be explained in the arrangement note or general collection note about "processing information."

Constituent Service Records

Issue mail, which is typically bulky, reflects a wide array of citizen opinion and thus captures the voice of the people during any given period. Incoming constituent mail and computer-generated response letters deserve special discussion: generally, in the introductory scope and content note, and more specifically, at the series level. Any numbering schemes for the office's responses, called "robos" (for the robo-typewriters that generated the multiple copies of one response) in the 1970s and subsequent decades, should be explained, as should any indexes of the responses. If statistical reports about dates of use for a robo are present, or if electronic records for later correspondence management systems are available, explanation is essential. Matching responses to actual incoming letters from constituents may be difficult if no coding is apparent. Stating this situation can be helpful. The arrangement of bulky constituent correspondence is another situation to describe; for example, it may occur by date and then by issue, or it may be arranged topically and subarranged chronologically.

Then again, retention of *any* constituent correspondence is frequently debated, and the discard or appraisal standards for the series should be explained to account for what was not kept. Pressure mail from constituents often consists of nearly identical or exact form letters or postcards. Sampling is recommended with the bulk destroyed, a process that should be noted with a statement summarizing the original amount of mail. For both the constituent correspondence and pressure mail, scope notes should include description that gives a sense of the issues that received the most mail. In later congressional collections from offices using electronic file management, summary data or reports may be compiled and preserved without keeping the original electronic issue mail.

Correspondence with federal agencies, usually on behalf of constituents, may be a distinct series. If it includes personal case files that have been restricted or discarded to protect personal privacy, that situation should be explained. Because federal government has been reorganized over time, it helps to explain the agencies' jurisdictions and the type of services and cases that are documented in the scope note to this series.

Another series, which may include correspondence with local and federal agencies, documents public works and a host of issues that affect the member's district. Often it includes the effects of federal policy on the state or district. Identifying the content and expanding abbreviated headings to help identify significant projects will greatly enhance the research value and usefulness of material in this series.

Appointment files, as for federal judges, may occur and these, too, should include specific description in the scope note and folder headings to increase accessibility for research. If correspondence for some offices, such as federal marshals, has not been retained, that fact should be stated.

Press Relations and Media Activities

The member's mailings to constituents may consist of formal newsletters or mass mailings, the latter during a more automated era. Clarifying the content of these mailings is useful, as they may summarize the member's positions and leadership on issues at particular times. Stating what kinds of background material are included for the staff's preparation of the newsletter is also helpful. Since the late 1990s, virtually every office has maintained a Web site with increasingly valuable information about the member's positions and services. In the first decade of the twenty-first century, several members have maintained Web logs or "blogs," reflecting personal commentary on all manner of issues. Web capture—preservation of and access through metadata to the digital content of these public relations products—is a challenge for the future already being addressed by the Library of Congress.[14] (See figure 19.15.)

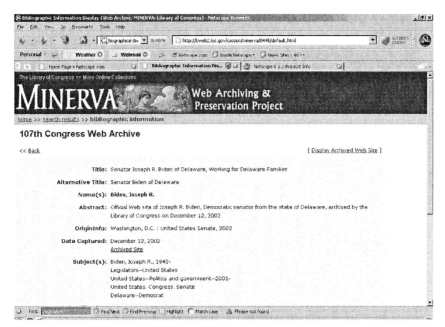

Figure 19.15.   Web capture, Library of Congress

Speeches may constitute an independent series or may occur as a subseries within others, such as Legislation or Campaign files. For those rare legislators who do not rely on speech texts, there may be no such documentation. Possibly speech notes have been kept, however; in such cases their existence and location should be stated.

Supplementing speeches or compensating for lack of them may be recorded speeches on audiotape, videotape, film, or in digital media. They may be within a press office subgroup, a campaign series, or a media series. If office staff or archival processors have listed them, the description can incorporate this information and such details as length of the recorded segment, names of other speakers, audience and place, and date. Such detail is incorporated in the audio speeches series of the Henry "Scoop" Jackson papers at the University of Washington. (See figure 19.16.) Photographs similarly merit considerable effort to identify the people or the group, the event, the photographer, and the date, even if the date is approximate.

Office Administration Records

Other series may have been weeded during processing or not retained at all. They may include invitations, military service academy appointments,

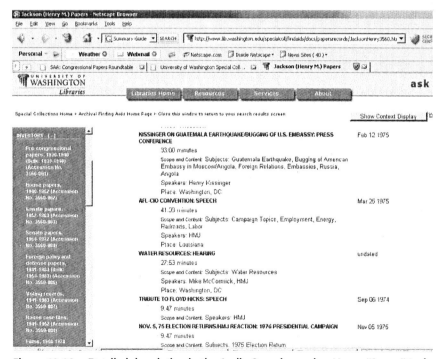

Figure 19.16. Detailed description in the Audio Speeches series, Henry "Scoop" Jackson papers, University of Washington Library

requests (for flags, visitor passes, tours, and other routine services), and various three-dimensional objects (such as plaques). Usually within the section "Processing Information," such actions should be explained. If kept, other routine office administration files such as policy memos, file manuals, or staff lists should be described in a way to determine their usefulness in context with other information in the collection.

Personal/Political/Official Records

Daily schedules and briefing materials are variously organized and exist in more or less completeness, but these record types appear in all congressional papers. Daily briefing memos provide the chronological thread of a member's legislative life and are often most revealing of the individual. These important records merit description at a level reflecting their usefulness to the researcher. Personal diaries, when they exist, should be noted for completeness, reflective content, or other substantive characteristics.

Trip files, which may occur within another series or independently, often contain speeches and background material that the legislator took along on a trip. Sometimes they contain correspondence before, during, and following the trip. Explaining the extent and content of such files and detailing the purpose of the trip will help researchers evaluate the relevance of the series.

Campaign files, mentioned previously, may be subsumed in a broad subgroup called "Political." Such a category may also include correspondence, press releases, newspaper clippings, and a variety of other materials. Regardless of where such files occur, it is helpful to describe the campaign issues, party platforms, and contestants involved to the extent that they are documented in the series.

Papers, photographs, scrapbooks, and realia from other periods of the individual's life and career may form distinct series of the papers. By the nature of their format, they may have quite different filing schemes and levels of description which need to be explained. Specificity in description is helpful, given the usefulness of visual content from these materials for exhibitions, publicity, or publications.

Processing Information and Administrative Notes

Processing information results from notes kept by archivists documenting various aspects of their work. If the current finding aid replaces an earlier one, especially one used by prior researchers, it is important to point out this situation. Processors may have shifted and consolidated widely separated but similar files to produce a more coherent arrangement. Very likely they have made appraisal decisions to reduce the bulk of constituent letters and pressure mail. They may have eliminated files of requests (for flags and calendars) and files about service academy appointments. They may have kept some but not all invitations. These actions should be explained after the introductory scope and content note in a general narrative about important decisions made in processing the collection. If a sampling technique was used, it should be described at least in terms of the approximate amount of material retained in proportion to the original volume. If an additional accession has been received since the original bulk of the papers was processed, it is important to alert the researcher to this new cache of papers.

"Related Material" indicates the existence other personal papers—perhaps created by the same entity, by political contemporaries, or by key aides—or other archival collections with topical relevance. A member of Congress may have been a state governor, for example, before or after service in Congress. A statement drawing attention to his or her papers in the state archives will alert users to this fact. If the member chaired a congressional committee, those records will be available at the Center for Legislative Archives. Occasionally a legislative aide may have kept papers from his or her service and donated them to the repository years after the member's papers have been processed. Calling attention to such related papers will draw users to valuable documentation with complementary or comparative content.

Access statements are short but provide vital information to prospective users, especially distant researchers who plan a repository visit to explore a collection. Access restrictions identify any limitations on physical access to parts of the collection, whether the papers are open to all users or whether part of them are physically restricted in some manner (and for how long). Proactive archivists will identify classified material in the collection, submit it to the Information Security Oversight Office at NARA for review, and note the restrictions on access to these sources in the finding aid.[15] Other limitations on use may also indicate restrictions on quotations or term-limited access to parts of the collection, as specified by the donor in a deed of gift.

CONCLUSION

As the chief source of information, the completed finding aid should enable a synopsis and abstracts to be distilled from it. Thus where appropriate in narrative sections of scope notes, statements such as "Significant topics include . . . " or "Of particular interest is documentation related to . . . " will be useful to catalogers, reference staff, and researchers who need quick information about career highlights, full personal names of key players, and multiple subject headings. Processors will use this information to determine access terms for the repository's encoded finding aids, also supplying standardized data elements, from which catalogers may generate collection-level records for submission to the parent institution's OPAC and forwarding to national databases. Whether for management, access, interpretation, or promotion, the archivist's role in describing a collection is to tease out distinctive and more typical features of the papers and to highlight them with care, exercising options about level of detail according to intended audience and purpose. Only then can an accurate descriptive summary be written and offered through a variety of access tools to attract researchers, repository staff, and the world of scholars interested in these sources.

NOTES

1. The Advisory Committee on the Records of Congress was established under Authority of Public Law 101-509, November 5, 1990. Ex officio members of the committee include the secretary of the Senate, clerk of the House, archivist of the United States, historian of the Senate, and historian of the House. Six additional members serve, each appointed by one of the following: the speaker of the House of Representatives, the minority leader of the House, the majority leader of the Senate, the minority leader of the Senate, the secretary of the Senate, and the clerk of the House. In its Third Report to Congress, the committee focused on "preservation of members' papers, the development and preservation of electronic records in Congress, and research access to congressional archival information." The Fourth Report advocates ongoing coordinated and collaborative approaches to provide access to both official records and personal papers—between the Center for Legislative Archives (CLA) at the National Archives and Records Administration (NARA), member institutions of the Association of Centers for the Study of Congress (ACSC), and the community of congressional archives. Advisory Committee on the Records of Congress, Third Report, December 31, 2000 (S. Pub. 106-52), and Fourth Report, December 31, 2006 (House Document No. 109-156).

2. Julian Zelizer, Sarah Binder, Joanne Freeman, and Paul Milazzo, panelists at a 2005 ACSC conference, all agreed on these points. Zelizer described the predicament of the congressional scholar: "part of the trick of congressional history is looking at multiple archives." "One thing you can definitely do is have the finding aids on the Web if you don't already," said Milazzo. "I really want to know what's there. . . . The more descriptive, from my perspective, is better, just because various people have different ways of interpreting broader categories," added Binder. Freeman elaborated: "as much sort of descriptive information as is possible is something that all of us, I think, would find useful . . . whether it's descriptive, or whether it has more do with searchability . . . to get a sense of the breadth and depth of something." Comments excerpted from "Congressional History: The State of the Art," transcript, ACSC Conference, Washington, D.C., May 4, 2005.

3. See Minnesota Historical Society Division of Library and Archives, Report of Congressional Papers Appraisal Committee (St. Paul: Minnesota Historical Society, 1993). Mark A. Greene, then curator of manuscripts acquisitions, and Dennis Meissner, archival processing manager, were two of the experienced archivists who

served on the Congressional Papers Appraisal Committee at the Minnesota Historical Society, a repository which holds one of the largest and most complete sets of congressional papers for any state's delegation.

4. Mark A. Greene and Dennis Meissner, "More Product, Less Process: Revamping Traditional Archival Processing," *American Archivist* 68, no. 2 (2005): 208–63.

5. Archivists from the House Office of History and Preservation and the Senate Historical Office are available with guidelines for preparing an office for closing as well as for transfer of records early in the member's term of office. *Managing Congressional Collections* (Chicago: Society of American Archivists, 2008) advocates establishing a strong working relationship between the archival repository and the member's office before records are transferred.

6. Bentley Historical Library (University of Michigan) archivist Thomas E. Powers provides a case study of preliminary arrangement and appraisal decisions based on surveying box lists for several hundred feet of "disrupted records" in his article "Processing as Reconstruction: The Philip A. Hart Senatorial Collection," *American Archivist* 46, no. 2 (1983): 183–5.

7. With the exception of individual manuscript items (when the piece itself is the chief source), the sources of descriptive information for archival collections "are, in the order of preference, the finding aid prepared for the collection, provenance and accession records, the materials themselves, and reference sources." Michael J. Fox, "Describing Archival Materials" in *Describing Archival Materials: The Use of the MARC AMC Format* (New York: Haworth Press, 1990), 22. DACS evolved to provide rules for the data elements behind all descriptive output for "any type or level of description of archival and manuscript materials." *Describing Archives: A Content Standard* (Chicago: Society of American Archivists, 2004), vii.

8. Archives, Personal Papers, and Manuscripts (APPM) was compiled by Steven L. Hensen and based on Anglo-American Cataloging Rules. It was first published by the Library of Congress in 1983, and a second, revised edition was published by the Society of American Archivists in 1989. Encoded Archival Description (EAD) is a technical standard used to mark up the data elements found in collection descriptions (finding aids); it also provides navigation through the descriptive components. Its development (Version 1.0 was released by SAA in 1999) raised awareness of consistent, core descriptive elements and preserved the hierarchical presentation of archival arrangement in online access tools. *Describing Archives: A Content Standard* (DACS, first edition 2004) is the latest description standard, developed to encourage consistency in use of data elements for access tools such as finding aids or collection-level records.

9. See "Congressional Collections Web Site Moved," *Congressional Papers Roundtable Newsletter* (February 2003), www.archivists.org/saagroups/cpr/newsletters/winter_2003.pdf.

10. ArchiveGrid shows promise as a national union catalog as it begins to harvest Web sites for archival collection descriptions, but future development and commitment for this much-needed tool is still uncertain after the 2006 merger of RLIN and OCLC.

11. The DELMAS foundation-funded Irish Literary Portal is a model for this type of subject-focused database. Hosted by Emory University, other institutions including Boston College, University of Delaware, Indiana University, University of

Texas Austin, and Wake Forest University are contributing collection descriptions of their strong Irish literary holdings using the EAD standard for finding aids. http://irishliterature.library.emory.edu.

12. The practices have particularly evolved since publication of the first edition of Karen Dawley Paul's *Records Management Handbook for United States Senators and Their Archival Repositories* (Washington, D.C.: U.S. Senate, 1985). Paul's handbook melded records management tools with archival goals by identifying common record types found in congressional offices and prescribing retention guidelines for those records. These appraisal guidelines and the opportunity to apply arrangement schemes to functional record types were a real boon to progress in congressional papers management for processing archivists.

13. The relationship of staff organizational structure and record types is described in Paul's *Records Management Handbook* (1998) as well as in "Senators' Papers: Management and Preservation Guidelines," a trifold brochure prepared under the direction of the secretary of the Senate by the Senate Historical Office.

14. In 2000, the Library of Congress established a pilot project to collect and preserve digital materials, including Web sites, in fulfillment of its mission to provide enduring access to primary sources of historical importance to the Congress and the American people. Information about this project is available at www.loc.gov/webcapture/, including access to a Web archive for the 107th Congress.

15. Information about the Information Security Oversight Office at NARA is available at www.archives.gov/isoo.

20

Classified: What to Do If National Security Officials Visit

Karen Dawley Paul

The donated papers of members of Congress can sometimes contain classified information; many definitely contain sensitive information. Sensitive and classified information may be received or created by staff in the course of conducting research and investigations. It can be sent to congressional offices by constituents seeking assistance with problem solving. It can be contained in documents or stored electronically. Whether provided by executive agencies, acquired from private sources and individuals, or originated within Congress, such information should be safeguarded and protected. It is vital that archivists who administer members' papers collections be thoroughly conversant with the law and with appropriate procedures to follow when such information is identified. This chapter provides necessary background and advice.

IDENTIFYING SENSITIVE OR CLASSIFIED INFORMATION

Sensitive information is defined in numerous statutes and regulations and can generally be described as information that, if prematurely disclosed, could result in the conveyance of an unwanted political, military, or economic advantage to others. Alternatively, release might be regarded as an undue invasion of personal privacy, contrary to sound business practices, or could reveal investigative information or techniques.

Classified information originates in the executive branch or is received from foreign governments and is presented to Congress with a clear indication of its protected status. Additionally, Congress can generate classified documents internally. For example, notes, briefing memos, questions, or talking points derived from a classified briefing or made from a classified memo are classified at the same level as the original information. National Security Classified documents are marked with the identification labels "Top Secret," "Secret," and "Confidential," indicating that their contents meet prescribed standards for the creation of official secrets.

More specifically, the following types of information warrant protection within the executive branch and, therefore, should be regarded as "sensitive" within the papers of members of Congress.

- Bank examination reports and related documents: 5 USC 552(b)(8)
- Classified information: 18 USC 798; 18 USC 952; 18 USC 1924; 50 USC 783; 5 USC 552(b)(1); 50 USC 421–426; E.O. 12958, as amended by E.O. 13292
- Commercial or financial information: 5 USC 552(b)(4)
- Information relating to the national defense information: 18 USC 793–798
- Diplomatic codes: 18 USC 952
- Electronic surveillance information: 50 USC 1801(f),(h); 50 USC 1806; 18 USC 2511; 18 USC 2515; 18 USC 1517
- Geological and geophysical information concerning wells: 5 USC 552(b)(9)
- Grand jury proceedings: 18 USC, Rule 6, Federal Rules of Criminal Procedure; 5 USC 552(b)(3)
- Identities of certain U.S. undercover intelligence officers, agents, informants, and sources: 50 USC 421–426)
- Intelligence sources and methods: 50 USC 403-3; 50 USC 413; 50 USC 413a; 50 USC 413b
- Law enforcement investigatory files: 5 USC 552(b)(7)
- National defense or foreign policy: 5 USC 552(b)(1); E.O. 12958, as amended by E.O. 13292
- Personal privacy: 5 USC 552(b)(6); 5 USC 552(a)
- Identifiable census data: 13 USC 8; 13 USC 9; 13 USC 214
- Restricted data regarding atomic energy: 42 USC 2274–2276
- Tax return information: 26 USC 6103; 5 USC 552(b)(3)
- Trade secrets: 18 USC 1905; 5 USC 552(b)(4)
- Vulnerabilities of sensitive programs, systems, or facilities, including infrastructures, computer systems, stockpiles, and other sensitive data: 5 USC 552(b)(2); 6 USC 121 note; 6 USC 133; 42 USC 247d-7e; 42 USC 300i-2;46 USC 70103(d); 49 USC 40119
- Information obtained in confidence from foreign governments: E.O. 12958, as amended by E.O. 13292

Congressional staff may acquire certain types of sensitive information when they review nominations (e.g., IRS returns), process casework (e.g., medical information, confidential business information, trade secrets, personal information provided in confidence), or attend classified briefings (notes from such briefings). Other types of information that may be of sensitive nature include documents not routinely available to a party in litigation with an agency, such as memos prepared for administrative proceedings or litigation before a federal or state court. Certain types of investigative information related to law enforcement may also need to be restricted.

Staff may also acquire certain types of "Sensitive But Unclassified" (SBU) information from the executive branch, which is now designated as "Controlled Unclassified Information (CUI), rather than SBU. A new framework has been established for designating, marking, safeguarding, and disseminating information designated as CUI under former President Bush's May 9, 2008 memorandum for the heads of Executive Departments and Agencies on Designation and Sharing of Controlled Unclassified Information (CUI).

The National Archives has developed guidance for the protection of information that might aid terrorist or other groups that wish to harm the government or individual citizens. These four categories are:

- *Personal identity information*—records that are name retrievable and include Social Security numbers that could be used to steal a person's identity.
- *Detailed information about critical infrastructure or public sites*—records that could assist in planning or executing a terrorist attack.
- *Information about security, evacuation, or other emergency planning*—records that could assist in planning or executing a terrorist attack.
- *Technical information concerning weapons of mass destruction*—records that could be used to build weapons.

The following nine categories of information help identify such records.

- Plans or detailed photographs of government facilities or other sensitive infrastructure.
- Materials relating to emergency action/planning, civil defense, and continuity of government.
- Materials relating to nuclear technology.
- Materials relating to weapons technology, including biological and chemical agents.
- Presidential/congressional member protection records.
- Materials relating to intelligence gathering and studies.
- Studies on terrorism and counterterrorism.
- Information on natural resources, such as oil (the strategic petroleum reserve, the Alaska pipeline), uranium, water.
- Materials relating to the Middle East that include information on current topics.

CLASSIFIED RECORDS IN
DONATED PAPERS: TWO CASE STUDIES

During 2004–2005, two instances of federal officials visiting repositories for the purposes of securing classified donated papers were reported to members of the Congressional Papers Roundtable of the Society of American Archivists. Because of the relative rarity of these occurrences, and because both institutions sought "advice and counsel" from the roundtable membership, the Information Security Oversight Office (ISOO) at the National Archives and Records Administration (NARA) was consulted. The ISOO is charged with oversight of agency actions with regard to the classification, safeguarding, and declassification of national security information. The office considers and acts on complaints and suggestions from persons within or outside the government with respect to the administration of the classified national security information program.

First, some background on the two incidents of document review conducted by government officials in private collections. The University of Washington Special Collections Division was visited the week of February 7, 2005, by a team of five people, led by the CIA. Over a three-day period, they reviewed around 400 boxes of the Henry Jackson papers and removed eight documents for declassification review. As reported by the head of special collections, Carla Rickerson, in the March 2005 issue of the *Congressional Papers Roundtable Newsletter*, each classified document was removed and replaced by a withdrawal form, indicating the type of document, date, number of pages, author or correspondents, and why the document was removed. The documents were then placed in the custody of the University of Washington's security officer, who proceeded to process the documents for declassification review with the appropriate federal agency. In this instance, a member of ISOO was part of the reviewing team.

Rickerson surmised that the visit was sparked by the return to the collection of a declassified document. Despite a tense and strained first meeting with a CIA employee the previous summer when the declassified document was returned (initially the officer said he wanted 400 boxes closed to researchers even though they had been open for 10 years), Rickerson found the full review by the team in February to be "professional and accommodating."

A similar situation arose at the South Caroliniana Library, University of South Carolina, where a team from the State Department reviewed a former governor/ambassador's papers and removed documents for further study. Although the final assessment by the library's director, Herb Hartsook, was that the team "acted responsibly," the initial contact did not start out smoothly. As Hartsook wrote on February 10, 2005:

We hold the papers of a now deceased SC governor, 1971–1975, and U.S. ambassador, 1977–1981 [John Carl West]. Among a recent addition was a file of classified documents from his period as ambassador, which he had sent to the State Department with an inquiry about their current status, and related correspondence. This dated from the early 1990s. Much of the material was returned declassified but other documents remained classified. Included in the latter were selected portions of a personal diary which he kept while ambassador.

Now, over ten years later, we contacted the State Department about the material which had remained classified and were told to send it to them for review, as well as other documents from the addition that were marked "classified" or "confidential." Shortly after sending this material, we received a call from a State Dept. staffer who informed us that the world had changed after 9/11, that an Executive Order which postdated the earlier review was now in effect, and that the collection should be closed in its entirety until further notice. She said that other collections were also impacted by this more rigorous classification, particularly congressional collections but even gubernatorial collections, and referenced an incident involving the Muskie papers. It all sounds very draconian and I'm surprised I haven't heard discussion of this among CPR (Congressional Papers Roundtable) folks.

The State Dept. official asked for a copy of the deed of gift, said the donation of the collection was "highly illegal," and that the personal diary, and I assume the rest of the collection, was subject to seizure. She said that once someone receives a security clearance, all materials generated subsequently are subject to review since the person may draw on knowledge gained from classified information.

The State Department officials soon softened their position when Hartsook asked for a written statement of their position. Hartsook then consulted with Records Declassification staff at the National Archives to get a better understanding of the process and learned that what the State Department was by then proposing to do was not "out of line." The State Department's final position on how best to proceed was that they preferred "to keep things informal," as it would benefit both parties.

WHAT TO DO

Given the confrontational nature of the initial meetings between the archivists and agency personnel in these two instances, how can archivists prepare themselves to deal with assertive agency officials who seemingly materialize from nowhere, demand that collections be closed, and proceed to take away documents for further review?

First, it is helpful to know that the director of the ISOO maintains there currently is "no concentrated effort under way" to go through everything that exists outside of federal custody, and in the view of that office, it is somewhat remarkable that two such cases occurred so close together. The ISOO points out that in most instances, it is either the donor (because of agency requirements) or the repository (because something classified is discovered in a donated collection) that initiates contact regarding declassification. Sometimes this has happened years before current staff came on board. In both the University of Washington and University of South Carolina cases, this is true.

Second, it is important to know that classified records, regardless of age, must be protected and undergo official declassification by the appropriate federal agency. Classified records that are over 25 years old and are outside federal custody are not subject to automatic declassification under Executive Order 13292. It is therefore the responsibility of repository archivists who discover classified material to remove it from publicly available materials, contact appropriate agency officials, and arrange for its storage in certified secure space. The repository may contact the Center for Legislative Archives (CLA), which serves as the liaison to ISOO, whose staff will propose a protocol for storing and ultimately declassifying the records. Archivists should not assume that just because the documents are filed with open material that the classified documents are declassified. If they have been declassified, they will be definitely marked as such by the declassifying agency.

Should an archivist happen to be "taken by surprise" by an unannounced visit of an agency individual or team of reviewers, the archivist should ask for copies of the legal authority by which the agency is operating and share this information with the office of legal counsel. Also a consultation with the National Archives prior to allowing their review to proceed is advised. If the collection is a congressional collection, the point of contact should be the Center for Legislative Archives at the National Archives. The CLA currently acts as liaison between the repository and NARA's Declassification Division for members' papers. The CLA is happy to extend this courtesy to former members.

Classified materials in members' papers can be handled in one of two ways. First, before the records are donated, they are deposited at the CLA, which transfers them to NARA's Declassification Division for declassification review by agencies. Second, if the papers already have been donated and are later found to contain classified records, the repository should contact the CLA, which will work with ISOO to arrange for declassification review. When the documents are declassified, the originals are forwarded to the member's repository for inclusion with the member's collection. In this way, both the repository's and a member's needs to get the material declassified will be met. In addition, any congressional equities in the material are also monitored should the material in fact be records of a congressional committee.

For classified material found in noncongressional collections, the ISOO office should be the point of contact. The ISOO office will act as a clearinghouse to assist the repository in processing the declassification review and will help to expedite the process. The office facilitates review of such materials so that they can be lawfully opened for research.

Finally, if your repository, unlike the University of Washington, does not have a classified holding facility on site, on a case-by-case basis the National Archives regional facilities, Presidential Libraries, or some other approved repository for classified information may be able to serve in that capacity, storing the originals while copies are sent out for review. This service can be arranged through assistance from the ISOO office. There should be no need for archives staff to allow original documents to "walk out the door," or for staff to feel uneasy as to where those documents are going or when they will be returned. Through the ISOO, the National Archives oversees and facilitates the declassification process and serves as an honest broker.

FURTHER READING

A variety of sources may be consulted for further clarification and definition of sensitive information. A concise discussion of the five most commonly restricted categories (privacy, business information, personnel data, investigative information, and statutory restricted) appears in *Archives and Manuscripts: Law* (Chicago: Society of American Archivists, 1985) by Gary M. Peterson and Trudy Huskamp Peterson. Heather MacNeil's *Without Consent: The Ethics of Disclosing Personal Information in Public Archives* reviews the "theoretical and practical issues associated with the administration of access to government-held personal information generally and to personal information held in government archives specifically." Another useful discussion of categories of information which may be protected from public disclosure under the Freedom of Information Act (FOIA) and the Privacy Act appears in *A Citizen's Guide on Using the Freedom of Information Act and the Privacy Act of 1974 to Request Government Records*, House Report 109-226, 2005. This report contains sections discussing reasons access may be denied under the FOIA and Privacy Act.

Additional sources that discuss "sensitive security" and "sensitive but unclassified" information include: *Security Classified and Controlled Information: History, Status, and Emerging Management Issues* by Harold C. Relyea (CRS Report RL33494), which examines the security classification regime in use within the federal executive branch; *Information Sharing for Homeland Security* by Harold C. Relyea and Jeffrey W. Seifert (CRS Report RL32597); and *The Protection of Classified Information: The Legal Framework* by Jennifer K. Elsea (CRS Report RS21900).

Legal Issues Related to the Possible Release of Classified Information by Senators, Representatives, or Members of Their Staffs by Elizabeth B. Bazan (CRS Report 89-322A) discusses the protection of members and aides engaged in legislative acts under the speech or debate clause of the United States Constitution, Art. 1, sec. 6, cl. 1, and the applicability of criminal sanctions for disclosure of national defense information under statutes dealing with espionage and restricted data on atomic energy. *Protection of Classified Information by Congress, Practices and Proposals* by Frederick M. Kaiser (CRS Report RS20748) discusses mechanisms established by Congress to safeguard controlled information in its custody. These arrangements have varied over time between the two chambers and among panels in each.

Protection of National Security Information by Jennifer K. Elsea (CRS Report 33502) discusses previous legislative efforts to criminalize the unauthorized disclosure of classified information; describes laws that potentially apply, including criminal and civil penalties that can be imposed on violators; and explores some of the disciplinary actions and administrative procedures available to the federal agencies that have been addressed by federal courts. In addition, the report examines possible First Amendment implications of using the Espionage Act to prosecute newspapers for publishing classified national defense information.

Protection of Security-Related Information by Gina Marie Stevens and Todd B. Tatelman (CRS Report 33502) provides an in-depth discussion of the history, requirements, and litigation that has developed with respect to information protection regimes for security-related information.

21

An Embarrassment of Riches: Access and the Politics of Processing Congressional Collections

Larry Weimer

Documentation of proposed local projects throughout one's state—from highway construction and other public works to health care and other human service programs. An archival repository would swoon at the opportunity to acquire such a collection.

Primary source material with "on the ground" responses of everyday people to national issues, large and small. A trove for social and cultural historians that a repository would accept gladly.

The papers of a political leader from one's state, perhaps an individual of national stature, that include contextual and legislative material from that politician's career. Repositories actively seek, and pride themselves on acquiring, such collections.

Finding all this rich material in *one* collection? Priceless!!!

A wealth of "priceless" material, however, is not exactly cost free. The papers of U.S. senators and representatives from the late twentieth and early twenty-first centuries—though desirable and valued acquisitions—pose significant and costly challenges to those repositories that seek to satisfy their fundamental mission, that is, to provide access to the materials they collect. In conducting the specific tasks involved in arranging and describing congressional papers for research access—in other words, processing the collection—an archivist confronts challenges ranging from the unwieldy bulk of the collection as a whole to the various sensitivities potentially offended by specific documents lurking in some innocuous-looking folder. Mediating the competing demands of providing timely access to the rich documentation found in a congressional collection and of respecting material of a national security or otherwise sensitive nature is a professional challenge for the processing archivist. Providing access to a collection recklessly and restricting a collection excessively through being overly cautious are twin professional embarrassments for an archivist.

Congressional papers archivists have long recognized the particular challenges they face in processing these collections, and they have sought ways to deal with the issues. This chapter surveys these challenges, providing an overview of issues that confront archivists processing political collections. Archival management issues related to the size and complexity of congressional papers are discussed first, followed by considerations of more problematic document types commonly found in these collections. Finally, the chapter looks at collections in light of donor relations, where the politics of processing political papers is most apparent. The chapter is informed both by case studies documented in archival literature and by interviews conducted by the author with several archivists experienced in processing congressional papers.[1] The reader is forewarned that this chapter provides no road map with the single best approach to all collections. More like a topographical map, it offers archivists a sense of the congressional collections landscape so they may negotiate their own processing route through rough terrain.

"MORE PRODUCT, LESS PROCESS"

On January 3, 2002, New York's *Daily News* reported that the city's Records and Information Services Department had agreed to permit Rudy Giuliani, who had left the mayoralty just a few days earlier, "to create a plan to archive the documents" from his eight years in office.[2] In the following weeks, additional details of the arrangement with Giuliani were disclosed in the press. A private corporation—the Rudolph W. Giuliani Center for Urban Affairs, Inc.—had been formed and had contracted with New York City to take custody of the former mayor's papers, rather than have them placed immediately with the Municipal Archives. The Winthrop Group, a provider of archival services, had been enlisted by the center to undertake a three-year project to process and microfilm the 2,114 boxes of material before turning the originals over to the Municipal Archives. Historians, archivists, government watchdogs, and others vehemently and publicly protested the removal of these public papers from the chain of public control. Nevertheless, although agreeing to some amendments to the original contract, Giuliani and his agents retained unprecedented control over the papers before eventually sending the bulk of the papers to the Municipal Archives by late 2005.[3]

How did Giuliani justify his actions? In addition to emphasizing the city's continued ownership rights and the contractual safeguards against the removal or destruction of any of the papers, Giuliani argued that he could deliver what the Municipal Archives could not: public access to the records. According to Saul S. Cohen, president of the Giuliani Center for Urban Affairs, "The purpose of having a private, professional archivist [Winthrop Group] to archive the mayor's papers is to make them available to the public in an accessible manner far more quickly than the years it usually takes New York City to archive mayoral documents. The city is still working on the papers of David N. Dinkins, although his administration ended more than eight years ago."[4] In addition, the work was privately funded, thereby avoiding the delays expected of an "understaffed and underfunded Municipal Archives."[5] Indeed, the *Daily News* found that the records of two recent mayors, Dinkins and Abe Beame, were not "well kept."[6]

In advancing his own interests, Giuliani struck at the archival profession's Achilles heel—its appetite for collecting documents often outstrips its ability to make those documents accessible to the public in a timely manner, resulting in large backlogs of unprocessed material. For example, a 1998 survey found that over one-half of congressional collections were unprocessed at 13 percent of repositories holding such papers.[7] Among the results of a survey conducted in 2003–2004 by Mark A. Greene and Dennis Meissner were the findings that "60 percent of repositories have at least a third of their collections unprocessed" and "59 percent of repositories acknowledge that their backlogs are a 'major problem.'"[8] Despite the archival profession's protests over concepts like public property, chain of control, and custody, Giuliani was able to promise what many, perhaps most, archivists could not—that the papers of an important political figure would be available to a wide public in a reasonable period of time. Indeed, Greene and Meissner's survey concluded "large backlogs are hurting the archival profession in the eyes of our researchers and resource allocators" and "51 percent of repositories, researchers, donors, and/or resource allocators had become upset because of backlogs."[9] Giuliani's case may have been exceptional in its high profile, but it exposed a sore point common in the archival world, where the struggle, and often inability, to provide timely access to archival resources has escalated as a pressing collections management issue.

Archivists have not been blind to the challenges that unprocessed congressional collections present. It is impossible to ignore their sheer physical mass. The papers of Senator Frank Murkowski (R-AK) amounted to 1,500 cubic feet when they arrived at the University of Alaska at Fairbanks in 2002.[10] Representative Richard Gephardt (D-MO) donated about 1,200 cubic feet to the Missouri Historical Society in 2005–2007.[11] The papers of Senator Gaylord Nelson (D-WI) at the Wisconsin Historical Society totaled 1,000 cubic feet.[12] Larger collections, such as the 2,000 cubic feet of papers from Senator Harrison A. Williams (D-NJ) at Rutgers University, are common.[13] Even "smaller" collections typically run in the hundreds of cubic feet, such as the 260 cubic feet of papers of Representative Robert L. F. Sikes (D-FL) at the University of West Florida or the approximately 500 cubic feet from Representative Sherwood Boehlert (R-NY) at the University at Albany.[14]

The emergence of electronic records has only compounded the critical mass problem. Not only do important records, such as staff notes and constituent correspondence, exist in e-mail and other digital forms with their own challenges for preservation and access, but this has not necessarily decreased the paper-based challenges. The papers of Senator Thomas Daschle (D-SD), acquired by South Dakota State University Library in 2005, included more than 1 terabyte of digital objects in addition to the 2,000 linear feet of physical material.[15] The papers of Senator Trent Lott (R-MS) received by the University of Mississippi in 2008 totaled 3,051 linear feet of material, several boxes of which contained various electronic formats.[16] In 2007, the Center for Legislative Archives (CLA) at the National Archives and Records Administration (NARA) received 5,000 cubic feet of material from House and Senate committees despite the increasing quantity of electronic records the committees also generate.[17]

Splashing into this mix of massive accessions and accumulating backlog came Mark Greene and Dennis Meissner's seminal 2005 article in *American Archivist*, "More Product, Less Process: Revamping Traditional Archival Processing." In surveying and critiquing archivists' processing activities, especially as they related to large twentieth-century collections, Greene and Meissner concluded that "processing projects squander scarce resources because archivists spend too much time on tasks that do not need doing, or at least don't need doing all the time."[18] The authors pointed out that many standard archival practices "make no sense": seeking out and removing all metal fasteners from papers held in climate-controlled storage, removing acidic paper from their equally acidic original folders, or physically arranging and describing collections at levels of detail that provide minor value in making the papers accessible.[19] Greene and Meissner sought to "redefine" processing *"to make backlogs more embarrassing to the profession than failure to remove paper clips."*[20] In doing so, they "articulate a new set of arrangement, preservation, and description guidelines that 1) expedites getting collection materials into the hands of users; 2) assures arrangement of materials *adequate* to user needs; 3) takes the *minimal* steps necessary to physically preserve collection materials; and 4) describes materials *sufficient* to promote use."[21]

As Greene and Meissner acknowledged, the essence of their observations and recommendations, and even real-life applications, could already be found in pockets of the archival profession.[22] For example, in 2003, faced with a tight timeframe and budget for processing the papers of Senator Hiram L. Fong (R-HI), the University of Hawaii completed processing the 660 cubic feet collection within eight months with one part-time archivist by employing varying levels of processing and description, depending on the priority of the series or subseries. The processing project's rallying cry of "using shovels, not teaspoons" would resound a year later in Greene and Meissner's article.[23] In 1998, archivists at Yale University Library, who faced at least 10–15 years of dedicated processing just to catch up on the unprocessed backlog, implemented a program of "minimum standards."[24] Originally consisting of basic arrangement, addressing only major preservation issues, segregation of restricted materials, a MARC record, and a finding aid with an overview and box/folder inventory, the minimum standards for processing were pared down even further for some of the collections that did not merit much resource commitment.

For many archivists who had long attempted to tackle these awesome collections with a variety of strategies, the Greene and Meissner approach served as a coherent framework that provided an understanding and justification of individual efforts to apply "rapid processing" techniques. With shorthand references to "Greene-Meissner," "MPLP" (the acronym derived from their article's title, "More Product, Less Process"), and "minimal processing," archivists now had a grammar to use to refer to their actions and to place them within a larger shift in professional archival practice. The practical impact was substantial. Two examples illustrate the point.

The 2,400 linear feet of papers from Representative Jim Wright (D-TX) received in 1989 outstripped Texas Christian University's resources to process using traditional approaches. TCU archivists applied Greene and Meissner's guidelines to two of the largest paper-based series in the Wright collection—constituent correspondence and subject files. A sizable portion of the constituent correspondence had been previously fully processed, but that processing had not resulted in significant researcher interest. Hence, TCU applied minimal processing to the remaining 353 feet, including container description only to the box level and no rehousing. This aggressive processing was completed in 80 hours, or 4 feet per hour. On the other hand, the 540 feet of subject files received folder-level descriptions and other processing steps (though not rehousing), given their higher research use. This level of processing consumed about 1 hour per linear foot.[25] Similarly, archivists at the University of Alaska at Fairbanks applied the Greene-Meissner approach to over 1,000 feet of various collections of state legislators' papers. Limiting the amount of item-level preservation work and arranging and describing collections at varying levels, the full-time equivalent of 1.25 staff completed the 1,000 feet in two years.[26]

The cultural and even psychological impact in the profession was profoundly affected by the Greene and Meissner article. Reflecting on the progress afforded by minimal processing, the senior archivist for the Jim Wright papers noted the "positive effects" on the staff which had previously "thought of the papers as an albatross."[27] The archivist at the University of Alaska at Fairbanks, appreciating MPLP's "flexibility," found in the concept "permission not to feel guilty when a collection wasn't 'perfect,' but was 'good enough.'"[28] The head of archives at the University of Montana at Missoula found the ability to swiftly process materials "a very liberating feeling."[29]

At this writing, the influence of the Greene and Meissner article continues to spread as real-life experiences with the concepts are beginning to be reported to the profession through articles, presentations at Society of American Archivists (SAA) conferences, and regional and local gatherings. Rather than applying MPLP principles on an ad hoc basis to individual collections or sets of collections, some repositories have institutionalized the practices as standard operating procedures. Calculating its backlog to be 3,000 feet and requiring over a decade of full-time traditional processing, the University of Montana reconstructed their practices so that minimal processing is the assumed level of processing for a collection. Early results included the completion of about 800 feet of material, spending about 2 hours per foot.[30] At Columbia University's Rare Book and Manuscript Library, the new curator confronted a backlog of unprocessed and partially processed collections stretching figuratively for eight miles. Altering the repository's standard practices to revolve around less detailed "default" processing, the library's productivity leapt from roughly 7–10 feet processed per month to over 200 feet per month.[31] Yale University Library's Manuscripts and Archives unit, realizing that sufficient resources would not be available to improve on the skeletal descriptions of its entire backlog, shifted its focus to ensuring that the situation was improved going forward. Hence, Yale moved essential processing steps into the accessioning stage, so that new accessions were not added to the backlog but were promptly ready for access.[32]

How widespread is the implementation of Greene and Meissner's recommendations for congressional papers? Michael Strom's use of MPLP on the Wright papers is one of the few instances documented in the professional literature. Through February 2008, none of the institutional updates in the *Congressional Papers Roundtable Newsletter* refer to the influence of Greene and Meissner's article on their projects. None of the interviewees for this chapter was systematically applying an MPLP approach.[33] But this is a bit misleading.

If Greene-Meissner means "minimal processing," especially in the sense of avoiding item- or even folder-level handling, indications are that many or most congressional papers archivists will say they are not adhering to Greene-Meissner (though they might apply specific recommendations, such as not refoldering all material). However, the Greene and Meissner article was not an exhortation to do minimal processing. It was an exhortation to be flexible, and to do the minimum *necessary* or *sufficient* for preservation of material and making it accessible to researchers. The trick is in determining what is adequate for the user for a given series. Greene and

Meissner acknowledge that some collections will deserve more processing than others, but that deviation from the "golden minimum" should be justifiable.[34] Archivists of congressional papers generally do more work on their collections and do express reasons for that. So, in that sense, archivists are in concert with Greene and Meissner's essential point, if not routinely with their specific recommendations.

From my own experience processing congressional papers, I would argue that processing to some absolute minimal level is inappropriate, for a number of reasons discussed below. I would also argue against the other extreme, that congressional papers are so unique as to rule out the possibility of taking measured risks and shortcuts in select portions of a collection. This chapter will turn toward some of the challenges that congressional archivists face in processing, all of which push against the ability to implement "minimal" processing and often imply the need for item-level handling. But I do not want the reader to lose sight of the need to approach processing with a creative mindset and strategic vision. Ultimately, the purpose of processing is to make a collection accessible to researchers. The fact that minimal processing may be inappropriate for sizable portions of congressional collections does not negate the power of the MPLP concept. Rather, the challenges of congressional papers increase the demand on archivists to think harder about processing tasks in order to ensure that they do not overprocess hundreds or thousands of feet of material because of the potential for some landmines in some parts of the collection. The archivist needs to look for opportunities to prudently employ a minimally necessary level of processing, not rationalize away the opportunity to gain processing efficiencies.

"ACCESSIONING AS PROCESSING" AND ELECTRONIC RECORDS

One mode of expeditious processing—that of "accessioning as processing"—may be especially applicable to congressional papers and appealing to their archivists. The concept involves arranging and describing collections to a sufficient level for access as they enter the repository.[35] Central to the success of this strategy is engaging with the donor or their agents, such as a member's office staff, in order to have them actively participate in providing inventories, identifying sensitive materials (or removing it from the accession altogether), documenting scope and content, describing relations among portions of the collections, and other activities.[36] This engagement can serve to reduce the processing resource requirements and ensure that finding aids include descriptions of the collection's provenance as viewed by the donor (who is often the creator) rather than the view reconstructed or perceived by the processing archivist.

Examples of this approach are increasingly found with congressional papers as archivists work with office staffs on the appraisal and description of material. The speakers at the Congressional Papers Roundtable (CPR) preconference of the 2007 Society of American Archivists annual meeting focused on the acquisition phase and included remarks by University of Vermont archivists on their preprocessing of the papers of Senator James Jeffords (I-VT) "before they even left the office."[37] Other repositories have worked with congressional offices or with archivists hired by a member to identify materials of interest to retain or to arrange periodic accruals to be shipped to the repository.

Such work with the congressional office staff is not always possible because of geographic distance, unwillingness of a member to engage in front-end discussions with a repository, resource constraints within the repository, or other reasons. Nevertheless, efficient processing of these sprawling collections is increasingly dependent on some front-end work. In the case of electronic records, the front-end work is vital. The archivists of the Ronald V. Dellums (D-CA) papers could not access information on computer tape in the collection because they lacked the appropriate hardware or software. Thus they were puzzled "how to document it in a human-readable manner, and determine whether or not they are records at all."[38] Tape might be the toughest format for a repository to cope with, but there are also zip drives, floppy disks of various sizes, external hard drives, DVDs, CDs, and whatever other media an office may have used to store material in digital form. Given the inability of repositories to work with many of these formats, negotiating with a donor's congressional staff for a useable format (even if in paper printout form) is essential.[39]

Software applications also range widely, and various versions of each product can be in use. Offices maintain their own servers with their own set of applications, so repositories cannot rely on common resolutions emanating from the House and Senate, from other archivists, or even from their own experiences with other political collections. Acquiring the software applications and downloading data from the office servers and computer hard drives to a format readable by the repository can at least place the records in the repository's possession where issues of identification, appraisal, description, preservation, and user access can be addressed. Working in advance with the staff will also enable the archivist to learn the digital file structures, file naming conventions, and the relation, if any, of the digital records to paper records.

E-mail also involves multiple proprietary applications employed by the individual offices. There are options for retaining e-mail, such as printouts, PDF files, forwarding to the repository as e-mails, or retaining offline in another file format. However, these solutions each have their technical difficulties and need to be worked out in advance of a member leaving office.

Beyond technical difficulties, the frequent use of office e-mails for at least some personal matters may cause resistance toward the repository getting all staff e-mails. The archivist will need to consider those sensitivities in pressing for acquisition of e-mails with archival value.

Constituent correspondence is often received via e-mail or input to a member's Web site, fed into correspondence management systems, and answered systematically. Capturing the data in readable form will need to be worked out with the office staff. Much of this correspondence is high in quantity and often low in research usefulness at the item level to the extent that it consists of redundant pressure mail. How this material will be appraised, described, and made accessible to researchers remains an unresolved challenge. Consider that the House received 88 million e-mails in 2005.[40]

Overall, electronic records pose enormous implications for archivists. The most valuable portions of congressional collections—staff analyses, meeting summaries, intra-staff notes, memos, directives, constituent correspondence, and more—are now likely to be in digital format, perhaps exclusively and perhaps in transient e-mail files. There is an upside: In an earlier age, much informal business was handled by phone and not reduced to writing; with e-mail now a preferred communication tool in the culture, and with its often unguarded language, the digital material could provide rich material not previously included in collections. Nevertheless, without making arrangements prior to a member leaving office, all of this rich digital material will be erased from the servers and the computers and their hard drives abandoned with the office space. Even if captured, the repository needs to receive hardware and software formats that are at least readable by the archivist. Issues of description, preservation, and user access all need to be resolved. Most fundamentally, the centrality of digital records forces a shift in accessioning practices. In a simpler age, boxes of paper would stay sitting on a shelf, ready to be sent at any time to a repository, which could readily grasp their content from a physical survey. In the digital age, no such luxury exists. Acquisitions of digital matter must be negotiated and discussed with a member's office well in advance of their departure from office, or else files will be deleted, contextual messages lost, and file structures and naming conventions rendered unintelligible.

No one has fully figured out how to resolve the challenges of electronic records. But the processing archivist needs to be aware of the importance of these records to a collection and work closely with a congressional office to survey what electronic records are being created, and by whom. Archivists need to manage the issue to the extent possible and in ways that suit their repository's resources, even if they work with the office staff to have digital material printed in hard copy for the repository. Otherwise, archivists face two unfortunate scenarios: either they will accession much digital media that they cannot read, process, preserve, and make available, or they will accession no digital media, thereby missing what are likely the most important and unique portions of a congressional collection.

IMPACT OF APPRAISAL DECISIONS ON PROCESSING

The fundamental fact about congressional collections remains that they are massive. For many repositories, this is an issue because of the lack of extensive storage space, or a lack of funds to pay for rented space.[41] Hence, it becomes imperative that collections be reduced in size to the extent possible without compromising their overall integrity or losing useful materials. Such reduction is not only possible but expected. Indeed, since the publication in 1985 of the first edition of Karen Dawley Paul's *Records Management Handbook for United States Senators and Their Archival Repositories*, congressional archivists have had detailed guidance as to which record types are worthy of retention and closer scrutiny in processing.[42] Former Senate Historian Richard Baker reported the view of researchers that "as much as 80 or even 90 percent of a given collection is of marginal value."[43] Processing archivists routinely slice their collections to half or less of their original size through weeding, sampling, and removal of select series. An especially well documented example of this is the appraisal of the papers of Senator James McClure (R-ID), which were reduced by 52 percent, from 1,515 to 732 cubic feet.[44] Appraisal activities were similarly documented for the papers of Senator John J. Williams (R-DE), which were reduced by 70 percent, from 481 to 143 linear feet.[45]

An extended discussion of appraisal concepts in relation to congressional papers is outside the scope of this chapter, with its focus on the challenges of processing such papers. Nevertheless, certain types of appraisal decisions are implemented during processing and are worth considering here. Further, the need to appraise extensively in these large congressional collections operates at points against minimal processing, so choices of which resources to spend (labor vs. space) need to be balanced.

Appraisal approaches have emphasized the need to reduce the size of congressional collections to the unique material of research value found embedded within a collection. Developing clear appraisal criteria and discarding "ruthlessly" in implementing those criteria are essential to avoid being "swamped in a sea of paper."[46] Over time, archivists have come to some broad agreement regarding common record types and the materials that are prime candidates for removal from a collection, including copies of the *Congressional Record*, federal agency press releases, routine requests for gallery passes, and similar material readily available elsewhere or of low research value. Nevertheless, there is a great deal of difference of opinion as well.[47] In some instances, these differences center on the perceived research value of the material itself; case files and invitations might be examples. In other instances, there is general agreement on value but disagreement on the extent to which the material should be retained. Constituent correspondence, clippings, and photographs might fall into this category. Finally, disagreement on archival value sometimes centers on the context of the material. Even though the material may not be unique, it might be useful in its unique context within the collection. Published reference material falls into this category.

Appraisal decisions that send entire series of content to the dumpster reduce collection bulk without impact on processing time. For example, some institutions take advantage of overlapping congressional collections. The University of Washington, holding both the Warren Magnuson (D-WA) and Henry M. Jackson (D-WA) papers, discarded all the case files from the Jackson papers for the period his tenure in the Senate overlapped that of Magnuson, retaining those in Magnuson's files.[48] The Minnesota Historical Society retained issue mail from Senate offices on a sample basis but discarded that from House offices.[49] Yet many appraisal decisions in congressional papers are made at the item level during processing. For example, government publications are routinely removed from collections. But these are not found all together in a library series that can be readily discarded. Rather, they are found in subject, case, project, correspondence, bill, and other files. Avoiding item-level appraisal means retaining the substantial bulk these documents add.

Constituent correspondence (meaning, for this discussion, issue-oriented mail) is another appraisal-related processing challenge. Typically, physical forms of redundant pressure mail (e.g., postcards, form letters, etc.) are discarded. The processing archivist needs to identify and remove the relevant mail (which is often mixed in with the unique correspondence), document the extent of the discarded material, and ensure that the items retained are representative of the discarded population.

Trickier to implement for the processing archivist are sampling strategies for the unique constituent correspondence.[50] Generally, two types of sampling approaches are available to the archivist: (1) applying quantitative techniques across a population of homogeneous correspondence at the level of box, folder, or other grouping; or (2) reviewing individual pieces of correspondence to generate a qualitative sample. The first approach is faster and easier to implement, and it is more objective, but it is a blunt instrument that risks discarding notable items while retaining much chaff. The second approach can result in a richer sample of correspondence, but at a steep cost in time and risk of unexamined archivist biases shaping the retained material. Given these risks, many archivists balance the approaches or, if it is a viable option for their repository, retain all the unique correspondence. The appraisal of Senator John Williams's constituent correspondence included such a blending of sampling approaches, based on the filing structure, range of issues in a file, substance of issue, and other considerations.[51] My interviewees indicated that a similar range of approaches continues, with some repositories retaining all issue correspondence after removing redundant forms, others sampling at the item level on subjective bases such as significance of issue or correspondent, and others selecting random blocks of correspondence.[52]

Driving these appraisal and processing approaches are not only the practical considerations of resource availability (storage space and labor time) but, more important, a *view* of the potential research value of the correspondence. This view is informed by a variety of sources, including the Senate and House records management guidelines and lines of inquiry by historians. Emerging interest in congressional collections from political scientists supports the usefulness of quantifiable data in issue correspondence files.[53] Target audiences, strengths of the collection, and usage patterns are among the other considerations informing an appraisal and processing view. An example from my own experience may serve as a useful illustration.

The Harrison Williams papers included 155 cubic feet of unprocessed issue correspondence from 1977–1982, foldered by sequential Correspondence Management System (CMS) code. This particular series included only correspondence receiving standard text responses, usually on topics generating a high volume of mail, much of it in redundant forms. However, because of the filing structure, all mail on a topic was not found together but was mixed with other topics in essentially chronological order across scores of boxes. By plodding through the scores of boxes, or by identifying potentially relevant items from the CMS computer output microfilm and tracking the hundreds of individual documents in the boxes, a researcher could use the files as originally structured, albeit with significant logistical burdens on both the researcher and the repository. Nevertheless, the file structure and coded labels made a potentially valuable resource essentially inaccessible to all but the most patient and sophisticated researcher. Further, 155 cubic feet was too much to retain, given both space constraints and the obvious quantity of redundant mail that could be seen in the boxes.

Appraisal in this instance sought to accomplish the twin objectives of winnowing the correspondence down to a core of unique correspondence (thereby eliminating redundant forms and gaining space) and rearranging file order from document sequence to subject (by translating the CMS text code) to make the subject content discoverable via the finding aid container list. The time needed to rearrange the material from CMS document sequence code to text code/topic, discard the redundant mail, sample unique correspondence for high-volume issues, document the extent discarded, refolder the retained material by topic, and record the folder description in an Access database took 2.5 hours per cubic foot. Not bad, but that was still an investment of about 60 days. The pay-off was a reduction of 60 cubic feet in space used by this portion of the collection, and folder-level subject descriptions readily accessible to researchers, including undergraduates, local historians, and other nontraditional users of congressional collections. This was certainly not minimal processing, but it was the minimum *necessary* to provide researcher access to the content and to free up significant storage space. Clearly, the resource and access stakes are significant, and no doubt archivists will come to different conclusions based on their view of the research usefulness and accessibility of the material at hand.

Contrast my approach with that of Michael Strom with the Jim Wright papers. Strom's experience with 135 feet of processed constituent correspondence was that it was seldom used, despite having been processed to a detailed level of arrangement and description. Hence, Strom applied box-level minimal processing treatment to the remaining 353 feet of correspondence, investing only 15 minutes per foot, for a total of 80 hours.[54] Neither of us was right or wrong in this approach. Rather, I highlight this to emphasize the direct linkage between appraisal and processing, and the fact that the specific challenges faced by a processing archivist will vary based on the objectives set by appraisal. Appraisal decisions not only shape the size and content of a collection but also impact the specific tasks in arranging and describing the collection. Appraisal, in articulating a view of the research value of the material, needs to consider that value in light of its consequences for processing activities and costs. On the flip side, processing needs to be conducted in ways that satisfy the objectives for the collection established during appraisal.

This point extends throughout a congressional collection. Take clippings as an example. Many archivists of congressional papers retain clippings, especially if they are found in scrapbooks or otherwise organized in subject form. Such an appraisal decision has the implication of leading to item-level preservation work (generally, photocopying or microfilming), especially where newsprint clips are glued or taped to paper backing that holds contextual data such as newspaper name and date. As with constituent correspondence, a view of the research value relative to the time and cost of processing needs to be considered. Case files fit as well, to be discussed later in this chapter.

LANDMINES IN THE ARCHIVES: COMMITTEE, CLASSIFIED, AND SENSITIVE RECORDS

Usually the archival repository is free to decide on the level of processing, to control the timing and extent of access, and to make and implement appraisal decisions. Yet many circumstances common with congressional papers either directly or indirectly impinge on the archivist's discretion in processing. Often largely outside the archivist's control, they present their own set of processing challenges. Their general effect is to force a more detailed level of processing than an archivist might otherwise think necessary or than is in concert with a zeitgeist of "more product, less process."

One such circumstance is the possibility of a collection holding original Senate or House committee records.[55] Generally, committee records, which are the property of the House or Senate, are held separately from the offices of the committee members. Occasionally, though, committee records have found their way into a member's office and then into their personal papers donated to a repository. This happened, for example, in the case of Harrison Williams. Some committee records related to specific legislative matters of interest to Williams were held in his office. When he resigned suddenly in March 1982, his office was emptied within days, with little time to review the material taken. In the rush, about 200 cubic feet of committee records were carried away to New Jersey and placed in storage with the other 1,800 feet of Williams's papers. Years later, when processing began, the records were identifiable as, predominantly, those of Labor Subcommittee counsel and were returned to the Senate.[56] A few other repositories have returned committee material to the Center for Legislative Archives, which oversees congressional records at the National Archives and Records Administration.[57]

Identification of committee records need not require an intense item-level review throughout the collection. Scanning folders and some contents to develop a series scope and content note can be enough to create suspicion if one finds, as happened with the Williams papers, original intra-committee staff memos, original correspondence and publications addressed to committee staff, materials date-stamped into the committee, and working drafts of legislation. Nevertheless, while committee records can be readily identifiable in general, it can be difficult to determine whether specific folders and sets of material in boxes of mixed material are personal or committee papers. One challenge for the processing archivist is to be alert to the possibility of committee records in the collection and, should any be found, to survey folders to identify materials for return. Appraisal choices impact here as well, specifically, the extent to which resources should be expended to copy committee material for the repository before returning it to the House or Senate. Perhaps the toughest challenge for the archivist will be doing what must be done—actually making the call to House or Senate archivists to inform them of the committee records and letting go of this rich legislative material.

A second circumstance that might serve to press an archivist to process in greater detail is the possibility of classified material held in a collection. Although unusual, federal officials, including those from the Central Intelligence Agency and State Department, have visited repositories to seek classified documents in political collections. The most recent and publicized of these instances occurred in early 2005. Five government officials spent three days poring through 400 boxes of Senator Jackson's papers at the University of Washington, removing eight documents and redacting several others.[58] Two officials spent a week at the University of South Carolina reviewing the papers of former ambassador to Saudi Arabia John West, removing 1.5 boxes.[59]

Archivists can learn some lessons from these two experiences. First, both seem to prove the adage "No good deed goes unpunished." In both instances, the government review is believed to have been triggered by the diligence of the repositories' reporting classified material found in the collections and seeking a declassification decision.[60] That is not meant to recommend nonreporting of classified material. Rather, it points out that repositories can expect, and should be prepared for, more intense government interest in their collections once some classified material is reported. A second lesson is that the government can be expected to be aggressive and intimidating in their initial approach to the repository, but the repository does have room to push back in protecting their interests. In both the Jackson and West cases, government officials wanted the collections (or at least their potentially sensitive portions) restricted from use, a position that softened somewhat when challenged.[61] The actual review process seems to have been less confrontational and more businesslike.[62]

For the processing archivist, the point is that classified materials do find their way into congressional collections, and it is during processing that these materials have the best chance of being identified and the situation managed proactively by the archivist. Not taking advantage of the opportunity available during processing exposes the archivist to the risk of providing classified material to the public or of being unnecessarily surprised during an unannounced visit by government agents concerned with matters of national security. Including a focus on classified items during processing need not be extremely time consuming. The government took 15 person-days to complete an item-level review of 400 boxes in the Jackson collection. That is not huge relative to the amount of time needed overall for processing these collections, especially the richest series where, presumably, classified material is most likely to be found, and where archivists could get the biggest pay-off for item-level processing in any event.

John West's papers were more complicated as they concerned personal diaries and other papers not necessarily stamped with the can't-miss "Top Secret" or other security designation. Christine Weideman's approach at Yale, discussed above, of working with a donor intensively during "accessioning as processing," certainly has applicability here as the best chance at highlighting potential hot spots for classified material such as these. That approach does seem to have been taken with the West papers. Prior to their donation to the University of South Carolina, the materials were submitted to the State Department in 1991, though they were not declassified at that time. In preparing to open the collection in 2005 in accordance with the deed of gift, the university contacted the State Department regarding the 1991 correspondence, leading to the State Department's renewed interest in both the original materials and other matter in the collection.

In any event, the repository and processing archivist have a responsibility to conduct due diligence to determine if classified material is in their collections and, if found, sending it through the proper declassification channels.[63] Not every piece of paper in every folder needs to be reviewed; not even the government does that. A risk-based approach driven by the particular portions of a collection, the member's committee assignments, or other factors can drive the intensity of the review. Of course, just as the risks will vary among collections or parts of a collection, so too will the extent to which the repository implementing the review accepts risk.

Some combination of a repository's willingness to accept risk and appraisal considerations comes into play with the most provocative portion of a congressional collection—case files. Casework contains a broad range of issues of personal interest to a constituent, such as health, taxes, finances, military service, immigration, criminal justice, employment, and social welfare payments. All such files will include personally identifiable, often sensitive, data about the correspondent or others discussed by the correspondent. Clearly, special handling is called for.[64] The first question is whether case files have sufficient research value to justify the special attention and uncertain level of risk to the repository should case details be publicized. Archivists' views on this point are decidedly mixed.

Frank Mackaman has argued compellingly for the value of case files in "document[ing] the confluence of three prevalent government-related activities: individual citizen appeal, congressional action on behalf of a constituent, and bureaucratic response."[65] He also sketched several potential lines of inquiry for various types of cases.[66] Indeed, just as Mackaman suggested, a very small amount of descriptive information about case files in the Senator Hiram L. Fong papers at the University of Hawaii was sufficient to attract a researcher of immigration issues.[67] One of the interviewees for this chapter reported use by individuals of their own case files. I had a similar experience assisting the family of a deceased serviceman who had turned to Senator Williams for help 43 years earlier.

Nevertheless, there was no consistency of perspective on case files among my interviewees. Some once thought that the cases would be useful in quantitative analysis, but the small, self-selecting number of case correspondents and the demonstrated lack of use in many instances changed minds on that point. While one interviewee shifted over time from retaining case files for their research value to discarding or no longer accepting them, another moved in the opposite direction, actively seeking case files. The perspectives and practices expressed by my interviewees ranged widely regarding case files. Some thought they had great value, or no value, or maybe unproven value. Some believed in keeping all (if small volume), or keeping none, or keeping a representative sample (perhaps the most common view). Should a donor not offer to donate the case files, most would seem to be satisfied with that result, while some would request the files. The Senate and House records manuals reflect this diversity of perspective as well. The suggested disposition in the House manual unambiguously calls for the destruction of resolved cases. The Senate's suggestion is more ambivalent, calling for the destruction of routine cases but suggesting alternative approaches in acknowledging the potential for archival value.[68] In short, the privacy concerns, the need for access restrictions of some kind, and the storage space and processing demands are clear, while the research use and value relative to these costs is uncertain. Archivists continue to feel their way through this thicket.

As discussed above, an appraisal decision favoring the retention of case files has several implications for processing. First, many (though not all) politicians are reluctant to donate case files to a repository because of privacy concerns. Archivists desiring to acquire and retain cases will need to work with the donor up front to ensure they obtain the files and that the deed of gift is structured to permit the repository discretion over the appropriate restrictions to place on case files.

Next, archivists will need to translate the appraisal decision into sampling and processing techniques that accomplish the appraisal goals. For example, a decision to keep case files because of an interest in documenting constituent experiences with, say, social welfare programs during a period of cutbacks would suggest heavy sampling of those types of cases, and little or no retention of other types. An appraisal decision based on an interest in military cases in a time of war means ensuring a sample skewed in that direction. For the archivist with no view on the research value of specific types of cases, selecting a sample that fairly represented all types would be warranted. An appraisal focus on the actions of a member's staff or the political connections underlying much casework, rather than the actual details of constituents' personal problems, would lead to a sample selection of cases where staff notes and correspondence with the member and staff were dominant, rather than the thick files often filled with copies of tax forms, benefit applications, and other administrative forms that contain the troublesome personal details. Older cases may be in formats such as Thermofax, requiring photocopying if retained.

Processing collections with case files, and the case files themselves, will take longer than situations where there are no such sensitivities. However, those sensitivities need not negate using accelerated processing methods judiciously. For example, Kenton Jaehnig, formerly of the American Heritage Center at the University of Wyoming, applied the minimal processing recommendations of Greene and Meissner to a manuscript collection of 162 cubic feet which held what proved to be 31 cubic feet of sensitive personal records that required removal or restriction according to the deed of gift. Methodically searching out sensitive documents wherever they might be hiding, while rigorously applying the MPLP approach in other respects, Jaehnig completed the 162 feet in four months. Reflecting on an earlier collection he had processed, the papers of a former U.S. ambassador to Guatemala, Jaehnig concluded that a diligent search for sensitive documents and an accelerated schedule for processing and researcher access were not mutually exclusive.[69] While case files are commonly well identified in collections, that is not always so. Case matters are often found mixed with departmental or other types of constituent correspondence. Jaehnig's conclusion is especially encouraging for those situations.

The processing archivist will need to place restrictions of some kind on case files. The most common restriction is that personally identifiable information not be used. The University of Hawaii's requirement along these lines has been well publicized.[70] Some repositories also restrict access for a number of years, typically 50 or 75. For the Harrison Williams papers, cases involving military, health, criminal justice, and other especially sensitive matters are restricted for 50 years from the case's original "closed" (i.e., resolved) date; cases involving consumer complaints, grants and contracts, land acquisitions, labor relations, and other items with less intensely personal details are open to research. Similar to the requirements placed on researchers at the University of Hawaii, researchers agree in writing not to cite personally identifiable data in their work.

DONOR-IMPOSED RESTRICTIONS AND EXPECTATIONS

We have discussed sensitive material and restrictions as defined in law or in the context of personal privacy, but there is another source of restrictions on material—the donor. Not surprisingly, many donors place restrictions on their collections. Indeed, the records management handbook for senators all but encourages restrictive deeds of gift "to provide a temporary delay to protect sensitive data and to guarantee confidentiality to living persons."[71] Perhaps the most common type of restriction is a closing of all or parts of a collection for a period of time. My interviewees mentioned experiences with donor-imposed restrictions of 20, 25, 30, and 50 years, as well as donor lifetime. A second form of restriction relates to usage reporting and permissions. Some interviewees reported the need to inform donors of usage of the material, with at least one instance requiring the donor's permission for use (a requirement that ends with the donor's death). No interviewee reported that access was denied in these instances. A third form of restriction requires the donor's involvement in the removal of material from the collection, perhaps being given the opportunity to take the unwanted material back or requiring the donor's permission for removals. Yet another form is the requirement for the archivist to identify, remove, and return any material harmful to living persons, constituting an invasion of privacy, or other such concepts.

The challenge for the processing archivist is in ensuring that these donor-imposed restrictions are respected. This is more difficult than it might appear. Complying rigorously with the conditions of the deed of gift may run against what might be taken as commonsense assumptions. For example, if a restriction is in place denying access for a time or requiring permission to access the papers, an archivist might assume that the restriction applies only to outside parties, not the archivist, assistants, and student workers. As reasonable as that assumption sounds, it may be entirely wrong. One interviewee reported the need to obtain a donor's approval simply to unseal boxes of restricted papers on their arrival at the repository in order to look for obvious preservation problems, such as mold or bugs.

Generally, donors are accepting of a clause in the deed of gift that disposition of materials will conform to standard archival practices, such as discarding duplicates and other material with no permanent research value. But this cannot be taken for granted. If the deed includes a condition requiring donor approval for removal of any material from the collection, that condition should be taken literally. Archivists would obviously respect such a condition for substantive material, but they might not think "any material" extends to blank stationery, old folders, envelopes, duplicates, paper clips, and the detritus usually discarded from a collection. One interviewee reported that a handful of donors intended their restriction on the archivist's discretion to extend to such material. Eventually, the donor will likely stop requiring notice of such routine removals, but until then, it is the archivist's responsibility to build the relationship through diligent adherence to the deed of gift. At the very start of surveying a collection, archivists should be sure to obtain a copy of the deed of gift, ensure they understand the terms, and apply the conditions.

Often a donor places no restrictions on the papers and may expect them to be immediately accessible to researchers. One would expect archivists to be happy about that. However, the lack of donor-identified restrictions creates its own challenges for an archivist. One such challenge is a practical one: given the size of these collections, and the lack of funding for processing many of them, the collections will be unprocessed for years. The archivist then is faced with the question of whether to permit use of an unprocessed collection and, if so, how to manage the potential for inappropriate disclosure of classified or sensitive records. Many archivists do not permit access to unprocessed papers. Others do, perhaps especially with older large collections with no real prospect in sight for processing. In these instances, user requests are handled on a best-effort basis, with the archivist often assessing individual requests and scanning requested material for potential problems.

The University of Florida's experience with the papers of Senator Lawton Chiles (D-FL), while perhaps exceptional in its intensity, is illustrative of the challenges faced by the archivist. Donated with no restrictions by Chiles after he left the Senate in 1988, thousands of feet of material were unprocessed when he decided to run for governor in 1990. Correctly anticipating demand for the records, the archivists identified the materials most likely to be of interest and those that could be processed most expeditiously. Position papers from the well-ordered press office files, campaign files, financial reports, and selected legislative aide files were among the most requested record types. Processed papers were made available to journalists on the same basis as any open collection; requests for unprocessed materials were satisfied by the archivists to the extent possible. This was done with Chiles's support and in conversation with his campaign staff. While somewhat unique, this instance illustrates that the challenges to the archivist of providing immediate access to an unrestricted collection may be as daunting as ensuring that restrictions are observed.[72]

The experience with the Chiles papers serves also to remind that political papers cannot be divorced from their political context. And that political context includes not only the donor politician, but also other political figures found directly or indirectly in the collection, including other politicians, political powerbrokers, campaign staff, and legislative and other office staff. Each of these parties will have their own level of comfort or concern about immediate public access to the materials. Some former members of Congress who went on to other public office, like Chiles or Representative James Florio, who became governor of New Jersey, placed no restrictions on their congressional papers.[73] Some who moved on to other public offices restricted access (although it is not necessarily known if continuation of public service was the specific motivation for the restriction).

Many archivists counsel donors to consider some time restriction, say, 10 or 20 years or even longer. This provides a level of privacy and confidentiality to the politician and to his or her staff, associates, colleagues, and constituents, at least for a time. Such treatment is likely most desirable for younger politicians who may return to public office, but the potential for older politicians remaining in some form of public service should not be discounted. Beyond the politician, staff members or political correspondents who remain active in their careers may be adversely impacted by documents emerging from the collection. Delaying the opening of papers takes them out of the realm of current events and the latest news cycle and moves them into the less heated realm of historical research.

If a donor expresses a willingness to have the papers opened immediately, why should the archivist counsel against immediate access? Because the issue transcends the collection in hand. Several of my interviewees explained their role as that of an honest broker, doing what is best for the repository but also acting in good faith in dealing with the donor. This might call for the archivist to advise the donor against excessive or vaguely worded and open-ended restrictions. Or it might mean reminding a politician of the potential sensitivities in the papers and advising a cooling-off period before opening the papers. A repository, especially one that specializes in the collection of political papers, will want to develop a positive relationship with the donor and to establish credibility as a discrete and trustworthy steward in order to attract other collections. Having a tin ear for the politics of political papers will hardly endear the archivist to future donors. In one case, restrictions were placed on the previously unrestricted papers of a former congressman after he returned to public office. In another instance, a congressman, having lost reelection at a relatively young age, was advised by the archivist to apply a not uncommon 30-year restriction to his papers, rather than a 15-year restriction with an option to extend it another 15 years, which he originally requested.

There are two cautionary tales in this regard. In the one case, the Library of Congress opened former Supreme Court Justice Thurgood Marshall's papers immediately upon his death in early 1993, as stipulated by Marshall's deed of gift.[74] Because Marshall died little more than a year after his resignation from the Court, his papers contained matters of recent interest which drew press attention. The Library of Congress's action attracted opposition from Marshall's family, and Chief Justice William Rehnquist wrote a letter to Librarian of Congress James Billington indicating that "a majority of the active Justices of the Court . . . are both surprised and disappointed by the library's decision" and that "we think it is such that future donors of judicial papers will be inclined to look elsewhere for a repository."[75] The Library of Congress's action was a principled one, and it was supported by the archival profession, including the Society of American Archivists council.[76] Nevertheless, one interviewee also recalled how such unrestricted access raised concern, at the time, from potential donors of political papers who worried how their papers would be handled if given to a repository.

On the other hand, restricting access also creates problems. In responding to a Freedom of Information Act (FOIA) request from *USA Today* regarding presidential pardons by Bill Clinton, the National Archives partially redacted or withheld 1,500 pages that it perceived as falling within the restriction on confidential communications allowed under the

Presidential Records Act of 1978. The newspaper reported, "The decision to withhold the records could provide fodder for critics who say that the former president and his wife, Sen. Hillary Rodham Clinton, now seeking the Democratic presidential nomination, have been unwilling to fully release documents to public scrutiny."[77] The National Archives maintained they were following Bill Clinton's restrictions, which could have been, but were not, waived by Clinton's legal agent, Bruce Lindsey. Lindsey and the Hillary Clinton campaign both asserted that the determination to redact and restrict the material was made by the National Archives. No one came off well here. Clinton's political opponents claimed she was suppressing information relevant to the campaign. And the archivists appeared as overly secretive and cowed by the restrictive attitude toward presidential records expressed by the administration of President George W. Bush.[78]

In short, the papers of a public figure, particularly those of one with continuing political relevance or those concerning issues of continuing public interest, will face a demand for access. The potential for embarrassment lies in both opening the collection recklessly and restricting it excessively. The archivist will need to work with the donor to steer between the rock and a hard place of too swift and too slow access. The calculus will differ under the circumstances of each collection. The purpose of collecting materials is to have them used, so a bias toward access is warranted. Yet longer range collection development goals may depend on the archivist's ability to manage effectively the politics of political papers.

Such politics extend beyond access issues to the nuts and bolts of processing. Donors, project funders, or resource allocators may have expectations of their own that will influence processing directions. Donors may contribute their papers to a repository with the expectation that they will receive a certain level of processing. Contributors funding a political papers project may provide enough money to do more processing than perhaps is minimally necessary. This is a fortunate luxury enjoyed by some projects, but such funding also creates processing expectations that the archivist needs to be aware of and satisfy. While the professional literature may indicate a movement against spending time pulling out metal fasteners at the item level, if the project funder or donor is paying for, and expects, that type of high-end work to be done, so be it. Not to do so will dissatisfy a client and, worse, may threaten the repository's ability to garner funding and to gain a reputation as a good steward of political collections.

Such expectations of the processing archivist may come from within the organization as well. It is not uncommon for senior management of a repository to request or accept the papers of a political figure whether the repository wants them or not. Such "flagship" collections may warrant close processing merely because of the high public visibility of the individual, the expectations of senior leadership, and the potential that good stewardship of the high-profile collection will lead to other collection development and possibly funding opportunities. The challenge for the archivist is in managing expectations and resources and negotiating deliverables in relation to the collection to ensure that the final processed product meets the objectives of the interested supporters.

The processing archivist may also be faced with a donor who expects to take a tax deduction for the appraised value of the collection. This is especially likely with donors who are the heirs of the politician, but the potential for some tax benefit might be found in any collection.[79] When an appraisal for tax purposes is performed, the archivist will be called on to assist, most significantly in providing inventories to an adequate level to support the appraiser's work.[80] Eventually, the appraiser will need to drill down to the item level to identify and describe in some detail the high spots of the collection, including autographs, stamps, important draft documents and other manuscripts, collectibles, artwork, editorial cartoons, photographs, and other material. The support role of the archivist will need to be coordinated with the donor and appraiser. Unlike traditional archival practice of describing a collection top-down through its hierarchy and stopping at the level sufficient to make it accessible to a researcher, the appraiser will be interested perhaps above all in item-level information. Whether the appraiser ferrets out those individual items based on high-level (box) inventories provided by the archivist, or whether the archivist is called on to do the detailed schedules, can be negotiated with the donor (who is paying for the appraisal work). Although the archivist will need to satisfy the donor's expectations, managing the timing and process of the financial appraisal may permit the archivist to complete a survey and high-level description in addition to the item-level description. The financial appraisal work for a large collection can be expected to take several weeks, and likely months, so the archivist will need to identify ways of tying that effort into the processing project, rather than operating on completely separate tracks.

The overarching challenge for archivists processing congressional papers is finding the proper balance among the three primary goals: (1) performing a level of efficient and expeditious processing that permits timely and effective access to the papers, (2) conducting the due diligence of collection material expected of a responsible steward to ensure that materials deserving exceptional treatment are handled accordingly, and (3) managing and meeting the expectations of the donor and program supporters for both the benefit of the collection in hand and for future collection development potential. At many points in this tension among access, restriction, and political context, the elements may push hard against one another in competition for priority. Good news: the three goals are not mutually exclusive.

NOTES

1. The author wishes to acknowledge the invaluable contributions of Senate Archivist Karen Dawley Paul in developing the concept and shape of this chapter and in providing guidance and leads during its research. The author also thanks L. Rebecca Johnson Melvin of the University of Delaware for her helpful comments on the draft of this chapter. The author thanks the following archivists for sharing their experiences and perspectives in interviews conducted in March–April 2008: Ronald Becker (Rutgers University), Nathan Bender (University of Idaho), Janet Bunde (New York University), Morgan Davis (Missouri Historical Society), Matt Fulgham (National Archives and Records Administration), Edward Gaynor (University of Virginia), Jennifer Graham (Wisconsin Historical Society), Herbert Hartsook (University of South Carolina), Kenton Jaehnig (University of Virginia), Leigh McWhite (University of Mississippi), Naomi Nelson (Emory University), Carla Summers (University of Central Florida), Sheryl Vogt (University of Georgia), and Jan Zastrow (University of Hawaii).

2. Joanne Wasserman, "Thinking Cap for Rudy," *New York Daily News*, January 3, 2002, 9.

3. Joanne Wasserman, "Giuliani's Paper Play Irks Some Historians," *New York Daily News*, February 5, 2002, 22; Joanne Wasserman, "Rudy Keeps Papers but City Decodes What's Private," *New York Daily News*, February 15, 2002, 21; Frank Lombardi, "Council Panel Eyes Rudy-Papers Plan," *New York Daily News*, February 21, 2002, 14.

4. Saul S. Cohen, letter to the editor, *New York Times*, July 2, 2002, A-20.

5. Joanne Wasserman, "Won't Keep My Papers Private: Rudy," *New York Daily News*, February 6, 2002, 6.

6. Wasserman, "Won't Keep My Papers Private"; see also Saul S. Cohen, letter to the editor, *New York Times*, January 29, 2002, A-20.

7. Mark A. Greene and Dennis Meissner, "More Product, Less Process: Revamping Traditional Archival Processing," *American Archivist* 68, no. 2 (2005): 210.

8. Greene and Meissner, "More Product, Less Process," 210–11.

9. Greene and Meissner, "More Product, Less Process," 212.

10. Anne L. Foster, e-mail to CPR mailing list, March 13, 2008.

11. Morgan Davis, "Missouri Historical Society," *Congressional Papers Roundtable Newsletter*, March 2007, 3.

12. Jennifer Graham, "Wisconsin Historical Society," *Congressional Papers Roundtable Newsletter*, March 2007, 4.

13. Larry Weimer, "Rutgers University Libraries," *Congressional Papers Roundtable Newsletter*, March 2006, 3.

14. Dean DeBolt, "University of West Florida: Papers of Congressman Robert LF Sikes," *Congressional Papers Roundtable Newsletter*, March 2005, 9; Brian Keough, "University at Albany," *Congressional Papers Roundtable Newsletter*, March 2007, 8.

15. James Borchert, "South Dakota State University (SDSU) Library," *Congressional Papers Roundtable Newsletter*, March 2006, 4.

16. Leigh McWhite, e-mail to CPR mailing list, March 14, 2008.

17. Matt Fulgham (assistant director, Center for Legislative Archives, NARA), in discussion with author, March 13, 2008 and April 23, 2008.

18. Greene and Meissner, "More Product, Less Process," 209.

19. Greene and Meissner, "More Product, Less Process," 235.

20. Greene and Meissner, "More Product, Less Process," 239.

21. Greene and Meissner, "More Product, Less Process," 212–3.

22. Greene and Meissner, "More Product, Less Process," 212, 214–5, 255–6.

23. Jan Zastrow, "University of Hawaii at Manoa Library: 'Using Shovels, Not Teaspoons': The Rapid Processing of Hawaii's Senator Hiram L. Fong Papers," *Congressional Papers Roundtable Newsletter*, March 2006, 5; Greene and Meissner, "More Product, Less Process," 240.

24. Tom Hyry, "More for Less in Archives," *Annotation* 33, no. 2 (2007): 8. The author thanks Karen Paul for referring him to this article.

25. Michael Strom, "Texas-Sized Progress: Applying Minimum-Standards Processing Guidelines to the Jim Wright Papers," *Archival Issues* 29, no. 2 (2005): 107, 109–10. The author thanks Karen Paul for referring him to this article.

26. Anne L. Foster, e-mail to CPR mailing list, September 19, 2007.

27. Strom, "Texas-Sized Progress," 110.

28. Foster e-mail, September 19, 2007.

29. Donna E. McCrea, "Getting More for Less: Testing a New Processing Model at the University of Montana," *American Archivist* 69 (Fall/Winter 2006): 289.

30. McCrea, "Getting More for Less," 284–5, 287–9.

31. Susan Hamson, "Wrestling with the Backlog: Applying Greene-Meissner to the Rare Book and Manuscript Library, Columbia University," presented at the program meeting of the Archivists Roundtable of Metropolitan New York, Columbia University, March 27, 2008.

32. Christine Weideman, "Accessioning as Processing," *American Archivist* 69 (Fall/Winter 2006): 274–6.

33. A note on my methodology and use in this chapter of the results of my interviews is appropriate here. During March and April 2008, I interviewed several archivists of congressional papers. Some were project archivists for particular collections, others were managers of repositories with a political papers focus, and others were managers of manuscript repositories that held congressional papers but with no specialized focus in that area. The interviews took a conversational form touching on the issues discussed in this chapter, varying depending on the circumstances of the interviewee. If an interview yielded a specific example used in the chapter in a way that identifies the associated institution or collection, that example was used with permission of the interviewee and is cited in the endnotes. Otherwise, perspectives gained from the interviews are reported in the chapter more generally without specific attribution.

34. Greene and Meissner, "More Product, Less Process," 240, 254.

35. Weideman, "Accessioning as Processing," 274.

36. Weideman, "Accessioning as Processing," 276–7.

37. "Congressional Papers Roundtable Pre-Conference Program," *Congressional Papers Roundtable Newsletter*, February 2008, 12.

38. Lori A. Lindberg and Supriya V. Pidady-Wronkiewicz, "African American Museum and Library at Oakland," *Congressional Papers Roundtable Newsletter*, July 2007, 5.

39. The following discussion of electronic records is informed largely by the author's interviews with Ted Clark of NARA (March 14, 2008) and Naomi Nelson

of Emory University (April 14, 2008). For a sense of the electronic records environment on Capitol Hill, and the technical recommendations made to congressional members for preserving and transferring their digital material to repositories, see Karen Dawley Paul, *Records Management Handbook for United States Senators and Their Archival Repositories* (Washington, D.C.: U.S. Senate, 2003), 50–62.

40. Office of the Clerk, House of Representatives, "E-mail Me: Congress and the Internet," http://clerk.house.gov/art_history/house_history/technology/internet.html.

41. See, for example, Mark Greene, "Appraisal of Congressional Records at the Minnesota Historical Society: A Case Study," *Archival Issues* 19, no. 1 (1994): 33.

42. At this writing, the current edition of Paul's *Records Management Handbook* is the 2006 edition.

43. Richard A. Baker, "Managing Congressional Papers: A View of the Senate," *American Archivist* 41, no. 3 (1978): 295.

44. Richard C. Davis, "James A. McClure: Notes on Appraisal and Processing," www.lib.uidaho.edu/special-collections/Manuscripts/jam/appraisal.htm. The author thanks Nathan Bender for referring him to this Web page.

45. L. Rebecca Johnson Melvin, "The Appraisal of Senator John Williams's Papers," *Provenance* 10, nos. 1–2 (1992): 41–56, especially 52.

46. Lydia Lucas, "Managing Congressional Papers: A Repository View," *American Archivist* 41, no. 3 (1978): 277, 278.

47. See, for example, Lucas, "Managing Congressional Papers"; Patricia Aronsson, "Appraisal of Twentieth-Century Congressional Collections," in *Archival Choices: Managing the Historical Record in an Age of Abundance*, ed. Nancy E. Peace, 81–101 (Lexington, Mass.: D. C. Heath, 1984); Greene, "Appraisal of Congressional Records"; Faye Phillips, *Congressional Papers Management: Collecting, Appraising, Arranging, and Describing Documentation of United States Senators, Representatives, Related Individuals and Organizations* (Jefferson, N.C.: McFarland, 1996), 35–44.

48. "Processing Info," *Guide to the Henry M. Jackson Papers, 1912–1987*, www.lib.washington.edu.

49. Greene, "Appraisal of Congressional Records," 35–36, 39; Phillips, *Congressional Papers Management*, 169.

50. For discussions of sampling techniques in congressional collections, see Phillips, *Congressional Papers Management*, 163–171; and Eleanor McKay, "Random Sampling Techniques: A Method of Reducing Large, Homogeneous Series in Congressional Papers," *American Archivist* 41, no. 3 (1978).

51. Melvin, "Appraisal of Senator John Williams's Papers," 49–51.

52. These approaches primarily reflect archivists' experience with paper-based correspondence. Alternative sampling approaches, or the use of summary reports, are likely with issue mail in electronic format.

53. See, for example, L. Rebecca Johnson Melvin, "Ready to Talk: Political Scientists and Congressional Archivists," *Congressional Papers Roundtable Newsletter*, March 2005, 11–13.

54. Strom, "Texas-Sized Progress," 109.

55. For information about committee records, see Karen Dawley Paul, "Congressional Papers and Committee Records: Private vs. Public Ownership," *Congressional Papers Roundtable Newsletter*, February 2004, 1, 8–13; and Paul, *Records Management Handbook*, 5–6, 114.

56. Karen Dawley Paul, "Rutgers University Returns Labor Committee Records to the Senate," *Congressional Papers Roundtable Newsletter*, March 2007, 13.

57. Matt Fulgham, discussion.

58. Karen Paul, "What to Do If You Find National Security Classified Documents When Processing a Collection of Congressional Papers or You Are Unexpectedly Visited by Agency Declassification Officials," *Congressional Papers Roundtable Newsletter*, July 2005, 1, 3; and Carla Rickerson, "Federal Team Reviews Henry M. Jackson Papers," *Congressional Papers Roundtable Newsletter*, March 2005, 11.

59. Paul, "What to Do," 3; "Annual Congressional Papers Roundtable Meeting," *Congressional Papers Roundtable Newsletter*, March 2006, 13.

60. Paul, "What to Do," 4.

61. Paul, "What to Do," 3.

62. Rickerson, "Federal Team Reviews Henry M. Jackson Papers," 11; "Annual Congressional Papers Roundtable Meeting," *Congressional Papers Roundtable Newsletter*, March 2006, 13.

63. Still useful for a concise summary of classification markings and declassification matters, though dated with respect to current regulations, is Kenneth Schlessinger and Marvin F. Russell, *Identifying and Handling Classified Documents in Archives*, Technical Leaflet Series 7 (Mid-Atlantic Regional Archives Conference, 1992). Also see Paul, "What to Do"; for detailed information about classification and declassification matters generally, see the Web site of the Information Security Oversight Office, www.archives.gov/isoo/.

64. Among the literature relevant to privacy and confidentiality issues in congressional papers are Mark A. Greene, "Moderation in Everything, Access in Nothing?: Opinions About Access Restrictions on Private Papers," *Archival Issues* 18, no. 1 (1993): 31–41; David Klaassen, "The Provenance of Social Work Case Records: Implications for Archival Appraisal and Access," *Provenance* (Spring 1983): 5–30; and selected essays in Menzi L. Behrnd-Klodt and Peter J. Wosh, eds., *Privacy and Confidentiality Perspectives: Archivists and Archival Records* (Chicago: Society of American Archivists, 2005).

65. Frank H. Mackaman, "Managing Case Files in Congressional Collections: The Hazards of Prophecy," *Midwestern Archivist* 4, no. 2 (1979): 98.

66. Mackaman, 100–101.

67. Mackaman, 101; Jan Zastrow, e-mail to CPR mailing list, April 3, 2007.

68. *Records Management Manual for Members* (Office of the Clerk, U.S. House of Representatives), 7; Paul, *Records Management Handbook*, 38.

69. Kenton G. Jaehnig, "MPLP and Privacy: The Walter Doniger Papers and Thomas F. Stroock Papers," presented at the annual meeting of the Society of American Archivists, Chicago, August 31, 2007. The author thanks Kent for sharing this work and another he wrote regarding the papers of Thomas Stroock at the American Heritage Center at the University of Wyoming.

70. Jan Zastrow, e-mail to CPR mailing list, March 9, 2006.

71. Paul, *Records Management Handbook*, 108–9.

72. Carla Summers (archives consultant), in discussion with author, April 4, 2008.

73. Ronald Becker (head, Special Collections and University Archives, Rutgers University), in discussion with author, March 19, 2008.

74. The author thanks Herb Hartsook for calling his attention to this incident.

75. "... and Rehnquist's Protest," *New York Times*, May 26, 1993. For an overview of the matter, see Barbara Bryant, "Thurgood Marshall Collection: Press Stories Stir Furor over LC's Opening of Papers," *Library of Congress Information Bulletin*, June 14, 1993, www.loc.gov.

76. "Council Meeting 6/11–13/93," *American Archivist* 56, no. 4, www.archivists .org.

77. Peter Eisler, "Clinton Papers Release Blocked," *USA Today*, March 6, 2008, www.usatoday.com.

78. Eisler, "Clinton Papers Release Blocked."

79. For an overview of tax issues, see Paul, *Records Management Handbook*, 110–12.

80. Kenneth W. Rendell, "Tax Appraisals of Manuscript Collections," *American Archivist* 46, no. 3 (1983).

Part V

BUILDING RESEARCH CENTERS

22

Raising Private Monies to Support Archival Programs

Herbert J. Hartsook

Legislative collections, and particularly congressional collections, present unique problems to archivists. They are often among the largest collections any repository will ever receive, they contain a diverse array of record formats, and their makeup is complex. Even larger well-established repositories will find these collections a challenge. Thankfully, archivists working with the papers of legislators, particularly those of national prominence, have a real advantage in raising funds to support their work. If those legislators are willing to help in soliciting gifts, the sums raised can be quite substantial. Raising money involves building personal relationships with potential contributors, and that takes time. But over a period of as little as five years, a legislative papers archivist can expect to raise sufficient money to have a significant impact. To be a successful fundraiser, you must invest time, energy, and some money. And remember, "ask and you shall receive." If you don't ask, you don't get.

During the first 10 years of our fundraising effort to support the work of South Carolina Political Collections (SCPC), we raised an endowment of more than $1.3 million divided between six endowed accounts. Endowment income supports two to four graduate assistantships and underwrites professional travel, summer internships, and other expenses. This chapter outlines the basic tenets of professional fundraising using our success at SCPC as a model.

SCPC was founded in 1991 as a division of the South Caroliniana Library, a fine special collections library at the University of South Carolina.

Previously published as "Raising Private Monies to Support Archival Programs" in *Archival Issues*. Reprinted with permission.

In 2005, SCPC became an independent unit of the USC Libraries. By 2010, SCPC should move into a new state-of-the-art home at the center of the USC campus. SCPC holds 80-plus manuscript collections of individuals and organizations playing significant roles in politics and government since 1945. Our collections include the personal papers of a number of former governors, members of the state's congressional delegation, the Democratic and Republican state parties, journalists, and editorial cartoonists. Because we collect broadly and across party lines, we fit, in many ways, the description of a public policy center as outlined by the Advisory Committee on the Records of Congress (ACRC) in their Third Report (S. Pub. 106-52, December 31, 2000). In that report, the ACRC recommended the establishment of a public policy center in every state or region as the most cost-effective and efficient way to preserve and make available contemporary collections relating to government, and particularly the papers of members of Congress. Archival processing of a single major collection is a significant and expensive undertaking. The creation of a center, involving many such collections, typically will require creative and effective programs raising private funds to support the project.

As noted above, it is a truism that if you don't ask, you'll never get. For many years, I was perplexed about the fate of the personal papers of James F. Byrnes, one of President Franklin D. Roosevelt's top lieutenants. Byrnes was one of South Carolina's leading public figures from the 1930s to the time of his death in 1972. A resident of Columbia, the home of the University of South Carolina, he was closely associated with the school. After his death, his home and all its furnishings were donated to the university. However, his rich collection of personal papers was given to Clemson University, which is USC's chief rival in the state. One day, I met a former associate of Byrnes and asked if he knew why Byrnes had given his papers to Clemson rather than USC. The associate responded simply, "Clemson asked." The former associate went on to say that Byrnes must have known USC wanted the papers but was irritated that the university seemed to take it for granted that it would receive all of his property. Thus, when Clemson asked, and asked nicely, Byrnes acceded to their request, and USC lost one of South Carolina's most important manuscript collections of the twentieth century. That story illustrates a lot about fundraising. You have to ask to receive, you have to establish and then maintain relationships with donors and potential donors, and you must never take a donor's good will for granted.

Former U.S. Senator Ernest "Fritz" Hollings (D-SC, 1966–2005) says that the only thing harder than asking for money is giving money. There is a lot of truth to that simple statement. Asking for money is difficult. Yet development work can be richly rewarding. In absolute terms, the money raised and income from endowed funds will help mount exciting programs and add or retain staff. There can also be a career benefit, as some administrations place greater significance on fundraising success than on success in acquiring or processing collections and other archival achievements. And there are added benefits. In building relationships with potential donors, archivists engaged in development work create strong personal ties with a network of valuable supporters invested in the success of the repository's programs. Some of these individuals may even become valued personal friends. All these factors can make fundraising worthwhile and very rewarding.

When established in 1991, SCPC was given a budget sufficient to fund a curator (namely myself) and either a full-time assistant or a team of graduate assistants. I was also encouraged to work with the library's development officer to raise endowed support for the division. My first few years were spent in getting established, building a track record in processing an inherited backlog of collections, and soliciting significant new collections.

When late in 1995 we were ready to begin raising money, we started off like many new to development work. A general solicitation letter was sent to a list of almost 1,000 SCPC friends and people we had identified as potential supporters. Approximately 5 percent of those solicited responded with gifts ranging from $10 to $500. Most gifts were in the $25 to $100 range. The total raised through this mailing was approximately $1,500. Professional fundraisers believe that a response of even 3 percent to this kind of mailing is good; 5 percent was extraordinary. Professional fundraisers will also tell you that such a mailing is rarely worthwhile, and certainly the amount we raised was barely worth the effort that went into the solicitation. But we did receive one side benefit—a great many people from a carefully defined group with an interest in government, politics, and libraries were made aware of SCPC's existence.

In reading the literature on fundraising and working with the university's development staff, I became much more sophisticated in and opinionated about development work. I carefully considered my division's needs and the nature of our donors and their friends and associates. I also weighed the potential for success in seeking private support as opposed to seeking grants, or dividing my efforts between grants and direct private support. Given limited time and resources to devote to fundraising, I decided to direct all our energies to developing private support and to ignore the grants that might be out there. I focused on developing relationships with individuals who might contribute directly to our cause or help us raise money from other individuals who might find our work of interest.

Our endowments are chiefly administered by a private organization affiliated with the university. The funds are invested and can be compared to a mutual fund. We normally receive an annual income equal to 5 percent of each account's balance. The process becomes fairly complicated though, as typically the fund's performance reflects the gyrations of Wall Street. If the fund performs well and earns more than 5 percent, the excess is ultimately added to the principal. One year, the principal grew by 33 percent as the account generated income of 38 percent. In other years, our principal has fallen, in some instances significantly, as the stock market declined. Over time, as with a mutual fund, we anticipate the fund will continue to grow and that earnings will be sufficient to provide us with 5 percent in expendable income for the foreseeable future. Most nonprofit organizations with endowments operate similarly.

Endowed accounts are typically regulated by guidelines drafted when the account is established. These guidelines may set a target amount pledged to the account and usually set forth the purposes for which income generated by the account may be used. Normally, the institution seeks to make these guidelines as broad as possible. In the case of a significant contribution, the donor may wish to restrict the expenditure of the income to some project close to his or her heart. The institution must then weigh the benefit of the gift to the organization's purpose. While it is difficult to decline a donation, sometimes it is necessary if you believe the donor's desired use for the endowment will not move your institution toward its overall goals. For instance, a donor might wish to endow an annual symposium on a certain issue of great personal interest, but the institution may believe that the issue is not appropriate or relevant to its mission, or there may be some other reason not to accept those limits on fund income.

Our current endowment income, approximately $75,000 annually, supports one full-time special projects archivist, three graduate assistantships, a small research award program, and professional development such as attendance at the annual meeting of the Congressional Papers Roundtable, hosted by the Society of American Archivists. One benefit from this kind of private support is that it is free from the ebb and flow of an overall university budget. Not too long ago, the USC libraries were forced to spend a great deal of energy planning for a tough budgetary environment which made it likely that the libraries would have to cut all or most of its student labor. As the students employed by SCPC are all paid from endowment income, SCPC would have been the only unit within the libraries to retain its student workforce.

Any archival program can replicate our success. Nothing accomplished at SCPC is exceptional in any way. You simply must show that you represent a strong archival program with real needs for private support, and then locate and target people who are likely to approve of what you are doing and who have the wherewithal to support you. Specializing in political collections provides a natural advantage in raising money because many of our donors are active and successful fundraisers themselves, or employ or count fundraisers among their close associates. But everything discussed here can also be applied to raising money for general archival endeavors.

As noted above, it is wise to concentrate fundraising appeals to donors capable of making a major gift. What constitutes a major gift differs from institution to institution. A small repository might set a major gift as being $10,000 and above. A large institution might set a major gift as being any amount over $100,000. All appeals share certain characteristics, but each is also unique, matching a particular appeal to a specific donor.

THE BASIC TENETS

There are some fairly simple tenets of fundraising that should shape planning and efforts. Based on my experience at SCPC, I identify six basic tenets of successful fundraising.

1. *Identify clear, concise fundraising goals that relate directly to your organizational goals.* Development experts tell you that people give to people, and the personal relationships you develop will define your fundraising success. But you cannot raise money without having a clear and valid need for support.

A clear and cogent long-range plan for your institution or unit is critical to successful development. Every time you approach a prospective donor—"a prospect"—seeking a contribution, you must share your vision and plans for your organization, strive to convince that prospect to buy into your vision, and show why the funds you seek are necessary to achieve that vision. If the prospect is sufficiently excited by your plan, he or she will contribute. In communicating with potential donors, you must express your need for contributions clearly and concisely. Your statements should describe the benefits that will result from each gift and, usually, what acknowledgment you will make of that gift.

The initial goal for our endowment was $1 million. At that level, endowment income would support a badly needed full-time project archivist, three graduate assistants working half-time during the school year, and some special expenditures. Our current total goal is $7 million. At that level, the endowment will also support a major annual outreach activity (such as a symposium), a special projects archivist to assist with digitization and other projects, research fellowships, additional graduate assistantships, and an expanded summer archival internship program.

Many of us work in state-supported institutions and, as a result, we have to address the misconception that tax dollars provide full support for our programs. The University of South Carolina is a state-supported institution, but in speaking with potential donors, I point out that less than 30 percent of the university budget comes from tax dollars, a percentage that has been in steady decline in recent years. That statistic is a good starting point in convincing potential donors of our real need for private support.

Fundraising success is also dependent on your ability to share your passion for your work. I believe in what I am doing, and it has been easy for me to speak persuasively about the future of South Carolina Political Collections. Also, I can show that we have been successful in raising funds and have been an excellent custodian of our endowment. People want to be associated with successful programs, and they appreciate seeing that early gifts have been used effectively. Indeed, if you are a good custodian of your gifts, it is likely that past donors will make repeat contributions to your program and may become volunteers helping you to raise additional funds. Many of our donors have followed initial gifts with additional, often larger, contributions. Several have also played critical roles in convincing prospective donors to give their personal papers to South Carolina Political Collections.

2. *Identify and cultivate prospects able to make a major gift.* It is far more rewarding to concentrate on potential major gifts than to expend great energy on mass appeals for support. I get more "bang" for my time and energy by seeking major gifts rather than many small contributions. If this does not seem right to you, consider all the time and energy spent in receiving a $10 check, processing that check, and sending a personal acknowledgment to the donor.

Donors of collections and materials are likely prospects for monetary contributions to support the repository. These donors have invested themselves in your program through the gift of their papers and their contacts with staff. As you consider your potential universe of supporters, it is helpful to think in terms of people of affluence and people of influence. People of affluence are those capable of making a major gift. While you do not turn away $50 gifts, your energies should be focused on donors who have the potential to make a major gift.

At one development meeting, we were told that 72 percent of all higher education gifts come from individuals, as opposed to foundations or corporations; we were also told that most of these gifts are from people age 60 and above. This is your target audience. Typical gifts to SCPC have ranged from $2,000 to $10,000. We have also received several six-figure gifts. Obviously, these gifts originated from people of affluence. People of influence are also worth cultivating. A person of influence is someone who has access to people of affluence and who can help you identify and cultivate potential major donors.

In one case, a high school student came to me for help with a National Endowment for the Humanities scholar project, and the student's parents decided I had gone "beyond the call of duty" in working with their child.

Later, I learned that the father, a prominent attorney, had once worked as a staffer for one of our donors, a former member of Congress. The donor had been retired for many years, but I approached the father, hoping that he might consider helping us raise money for an endowment to be named for his former boss. He declined but referred me to two other people of influence he thought might take on this project. Those gentlemen did agree to help us and became very energetic in targeting industries that had been championed by our former congressman. Within about six months, over $75,000 had been raised, chiefly through these men's efforts. This endowment currently stands at over $90,000. Accepted wisdom is that once out of power, a congressman's fundraising potential sinks to nothing. Clearly, that is not true, especially if people of influence are working on your behalf.

Target your energies at people of affluence and influence who have some natural connection to your repository's collecting theme. Some names will jump out at you. They may be donors of collections, users of your repository, or even personal acquaintances. As you work with these people, they can suggest others you might contact, but they probably will not help unless you ask. Always ask contributors for leads to other prospects and for help in approaching those newly identified prospects.

3. *Take advantage of any assistance your organization or friends can provide.* If you are part of a large organization, you will rarely work alone in development. Your administration or a development office often will be actively involved in your fundraising efforts. You may need to clear your prospects with higher-ups in your organization before approaching the potential donor. The work of a development officer has been compared to that of a Sherpa guide. The development officer cultivates potential donors and connects those prospects with people within the organization who have the status and expertise to ultimately make what is known as the "ask," the formal request for a contribution. Your institution's top administrator probably has development among his or her top priorities. University deans may be required to spend up to 50 percent of their energies on fundraising. Development officers want to help your efforts, and they or some other highly placed individual within your organization might join you and your prospect at a dinner or other event to help you in cultivating that prospect. Prospective donors are often impressed that a dean or even the university president is interested in meeting with them. Also, additional people at the table make for livelier conversation. The downside is that at times you will need to work to control the conversation to ensure that you have the opportunity to present your appeal.

Be alert to relationships that may exist between prospects and current donors and supporters. Several donors of collections have become active in wooing collections and money for SCPC. When successful politicians meet someone for the first time, often they ask about that person's family and connections, trying to identify some mutual association. A good development officer will do the same thing, and you should too. Having a common acquaintance or a shared hobby does wonders to break the ice and helps with the initial steps in forming a relationship with the new donor.

Timing your request is difficult and often a matter of following your gut feeling. Conventional wisdom states that the "ask" should only be made after a relationship has been established. This could take a year or more. But I have had success with requests made fairly early in the relationship. When I approach someone regarding his or her papers, I mention the endowment and describe our vision for South Carolina Political Collections. I explain that we want their collection regardless of any promise of financial support, but that we hope they will consider making a contribution equal to our anticipated processing costs for their collection. If we plan to mount an exhibit or publish a collection guide, I will estimate and note the added expense involved in such projects. As a result of these early "asks" and sharing our honest estimate of the costs of dealing with these collections, over half of SCPC collection donors have contributed to our endowments. Possibly, we have enjoyed success because (a) we typically seek amounts less than $50,000; (b) we link the amount clearly and precisely to the work we will perform on the collection; and (c) we point out the real value of the services we offer in processing and preserving their collection.

An ongoing oral history program supplements the documentary record collected at SCPC. This program has been a great help in developing the strong personal relationships necessary to successful fundraising. We have recorded over 100 hours interviewing donors of papers and key associates. The hours spent with these individuals help to create bonds that are otherwise difficult to forge in a donor/archivist relationship. Relationships with donors who are also interviewees are uniformly stronger than those with donors who have not been interviewed.

Relationships with prospects capable of a major gift typically develop over a period of years, and development continues after receipt of the initial gift. As noted above, past contributors are prime candidates to make future gifts. Sometimes, unexpected gifts arrive. One prospective donor of a collection was reputed to be rather tight with his money, and I decided not to seek financial assistance along with the gift of papers, for fear of offending this particular donor. Over a year after we began receiving the papers, without any urging on our part or any discussion, we received a check for several thousand dollars. The donor continues to make regular gifts, which have ranged from $2,000 to $5,000, without us ever having asked for a contribution. Another donor completed a multiyear pledge and immediately volunteered his intention to make an additional, more substantial gift. With a third donor, we requested and received an annual gift in the range of $5,000 to $7,000. Our relationship has developed and we recently requested and have been pledged a six-figure gift. So, once papers and even a generous gift are in hand, the door does not close to future gifts. Indeed, over time, as your relationship matures and you prove you are a good steward of both papers and contributions, the donor's ties to and stake in your repository grow. Future gifts become more rather than less likely. And you may well find that donors of collections and donors to your fundraising efforts offer you much more than money and their papers. They also prove valuable for the help that they can offer in reaching out to other prospective donors and contributors.

4. *You cannot thank donors enough.* Once you receive a gift, your development work continues. It is a truism in development that you cannot thank donors enough. Nor can you be too effusive. Typically, on receipt of a gift, I will send a personal note of appreciation, and the development officer also sends a personal communication. For a major gift, the dean and even the president may send personal thank-you notes. A personal note is brief and written by hand. If others have been involved in soliciting the gift, you should write and update them as well.

Donors are invested in your program. Keep them apprised of what you are doing and particularly aware of any progress made as a result of their support. Donor names and addresses should be maintained in a VIP mailing list. You should provide these people with regular updates on progress in general and alert these important people to special events that might interest them in particular. If you do not have a newsletter, consider establishing one or piggybacking on an existing publication. This provides a superb venue in which to inform the public about your progress and excite interest in your work. It is nice to be able to acknowledge support provided by major donors in publications, perhaps illustrated with a photograph.

5. *Never make a promise you cannot keep, and always do what you say you will.* Remember, your current donors are a primary source for future gifts and a key resource in encouraging peers and associates to support your program. Do not disappoint them. And do your best to ensure that your administration does not make a promise that you cannot keep. I routinely provide donors of collections with estimated target dates for completing work on their papers. These are always conservative estimates, and I expect to please the donor by coming in well ahead of schedule. If the situation changes and I fear we might miss a deadline, I try to alert those donors of that fact as soon as possible and discuss why we are running behind schedule.

Donors of collections can serve as your most capable field representatives. They can play leading roles in convincing associates to place their papers in your care or contribute to your endowment. It is easy to understand why people might not respond to an unsolicited letter from an unknown archivist seeking their papers. The prospective donor might not even be familiar with the concept of placing personal papers in a manuscripts repository and not appreciate the honor the request represents. But he or she will not ignore a call from a good friend and respected associate; a strong recommendation from such a person will carry great weight.

Many development experts argue that you should consider establishing an advisory committee or board for fundraising. This will help to cement and formalize your relationships with supporters of affluence and influence. People of affluence should dominate such committees. The committee size relates to the amount of money you hope to raise—the larger the amount, the larger the committee. Typically, these committees consist of at least 12 members.

6. *It takes money to raise money, and fundraising is time consuming.* Development costs are often 8–16 percent of the total amount raised. This includes the overhead for your development office. You will incur expenses wining and dining your prospects. Working lunches are a staple of development. Use good stationery and consider having it personalized. Plan for out-of-town and possibly out-of-state travel. You may even plan overnight trips to maximize your time in a distant city; overnight stays allow you to arrive fresh and on time for an early meeting away from home. And you will spend lots of time on development. As director of South Carolina Political Collections, I spend about 15 percent of my time on development. Many of our gifts are received years after I first targeted a prospect. Of course, sometimes you invest a great deal of energy on a prospect and the prospect fizzles out. We once had a couple seriously considering a seven-figure gift. The couple would have benefited from specific tax breaks that would have accrued to them had they made the gift. I had cultivated them for several years and at one meeting brought in one of our top development officers to make a formal proposal. The couple never responded. I do not regret the time invested in them and continue to reach out to them. They may yet come back into our fold.

To reiterate my six tenets of fundraising:

1. Identify clear, concise fundraising goals that relate directly to your organizational goals.
2. Identify and cultivate prospects able to make a major gift.
3. Take advantage of any assistance your organization or friends can provide.
4. You cannot thank donors enough.
5. Never make a promise you cannot keep, and always do what you say you will.
6. It takes money to raise money, and fundraising is time consuming.

Following are some other pragmatic tips for development work:

- Never criticize another person or institution in front of a prospect.
- Never miss an opportunity to break bread with a prospect or donor; this creates a special bond.
- Donors may ask you, personally, to support one of their favorite charities. If asked (and allowed to do so by your institution's guidelines), make a contribution. Even if your contribution is not as generous as what the donor hoped for, he or she will appreciate your support.
- Do not give up easily on prospects. If you receive no response to an inquiry, that is not the same as a "no." Follow up.

Archivists can succeed in raising private funds to support their programs. A good development program will be time consuming, but a strong program will benefit the bottom line and provide unexpected benefits in collection development and, perhaps, in areas such as staff development and general support for archival endeavors. The relationships developed in building private support can be personally and professionally rewarding, and development work will help focus and clarify your institutional goals. As Samuel Pepys noted in his diary on March 21, 1667, "It is pretty to see what money will do."

FURTHER READING

The following are helpful, pragmatic articles and books on development. Each will suggest further reading, much of it in the areas of sales and marketing.

Becoming a Fundraiser: The Principles and Practice of Library Development, by Victoria Steele and Stephen D. Elder (American Library Association, 1992). This small (129 pages) book provides an expert, readable, and pragmatic analysis of fundraising for libraries. The book is aimed at library directors and deans, but the commentary applies equally well to administrators in archives and special collections repositories. One key point the authors make is the need to evaluate success on the basis of both the total amount of the contributions received and the utility of those gifts in moving your organization toward its goals. A minor gift to a discretionary fund may be more valuable to the organization than a major gift that binds the organization to some activity only marginally connected to the organization's goals.

"By Fair Means If You Can: A Case Study of Raising Private Monies to Support Archival Programs," by Herbert J. Hartsook, *Archival Issues* 25, nos. 1 and 2 (2000). This article illustrates basic development tenets as they apply to special collections repositories.

The Millionaire Next Door: The Surprising Secrets of America's Wealthy, by Thomas Stanley and William Danko (Longstreet Press, 1996). This is a popular book of great utility to the fundraiser, opening our eyes to opportunities and prospects we might otherwise ignore. The book points out that the wealthy are all around us, and indeed often look like us, shunning trappings of wealth such as fancy homes and cars. As a fundraiser, you must be attuned to people's potential for a major gift.

Library Fundraising: Models for Success, edited by Dwight Burlingame (American Library Association, 1995). This volume uses case studies to show the variety of tools available for library fundraising. The seventh and final chapter, "The Role of Special Collections in Library Development," by Victoria Steele, is a synopsis of her earlier book, described above.

Building Bridges: Fundraising for Deans, Faculty, and Development Officers, edited by Mary Kay Murphy (Council for Advancement and Support of Education, 1992). This book presents a comprehensive outline for developing a fundraising program in an academic setting. Murphy notes in her introduction that the major focus of the book is on the dean's and the faculty member's role in development work. A secondary focus is on the teamwork and synergy that develop in the best efforts among deans, faculty members, and development officers.

23

Creating the Howard Baker Center

Alan Lowe

As the first executive director of the Howard Baker Jr. Center for Public Policy at the University of Tennessee in Knoxville, the two most fundamental tasks I have undertaken since our founding have been (1) establishing the center's vision and mission, and (2) creating a range of individual and institutional relationships. This chapter provides information on the paths the center has taken and some of the lessons learned over the first four years of building a new institution.

The succinct statement created at the very beginning of the center's operations still forms the core of its mission: "The Baker Center develops programs and promotes research to further the public's knowledge of our system of governance and of critical public policy issues, and to highlight the importance of public service."

Since then, to help people better understand the center's focus, subject areas have been added to the mission statement: "Areas of special interest include the media, energy, environment, the teaching of civics and history, health care, political communications, national security, and the future of representative government."

Given that the center is named for a prominent Republican, though Senator Baker has a wonderful bipartisan reputation, there are occasional concerns that the center will become a partisan, Republican organization. Therefore, another note is sometimes attached to the mission statement: "The Baker Center is and will remain a nonpartisan institution. In all of our programs and activities, we seek to include and discuss many perspectives.

Derived from a presentation at the annual meeting of the Association of Centers for the Study of Congress at the Thomas Dodd Research Center, University of Connecticut (May 10, 2006).

In the best tradition of Howard Baker, the Center embodies his genuine respect for differing points of view. The Center neither advocates nor endorses specific policies or individuals. Instead we serve as a forum for discussion, debate, education, and unbiased research."

That is the Baker Center's mission on paper. I first came on board as a one-person staff, but we are now up to the outrageous size of six staff members plus student workers. The Baker Center was brand new when I joined it, but ideas on what it should be and what it should do had been around for over a decade. Those discussions had led UT and the senator from an original proposal for a school of government to something different, a center for public policy. Senator Baker, the Baker Center Board of Directors, and UT determined in broad outline that the center would (1) discuss important public policy issues, (2) stress the importance of public service, (3) provide some focus on journalism, (4) house an archives, (5) seek student involvement at UT and at high schools and middle schools, (6) stress community involvement, and (7) be useful to UT. This broad mission was very useful because it provided plenty of room to run and to grow, while still pointing in some very important directions.

I also liked it because of my background in presidential libraries at the National Archives and Records Administration. I worked with the Ronald Reagan Library, the Office of Presidential Libraries, and the Franklin D. Roosevelt Library for almost 14 years before arriving in Knoxville. When I interviewed for the Baker Center job, I told both UT and the Baker Center Board of Directors that they should use the presidential library model as much as possible, taking all of the good parts and changing them as necessary. That focus in turn led to a proposal to establish a center that put emphasis on public programs, education, research, and archives. Since its first days of operation, the Baker Center has been able to move from a near total emphasis on public programs to a continued emphasis there but with additional resources to archives, education, and research, and a constant searching for ways to combine these activities. The question still remains not only how to balance these elements, but how to have each strengthen the other. We reject the idea that quality public programs can be created only at the expense of serious research efforts, or vice versa. Instead, the center has had success in reaching a critical mass in which all of the elements work together very effectively.

Since those early days, the Baker Center's mission has evolved—sometimes because of direction from Senator Baker or others, sometimes due to natural selection, and sometimes just because of good fortune. For example, the center's focus on energy and the environment comes directly from Senator Baker's desire that we look closely at those issues, which is understandable given his stellar record in both areas.

Our focus on issues such as foreign policy, the role of the media, or the interplay of science and the making of public policy stems from natural selection. Those issues were so vital in the current national discussion that we simply could not ignore them as a public policy center, especially when there are members of our board and partners within UT and at other organizations, such as Oak Ridge National Laboratory, with tremendous expertise in those policy areas. For example, the Baker board includes Cynthia Baker, a vice president at Tribune Media; Tom Griscom, editor of the *Chattanooga Times Free Press*; and John Seigenthaler, renowned journalist and now head of the First Amendment Center at Vanderbilt University. The College of Communication and Information at UT is also very strong. With that type of built-in knowledge, it is natural that we should discuss the role of the media. As a matter of fact, the center's inaugural conference in the fall of 2003 examined the role of the embedded press in Iraq.

Some of the Baker Center's programs, such as the very successful Churchill conference in March 2006, stemmed from the good fortune of having friends who were comfortable proposing what seemed a fantastic idea—a partnership of the Baker Center with the Churchill Archives Centre at Cambridge University. The result after a year of planning was a partnership that started with a blockbuster conference attended by roughly 2,000 people and featuring speakers such as Henry Kissinger, Brent Scowcroft, Winston S. Churchill, Sir John Boyd, and Lord Charles Powell. This event was a great example of how programs, and even mission, can be altered by good fortune and good networks. The center has established a wide variety of audiences and friends, and they have helped define the center and its future.

That is how the Baker Center's mission in general has developed over three years. No doubt it will continue to evolve. Turning now to the center's management and institutional relationships, it first must be emphasized that Senator Baker has given the center his constant support, and he has maintained a high, consistent level of involvement in its operations. Together with his superb staff, he has provided both general guidance on the direction of the center and specific help in lining up speakers, establishing new partnerships and initiatives, and raising money. With his reputation and long record of accomplishments, Senator Baker gives us our vision and our inspiration. He has been absolutely essential to the center's success.

The Baker Center Board of Directors is made up of very successful individuals who have been close to Senator Baker for many years. With Chairman James Haslam's leadership, and the help of Senator Baker, our board meetings typically include excellent discussions on a multitude of ideas for center initiatives and fundraising possibilities. Chairman Haslam and the other board members have proven invaluable in fundraising, in helping us with our programs, and in providing community support for the center. As of this writing, the board is composed of Chairman Haslam, Senator Baker, Senator Fred Thompson, Tennessee Governor Donald Sundquist, Tennessee Governor Ned Ray McWherter, Cissy Baker, Tom Griscom, John

Seigenthaler, Bill Swain, Fred Marcum, Don Stansberry, Sam Browder, and Dr. Bob Waller. Ex-officio members include UT President John Petersen, UT Knoxville Chancellor Loren Crabtree, UT President Emeritus Joe Johnson, and the president of the UT Student Government Association. Other members of UT management also attend board meetings, including Dean of Libraries Barbara Dewey.

Within the university structure, the executive director reports to the chancellor of the Knoxville campus, Loren Crabtree, and the center receives good support also from the president of UT, John Petersen. In addition, the center is assisted by faculty associates drawn from a variety of academic departments. Overall, we have received good support from the university, but there is always the question of personalities and of fitting into campus priorities. After three years of existence, the center is being recognized more and more as part of the life of the campus, and therefore it has become more involved in general campus activities. This increased activity and involvement is due to the center's success, visibility, and growing network of campus friends.

The Baker Center receives great benefits from being on campus and from being a part of UT. This association gives the center added credibility; access to tremendous faculty, alumni, and students (including the wonderful Baker Scholars); support services such as legal counsel and endowment management; increased connections with local, state, and federal officials; and the ability to be part of the very rich and vibrant traditions of UT. A big question continues to be how to fully involve university partners and make them feel that the center is an asset. There is a constant assessment within the center of how it can be integrated into the campus without losing a certain sense of autonomy.

At first, the main access to the university was through the Advisory Committee. This mechanism proved unwieldy due in part to time constraints, but those faculty contacts have been maintained without convening meetings, and they have proven absolutely invaluable. In addition, we have expanded our group of faculty associates to be much larger than the committee. For example, the center now has a senior teaching fellow, Michael Fitzgerald of the Political Science Department. He is organizing classes to accompany our public events and is very involved in our program planning. The center also recently hired on a part-time basis the former head of UT's Joint Institute on Energy and Environment, Robert Shelton, as senior associate for energy policy. We maintain close relations with the dean of libraries, with the head of the Department of Political Science (who also heads up the Public Administration program), with several professors in communications, with faculty attached to Oak Ridge, with the UT Press, with our Public Relations Department, with the excellent staff of the University Center, where many of our events currently take place, and many others. We have effectively created a network of supporters who have proven to be invaluable allies.

We are continuing to create logical connections between our university colleagues and other partners, such as city and county leaders, state officials, business leaders, friends of Senator Baker and of our board members, partners at the Oak Ridge National Laboratory and the Tennessee Valley Authority, and at other organizations like the Center for Civic Education, and colleagues at other universities like Harvard and Cambridge. Sometimes it is challenging to bring together different groups. At times the center's academic and nonacademic partners have had different goals and different assumptions. A big issue is that of balancing, in the center's programs, the perceived academic heft of the topic and our approach to it versus broader public interest. For example, some of our faculty may prefer that the center have a noted scholar on campus talking about health care, whereas members of our community would be much more interested in hearing from a public policy maker or practitioner. The center has tried to balance this by including both types of speaker whenever possible.

The center also involves people of varying political persuasions, and it is always a delicate balancing act, making sure that the center is not perceived as partisan in any way. Having a Republican leader as our namesake sometimes leads people to assume that we are partisan even when all evidence shows that is not the case. But overall feedback from the public and from UT faculty and students has been overwhelmingly positive and supportive.

The center also has faced some issues within the university's bureaucracy because it has occasionally challenged traditional ways of doing things. UT has been good about exploring options, though sometimes it has taken some convincing. At the same time, we have had to learn the rules of the university and the oftentimes good reasons for current practices.

Finally, because we are a new center, fundraising has assumed a high level of importance in planning. A dedicated Baker Center facility on UT's campus has been constructed at a cost of approximately $17 million. This building will include state-of-the-art archival storage, processing, and research areas, public program spaces, classrooms, administrative areas for the Baker Center and for Senator Baker, and a wonderful museum that will be key to our educational efforts. In addition to building funds, there are plans to increase the current $6 million endowment to at least $10 million in the short term, and $20 million in the long term. Therefore, it is always important to craft programs and other initiatives that will create interest among potential donors. Thanks to the incredible work of Senator Baker, our board, and UT, the center is making great progress on monies for the facility. The endowment, however, has understandably been a lower priority. The center's big concern has been increasing the endowment so that staffing and programming levels for the new facility can be maintained and, in some areas, increased.

These fundraising efforts have created a set of institutional relationships that are obviously fundamental to the success of the center, and that is not only due to the money provided by these groups. The people who have provided the most support often have been those most involved in the center's programming and desirous of helping in nonmonetary ways as well. Their general support throughout the community has given the center a credibility and visibility that has been instrumental to the success of its many initiatives.

Creating the Baker Center certainly has been a labor of love. Our success thus far has been possible only because of the outpouring of support from a huge variety of friends who believe in our mission and find our programs exciting and useful. Thanks to those supporters and especially to Senator Baker, the center quickly and proudly has assumed a vital role in our community and in the national discussion of public policy issues.

24

Richard B. Russell Library for Political Research and Studies: An Evolutionary Model

Sheryl B. Vogt

In a period just short of 35 years, the holdings of the Richard B. Russell Library for Political Research and Studies at the University of Georgia Libraries have expanded from a cornerstone collection to include nearly 300 collections of papers of individuals and groups representing, persuading, or observing the political and public policy processes in Georgia and the nation since 1900. In 1974, the Russell Library was established through the efforts of the Richard B. Russell Foundation, Inc., the Georgia General Assembly, and the University System of Georgia Board of Regents. Its original mission was to collect and preserve materials documenting the life and career of the late Richard B. Russell, a U.S. Senator from Georgia from 1933 to 1971.[1] The library's steady growth and development has evolved into research, exhibit, and public programming activities that now draw thousands of visitors yearly.[2]

To understand the Russell Library's success and its reputation as a model congressional repository, it is necessary to understand the context of its development. This chapter provides an overview of the library's growth and highlights key periods that were directional turning points. As background, it is important to understand certain factors that make the library unique among its peer political collection repositories.

The Richard B. Russell collection, like many prominent political collections, found a home in the academic library on the campus of its namesake's alma mater. The designation of the Russell Library as a university libraries department, though, was unusual. Most collections placed in academic libraries become part of a larger special collections department, while some combine with other political collections to form a unit within a department. Because of its administrative placement and its continued affiliation with the Russell Foundation, the "Russell Collection" had resources to evolve into a strong research library with some public programming. On the other hand, many institutes or centers that are generated from a congressional collection are placed administratively either in or adjunct to an academic department where faculty pursuits are primary, and the collection and the question of its growth become secondary.

Another distinguishing factor has been my tenure as the director (department head). Having begun work as an archivist one month after the library's dedication, I was interim department head within four years, and four years later, department head. More rewarding than the benefits of seniority have been the strong relationships with the executors of the Russell estate, members of the Russell family and other donors over the years, and Russell Foundation trustees, including the most recent, longtime foundation chair. While direct access to the executors has been a necessity for managing the Russell collection, my responsibility for writing and presenting the library's annual report has given equal access to the foundation meetings.

Finally, after establishing the library and a chair in history, the Russell Foundation set up other programs over the years that one expects to find in a public policy research center. Designed to promote the Russell name, foundation programs are widely distributed across the university campus. They consist of scholarships for the debate team, teaching awards for younger faculty, Leadership UGA for third- and fourth-year students, a biannual symposium, a professorship in agriculture, and a Blue Key Honor Society scholarship. The foundation also sponsors the Georgia High School All-State Debate and four scholarships in the Russell name at his prep school, Gordon College. Although the Russell Library enjoys a national reputation among its peers, it is largely because of this competing factor of Russell recognition on campus that the library works steadily to improve public relations about its existence and activities in its own community.

BEGINNINGS

Although the university libraries had corresponded with Senator Richard B. Russell on several occasions in the 1950s and 1960s about donating his papers, there was no movement in that direction until 1969. A group of Senator Russell's friends persuaded him that a foundation in his name be established; one of its goals was to document his life and career. The following June, the Richard B. Russell Foundation was incorporated under the laws of the state of Georgia, but Senator Russell would not agree to fundraising while he was living. This was one of two signal points in the library's development—a living senator would have yielded more donations and brokered the independent library or institute that the foundation proposed. The second was that the Russell collection never received federal appropriations like some of its contemporary collections, such as those of Everett Dirksen, Hubert Humphrey, and Carl Albert.[3] Following the senator's death in 1971, it is all the more commendable that the Russell Foundation and its first chair, Senator Herman E. Talmadge, raised a significant endowment to establish the library and to fund a Russell chair in history at the university.

Working with the University System Board of Regents and the University of Georgia officials, the foundation trustees agreed to locate the Russell Library with its own entrance on the ground floor of the main university library's new annex. (It would have the façade of being a separate library.) Allocated over 13,000 square feet, the library's physical layout included two galleries, a multipurpose room that could seat 100, a reading room, staff offices, and work and stack areas. The Russell Foundation furnished the library, purchased equipment, and agreed to fund student assistants. In 1973, the executors of the Russell estate conveyed the Russell collection to the foundation, which then transferred it to the University of Georgia. In June 1974, the Russell Library was finally dedicated, and in January 1977 it opened for research.[4]

The Russell Foundation remains in an advisory and limited fiscally supportive role. The university president and the university system chancellor are members of the foundation's board of trustees; the university librarian is ex officio. Since the Russell Library is a department within the university libraries, I report to the university librarian, and as previously noted, I present the library's annual report to the Russell Foundation.

Early on, it was evident that the Russell Foundation expected use of the library by researchers and visitors as though it were a presidential library. In the 1970s, the presidential libraries provided the closest model for a repository honoring someone in public service. There was little chance of this type of research happening with one major senatorial and a few contemporary collections, nor were crowds expected to find the library's separate entrance on the west side of the library annex in the midst of north campus. From the library perspective, growth of the collections and outreach were the means to attract a constituency. Thus, the 1980s were marked by slow, steady progress through trial and error. All post-1900 political collections were transferred from the general special collections department to Russell Library, and we began actively soliciting papers. I started with contemporary congressional collections, calling on offices and camping in hallways between appointments, and then moved to related papers. By making one to two trips yearly to Washington, D.C., I built stronger relationships with the Senate and House historical offices and became active in the Congressional Papers Roundtable of the Society of American Archivists.

Russell archivists developed a formal outreach plan based on the library's strengths and weaknesses at the time, and they began working with university classes and civic groups as well as expanding exhibits and offering some public programming based on collections. Gradually, growth and use increased. A significant lesson from this period was the value of cultivating the library's relationship with the foundation. Through observation and experiment, we learned what the trustees liked and wanted. Annual reports became more dynamic and included library "press kits." Most attention-getting, however, was a project to list publications supported by research in the Russell Library.[5] Done 15 years after the library opened for research, the project was labor intensive but proved more than worthwhile, for it was proof positive to the trustees of collections use. Following distribution of the list, the trustees' attitudes toward the library's work changed dramatically.

In the late 1980s, the foundation elected its fourth chair, and the group evaluated its programming support. Since the library had recently completed a program review and strategic plan, the timing was perfect for my meeting with the new chair. As a result, the library's support tripled, with an annual allocation for unmet equipment needs and students as long as the university libraries did not decrease their support. Prior to this time, the foundation only funded student assistants, which generally had cost less than $8,000 per year. With the additional funding, the library could at last move fully into the computer age.

DEVELOPING A FOCUS

Speaking at a 1989 bicentennial research conference on understanding Congress, Senator Robert C. Byrd, a noted student of the institution, observed: "what we ought to know is that Congress is the people; that it reflects the incredible diversity of this Nation and that it does a creditable job of reflecting local public opinion on national issues."[6] Archivists, experienced in working with congressional collections, would agree with the venerable statesman that the overall documentary record for the institution, though complex and fragmented, reflects that diversity and reveals the multidisciplinary nature of the nation's ever changing historical and cultural landscape. Very few would dispute the significant yet often untapped historic research value to be found in congressional papers.

A truly defining period for the Russell Library came in 1992 and 1994, as the power structure changed in Congress. Nine Georgia congressmen leaving office donated their papers, and holdings more than doubled. My efforts to solicit collections on Capitol Hill were bearing fruit. For the first time, materials had to be moved off-site for storage. To denote the scope of the library's collections and its evolution, we proposed a name change in 1994.[7] In the space of two decades, what began as a memorial to one of the most influential U.S. senators in modern times had evolved into a major repository for papers of individuals and organizations that document the American political system, by specifically supporting research and study of politics and policy in Georgia and the nation.

The library now offered opportunities for research in a broader area of subjects covering a much longer period of time than most comparable libraries. The holdings were beginning to demonstrate the breadth, the diversity, and the full spectrum of Georgia's political life for over a century. It was time to revisit collecting activity and establish a systematic and inclusive policy. The Russell collection was the cornerstone, but the newly developed strength was the comprehensive, interrelated nature of the public policy collections and the ability to support research of politics and policy in the broadest sense. A major endorsement, the Russell Foundation was in accord with the library's new focus. The trustees realized the greater legacy was the growth of the library, that formal collecting did not have to focus exclusively on the senator.

For collection development, the Russell Library adopted the guidelines recommended by the Congressional Archivists Roundtable Taskforce on Congressional Documentation in Karen Dawley Paul's *The Documentation of Congress*.[8] This proactive strategy became the underpinning of the library's approach to acquiring and appraising congressional papers: that Congress cannot be documented without documenting the expansive political framework in which it exists. The Russell Library collected both synchronically (documenting historical events and people that indicate coincidence or occur simultaneously in a chronological arrangement) and diachronically (documenting phenomena as they occur or change over a period of time). Most significantly, we wrote a full collection development policy, one of the documentation task force's recommendations, which is discussed more completely in Faye Phillips's *Congressional Papers Management*.[9] With particular emphasis on the role of Georgia and the U.S. Congress, collection development and programming were expanding the focus on the dynamic relationship of politics, policy, and culture—generated wherever public interest intersects with government. The scope of the Russell Library collections was beginning to provide an interconnected framework of people, events, and ideas for understanding Georgia's increasingly diverse and ever changing political and cultural landscape.

A well-defined collection policy, established procedures for working with political offices, observation and tracking of research use, and institutional growth and development of expanded educational programs are primary factors now shaping appraisal decisions at the Russell Library. This process has formed in the last 15 years as we periodically evaluate goals, acquisitions, and resources in light of the overarching mission. If the collection or certain of its components were questionable when acquired, archivists will review the materials according to its relevant appraisal factors at the time of processing or a reappraisal project. If the materials are to be maintained, there is an obligation to promote their use; otherwise we will arrange for deaccessioning according to the gift agreement. The challenges of storage requirements and concerns about access restrictions that some repositories find problematic or insoluble do not override appraisal decisions at the Russell Library.

Among the Russell Library's nearly 300 collections are the papers of 12 senators, 33 representatives, 55 state legislators, and numerous governors, federal and state judges, elected officials, and political appointees, as well as journalists, the state Democratic and Republican parties, the Georgia Public Policy Foundation, Leadership Georgia, and the Georgia ACLU. Today, the collections concentrate not only on those who represent, persuade, or observe the political and public policy arena but also on the grassroots and civic groups that foment or nurture new ideas, workers, and leaders.

A MODEL PROGRAM

Challenging to many repositories, and especially to those inexperienced in acquiring such collections, are the tasks of preserving and managing collections that are voluminous and complex. Congressional and political papers archivists must be familiar with federal and state laws and statutes that govern ownership and access to the papers they hold. To be effective in soliciting new collections or in building relations with donors still in office, archivists must have access to members and their offices and participate in the records management of a donor's office if possible. They must be knowledgeable about the broader universe of political holdings at other repositories and current professional standards, and they must have good liaison with federal and state resource offices and personnel. One collection of a long-term member can easily overwhelm the limited staff resources of some special collections. When appraisal is inadequate, the amount of material to sift through that may or may not be useful can delay the opening of a collection and, when open, can even overwhelm the inexperienced researcher.

When Russell Library archivists visit Washington, D.C., they solicit every member of the Georgia delegation. Because there is stiff competition from other Georgia institutions, a list of priorities has been developed for use in solicitation. These include whether the Russell Library holds the precongressional papers of the member, whether it holds the member's predecessor papers, or whether the member has experienced certain events or dealt with particular district issues that intersect with other Russell Library holdings and resources. Once the member makes a commitment for deposit, the library's primary goals are to document (1) the member, (2) the function of the office, and (3) Georgia's representation in Congress.

The library has developed a standard procedure for working with members' offices. This consists of conducting a full congressional staff interview where we meet the entire staff for an orientation, then follow up with separate units or individuals to determine specific responsibilities, files created, and filing system in use. In these interviews, we convey an awareness of what kinds of documentation we are seeking and discourage any destruction of significant files that may already be taking place. From the orientation and interview, we prepare records retention guidelines for each office. These are organized by office or member activity (administration, press, legislative, computer systems, district/state office, campaign). For each activity, we provide a records description, a retention decision, preservation recommendation, and comments. While the guidelines follow a basic pattern, they are unique to each office. The library asks for an office liaison and promotes specific intern projects aimed at the preparation of materials for transfer to the archives. For example, we supply guidelines for properly inventorying photographs, special media, and artifacts. We do refer to the Senate or House *Records Management Handbook*.[10] But experience has shown that the drafting of guidelines for each office encourages staff to supply insights that would otherwise be lost and results in more useful guidance for the library staff. Experience also has shown that this personalized type of guidance is more likely to be followed.

To reinforce a sense of trust, we promote the Russell Library as an extension of the member's office—and the idea that the papers have a life beyond the function of the legislative office, although the focus and life cycle will be different in the archives. A few minutes of each office orientation visit are spent introducing the staff to the Russell Library, its mission, the archivist's work, and how the member's papers will be managed and used once transferred. We emphasize working together with the common goal of documenting the member, the office, and its representation of Georgia in Congress, but we reassure staff that the commitment to the library will not add to the workload. Office staff members are usually intrigued with the thought that their files, rather than ending with their employment or the member's service, will serve a new purpose as historical documents that will be preserved for future generations to study. This concept has invested many in contributing to better recordkeeping practices in the office.

The importance of sustaining the office contact in D.C. and at the district/state level cannot be overstated. This is key to the Russell's experience in solicitation and acquisition. The records retentions guidelines that are developed for each office take into account the uniqueness of each office, an assessment of library resources and experiences, and the library's long-term documentation goals. By providing on-site recommendations, we also have the opportunity to assess each individual office's particular use of technology, something that is critical as more offices switch to electronic filing.

For various reasons, some archivists at repositories in academic settings cannot get, or have difficulty getting, administrative permission for direct access to congressional offices. Administrative hierarchy or development policies frequently keep the archivist out of an important decision-making loop in accepting such papers and specifying under what terms. Fortunately, as Russell director, I was given freedom and encouragement to act on behalf of the library in this regard and was "under the radar" for years, working with offices for papers before the "political" value of such activity was recognized. By the time the university became a major fundraising institution in the 1990s, the library's reputation was established with the university librarian and the Russell Foundation, and we were probably considered nonthreatening to any other brokers.

Today, the support of both the Russell Foundation and the university librarian has boosted my ability to negotiate the labyrinth of development and government relations policies regarding who represents the university for certain issues in Washington. The university librarian realizes our need to have direct access to the member and the congressional office staff to build trust and acquire the best documentation from each office. He has encouraged us to take the same leadership on campus to reach out to these other units and build partnerships or working relationships to achieve the library's goals for promotion and use of these resources. Since these university administrators frequently have been in politics prior to their current positions, they have given additional insight for approaching prospective donors. They have opened doors by providing an office contact, and they have provided a solicitation letter from the university president when requested. Over time, they, too, have become good colleagues and advisors.

A two-fold benefit from these relationships is well represented by a library-sponsored event in 2007–2008. When the university was approached to house the U.S. Senate Agriculture Committee chairmanship portrait of Senator Saxby Chambliss in the Georgia Museum of Art, it was one of the library's contacts who redirected the enterprise to where the senator's papers were housed on campus. As the project unfolded, the library worked with the fundraising committee by soliciting contributions to commission the portrait and provide an unveiling reception. The university libraries and the Russell Library appeared on the invitations as hosts for the unveiling in Washington.

The event organizers asked me to speak at the occasion, with an open invitation to talk about the library and anything I thought would give context to our participation in the portrait's commissioning. About 200 gathered in the Russell Caucus Room in the Russell Senate Office Building, including nearly 20 senators, on May 13, 2008. The university's two top government relations administrators as well as the dean of the School of Policy and International Affairs attended. With that captive audience, what congressional archivist could resist turning "lobbyist"?

After briefly describing the library and praising Senator Chambliss for making the decision to place his papers at the University of Georgia when serving in the House, I described how future scholars will research agricultural legislation and land-use policies by visiting the library and, depending on their topics, how they will visit any number of other repositories with relevant congressional collections. Since national history is made in Senate chambers daily, I noted that the only way to preserve this history is for senators and staff to consciously do so by making the same kind of commitment as made by this Georgia senator. Because on the following day I would join many colleagues at the Robert C. Byrd Center for Legislative Studies for the annual meeting of the Association of Centers for the Study of Congress (ACSC), I pointed out that the ACSC is dedicated to preserving the papers of members of Congress and making them available for educational purposes, and that it was a group that would greatly appreciate support for its work to preserve this documentation. I closed by reiterating praise for Chambliss, who had recognized the importance of documenting American history, and I noted that the portrait being unveiled was one more record of successful public service.

This occasion was also useful for conversations with the university's government relations administrators to focus on pending legislation relevant to archives, specifically funding for the National Archives, the National Historical Publications and Records Commission, and a new initiative, Preserving America's Historical Record (PAHR).[11] I was able to gain not only permission to advocate for this legislation on university letterhead but also the support of the university lobbyists to advocate for it as an interest of the university.

REACHING POTENTIAL AND BECOMING A "CENTER"

Collecting success and stakeholder expectations threatened to overwhelm the Russell Library as it moved into its third decade. An uncertain future loomed because collections continued growing and storage space remained static. Library administrators proposed a separate special collections building to solve the dilemma. Recognizing a prime opportunity, the Russell Foundation signed on with the initial pledge for the new building, which will be named for the senator. Subsequent development activities and fundraising introduced exciting new contacts and resources.

As a result, by the turn of the century, the Russell Library began to function like a "Center" as it promoted public programming. We developed academic partnerships with faculty groups including the Foot Soldier Project for Civil Rights Studies and the Center for International Trade and Security. The Foot Soldier Project enhanced the library's documentation of Georgia's rich history in the civil rights movement. While certain archivists serve as faculty in this interdisciplinary venture that focuses on the "unsung foot soldiers" of the movement, the library serves as the official repository for research materials gathered and generated by the project. The library also houses the records of the Center for International Trade and Security and co-sponsors programs with it and its parent institution, the School for Policy and International Affairs.

Oral history at the Russell Library recently developed as a formal interview and production program, no longer the passive collection of accepted interviews generated by the research of others or projects led by friends of donors. Although we are on a very limited budget (and looking for an endowment), we have partnered with a retired political staffer with a press background who is donating his time and conducting the interviews. We can now film and produce in house. The oral history we want is evolving into a dynamic series of unique programs, capturing in the first person the stories and lives of Georgia's history makers and those who reflect or give voice to the time and place in which they live. The memories of public officials, community leaders, farm families, business people, immigrants—any who have interest in the forces of public policy—will add value to the historical record. For example, an oral history series may feature the politics and policy of Georgia's Rural Development as a theme in which the relationship between land stewardship and economic interests could be detailed in great depth. Similarly, the series might examine the role of land use in Georgia's public policy making, a signal subject strength in Russell Library collections, with an emphasis on the growth of agribusiness, and the modern farm family, as well as ensuing agricultural legislation sponsored by interest groups such as the Georgia Pecan Commission or the Georgia Forestry Association.

Gradually, we have provided learning opportunities aimed at the broader-based communities that the library serves. Russell archivists have worked to facilitate and encourage research by improving access to the collections in national databases and by providing a more creative Web presence. We reached out to new constituencies by teaching more classes and by developing new public programs and thematic exhibits that, unlike the early exhibits, are based on expanded civic themes. In 2007, the library collaborated with the Kettering Foundation and others on campus to host its first Public Policy Institute and National Issues Forum. This new venue actively engaged the campus and wider community in civil discourse and was so successful that a contract was made with Kettering in 2008 to formalize an ongoing civic program, the Russell Forum for Civic Life in Georgia. Through its Kettering affiliation, the library is joining the Jimmy Carter Library and others to produce a series of forums related to the fall 2008 presidential debates.

Spearheading this major civic engagement initiative in Georgia, we contacted our newer constituencies around the state to solidify relations and fulfill the university's mission to respond to the evolution of the state's educational, social, and economic needs. Specifically, the university strives through its strategic planning for even closer contact with the citizens it serves. For example, we have worked through a donor to bring together community leaders in a small city in South Georgia to plan their own forum series as part of the library's Georgia Deliberations Fall 2008: What Policy Decisions Today Will Get Us a Better Tomorrow? Enthusiastic about the library's interest in south Georgia, these leaders have put forth ideas for three forums to deliberate critical issues in their community. At these forums, we will learn more about the people and the area; we will learn what is going well and what is at risk; we will promote civil discourse; and perhaps, as a greater reward, we will encourage an informed citizenry across the state. We will learn, too, what documentation is available and must be preserved, raising the visibility of our statewide collecting interests.

On the basis of past collecting performance and the certainty of a new building, we and our stakeholders anticipate continued growth for the Russell Library as a pace-setting repository. If the future collection were built on today's research strengths alone, Russell holdings should grow exponentially, and serious thought has been given to the security, integrity, and direction of the Russell Library. While I have enjoyed support from many in the upper administration, that support has been hard won over an extended period of time. Staff members have concerns that my successor might not be as fortunate with future administrations without a heightened presence for the library.

Two factors will determine the advantage: (1) an endowment to raise the prestige of the library locally and statewide, and (2) salary and benefits in the academic faculty range for the director that are highly competitive nationally. Believing that ongoing leadership from the director will be critical in fulfilling the Russell Library's potential, we want the director at a level to engage senior faculty and administrators from the outset. Looking ahead, our goals are to increase public programming and outreach efforts dramatically; appoint faculty, policymakers, and donors to a Russell Advisory Committee that will evolve into a support group of stakeholders; and ensure an environment of excellence that attracts prestigious donors, highly regarded and dedicated staff, strategic partners, funding sources, and the general public.[12] Rather than sponsor another salaried position on campus, the Russell Foundation responded to the library's stated concerns with a $1 million pledge for a programming endowment to support growing outreach activities when the new facility is dedicated.[13] The foundation also expressed its own shift to the future by appointing a long-range planning committee.

Within the next three years, all three of the university's special collections departments will move into the new building. Using private funding and a special allocation from the state, significant planning for the facility is already complete. A $45 million project, the building will encompass 110,000 square feet of space. As a major capital project approved by the University System Board of Regents, building construction should begin in late 2009. This impressive building will provide sufficient space for the rapid growth of the collections, for large-scale exhibition galleries, for a state-of-the-art conservation environment, and for creative programming.

The Russell Library's already ambitious exhibits program will occupy attractive space, encompassing several galleries. Equally, the new building will provide a variety of venues for public gatherings and dynamic learning tailored to the library's diverse constituencies. The library is committed to developing and presenting exhibits and public programs that educate and inspire visitors about the ways in which Georgia and its citizens have persuaded policy and shaped the political life of their communities, the state, their nation, and the world. In this modern setting, the Russell Library will be both a center for political research and study and a destination for cultural tourism and learning.

The Richard B. Russell Library for Political Research and Studies is an institution that has evolved over time, and its evolution perfectly mirrors the growth and development of congressional policy centers and the development of a group of dedicated archivists, the Congressional Papers Roundtable, who focus on the preservation of congressional collections and their research accessibility. Development of a documentation strategy also evolved naturally over time, and this strategy has directed the course of the library's collection growth. Throughout its history, the Russell Library has reflected the current standards of a model institution for congressional papers, one that is frequently studied by other newly established centers. Moving into a new building and accepting a $1 million programming endowment will allow the Russell Library to (1) achieve a higher profile with its own constituency, (2) validate its position as the repository of record for state political and public policy papers, (3) attract funding sources, (4) increase the base of influential political donors, (5) generate programming that contributes significantly to the mission to the university, and (6) confirm its national standing.

NOTES

1. Gilbert C. Fite, "The Richard B. Russell Library: From Idea to Working Collection," *Georgia Historical Quarterly* 64 (Spring 1980): 22–34.

2. Annual Reports, 2002–2007, Administrative Files, Richard B. Russell Library for Political Research and Studies, University of Georgia Libraries.

3. P.L. 95-270 set aside $2.5 million for development of the Everett McKinley Dirksen Congressional Leadership Center, Pekin, Illinois, on April 27, 1978. Up to $5 million was authorized in P.L. 95-270 to provide financial assistance in the development of the Hubert H. Humphrey Institute of Public Affairs. This was one-quarter of the total planned $20 million, largely being raised privately. In 1981, H.R. 4605 was proposed "In recognition of the public service of former United States Senator Richard B. Russell, and of the pressing need for national centers for congressional scholarship and the archiving of congressional papers." The bill was referred to the House Committee on Education and Labor's Subcommittee on Postsecondary Education, where it died. P.L. 97-377 (December 21, 1982) and P.L. 99-498 (October 17, 1986) together awarded $3 million to the Carl Albert Congressional Research and Studies Center to assist in further developing the center.

4. Fite, "The Richard B. Russell Library," 22–34.

5. See www.libs.uga.edu/russell/research/support.shtml to review the list.

6. Robert C. Byrd, "Introductory Remarks, Understanding Congress: A Bicentennial Research Conference," in *Understanding Congress: Research Perspectives*, ed. Roger H. Davidson and Richard C. Sachs (Washington, D.C.: Government Printing Office, 1991), xvii.

7. The Russell Foundation approved the name change from Richard B. Russell Memorial Library to Richard B. Russell Library for Political Research and Studies at its annual meeting in 1994. Minutes of the annual meeting of the Richard B. Russell Foundation, December 1, 1994, Administrative Files, Richard B. Russell Library for Political Research and Studies, University of Georgia Libraries.

8. Karen Dawley Paul, *The Documentation of Congress: Report of the Congressional Archivists Roundtable Taskforce on Congressional Documentation*, S. Pub. 102–20 (Washington, D.C.: U.S. Senate, 1992).

9. Faye Phillips, *Congressional Papers Management* (Jefferson, N.C.: McFarland, 1996), 8–18.

10. Karen Dawley Paul, *Records Management Handbook for United States Senators and Their Archival Repositories* (Washington, D.C.: U.S. Senate, 2003); Office of History and Preservation, Office of the Clerk, *Records Management Manual for Members* (Washington, D.C.: U.S. House of Representatives, n.d.).

11. H.R. 6056, "To authorize the Archivist of the United States to make grants to States for the preservation and dissemination of historical records," was introduced by Reps. Maurice Hinchey (D-NY) and Chris Cannon (R-UT) and referred to the House Committee on Oversight and Government Reform on May 14, 2008. PAHR would establish a program of formula-based grants to states for regrants and statewide services to support preservation and use of historical records. The program, to be administered by the National Archives, will provide a total of $50 million per year nationwide. Each state would receive a portion of these funds for redistribution to organizations within its borders.

12. Sheryl B. Vogt to Charles E. Campbell, September 14, 2005, Russell Foundation Correspondence, Administrative Files, Richard B. Russell Library for Political Research and Studies, University of Georgia Libraries.

13. A perpetual fund agreement between the Richard B. Russell Foundation and the Arch Foundation of the University of Georgia to establish the Richard B. Russell Programming Endowment was presented for final approval at the annual meeting of the Russell Foundation, October 21, 2008.

Part VI

USING POLITICAL COLLECTIONS

25

Trends in Scholarship on Congress: A Historian's View

Nancy Beck Young

My problem is simple: I can discuss extensively what the trends on historically driven congressional scholarship should be, but it is much harder to discern noticeable trends in a literature that is in its infancy. Think of this chapter as a call to arms for more historical attention to the study of Congress.[1] Certainly this new literature would have a home alongside the revival of political history. Indeed, under the guise of policy studies or American political development—both hybrid fields of historians, political scientists, and sociologists, to name a few—the explicit study of Congress by historians or from a historical perspective wants for attention.

The necessary correctives within the literature of American history in the 1960s and 1970s away from a strictly political focus to include a diversity of social and cultural modes of inquiry has made it unfashionable to examine high politics. When one looks at some of the most important new political history, the influence of social and cultural history is apparent and beneficial. Some examples include Lizabeth Cohen's *Making a New Deal: Industrial Workers in Chicago, 1919–1939* and Theda Skocpol's *Protecting Soldiers and Mothers: The Political Origins of Social Policy in the United States.*[2] Certainly, I could not undertake my current book project on Congress during World War II without the wealth of social and cultural history scholarship produced over the last four decades. For the field of American history to move forward in a healthy and a mature fashion, though, it is well past time for some remedial attention to the sort of high politics that has been ignored for too long. This renaissance should not occur at the expense of

Derived from a presentation at the Association of Centers for the Study of Congress, May 2004.

social and cultural history, but alongside its continued flourishing, for each will enrich the other.

Regarding the extant literature, historically driven considerations of Congress have followed two major directions—topical and biographical treatments of the institution and its members. Both historiographical trends can be subdivided. Among the latter, there are numerous cradle-to-grave biographies, partial biographies, and biographical studies that in reality examine a topic larger than the life of the particular member being considered. Any attempt to list work will be incomplete and will no doubt reflect my own bias toward the twentieth century, but nonetheless here are some recent biographical titles that merit attention. Scholars interested in studying Congress through the lens of biography would be well advised to examine Stephen Kantrowitz's *Ben Tillman and the Reconstruction of White Supremacy*.[3] This book departs from a more traditional approach to political biography in that the author uses Tillman's activities to tell a larger story about the nature of white supremacy at the turn of the twentieth century. Additionally, Byron C. Hulsey's *Everett Dirksen and His Presidents: How a Senate Giant Shaped American Politics* provides an assessment of how a key Republican lawmaker remained influential during an era of Democratic ascendancy.[4] More important, Hulsey's book reveals the continued vitality of Congress during an era supposedly dominated by the imperial presidency. In *Taxing America: Wilbur D. Mills, Congress, and the State, 1945–1975*, Julian E. Zelizer highlights the intersections between technocratic governance and postwar liberalism.[5]

An even greater diversity can be found in the various topical approaches to Congress studies. Key examples include policy evolution studies, analyses of particular eras, explications of key Congresses, and examinations of particularly significant issues and problems. Susan M. Hartmann's classic monograph *Truman and the 80th Congress* remains an important treatment of the intersections between congressional and executive power at a crucial moment of political transition.[6] A good example of scholarship that explores a particular issue, in part from a legislative perspective, is Elizabeth Sanders's authoritative work on progressivism, *Roots of Reform: Farmers, Workers, and the American State, 1877–1917*.[7] In it, she argues that radical agrarians pushed Progressive Era reform legislation in Congress. And Julian E. Zelizer's *On Capitol Hill: The Struggle to Reform Congress and Its Consequences, 1948–2000* promises to force a reconsideration of institutional reform.[8]

When looked at this way, the historical literature on Congress is not as bleak as I first hinted. Yet all is not rosy. Few apparent linkages—other than the obvious common focus on Congress—exist among the various books that have been produced. This problem results in no small way because the scholars who have produced or are producing this work tend not to think of themselves as foremost contributing to the literature on Congress but on some other topic within political history, such as the New Deal or the Vietnam War. More conferences and conference sessions on Congress and American political history will help, but ultimately what is needed is a renewed appreciation within the discipline of the many questions about the American past that can only be answered by an explication of national legislative politics. Put simply, if more scholars can be attracted to this fascinating and never-ending topic, the problem will solve itself with time.

For my own part, I will continue to try with my research to highlight the importance of congressional history. My biography of Wright Patman uses an individual life to study a larger problem—in this case the failures of agrarian economic liberalism to maintain its prominence within the political marketplace of ideas.[9] My current work is more ambitious. This project is large—in terms of archival research and in terms of argument. I expect that when I am finished, the bibliography for this manuscript will include well over a hundred manuscript collections.

First, a few general words about the importance of archival sources to historical studies of Congress: without drawing too fine a point, the historical evaluation of Congress without manuscript research is incomplete. I say that as someone whose scholarship would be impossible without the many archives either specifically devoted to congressional studies or that happen by chance to have the papers of a particular member. Certainly, no congressional history could be written without extensive consultation of key printed primary sources like the *Congressional Record* and the many published congressional hearings, but typically unheralded outside the discipline of history are the rich and insightful untapped manuscript collections of former members of Congress. While no two manuscript collections are equal, it is only through consideration of the letters, speech drafts, notes, and memoranda, for example, found in the papers of members of Congress that one can reconstruct the intent and the deal-making of the members with regard to policy and politics, especially when the lawmakers are long deceased. For most topics in congressional history, there are other equally significant manuscript collections necessary for consideration: the records of the various standing, special, joint, and other committees of Congress held at the National Archives. These records are uneven from committee to committee and chair to chair, but if they are read carefully, the researcher can discern committee work styles, legislative priorities, and constituent concerns as presented to the committees, for example. The manuscript materials in the relevant presidential libraries rank next in importance because they provide researchers with a sense of the interaction between the legislative branch and the executive branch.

So, what am I doing in my manuscript on Congress during World War II?

"Do you think they are going to liquidate the Jews?" Congressman Cliff Clevenger (R-OH) posed this question to a witness before the House Immigration and Naturalization Committee. The witness answered yes, and

Samuel Dickstein (D-NY), the committee chair, concluded, "At the rate
Hitler is going he can liquidate anything." This July 1939 exchange typified
countless hearings in the House Immigration and Naturalization Committee.[10] More important, this vignette encapsulating the reasons "Why We
Fight" will make a major contribution to the literature of American history: it reveals substantial congressional involvement in war policy debates
and congressional knowledge of the global threats to democracy. Little is
known of these events because one of the conventional arguments about
American politics is that Congress lost power to the executive branch in
war-making, but through my new look at World War II, we see this is not
the case. World War II then becomes the template for understanding the
new history of the twenty-first century. Indeed, as members of Congress
looked outward, they gained growing awareness of the rest of the world.
This new perspective changed the way lawmakers thought about legislative
governance and foreign policy, intensifying partisanship in the process.
As with any cataclysmic shift, political globalization caused Congress to
lose its equilibrium and struggle with its identity, throwing the whole of
national politics into turmoil.

    Before World War II, Congress was a provincial institution isolated
from international politics. As a result, war-induced political globalization
strained congressional politics. For lawmakers, politics soon had as much
to do with the affairs of Asia as it did Alabama. Congressional decisions
about issues ranging from price control to immigration affected people
around the globe, not just in the United States. This globalization rendered old political habits obsolete; the result was significant strife with the
executive branch, which seemingly had less trouble adapting to the new
conditions. The ensuing political flux became a compelling feature in the
government as lawmakers searched for an identity comparable to the imperial presidency. While World War II rendered insular thinking impractical
and dangerous, lawmakers nonetheless remained divided on whether and
how to participate in the politics of globalization. "Why We Fight" argues
that this wartime change remade both Congress and national politics.
Globalization exacerbated weaknesses within the legislative branch while
also encouraging social and institutional reform, a process that unfolded
gradually. The congressional response to globalization more than anything
else fractured legislative comity with the White House. Congress nonetheless came of age and addressed the governmental needs of the country as
an emerging superpower.

    The confluence of political globalization with wartime congressional
politics energized a power struggle between lawmakers and the executive
branch with both seeking control of public policy. Because "Why We Fight"
will analyze home-front politics from a global perspective, my book casts
a wholly new light on congressional politics and World War II. The search

for a new legislative identity produced interesting permutations within the constitutional system of divided powers, which has been ignored in the literature.[11] The imperial presidency jeopardized the historic balance of power between lawmakers and the president while also heightening partisanship. On the American home front, political globalization thus ignited a tremendous contest for the additional powers the United States was accruing. The many wartime fights among lawmakers and between Congress and the president exposed the systemic shifts to democracy.

The standard story of American politics during World War II celebrates Franklin D. Roosevelt as savior of democracy at home and abroad. This narrative obscures a more important story. During the war years, as more and more authority was granted to the federal bureaucracy, Congress seemingly became irrelevant. Such was not the case, though. Lawmakers brought important local and regional perspectives to mounting global issues. They fought to preserve the messy but democratic component of governance—the legislative process—and struggled to retain their identity within an evolving American system. Congress, for example, exerted power over the new agencies through the appropriations process and anticommunist investigations. This fight for congressional power was part of the larger quest for a new congressional identity. With political agenda development and legislative management shifting to the White House, could lawmaking, a historically localized endeavor, find a place for itself in the new order? Would investigatory and oversight endeavors sustain congressional power?

The early 1940s were perhaps the most critical period in twentieth-century American history. Scholars have airbrushed out of the story of Congress the numerous honest differences with the executive branch, negating continued congressional potency. Franklin D. Roosevelt seemingly consolidated the twentieth-century trend toward strong presidents and a weakened Congress, which began with the administrations of Theodore Roosevelt and Woodrow Wilson. Simultaneously, congressional governance shifted from the partisan era to the committee era, which featured omnipotent committee chairs and the problematic seniority system. While political scientists, and historians to a lesser extent, have written much about the committee era, few have addressed the legislative–executive collisions that resulted. Instead, most scholars have wrongly used examples of congressional compliance with the executive as proof of legislative impotence. However, they have ignored a different, more important story. Many of the choices the U.S. government made during World War II, about how to fight the war and about domestic programs, resulted from congressional decisions; failure to address wartime legislative politics makes it impossible to understand the American role in the war and the effect of the war on the country. Indeed, this contentious legislative–executive contest for power shaped congressional politics for the remainder of the twentieth century.

In this conflict over power and identity, Congress reflected the divisions within the country over the various war programs and, by extension, the new global politics, all the while asserting its continued importance to governance. The international perspective, though, challenged Congress in making domestic policy. Intense debate over issues ranging from taxation to rationing and manpower mobilization highlights the fragile American political infrastructure. The wartime convergence of global and domestic issues pressured the legislative process. Lawmakers who opposed liberalism at home and internationalism abroad used wartime problems as a shibboleth to terminate debate about controversial public policy measures, much as lawmakers would use the Cold War a decade later to halt domestic reform initiatives. In this way, the vulnerabilities born of wartime global politics created the contentious operating style of the postwar era, which featured even more frequent partisan bickering between lawmakers and the executive than had been the case during the war. Redirecting attention from the World War II myth of American political invincibility to the reality of American political vulnerability makes possible analysis of the tectonic shifts resulting from political globalization. "Why We Fight" evaluates the four key components of this process: a heightened, often negative conflict with the executive; the merger of nationalism and internationalism; wartime congressional partisanship; and consolidation of New Deal reforms.

American democracy (and history) cannot be appreciated apart from politics, especially congressional politics. Wrongly dismissed as irrelevant during World War II, Congress authored legislation and rewrote and curtailed executive branch programs. Congress, more than the president, encapsulated the national political consciousness, and lawmakers in the 1940s formalized the imperfect balance of internationalism with domestic liberalism that characterized the United States during the Cold War years. In so doing, they remained skeptical about the initial forays into political globalization. "Why We Fight" evaluates how and why Congress blocked what it perceived as an overreaching executive to preserve both the federal balance of power and local interests in a widening world.

Between 1939 and 1945, the United States moved from a nationalist neo-isolationism to an internationalist hegemonic superpower politics. Certainly this transition is well known, but a consideration of the congressional role reveals much that is new. Lawmakers commingled nationalism with internationalism to comprehend wartime domestic and foreign policy issues. While members of the executive branch spoke almost exclusively in the language of internationalism, lawmakers blurred nationalism and internationalism, often using the former to understand the latter and even seeing the two as synergistic, not antagonistic, forces. This tendency emerged in often partisan congressional debates about immigration and the formation of the United Nations, for example. Lawmakers typically viewed nationalist politics much more favorably, arguing against the introduction of "foreign" ideologies. "Why We Fight" will explicate this congressional blending of nationalism and internationalism and use it to evaluate the politics of globalization, the congressional identity crisis, and wartime partisanship.

In all the twentieth-century wars, and even in the more recent "war on terrorism," ritualistic invocations of nonpartisanship occurred just after the event or war declaration, and then politics as usual recurred immediately. Because World War II is understood as "the Good War" fought by the "Greatest Generation," the record of partisanship has been forgotten. This collective lapse of memory has impeded scholarship about wartime politics. Too much focus has been placed on sentiments such as those recorded in the *New York Times* on December 8, 1941: "Gone is every sign of partisanship in the Capitol of the United States. Gone is every trace of hesitancy and indecision. There are no party lines today in Congress."[12] The illusion of cooperative congressional behavior masked the internecine party warfare over issues ranging from strikes, economic regulation, and anticommunist red-hunting to race, gender, and the postwar peace, which resulted from political globalization. World War II has slipped into myth, and these home-front quarrels have been forgotten. My manuscript will disprove the fiction that partisanship and politics stop when the nation goes to war. A close look at Congress during the most consensual war in American history will reveal that politics thrived in World War II. In fact, partisanship intensified because the contested global terrain was an unrelenting factor in Capitol Hill policy deliberations. As a result, lawmakers both tempered and solidified the political realignments of the 1930s and rehearsed for the politics of the Cold War.

Other World War II myths posit that House and Senate members bent on killing the New Deal were ineffectual and unnecessary impediments to the wartime bureaucracies. Careful examination of Congress during World War II results in a different, more sophisticated interpretation that contrasts Congress favorably with the presidency. Conservatives attacked New Deal social and political modernizations, but liberal and moderate Democrats counterbalanced these forces. Members of Congress in the majority party fought and won a dual war in the 1940s: preserving the New Deal and providing for a global military victory. These actions made possible the postwar dawn of the American century, and they forever linked a mutated domestic liberalism with American intervention abroad. While these political developments might seem unremarkable at first glance, in actuality, war era challenges to the New Deal welfare state were much more intense than previous accounts recognize, prefiguring postwar attitudes toward liberalism. Furthermore,

Congress often used the perspective of global politics to evaluate whether certain New Deal experiments became permanent.

"Why We Fight" will not be simply an institutional history devoid of personality. To study Congress is to study the myriad individuals who prac-́ ticed democracy on a daily basis. The politicians who populated Capitol Hill at midcentury were among the most colorful and substantive ever to serve in Washington, D.C. Analysis of the congressional gadflies—such as Senator Theodore Bilbo (D-MS), Representative Vito Marcantonio (AL-NY), and Senator William Langer (R-ND)—cannot be divorced from consideration of the congressional workhorses like House Speaker Sam Rayburn (D-TX), Senator Robert A. Taft (R-OH), and Senator Robert La Follette (R-WI). A diverse cast of astute politicians with complicated motivations dominated Congress. They perfected the politics of hypocrisy, nationalism, and partisanship. The informal aspects of congressional life—the clubbiness, the fraternities, the socializing, and even the gender politics—played a significant, if often hidden, role in policy outcomes. These factors, as much as committee assignments and floor debates, determined the kind of institution Congress was at midcentury. "Why We Fight" will seamlessly integrate pertinent anecdotes and illustrative stories about informal Capitol Hill politics to demonstrate how lawmakers defended their power base within the new global politics.

Why has the congressional role in war policy of the 1940s, then, been so obfuscated? The answer to this question is complex. First, Congress appeared in late 1941 to have just pulled its head free from the sands of isolationism, while Roosevelt had warned for several years of the European and Asian war. Second, the speed and ease with which Congress declared war suggested presidential preeminence over the process. Third, the explosion of an executive bureaucracy hinted that maybe wartime economic and social problems were beyond the ken of Congress. Fourth, the continuation of premodern congressional mores compared unfavorably with a modernizing executive branch. Finally, Franklin D. Roosevelt has cast a larger-than-life shadow over the period 1933–1945. These would seem to be reasons enough to overlook Congress. Such a decision was foolish.

For too many years, political scientists and historians interested in questions of governance have employed a presidency-centered approach. Going to one archive is much easier than the multiarchival work necessary for any good political history of Congress. Furthermore, presidency-centered political history usually divides neatly into four- or eight-year segments. Biographies of representatives and senators require mastery of numerous, sometimes conflicting political eras, while studies of Congress at a particular moment in time necessitate understanding how the history of the members and their institutional service caused them to react as they did, be it during the Civil War, the Gilded Age, or World War II. Even when exploring a finite period in the institution's history, substantial appreciation of what came before is necessary to anchor the study.

Given the historiographical and research work needed to master a congressional history topic, it is easy to understand why so many scholars have shied away from the challenge. Despite the renaissance of political history, too few have foregrounded Congress in studies of national politics. In discussing modern American history, the Columbia University political scientist and historian Ira Katznelson argued recently, "It is hard to see how the American national state can be understood, or how such issues as legislative enactments, citizenship, bureaucratic organization, . . . voting rights, gender and the party system, . . . the rules of political economy, patterns of taxation, the federal qualities of public policy, the rise of antigovernment social movements, or the status of liberal and democratic values . . . can be reckoned and combined into larger syntheses without placing Congress at the center of historical investigation."[13] Certainly, Congress contended with each of these issues during the World War II era, a key moment of transformation within American government and society. But the serious neglect of Congress as an actor in American political history transcends World War II scholarship: it permeates the entire literature of modern American history.[14]

Over the past decade or so, some historians have encouraged a slow but steady revival of political questions. The methodological approaches and specific topics have been as varied as the practitioners, but one of the most significant has been in the area of policy studies. The rediscovery of political history has captured an even wider audience over the past several years with the reminder that politics and questions of governance still matter. "Why We Fight" will look at congressional politics, governance, and the policy formation process in what was the defining decade of the twentieth century. World War II catapulted the United States from a third-rate military power to one of two leading superpowers. Nevertheless, the story of Congress in this global transformation has yet to be told.

The World War II congressional generation saw everything—economic depression, war, and then Cold War. These incredibly varied experiences changed the members of Congress and the institution in which they served. The part-time lawmakers who informally and cordially shared quarters in the capital city's many hotels disappeared. Because of the politics of globalization, a professional, modern, even imperial Congress of full-time lawmakers unwilling to cede an ounce of control to the newly powerful imperial presidency emerged. These transformations to the politics of partisanship, nationalism, and policy formation beg for scholarly investigation. Indeed, it is well past time for an analytical and accessible account of how America's national lawmakers responded to and were transformed by the last great worldwide military conflagration.

NOTES

1. This chapter originated as a talk for the Association of Centers for the Study of Congress, held at the Woodrow Wilson International Center for Scholars, Washington, D.C., in May 2004. The manuscript "Why We Fight: Congress and the Politics of World War II," discussed in the chapter, is under contract to Princeton University Press.

2. Lizabeth Cohen, *Making a New Deal: Industrial Workers in Chicago, 1919–1939* (New York: Cambridge University Press, 1990); and Theda Skocpol, *Protecting Soldiers and Mothers: The Political Origins of Social Policy in the United States* (Cambridge, Mass.: Belknap Press of Harvard University Press, 1992).

3. Stephen Kantrowitz, *Ben Tillman and the Reconstruction of White Supremacy* (Chapel Hill: University of North Carolina Press, 2000).

4. Byron C. Hulsey, *Everett Dirksen and His Presidents: How a Senate Giant Shaped American Politics* (Lawrence: University Press of Kansas, 2000).

5. Julian E. Zelizer, *Taxing America: Wilbur D. Mills, Congress, and the State, 1945–1975* (New York: Cambridge University Press, 1998).

6. Susan M. Hartmann, *Truman and the 80th Congress* (Columbia: University of Missouri Press, 1971).

7. Elizabeth Sanders, *Roots of Reform: Farmers, Workers, and the American State, 1877–1917* (Chicago: University of Chicago Press, 1999).

8. Julian E. Zelizer, *On Capitol Hill: The Struggle to Reform Congress and Its Consequences, 1948–2000* (New York: Cambridge University Press, 2004).

9. Nancy Beck Young, *Wright Patman: Populism, Liberalism, and the American Dream* (Dallas, Tex.: Southern Methodist University Press, 2000).

10. U.S. Congress, House, Committee on Immigration and Naturalization, "Admission of German Refugee Children," unpublished hearings, 76th Congress, 1st session, July 19, 1939.

11. Michael C. C. Adams, *The Best War Ever: America and World War II* (Baltimore: Johns Hopkins University Press, 1994); John Morton Blum, *V Was for Victory: Politics and American Culture During World War II* (New York: Harcourt Brace Jovanovich, 1976); Alan Brinkley, *The End of Reform: New Deal Liberalism in Recession and War* (New York: Knopf, 1995); James MacGregor Burns, *Roosevelt: The Soldier of Freedom* (New York: Harcourt Brace Jovanovich, 1970); Thomas Fleming, *The New Dealers' War: FDR and the War Within World War II* (New York: Basic Books, 2001); John W. Jeffries, *Wartime America: The World War II Home Front* (Chicago: Ivan R. Dee, 1996); David M. Kennedy, *Freedom from Fear: The American People in Depression and War, 1929–1945* (New York: Oxford University Press, 1999); William L. O'Neill, *A Democracy at War: America's Fight at Home and Abroad in World War II* (New York: Free Press, 1993); and Richard Polenberg, *War and Society: The United States, 1941–1945* (Philadelphia: Lippincott, 1972).

12. "United We Stand," *New York Times*, December 9, 1941, 30.

13. Ira Katznelson, "The Possibilities of Analytical Political History," in *The Democratic Experiment: New Directions in American Political History*, ed. Meg Jacobs, William J. Novak, and Julian E. Zelizer (Princeton: Princeton University Press, 2003), 389.

14. See, for example, Karen Orren and Stephen Skowronek, "Regimes and Regime Building in American Government: A Review of the Literature on the 1940s," *Political Science Quarterly* 113 (Winter 1998–1999): 689–702. None of the scholarly works assessed in this piece takes Congress as a serious actor in the processes analyzed.

26

Congressional Archives and Policy History

Paul Milazzo

Increasing access to and interest in congressional archives on the part of scholars has transformed the landscape of political history. To trace the origins and evolution of influential government programs in education, the environment, civil rights, or national defense (to name just a few), historians who once focused exclusively on the executive branch as the engine of federal policy development now treat Congress as a coequal institution. We have been rewarded with new, comprehensive narratives detailing how the interplay between legislators, congressional staffers, interest groups, experts, bureaucrats, and mass movements led to the steady expansion of state capacity following World War II. The onset of "big government" in a big way after 1945, it turns out, owes much more to the deliberate efforts of legislators than previously admitted. Indeed, the institutional evolution of the legislative branch over the course of the twentieth century created a committee system and a concomitant set of professional incentives that enabled "legislative entrepreneurs" to expand the scope of federal entitlement and regulatory programs—quite often before the president, or even the public, demanded it.

Historians overlooked Congress for many years for a variety of reasons. Some stemmed from historiographical biases. Scholars interested in modernization gravitated to the executive as the more centralized and "muscular" branch of government and cast Congress as an inveterate opponent, rather than a willing architect, of the postwar state. Others, suspicious of "top-down" institutional histories that they thought marginalized the authentic experiences of ordinary people, deemed the legislative machinations

Derived from a presentation at the Association of Centers for the Study of Congress, May 2005.

of white males less vital than social movements or cultural transformations. From a purely practical angle, moreover, Congress looms as a daunting research subject, with two distinct chambers, dozens of committees, and hundreds of independent actors and agendas. That sense of the chaotic and centrifugal extends to archival sources as well, which reside in the National Archives and Library of Congress as well as in the private collections of individual legislators scattered across the country.

This multitude of materials can cause vertigo, but as I can attest, it also presents opportunities for rethinking and retelling the story of American political development after World War II. Drawing generously from legislative archival sources, my book *Unlikely Environmentalists: Congress and Clean Water, 1945–1972* (University Press of Kansas, 2006) recasts the rise of the environmental regulatory state through a congressional lens. It demonstrates how legislative entrepreneurs like Representative John Blatnik (D-MN) and Senator Edmund Muskie (D-ME) outpaced both the president and public demand, laboring to build a constituency for stronger federal water pollution control laws well before a mass movement had coalesced in the early 1970s. Moreover, this legislative focus reveals clean-water policy as a product of many unheralded actors, institutions, organizations, and agendas, whose contributions remained obscured by a conventional focus on grassroots activism. More careful attention to Congress's ingrained policy networks underscored the surprising continuity between older political priorities, such as economic development and the Cold War, and new ones like environmental protection. Thus, "unlikely environmentalists," including the House and Senate Public Works Committees, missile system designers, and even the Army Corps of Engineers, emerge as important players who shaped pollution control policy both before and after Earth Day.

Building this new narrative without congressional archives would have been unthinkable, but traditional published sources remained indispensible nonetheless. I relied, for example, on the *Congressional Quarterly Almanac*'s annual overview of specific legislation, which traced the background and progress of pending bills, summarized party positions, and tallied votes. Similarly, the *Congressional Record* provided the blow by blow on floor debates and served as a repository where members inserted newspaper articles, speeches, and other topical primary documents.

Although committees often conduct their hearings as choreographed events, published transcripts still offer a treasure trove of information. There is no better way to get up to speed on the major players involved in specific policy issues than to peruse a hearing's witness list. Committee members don't always question witnesses after their formal statements, but when they do, the exchange can clarify specific technical points as well as the legislators' underlying assumptions. The hearings of Senator Muskie's Subcommittee on Air and Water Pollution (Senate Public Works Committee) in the early 1960s tutored me on the basics of waste treatment technology, but also suggested Muskie's underlying concern that pollution control programs should bolster national water supplies and economic development while cleaning up the environment. While hearings can produce authentic conflict and drama, they also reward the diligent reader with moments of levity. When a witness representing the industry-friendly Manufacturing Chemists Association indicated that his organization actually supported a 1969 water-quality bill, Muskie was nonplussed. "As I understand your testimony, you have no objection to S. 7," the Senator said. "That is correct, sir, yes." "Maybe there is something wrong with it," Muskie replied.

Congressional researchers can never afford to overlook executive sources either. For insider details on the implementation of environmental regulatory programs Congress created, I turned to the records of the Environmental Protection Agency, the Department of Health, Education, and Welfare, and the Army Corps of Engineers. Likewise, presidential papers shed light on the interplay between the branches. Aides for the Johnson and Nixon administrations worked closely with the Muskie subcommittee, and their internal memoranda contain many important details about pending environmental legislation. In 1971, for example, Richard Nixon's top domestic advisors, John Ehrlichman and John Whitaker, kept the president up to date on the development of what would become the 1972 Clean Water Act. They highlighted specific provisions, explained why they opposed certain features, and gauged how receptive Republican members of Muskie's subcommittee would be to suggested revisions. Indeed, they expressed chagrin when those GOP senators, particularly Howard Baker of Tennessee, backed Muskie's version.

While the view from the White House can provide an up-close—and frequently oppositional—perspective on legislative policy making, there's no better vantage point than the committee chambers themselves. I'm a big fan of committee records and have had good luck with them. They are housed in the National Archives Center for Legislative Archives (CLA) in Washington, D.C., a wonderful place to do research. The CLA has its own dedicated staff, directed by Richard Hunt, which caters exclusively to congressional researchers. There are no preset "pull times," so staffers can retrieve records on demand or give individual researchers a good deal of personal attention tracking down specific items.

My work benefitted from the materials found in Record Group 46, the records of the U.S. Senate, and those of two committees in particular. The first, known as the Senate Select Committee on National Water Resources, convened between 1959 and 1961. Its objective was to study the future water needs of the United States and make recommendations to the Senate about what the government should do to meet them. On its face, the committee served as a vehicle for western Democrats to criticize the Eisenhower administration's crackdown on public-works spending on the eve of an election year. It was supposed to make a case for more dams and big water projects in the West that emphasized national economic growth while playing down criticisms of wasteful regional "pork." The committee's final report certainly did so, but by emphasizing pollution control, rather than irrigation or hydroelectric needs. It called for a multibillion-dollar national construction program of sewage treatment plants and dams to ensure that future waste loads would be processed and then diluted with the clean water stored in reservoirs.

The select committee's records helped explain how concerns about development, growth, and pork in Congress could somehow translate into calls for an "environmental" policy like water pollution control. Using various memoranda, letters, and draft reports, I reconstructed how the committee's staff chose from among various mathematical models to estimate the nation's water supply and demand. Although external consultants warned that the model they ultimately employed had flaws, it offered the quickest and most complete answers to the questions the committee's final report had to address. It became clear that the staff's work on the supply and demand equations subtly shifted the committee's emphasis toward pollution control, but in a way that pleased its chair, Robert Kerr (D-OK), because the final product succeeded in making federal water development look like a justified national undertaking. Moreover, the committee's records demonstrated how it managed to process enormous amounts of technical information despite the limited institutional resources it wielded (relative to the executive branch), by tapping an informal web of experts culled from universities, private think tanks, the Legislative Research Service, and federal agencies.

The interplay between experts, staffers, and legislators in congressional policy making also took center stage in the evolution of Edmund Muskie's seminal 1972 Clean Water Act. The records of the Senate Public Works Committee reveal how this long, complex piece of legislation was written, and the ideas that shaped its unprecedented regulatory features. The staff at the Center for Legislative Archives discovered 10 full-size cartons of materials spanning the committee's clean water deliberations in 1971 and 1972. Imagine my delight as I unfurled poster-sized committee prints of the bill as it progressed from draft to draft, replete with detailed EPA margin comments on the perceived strengths and weaknesses of various provisions, and notations by the committee staff pointing out features modeled after the 1970 Clean Air Act. As I tracked the changes in legislative language, I could match them to various internal staff memos explaining what they had done and why. The section on non-point-source pollution (urban and agricultural runoff not originating from an outflow pipe) changed dramatically in the summer of 1971, eliminating enforceable deadlines and standards while emphasizing regional planning. As staffers explained to Muskie, numerous factors influenced this shift, from the lack of suitable treatment technology to the opposition of agricultural lobbyists and the perceived cost to rural communities.

The Clean Water Act's many tough provisions, from its federal effluent standards and deadlines to the unprecedented goal of achieving "zero discharge" by 1985, stemmed from its overt grounding in ecosystems ecology. The committee's papers reveal how professional ecologists and ecologically oriented staffers introduced a professional scientific discourse that the senators ultimately found appealing. George Woodwell, an ecologist at Brookhaven National Laboratories, served as one of the Public Works Committee's scientific advisors, and in that capacity reviewed an early draft of the bill. In a letter addressed to Muskie, Woodwell offered a number of critiques but also noted the lack of an overall objective for the federal water pollution control program. He suggested that the legislation's rationale should be "the maintenance of the chemical, physical, and biological integrity of all waters." This language not only influenced how the staff crafted many of the bill's subsequent provisions, but it also ended up inserted as the Clean Water Act's literal statement of purpose.

The "integrity clause" helped transform the Senate bill's regulatory framework, leading to friction with members of the House Public Works Committee who preferred the existing system of ambient stream standards set by individual states. These disagreements became evident during the tense conference committee meetings in spring and summer of 1972. Staff memos, reports, and handwritten notes spelled out the differences separating the two sides in great detail and shed new light on how they eventually overcame them.

Although the Senate Public Works Committee presented a united front during the conference committee hearings, the turn to ecology generated considerable dissension among the senators during the summer and fall of 1971 as they worked to complete their own draft bill. The best evidence of this internal discord came not simply from memoranda but from the rarest of all finds for the legislative researcher: actual transcripts of executive session hearings. Behind closed doors, exchanges between the senators were more frank, less scripted, and thus immeasurably insightful. The transcripts reveal wonderful individual moments: the day, for example, when Muskie interrupted his colleagues to read the Woodwell letter and introduce the concept of integrity for the first time, suggesting both the staff's enthusiasm for the concept as well as his own. Muskie believed that "integrity" provided administrators with a sophisticated, scientifically valid means to describe extremely high standards of water quality, while offering the public a comprehensible and expressly ecological way to understand what the government was trying to do.

Indeed, "integrity" solved a number of practical, political, and legislative problems for Muskie, not the least of which was finding an alternative to a bold proposal introduced within the committee by a freshman senator from California, John Tunney. The executive session hearings divulge the impact that the "Tunney Standard" had on the committee's deliberations during the summer of 1971. Tunney suggested a national ambient standard that would restore virtually all waters to swimmable and fishable quality within a decade—an ambitious objective that appealed to environmental lobbyists but which Muskie considered prohibitively expensive and impractical. The two senators engaged in a number of frank (and entertaining) exchanges about the proposed standard. In the process, they hashed out broader issues of legislative intent and discussed how legislative language might best translate into clear mandates for administrators.

Ironically, Muskie's bill ultimately rejected "swimmable fishable waters" in favor of strict technology-based effluent standards and the "zero discharge" goal—features no less dramatic than the original Tunney proposal Muskie had rejected as impractical. The reasons Muskie chose the latter over the former are too intricate to describe here in full, but as the sources indicate, one had to do with the regulatory implications of "ecological integrity." Carried to its logical conclusions, the integrity concept discouraged *any* discharge of pollutants into waters, and judged ambient stream standards less useful than effluent standards as instruments of regulation and enforcement.

In fact, Muskie's staffers proposed to adopt an innovative and untried waste treatment technology as the cornerstone of the bill's sewage treatment construction grant program precisely because it promised to achieve zero discharge and ecological integrity. The technology, known as land disposal, used soil to remove up to 99 percent of the various impurities found in waste water. Its institutional sponsor, the Army Corps of Engineers, touted it as a replacement for conventional sewage treatment technologies that achieved lesser efficiencies and continued to allow waste disposal directly into water courses. As various draft bills, memos, and the executive hearings reveal, the staff's resounding enthusiasm for land treatment led them to rewrite major portions of the legislation, much to Muskie's surprise. The senator lit into his staffers for the sudden switch (which made for more entertaining reading), but he ultimately acceded to their innovations with minor revisions. The committee's faith in such technology—and the ecological principles underwriting it—facilitated the Clean Water Act's critical shift to strict technology-based effluent standards.

The transcripts of the executive sessions were not to be found in the National Archives. Instead, I discovered them on my last day of research in Lewiston, Maine, at Bates College's Edmund S. Muskie Archives. The overlap that exists between government and private congressional collections can foster confusion, as archivists readily admit. One staffer at the Center for Legislative Archives expressed surprise when I told him about the transcripts I had found at Bates. "We should have those here!" he exclaimed, with just a tinge of bitterness. Obviously, a senator or representative's personal files will contain more materials related to local offices, election campaigns, media coverage, and constituent affairs, as well as biographical or family-related memorabilia. But with respect to legislation and policy matters, committee and individual collections may offer invaluable nuggets to intrepid researchers—or not.

Of course, some of the most indispensible sources for congressional researchers do not reside in any archive. Former legislative staffers can provide critical insight and information that nothing on paper can match. Yes, faded memories and retrospective biases often render interviews less trustworthy than written documents. But staffers bring a special "insider" perspective that can distinguish the critical issues from those policy makers cared less about, flesh out subtle but influential interpersonal conflicts, or reveal important hidden players in policy-making process.

Moreover, when few written records remain, staffers may represent the last surviving witnesses to legislative history. Representative John Blatnik of Minnesota sponsored the first permanent federal water pollution law in 1956. The Minnesota Historical Society's Blatnik papers contained little information from that era, but Blatnik's loyal aide, Jerry Sonosky, stepped in to fill the yawning gaps in a fascinating story. He related how Blatnik's utter lack of interest in the subject of water quality suddenly became personal when one of his own Public Works Committee members, Georgia's Iris Faircloth Blitch, helped table an uncontroversial pollution control bill on behalf of industrial interests. The delay interfered with Blatnik's work on a subject truly dear to his heart—the Federal Highway Bill. His personal pique led him to embrace the issue in a way he might not have otherwise. Sonosky also revealed how important the support of organized labor was in getting the bill passed—an influence not immediately apparent in the written record. Unions saw pollution control in part as a jobs creation program, and Blatnik's major innovation, a federal grant program for sewage treatment plant construction, not only earned their support but provided the "pork" necessary to convince wavering legislators to back the bill over the opposition of industry.

The very existence of Jerry Sonosky came to my attention during another interview with the former staff director for the Senate Public Works Committee in the early 1960s, Ron Linton. Linton also directed me, in an almost off-hand way, to the most unusual primary source I used in the book. "You know about the movie, don't you?" he asked me near the end of our meeting. I did not. It turned out he was referring to *Troubled Waters*, a documentary produced by the Public Works Committee for the purposes of publicity and public education in 1963, soon after Muskie became chair of the Subcommittee on Air and Water Pollution. *Troubled Waters* was the first-ever motion picture produced by the Senate. Narrated by Henry Fonda, it took viewers on a Technicolor tour of water pollution across the nation, explaining its sources, noting the threat it caused to water supplies, and hinting that Muskie's committee had some legislative answers to address the problem. Once I viewed the film, located in the National Archives Motion Pictures, Sound, and Video Branch in Bethesda, Maryland, I realized that it represented the perfect example of legislative entrepreneurship: an attempt to build support for a government program designed to address a problem most of the public didn't realize was a problem yet. And I never would have found it without a tip from a staffer.

The most important question a historian can ask a legislative staff member is "Do you have any papers?" Thomas Jorling, the minority counsel for the Senate Public Works Committee from 1969 to 1972, pointed me toward his collection at the Williams College Library Archives. Jorling, trained in both law and botany, served as the most vocal staff advocate for ecology during his tenure. His papers trace his early career at the Interior Department and Smithsonian Institution and underscore the young attorney's efforts to bring professional ecologists together with policy makers in the late 1960s. Likewise, Jorling's memos, letters, and speeches between 1971 and 1973 highlight his efforts to draft a water pollution bill that would bring about "the orderly transition to an ecologically sound society."

Unlikely Environmentalists is just one of a number of new monographs employing a legislative focus and relying on legislative sources. But the time when historians could claim to break new ground merely by asserting the institutional relevance of Congress is coming to a close. With the publication of Robert Davis Johnson's *Congress and the Cold War*, even the last bastion of executive branch chauvinism has been breached. Johnson argues that Congress did not merely cede power to the "imperial presidency" in the post–World War II era. He demonstrates, rather, how legislators continued to shape foreign policy and check presidential aspirations through the power of the purse and the sophisticated manipulation of congressional rules and procedures.

The most recent work in the field of policy history tends to offer sophisticated syntheses of legislative, executive, and judicial activities, a trend that I expect will continue. One of my graduate students is writing a dissertation on the history of federal crime policy since 1945, a story that can be properly told only in reference to the reciprocal activities of judges, legislators, and executive law enforcement officials, not to mention their counterparts outside of Washington. Likewise, recent scholarly interest in postwar conservatism will likely expand beyond the current work describing its intellectual origins and grassroots development, or the spate of recent books on the Reagan presidency, to look more carefully at conservative contributions to policy development and governance in each of the three branches, particularly during the 1970s, 1980s, and 1990s. The congressional component of this story should prove particularly interesting.

Legislative archivists have an important role to play in this future scholarship, and I'd like to close with some humble suggestions for them. Historians have come to rely on Web-based finding aids for their convenience of access. Thus, archivists should invest the time to make these indexes as informative as possible. Anyone familiar with legislative archives knows that the "wheat to chaff ratio" tends to skew toward the low end; that is, collections that boast hundreds of cubic feet of material often contain fewer useful items than an intrepid researcher would hope. Optimism quickly fades as box after box offers little more than copies of bills or hearings testimony readily available in published sources. Finding aids should be as specific as possible about the substance of documents in a collection. As my own experience indicates, scholars get most excited about internal memoranda, personal letters or notes, executive hearings, marked-up draft bills, or any other record of internal interaction among elected officials and their staffs. Even constituent mail can be useful to gauge public concerns (with the caveat that letter writers tend to be more motivated or agitated than the average citizen). A finding aid that can inform us whether the contents of a particular carton is worth booking a flight and hotel room would be a useful tool indeed. Even better, if archivists could describe with some certainty how the private collection of a senator or representative overlaps with committee records in the National Archives, the process of legislative research would feel less scattershot.

Legislative archives should make it a priority to conduct oral histories with committee and office staff. Moreover, they should provide contact information so researchers can interview these individuals themselves. Donald Ritchie and Richard Baker at the Senate History Office perform these services to the best of their abilities, and rare is the congressional scholar who does not owe them a debt of gratitude. But Don and Dick cannot possibly keep track of everyone, and forging relationships with the men and women who loyally served Congress should be a priority for every archive that houses the papers of a former senator or representative. In my experience, congressional staff members have been eager to relate their experiences and would respond enthusiastically to your outreach.

Finally, remember to keep students in mind when planning programs and making archival resources available. When I teach modern American history, I rely on audio and video materials both in classroom lectures and as assignments. Consider posting video and audio clips online for viewing or downloading from your Web site. Old-fashioned paper documents are terrific, too. These sorts of primary sources not only provide great fodder for in-class discussions but will entice undergraduates into deeper examinations of historical issues and problems that your collections can nurture.

Graduate students, however, require a different kind of lure. In that vein, I will close by invoking (and paraphrasing) the disembodied voice of Shoeless Joe Jackson: "If you fund it, they will come." Well-advertised grants, travel fellowships, and even discounts on photocopying charges can make a huge difference for those with limited resources. Fundraising for this kind of support is often difficult, but it remains the best investment you can make. The future of congressional research lies with the next generation of young scholars, hungry for new stories to tell and unmined evidence to cite. I will be teaching my graduate research seminar in twentieth-century U.S. political history once again this fall, making the argument that congressional sources offer the path of least resistance to original scholarship. You will buttress my plea while serving your own interests—and those of the historical profession—by catering to this eager constituency.

27

Dataheads: What Archivists Need to Know About Political Scientists

Scott A. Frisch and Sean Q Kelly

> Political scientists have always quantified whenever and whatever they could.
>
> —Theodore J. Lowi, "The State in Political Science:
> How We Became What We Study"

At least once during their political science methodology coursework, budding political scientists hear the parable of the man who lost his keys:

> Walking down the street one night, one happens upon a man who is obviously intoxicated and is searching the sidewalk and street for something. Wanting to be a Good Samaritan, one asks the man what he has lost and if he would like some help. The man replies, "Yes, I dropped my house keys and I am having problems finding them." A detective by nature, one asks the man where he was standing when he dropped his keys. "Over there," says the man, casually pointing toward the darkness down the street while looking down and casting his head narrowly back and forth. Curious that the man is not looking in the area where he indicates that he lost his keys, one asks, "Why are you looking here when you lost your keys over there?" "Because," the man answers quite seriously, "it is dark over there, and there is a street light here so I can see better."

Laughing and shaking their heads in agreement, the students resolve then and there not to succumb to the allure of using data that are easy to obtain though inappropriate for their research question. Most proceed to forsake the resolution, either pursuing a research project because the data are easily available or using less than optimal data to address a research puzzle in the face of the work involved in collecting the appropriate data. Protecting themselves from the claim that they are acting like the drunken man in the story, they subsequently argue that more appropriate data do not exist or, if they do, they would be too costly to assemble.

In this chapter, we seek to provide archivists with a better understanding of the sociology of political science and explain why political scientists currently do not use archives more often. We are convinced that using archives can immeasurably improve the quality of political science research, but political scientists need to be convinced of the importance of archives.[1] By better understanding political science as a discipline, archivists can improve their outreach activities and entice political scientists into using political papers collections.

Before continuing, we should explain the nature of our experience with political papers and thus some of the limitations of this discussion. Since the year 2000, we have used more than 40 congressional papers collections, physically visiting 28 (70 percent) of the collections in 32 separate or combined trips. We have visited small universities with few congressional collections and extremely limited resources, and we have visited major congressional research centers, the National Archives, and presidential libraries. Our quest through this period has been for appropriate data that allow us to test the major theories of congressional organization. Because of our experience, our advice will focus on congressional papers collections. However, we believe that the insights we offer can be, with a little thought, easily applied to any political collection.

DATAHEADS

The most important thing to know about political scientists is that we like to count things: we are dataheads. During the 1930s–1950s, an important shift was taking place within political science, the "behavioral revolution." The most important elements of this revolution were an emphasis on methodological individualism and the adoption of the norms of the natural sciences, specifically the scientific method, to the study of politics. Methodological individualism holds that the appropriate unit of analysis in the study of politics is the individual, as opposed to concepts such as "classes," "parties," "elites," and the like, which were considered epiphenomenal to individual behaviors. The behavioral revolution sought to adapt some of the methods of the sciences—or at least political scientists' understanding of how science "works"—to the study of politics, especially the empirical tradition, which proceeds from direct observation of individual behavior, precise measurement of behaviors through quantification, and the use of statistical methodologies to analyze the resulting data.[2]

The behavioral revolution was—to use the language of psychology—an act of individuation; it was the point at which political science declared its independence, once and for all, from history and the humanities.[3] Central to the behavioral revolution was a focus on data collection methods distinct from those of the humanities. V. O. Key, a legendary political scientist, lamented the slowness of movement toward this new epistemic orientation:

> Professional students of public affairs, both by the limiting circumstances of their employment and the habits of work induced by the tradition and training, have been far too dependent upon the library, the document, and excogitation. Projects that rely on firsthand observation and utilize the appropriate techniques for the accumulation of data relevant to the analytic problems deserve priority. All this is not to deny the utilities of the printed or archival source. The point is simply that heavy reliance on such materials severely restricts the range of questions open to investigation. Over the past quarter of a century social scientists have in varying degree extricated themselves from the toils of the library, but the political scientists have made the least progress in this direction. (Key 1956, 30)

In many respects, the behavioral revolution marked an important and positive turning point for the discipline. Emphasis on observation and measurement allowed political scientists to seek out and discover regularities in political behavior and attain a more secure grasp on the actual practice of politics. For instance, the prebehavioral classic in the study of Congress was Woodrow Wilson's *Congressional Government*, which he wrote in 1885 as a dissertation while at Johns Hopkins University in Baltimore. Though less than 50 miles from Washington, D.C., and the Congress about which he wrote, Wilson never took the time to visit and observe Congress in person. While still a classic, Wilson's work is excessively normative and dependent on journalistic descriptions; it would be difficult to argue that the spirit of observation launched during the behavioral revolution did not have a positive impact on the study of Congress, at the very least.

By the same token, we believe political science took Key's advice a little too enthusiastically. Political scientists abandoned "the toils" of libraries and archival collections, leaving them to be mined by "prescientific" historians. Meanwhile political scientists, possessed by the behavioral spirit, sought out real data that could be analyzed using the latest statistical methods with their complicated calculations that could be completed by rapidly advancing computer technologies. Reliance on data and statistics completed the metamorphosis of the study of government into political science. Important strides were made in understanding the political attitudes and behaviors of voters through nationally representative surveys of American voters. For instance, in their ground-breaking book *The American Voter*, Campbell, Converse, Miller, and Stokes (1960) tested the prevailing wisdom that voters chose candidates based on well-defined ideologies and found that voters used cognitive shortcuts, primarily party affiliation, to make their choices at the polls. Through their work, Campbell and colleagues established survey research as a dominant data source in American politics.

Congressional studies qua political science was on the leading edge of the behavioral revolution. As a subfield of American politics, the development of congressional studies provides useful insight into the behavior of political scientists. Political science is pack oriented; once a relevant and significant research puzzle is identified, political scientists are magnetically attracted (Arnold 1982). This pack orientation is magnified when ready data are easily available. One example is the question of incumbency advantage David Mayhew (1974a) first brought to the attention of congressional scholars. Mayhew focused on the propensity of incumbent members of Congress to win reelection (incumbency advantage), usually by large margins, and hypothesized reasons for the increasing electoral security of incumbents (Mayhew 1974a, 1974b). As a result, congressional scholars began to mine electoral data—which are neatly and regularly generated in a democracy by the federal and other levels of government—in search of an explanation for the advantage. And a subsequent finding by Kernell and Jacobson (1981), which established a link between incumbent campaign spending and the incumbency advantage, led congressional scholars to campaign finance data (made far more easily available by the campaign spending reforms of the 1970s and now available for easy download on the Internet by the Federal Election Commission).

Another area intensively studied in congressional politics is the roll-call voting behavior of members of Congress. Studies of the voting behavior of members of Congress and other legislatures have a long pedigree. This is true, in part, because voting on proposals is one of the most important (and obvious) activities of a legislature. Because legislatures tended to keep careful records of votes, they could be easily translated into quantitative data. Reforms in the late 1960s made recorded votes far more common in Congress, and today they are reported and on the Internet almost simultaneously with the vote. Political scientist Doug Arnold (1982, 94) calculated that about 10 percent of the articles on American politics in the four top journals were on these two topics: incumbency advantage and congressional elections, and roll-call voting in Congress.

These examples point to another important insight into the behavior of political scientists: political scientists are lazy or rational (take your pick). Once a data set has been created and archived, making the data set available for disciplinary consumption, there is little incentive for political scientists to pursue the creation of new data. Why would a rational actor invest his or her resources into collecting new data? Collecting large new data sets is expensive. And except at the largest universities, it is difficult to find the resources to support new data collection. As Arnold points out (1982, 101), original data collections are

> in the first instance, very expensive, and someone must pay the bill. Once paid, however, it becomes very inexpensive to duplicate the data files and distribute them to interested scholars. Many universities pay for the automatic acquisition of such data through the Inter-University Consortium and then provide free computer time for analyzing them. . . . From the point of view of the individual scholar, then, doing research on elections is costless. Complete and automatic subsidization eliminates the need for either grants or the investment of personal resources. Small wonder that so many scholar are doing research [using surveys]. . . . It is free. (Arnold 1982, 101)

Unlike research that relies on analysis of existing survey data, archival research poses legitimate barriers for political scientists. First, political scientists are not trained in archival research (much less alerted of its existence), which may impose substantial startup costs (locating collections, learning how to use a finding aid, developing successful information seeking strategies, etc.). Archival research is expensive: the average cost of our trips has been about $1,000, including airfare, lodging, and photocopying. Archival research is time consuming: the modal duration of our trips is three days; trips of five days are not uncommon (nor is resistance from our families). Archival research involves elements of risk for political scientists. In a discipline unfamiliar with archival data, the prospect of publishing archive-based research is unclear. In the presence of established research questions and existing data, why bear the risk?[4] As Arnold (1982) puts it: "The competition is [between] plenty of free data . . . that scholars can analyze without ever applying for a grant, spending a dime, or leaving the comfort of the university" (103).

As if to prove how much political scientists like to count things (but aimed, in part, at demonstrating the quantitative nature of the discipline), we have performed a content analysis of two top journals in our discipline between 2001 and 2005; the results are presented in table 27.1.[5] One interesting finding is the large proportion in these two journals of articles that are quantitative: on average, more than 40 percent of the articles in the *American Political Science Review* and over 50 percent of articles in the *Journal of Politics* are primarily quantitative.[6] It is also worth noting that these percentages are reasonably steady over time; there is no indication that the dominance of quantitative studies is on the decline.

The table also reports the degree to which archival sources are not used in mainstream journals. Less than 3 percent of the articles published in these two leading journals involved the use of archival or unpublished sources; the modal number of papers drawing on archival sources in any given year

Table 27.1. Research Articles Using Archival Data, *American Political Science Review* and *Journal of Politics,* 2001–2005

	Number of Articles Published[a]	Pure Quantitative[b]	Archives/ Unpublished Data[c]	Historical[d]	Quantitative[e]	Not Significant[f]
			American Political Science Review			
Year						
2001	54	19	1	—	—	1
		35.2%	1.9%			100%
2002	33	11	—	—	—	—
		33.3%				
2003	40	20	2	1	1	—
		50.0%	5.0%	50.0%	50.0%	
2004	42	20	1	—	1	—
		47.6%	2.4%		100%	
2005	35	16	1	—	—	1
		45.7%	2.9%			100%
Total	204	86	5	1	2	2
		42.2%	2.5%	20.0%	40.0%	40.0%
			Journal of Politics			
2001	43	25	1	—	1	—
		58.1%	2.3%		100%	
2002	49	27	1	—	—	1
		55.1%	2.0%			100%
2003	53	29	0	—	—	—
		54.7%				
2004	53	27	1	—	1	—
		50.9%	1.9%		100%	
2005	53	25	0	—	—	—
		47.2%				
Total	251	133	3	—	2	1
		52.9%	1.2%		66.6%	33.3%

Source: Calculated by the authors from the *American Political Science Review* and the *Journal of Politics,* 2001–2005.

[a]Total number of research articles published in journal during that year.

[b]Pure quantitative research articles are those that center on the analyzing and reporting results of research employing quantitative data. Percentages represent the proportion of the total number of articles published in that year.

[c]Archives or unpublished data sources include those articles that rely on "archival and other unpublished documentary sources" (Skemer 1991). Percentages represent the proportion of the total number of articles published in that year.

[d]Archival sources were used for primarily historical purposes. Percentages represent the proportion of the number of archive-based articles published in that year.

[e]Archival data were used as a data source in a quantitative analysis. Percentages represent the proportion of the number of archive-based articles published in that year.

[f]Archival sources were utilized but did not constitute a primary source for historical or quantitative analysis. Percentages represent the proportion of the number of archive-based articles published in that year.

is one. Finally, the most common use of archival sources in published articles is to create quantitative data for analysis using quantitative analysis.

Analysis of quantitative data tends to dominate academic political science. Beginning in the middle third of the century, a premium was placed on measurable and observable behavior. This trend pushed political scientists out of the library and, increasingly, into the computer lab (and occasionally into the field); the methods of history, archives in particular, were to be abandoned once and for all to the gnomish historian—political science was prepared to join the ranks of more mature sciences: economics and psychology. Abandoning the archives was viewed as an indication of progress. While historical political science is experiencing something of a renaissance, as we heard an anonymous political scientist put it: "The battle is over, quantitative political science has won, and everyone gets to learn how to estimate maximum likelihood models." Even considering the bravado and overstatement contained in the statement, it illustrates an important point. If archival research is to enter the mainstream of political science research, it will be on the coattails of quantitative analysis; the majority of articles in top journals are quantitative and do not rely on archival data. We believe that the spread of archival research to political science is dependent on identifying quantifiable data in the preserved documents in the collections of public figures.

What does all of this mean for an archivist working with political collections? In the following sections, we hope to go beyond generic outreach advice like "sell your collection on campus" and instead offer practical advice that will help to get political scientists back into the library and into political collections. In short, we hope to illustrate how one might communicate with political scientists. We begin by describing how to think like a political scientist. We then describe some of the things that tend to pop up in political collections that may be of interest to political scientists. Using this knowledge, archivists will be prepared to reach out to their campus community and to the broader discipline.

THINKING LIKE A POLITICAL SCIENTIST

For several generations now—for reasons discussed above—historians have been the most intensive users of political collections. Rightfully, given the circumstances, archivists have come to think like historians. To make archives more relevant to political scientists, it will become necessary to be able to think like a political scientist. The primary rule of quantitative political research to remember is: When it comes to data, in political science less is not more; more is more. Because statistical research relies heavily on large numbers of cases, the more data that are available the better. This axiom has two corollaries. First, thinking cross-sectionally, the more information that is available for any given period (a Congress, in the case of congressional papers collections, a court term, and so forth), the better. Second, to the degree that complete information is available for multiple periods, even better; the longer time frame allows for examining patterns over time.

Two additional considerations may also help archivists to better understand how political scientists think: (1) If it can be counted (or better yet, has already been counted), it may be of interest to a political scientist. Many historians are interested in one or a few documents that are perhaps particularly revealing. For the political scientist, the number of documents, in part because it may be quantified, can be of particular interest. (2) If it has numbers in it, it may be of interest to a political scientist. Documents that contain numbers tend to catch the eye of a political scientist because they may contain data that can be entered directly into a data set or modified to be useful in a quantitative data set.

THE CASE OF CONSTITUENT MAIL

One enduring research puzzle in American politics is how public opinion shapes the behavior of politicians. Do representatives' votes in a legislature reflect the opinions of their constituents or do they represent the representatives' independent judgments? This is a research question that goes directly to the heart of democratic theory.

Trying to explain the voting behavior of legislators became (and persists as) a cottage industry mainly because of the easy availability of the data. Legislatures take care to record their votes; political scientists can count yeas and nays. Establishing a linkage to district opinion has proven to be trickier. It is exorbitantly expensive to conduct surveys with 1,000 or 2,000 respondents. Because only a few of the respondents will fall in any single district in the House of Representatives (or state in the case of the Senate), it is difficult to get an accurate measure of "opinion in the district." Even if it were possible to conduct such surveys, they would only reflect a slice in time, foreclosing the opportunity to observe if legislators adjust their behavior as opinion changes. This would be overcome by repeated samples of public opinion; however, conducting surveys repeatedly over time would be cost prohibitive.

A Potential Solution: Constituent correspondence could represent a means of examining the relationship between district opinion and the voting behavior of legislators. Policy-related letters from constituents might be conceived of as "activated public opinion." Constituents who are concerned enough to communicate to their representatives an opinion on an issue of public policy—taking the time and effort to write a letter and pay the cost of postage—reflect the opinions of voters in a district who are of great concern to a legislator: those who vote in elections. Counting up letters—based on the opinions they express—could serve as a barometer of district opinion. Certainly the letters do not represent a random sample of constituent opinion. The letters do provide an opportunity to reconstruct district opinion in the absence of modern survey data methods.

If constituent correspondence is to be used by political scientists, maintaining as much of the original material as possible is vital. The number of letters—remember, it is about counting things—is one of the first things that a political scientist might look at to get a measure of opinion, in addition to the tone of a letter. To be able to study change in district opinion over time—and to consider fully the implications of external events—having the dates of the letters is critical. If the tone of district opinion seems to change, we would be interested to know if some critical event outside the district might have prompted the change. The more years of material we have, the better. The longer the time span, the better able we are to measure change across time. Having the letters will allow us to determine the physical location of the writer. Of course we will be interested if the writer lives in the district (and many congressional offices destroy mail from outside the district), but with addresses we can map public opinion and potentially discover spatial regularities in opinion.

Collections that revolve around political figures have to deal with the issue of constituent mail. For some politicians, constituent mail may constitute 100 boxes or more. From the point of view of the archivist and the archival institution, space constraints and the time necessary to process these letters are in short supply. One seeming solution to the problem of constituent mail is to "sample" constituent correspondence. A handful of letters on each topic in the mail that seem to represent the views expressed by constituents are retained, thus reducing the burden of this part of the collection. This approach might serve historians well, allowing them to capture the flavor of constituent opinion well enough to convey the context they would like to express. Considered from the point of view of political scientists, we see this approach as the destruction of potential data. If we do not know how many letters of each type were in the original collection, it would be impossible to quantify local opinion.

We do not expect to convince archivists that they should keep all of the constituent correspondence that shows up with that next political collection. However, our discussion of constituent correspondence is convenient because it provides a point of high contrast between how political scientists and historians think. Depending on how an archivist thinks, the archivist might approach materials in a political collection differently. To an archivist thinking like a historian, the volume of material may appear as a nuisance; however, the political scientist sees an opportunity to generate data by counting.

HOW TO REACH OUT TO POLITICAL SCIENTISTS

Skemer suggests that a post-behaviorist wave in political science concerned with a historical interest in American institutions—what has come to be known as the American political development (APD) approach—implies a possible return to the "humanistic origins" of political science. Skemer argues that "there is reason to believe that archival research by political scientists will increase, chiefly in the areas of American political institutions, group politics, international relations, comparative public policy, political theory, and history of the disciplines" (1991, 367). However, as the results of table 27.1 demonstrate, our discipline is still heavily influenced (even dominated) by data and quantitative analysis. For a variety of reasons, it is unlikely that a return to our historical roots will lead large numbers of political scientists back into the library.

If political scientists are dataheads, selling them on archival research means selling them on the idea that there are data in those boxes in your collection. Part of the outreach effort, of course, is to have a good understanding of your collection: What in your collection might be conceived of as quantitative or potentially quantifiable? The other part is to know how your collection might appeal to a political scientist.

A GRASSROOTS APPROACH

Broadly speaking, a successful outreach strategy will focus on the potential data that reside in one's collection and the ability to communicate the value to potential researchers. Depending on the size of your university, or the universities in your area, there will likely be one or more specialists in American politics who will not be familiar with the use of archives. Step one is to convince faculty that archives are a potentially useful data source. Point them toward accessible discussions of the use of archives in political science (Frisch and Kelly 2003, 2004, 2005; Harris 2005c; Kelly 2005). In addition, suggest that they consider examples in the political science literature that demonstrate the use of archival sources in quantitative data analysis. Maltzman, Spriggs, and Wahlbeck (2000) use the papers of former Supreme Court Justice Harry Blackmun to great effect, and data from the same source have recently found their way into the *American Political Science Review* (Johnson, Wahlbeck, and Spriggs 2006). Evans and Renjilian (2004), Evans and Lapinski (2005), and Evans and colleagues (2005) use archives extensively to examine how legislative leaders and individual members use the legislative process to produce specific outcomes. Doug Harris's work on party leadership in the U.S. House makes extensive use of archival data (2005a, 2005b). Matthew Green (2006) and Doug Harris (2006) have used party leadership candidates' whip counts to help explain the systematic components of support for candidates. Also consider the work of Lawrence, Maltzman, and Wahlbeck (2001) on committee assignments at the turn of the twentieth century, and our work on House committees (Frisch and Kelly 2006a) and Senate committees (Frisch and Kelly 2006b).

Step two is to discuss how your political papers collections may benefit their research. American politics is a highly diverse field composed of a number of subfields. Very generally speaking, scholars tend to specialize in political institutions (further subdivided into the study of legislatures, executives, the courts, and bureaucracy), political behavior (the behaviors of individual voters and individuals within political institutions), interest groups, political parties, and public policy. In each of these subfields, archives have the potential to yield important data.

The intention in table 27.2 is to provide a suggestive listing for both the archivist and the potential user of the papers. What constitutes potential data? It is sometimes difficult to know without significant grounding in the political science literature, but some types of materials are easily identifiable:

1. *Attitudinal surveys conducted by politicians, political parties, or political consultants* within a political jurisdiction (city, county, state, or congressional district). Nationally representative samples allow us to make accurate inferences about national attitudes, but they do not allow us to understand how public opinion impacts the decisions of local politicians. Surveys focusing on a specific jurisdiction can be used to examine the relationship between public opinion and elite decision making.

2. *Whip counts, surveys of other politicians in the same institution*, which indicate support or opposition for pending legislation or actions. While the party leadership often engages in whip counts, it is not uncommon to find these counts in the collections of rank-and-file members who are pursuing specific legislative goals or an elected leadership or other institutional position.

3. *Letters from other politicians requesting help or support for a project or position.* These kinds of letters tend to be voluminous in the case of political actors who served in positions of formal leadership, such as party and committee leaders. Often these letters will be summarized in spreadsheets and binders that may have been used in formal decision-making meetings.

4. *Documents that contain information about money but are not typically made available to the public.* Money is the lifeblood of politics. In electoral politics, money helps to finance elections, and information regarding the when, where, and how of campaign contributions is of great interest to many students of American politics. In public policy, the battle over money (e.g., how much money will be allocated for particular policies and projects) is critical. Unpublished materials that document proposed

Table 27.2. Real Data and Latent Data in Political Collections: A Guide for Reaching Out to Political Scientists

	Ready Data[a]	Latent Data[b]
Public Opinion	• Surveys commissioned by the politician, institution, or group • Telephone logs recording opinion on proposed legislation • Staff analysis of constituent mail or telephone logs (summaries of pro and con opinion calculated by the staff)	• Constituent correspondence could provide an indication of activated opinion in the district on a wide array of policy issues, or evolution of opinion within the district over time on a selected issue or issues • Office phone logs that record phoned-in constituent opinion could similarly be a measure of activated opinion
Electoral Strategy	• Actual campaign contributions (especially before the campaign reforms of the 1970s): Who contributes? Where are they?	• District appointment books (how members choose to allocate their time in the district) during election periods compared to off years, or across election periods • Letters to potential campaign contributors: Who are they? Where are they?
Party	• Party campaign contributions to members of their caucus • Surveys commissioned by the party • Internally calculated party support scores • Party whip counts • Records of Senate holds	• Communications from party leaders indicate how the party leadership would like members to vote on legislation • Party "message" documents indicate how the party would like its members to talk about party programs • Party legislative agendas indicate which pieces of legislation are most important
Redistricting	• Precinct-level party registration information • Precinct-level demographic data	• Maps of proposed district lines • Memos regarding districting issues
Policy	• Party or office whip counts detailing how others may vote in the legislature on legislative initiatives of the politician • Vote estimates from interest groups	• "Dear Colleague" letters requesting support or opposition for particular pieces of legislation • Interest-group letters regarding pending legislation
Leadership Battles	• Whip counts of members intentions to support a particular leadership contestant	• Letters to colleagues requesting support • Letters from colleagues pledging support, sending regrets

	Ready Data[a]	Latent Data[b]
Career		• Bill co-sponsorship; correspondence with other members of a legislature may provide insight into which bills have strong co-sponsors (versus symbolic co-sponsors) • Office appointment books (how political actors allocate their time in the legislature) • Requests for committee assignments
Credit-Claiming Activities	• Listings of projects in the district that have received funding and amounts of funding	• Requests for funding sent to the appropriations committees: Which are funded? Which result in positive (or negative) stories in the local media? • Press releases/press clippings: When do press clippings result in actual stories in the local media? • Constituent newsletters: How much credit-claiming activity is included in newsletters? What types of activities are stressed?
Position-Taking Activities	• Listings of press conferences and topics • Listings of floor speeches, one-minutes, and topics	• Constituent newsletters: How much position-taking activity is included in newsletters? What types of activities are stressed?
Influence		• Recommendations for federal judicial appointments • Recommendations for executive-branch appointments • Requests for Senate holds • Rules Committee requests for special rules
Executive Relations	• Budget projections, cost estimates, etc., from OMB and other executive departments and agencies in response to individual request	• Communications from the White House regarding the president's policy preferences

[a]Ready Data are materials in a collection that are already expressed in numerical terms and would need only to be entered into a database.
[b]Latent Data are materials that would need to be translated into data by the researcher.

or actual public expenditures or campaign expenditures are of great interest to many scholars too.

Beyond prompting awareness of what may be in your collection, table 27.2 could be copied and sent to the potential researcher. If one has never used a collection, it is hard to imagine the vast potential of these collections and what might be there. It is all the more difficult for researchers who have limited experience working in practical politics; they may be surprised by the degree to which behaviors are documented and retained by offices.

A STRATEGIC APPROACH

For several years, we have worked with members of the Congressional Papers Roundtable (CPR) of the Society of American Archivists (SAA) on a strategic approach to encourage the use of political papers by political scientists. The purpose of our efforts is to build a bridge between political science and the archival world in hope of creating greater awareness in political science about the value of archival collections, and to make the archival world aware of the interests of political scientists in the content of archival collections.

The strategic approach has three components: advocacy, networking, and training. Advocacy focuses on the political science discipline and promoting the use of congressional papers by political scientists in their research. The means for achieving this is cross-disciplinary dialogue between political scientists and archivists; in other words, crossing over into each others' worlds to prompt dialogue. This includes attending each others' conferences. The Association of Centers for the Study of Congress is an ideal forum for bringing together institutions that have collections and those who use them.

Networking involves disseminating evidence more broadly across the disciplines. Information regarding collections that offer research funding for scholars can be found on the Congressional Papers Roundtable Web site at www.archivists.org/saagroups/cpr. We need to get to the point where archivists can communicate directly with the political science community about the availability of a new collection and some of the more unusual contents that may be of interest to the discipline.

Training is aimed at providing political scientists with some of the initial tools to begin using archival collections. In August 2005, the Legislative Studies Section of the American Political Science Association (APSA), the Congressional Papers Roundtable, and the National Archives co-sponsored a course at the APSA national meeting to provide initial training to political scientists. Approximately 40 people attended the sessions. Strategic cooperation between political scientists and the archival world can help to increase the use of archival resources, thereby increasing audiences at archival repositories.

OUR CONCLUSIONS

Our formal collaboration began in March 2000. Frisch called Kelly and told him of some of the wonderful things he had found while working in the Robert Michel Papers at the Dirksen Congressional Center in Pekin, Illinois. Among the wonderful things were hundreds of paper ballots used by the Republican leadership to vote on who would get assigned to congressional committees. One would assume that these were secret ballots, but "no," Frisch said, "the people casting the ballots put their names on the ballots." Intrigued by the possibility, and funded by a small grant from the Dirksen Center, Kelly traveled to Pekin, where these ballots had been carefully stored in envelopes by some diligent Republican staffer. Kelly spent almost three days entering the information contained in those thousands of ballots into a spreadsheet (there were far too many to make copies on our limited budget). At one point, the director and archivist of the center, Frank Mackaman, strolled over and said, "I always wondered if those were of any use." One chapter of our book is dedicated to an analysis of those data which allowed us to, among other things, empirically verify factions within the Republican Party in a way that likely would be impossible otherwise.

Political scientists are dataheads, as our experience illustrates. We love it when we can find things to count and then use them in quantitative analysis. Quantitative political science eclipsed historically oriented political science in the 1970s, and its dominance continues and is increasing. Though history-minded political scientists continue to work and publish, large-scale use of archival sources is most likely to come from the quantitatively minded wing of the profession. It makes some sense, then, for archivists to better understand the orientation of academic political science and to try to think about their collections—from time to time—from the perspective of the political scientist. Had Frank Mackaman considered what a political scientist might do with those little scraps of paper—and if a means of communicating that kind of information had been available to him—he could have let political scientists know about the availability of these data. (Thankfully for us, he did not!) Historians tend to value context over quantity; political scientists tend to value quantity—there is more to count that way. A political scientist prefers to have more data over time whenever possible; the greater the number of years that are available, the better.

Readily available political science data files filled with surveys, roll-call votes, campaign expenditures, and so forth are seductive. They offer the promise of ready data at one's fingertips: analysis is just a download away. Drawing political scientists back into the library collections means convincing them that there are data in your collections. Archivists should take some time to consider collections from a political science perspective and then reach out to local faculty. Refer them to the books and articles mentioned here, and send them table 27.2. On Web sites, note particular parts of collections that may be of interest to political scientists. Find ways to make contact with the political science community through e-mail lists and Web sites. Most of all, encourage political scientists to spend an afternoon looking through the finding aids and the collections.

We were both astounded about the research possibilities hidden in the many boxes during our first foray at the Dirksen Center, and we have been focused on archival research ever since. We expect many others could be hooked by a single visit that demonstrates the potential of archival research. From the time of our first trips to archival collections, we were convinced that archival research has the potential to significantly improve the quality of political science research. By offering new and improved data, archival research can improve our understanding of politics while creating new demand for political collections.

NOTES

We owe an enormous debt of gratitude to the many archivists and archival staff that we have had the opportunity to learn from, including Beth Bower, Rose Diaz, Michael Knies, Rebecca Johnson Melvin, Richard Hunt, Jessie Kratz, Frank Mackaman, Charlotte Walters, and Linda Whitaker, to name just a few. Our work in archives has been expensive and we have had the financial support of the Dirksen Congressional Center, the Carl Albert Center, the Gerald Ford Presidential Library, the Institute for Humane Studies, the Thomas S. Foley Institute at Washington State University, the Niagara University Research Council, and California State University Channel Islands.

1. For that reason, in the past several years, we have applied the zeal and enthusiasm of evangelists to spread the good news of archival research. This includes an article in a leading political science journal (Frisch and Kelly 2003), a joint political scientist and archivist roundtable at a major regional political science conference (the NE APSA in 2004), and a "short course" for political scientists on "doing" archival research at our 2005 American Political Science Association conference.

2. Shapiro (2005) argues that the deductive and the empirical elements of the "behavioral revolution" that we describe are distinct traditions; we present them as a unified tradition, which we believe is all the more appropriate given the rise of the EITM movement (Empirical Implications of Theoretical Models) that seeks to reconcile these two somewhat distinct traditions.

3. This is not to argue that political science has not maintained a strong attachment to history, as the American Political Development movement illustrates. However, it would be difficult to argue that the top political science journals are dominated by behavioral and quantitative political science.

4. For junior faculty under pressure to publish to achieve tenure, the risks may be even higher. The time-consuming data collection phase of archival research

could substantially slow the rate of publication, raising the eyebrows of more senior faculty.

5. The *American Political Science Review* is the flagship journal of the discipline and is considered an outlet for the most innovative and ground-breaking work in political science. As the flagship journal, it should be a good indicator of trends in political science research, though many political scientists will argue that it has a distinct bias toward logical-deductive and empirical approaches to political science. The *Journal of Politics* is one of the leading journals in the profession and has a reputation for promoting theoretical and methodological pluralism relative to the *APSR*.

6. To some, these percentages may seem low. Are the other halves of the journals mainly historical? The short answer is no. A concomitant development in political science was the logical-deductive approach. This approach focused on the development of general theories from which testable hypotheses could be generated. Formal theoretical papers make up a large portion of the articles in the top political science journals.

BIBLIOGRAPHY

Arnold, R. Douglass. 1982. "Overtilled and Undertilled Fields in American Politics." *American Politics Quarterly* 97:91–103.

Campbell, Angus, Philip E. Converse, Warren E. Miller, and Donald E. Stokes. 1960. *The American Voter.* Chicago: University of Chicago Press.

Clubb, Jerome M. 1975. "Sources for Political Inquiry II: Quantitative Data." In Fred I. Greenstein and Nelson W. Polsby, eds., *Strategies of Inquiry: Handbook of Political Science,* vol. 7. Reading, Mass.: Addison-Wesley.

Evans, C. Lawrence, S. Brown, K. Devereaux, K. Haase, W. Marlow, and J. McHenry. 2005. "Tax Cuts, Contras, and Partisan Influence in the U.S. House," presented at the annual meeting of the Midwest Political Science Association, Chicago, April.

Evans, C. Lawrence, and Daniel Lipinski. 2005. "Holds, Legislation, and the Senate Parties," presented at the Conference on the U.S. Senate, Rothermere American Institute, University of Oxford.

Evans, C. Lawrence, and C. Renjilian. 2004. "Cracking the Whip in the U.S. House: Majority Dominance or Party Balancing?" presented at the annual meeting of the American Political Science Association, Philadelphia, August.

Frisch, Scott A., and Sean Q Kelly. 2006a. *Committee Assignment Politics in the U.S. House of Representatives.* Norman: University of Oklahoma Press.

———. 2006b. "Committee Assignment Politics in the U.S. Senate: Democratic Leaders and Democratic Committee Assignments, 1953–1994." *Congress and the Presidency,* Spring.

———. 2005. "Five Reasons to Consider Taking the Road Less Traveled." *LSS Newsletter, Extension of Remarks* 28:28–33. www.apsanet.org/~lss/Newsletter/july05/EOR-July-2005.pdf.

———. 2004. "Political Scientists: Strangers in a Wonderland." *Congressional Papers Roundtable Newsletter,* July, 5–7.

————. 2003. "Don't Have the Data? Make Them Up! Congressional Archives as Untapped Data Sources." *PS: Political Science and Politics* 36:221–4.

Green, Matthew N. 2006. "McCormack Versus Udall: Explaining Intraparty Challenges to the Speaker of the House." *American Politics Research* 34:3–21.

Harris, Douglas B. 2006. "Legislative Parties and Leadership Choice: Confrontation or Accommodation in the 1989 Gingrich-Madigan Whip Race." *American Politics Research*, March.

————. 2005a. "House Majority Party Leaders' Uses of Public Opinion Information." *Congress and the Presidency* 32.

————. 2005b. "Orchestrating Party Talk: A Party-Based View of One-Minute Speeches in the House of Representatives." *Legislative Studies Quarterly* 30:127–41.

————. 2005c. "Recovering History and Discovering Data in the Archives: An Alternative 'Mode of Research' for Congress Scholars." *LSS Newsletter, Extension of Remarks* 28:1–10. www.apsanet.org/~lss/Newsletter/july05/EOR-July-2005.pdf.

Johnson, Timothy R., Paul J. Wahlbeck, and James F. Spriggs II. 2006. "The Influence of Oral Arguments on the U.S. Supreme Court." *American Political Science Review* 100:99–113.

Kelly, Sean Q, ed. 2005. "Using Archival Resources in Legislative Research: Choosing the Road Less Traveled." www.apsanet.org/~lss/Newsletter/july05/EOR-July-2005.pdf.

Kernell, Samuel, and Gary C. Jacobson. 1981. *Strategy and Choice in Congressional Elections*. New Haven: Yale University Press.

Key, V. O. 1956. "Strategies in Research on Public Affairs." *Social Science Research Council Items* 10:29–32.

Lawrence, Eric, Forrest Maltzman, and Paul J. Wahlbeck. 2001. "The Politics of Speaker Cannon's Committee Assignments." *American Journal of Political Science* 45:551–62.

Lowi, Theodore J. 1992. "The State in Political Science: How We Became What We Study." *American Political Science Review* 86:1–7.

Maltzman, Forrest, James F. Spriggs II, and Paul J. Wahlbeck. 2000. *Crafting Law on the Supreme Court: The Collegial Game*. New York: Cambridge University Press.

Mayhew, David R. 1974a. "Congressional Elections: The Case of the Vanishing Marginals." *Polity* 6:295–317.

————. 1974b. *Congress: The Electoral Connection*. New Haven: Yale University Press.

Shapiro, Ian. 2005. *The Flight from Reality in the Human Sciences*. Princeton: Princeton University Press.

Skemer, Don C. 1991. "Drifting Disciplines, Enduring Records: Political Science and the Use of Archives." *American Archivist* 54:356–68.

Vose, Clement E. 1975. "Sources for Political Inquiry I: Library Reference Materials and Manuscripts as Data for Political Science." In Fred I. Greenstein and Nelson W. Polsby, eds., *Strategies of Inquiry: Handbook of Political Science*, vol. 7. Reading, Mass.: Addison-Wesley.

28

Congressional Collections: Where the Mundane Becomes Compelling

Frank Mackaman

I have a selfish interest in writing about the uses of archival sources for legislative research. Frankly, the Dirksen Congressional Center is an underused resource. True, we have our share of historians and hobbyists who consult our collections, but political scientists are a rarer breed. Despite the relevance of our historical materials to studies of Congress, we don't get much use from scholars trained as political scientists. I would hazard a guess that the vast majority of the nearly 40 member institutions of the newly formed Association of Centers for the Study of Congress (ACSC) have the same experience.[1]

For the past 30 years, I have immersed myself in the collections of political figures as a graduate student, historian, staff member at the Dirksen Congressional Center, director of the Gerald R. Ford Library, and finally returning to the Dirksen Center in 1996. I worked my way through graduate school as an archivist. My first boss tried to make the job of poring through hundreds of boxes of the Thomas B. Curtis (R-MO) papers, page by page, attractive by appealing to my academic major: "You will discover a richness in the historical record by actually processing these papers—a perspective that even the most conscientious researcher can never achieve," she said. And she was right. So this is my bias: the papers of members of Congress provide unique, verifiable, reliable, even entertaining information about almost all things congressional.[2]

Although this chapter concentrates on members' personal collections, there are other archival resources about the host of legislative actors,

Previously published as "Congressional Collections: Where the Mundane Becomes Compelling" in *Extension of Remarks* Legislative Studies Section, American Political Science Association (July 2005). Published with permission.

processes, and outcomes. The universe of documentation about Congress includes committee and institutional records (e.g., the records at the Center for Legislative Archives at the National Archives), government records created by executive and judicial departments (e.g., the White House and executive branch congressional liaison offices), personal collections of those who once served in Congress but whose main career took some other form (e.g., the papers of Gerald R. Ford, a House member before he became president), and the business records of lobbyists, interest groups, think tanks, law firms, and so on. The list is almost endless.

WHAT ARE THE SCOPE AND
STRUCTURE OF A MEMBER'S PAPERS?

Variety is the key here. No two congressional collections are alike, because no two congressional offices function the same way. A congressional collection is the artifact of the congressional office, which in turn reflects the personality of the member, at least to some degree. Archival practice underscores this uniqueness. In processing a collection, archivists preserve, to the extent possible, the original nature and order of the collection. We do not file records in some archival equivalent of the Dewey decimal system.[3]

Having said that, most congressional collections if they are reasonably complete, share common elements. They consist of records relating to a member's representational role, records relating to lawmaking, files pertaining to the member himself or herself, and administrative records. In the first category, that of representation, fall issue mail, district or state office files (including grants and projects), casework, VIP correspondence, patronage, campaign and political files, accepted invitations, and a collection of "marketing" materials such as speeches, press releases, newsletters, the Web site, and television and radio files.

Congressional archives house records related to lawmaking, including legislative working papers, bill files, general reference materials, voting and attendance records, materials related to congressional membership organizations, and leadership files (if applicable). Member-centered records include appointment books and schedules, biographical and personal files, newspaper clippings, and diaries or personal journals (if you're very lucky). Administrative records document office management practices. Staff files, agency and department files, general correspondence, memorabilia, and audiovisual materials are types of records that span all four categories.[4]

Congressmembers' collections share something else: diversity in format. Actual paper still predominates, but many collections also include still photographs, artifacts, books, film and tape in their multiple formats, and increasingly, e-based formats.

There are, however, few complete congressional collections.[5] In the case of Everett Dirksen, for example, virtually all of the records from his 16 years in the House were destroyed. It is an oft-repeated truism: the primary purpose of a congressional office is not to preserve the historical record. Expect substantial gaps in most members' papers.[6]

WHAT ARE THE STRENGTHS AND WEAKNESSES OF MEMBERS' COLLECTIONS?

The scope and structure of congressional collections pose opportunities and obstacles. The primary strength of congressional collections lies in their uniqueness. I know of no other way to appreciate the life of a politician than to "soak and poke" in their archives. Following them around for a time comes close, but it's not quite the same. I'm reminded of a graduate student in the University of Michigan's School of Business who was conducting research at the Gerald R. Ford Library for a dissertation on organizational change. He called his work "theory-elaborative archival ethnography" (a phrase I've always wanted to work into print). To the extent that a high-quality congressional archive can allow a researcher to reconstruct past events in fine detail, ethnography is an apt word. Any archivist who has worked more than three months in a congressional collection can describe documentary gems that would crown the right research project.

One of my favorite gems from the Dirksen Collection relates to what may have been his most famous speech on the Senate floor (remember, these were the days before C-SPAN). After a record-breaking filibuster stalled passage of a civil rights bill in the Senate in 1964, the time came for the cloture vote. Head counts suggested the vote would be breathtakingly close. Dirksen, described by one journalist as "a collapsed ruin, drawn and gaunt" after weeks of 16-hour days, was to have the last word before the vote on June 10 (MacNeil 1970, 236). Very rarely did Dirksen prepare remarks in advance. This time, however, he and his wife, Louella, spent the late evening of June 9 preparing a 12-page script which Dirksen himself composed on his Royal manual typewriter. The annotations indicate that he reviewed the text at least three times before delivering it. When the cloture vote passed, Dirksen's remarks were widely credited with the outcome. My point is this: only a close reading of that raw text reveals the importance Dirksen attached to his remarks and the almost painful effort he made to perfect them. He knew what was at stake. He appreciated the power of language, of persuasion, in the legislative setting. Seeing the text in the *Congressional Record* is just not the same. The roll-call vote doesn't do the occasion justice either.

If these collections are so rich and unique and revealing, why don't scholars flock to them? Because they are not easy to use. The weakness of these collections is not their content per se. The obstacles are primarily external to the individual collections: political science as a discipline does not provide incentives for historically or archivally grounded research and publication, for example. Another difficulty is that the collections are spread out all over the country; it is costly to travel to more than a handful.[7] Some repositories do not place a high priority on getting the collections in shape to use, even if their content merits more attention. Moreover, the uniqueness of collections frustrates a standardized approach to doing research.

There is also the large size, which is an inherent quality of many political collections. Volume poses a problem both to archivists who must process the papers and to researchers who want to use them. Volume varies as widely as subject coverage. The Carl Albert Center houses 55 congressional collections ranging in size from one-tenth of a foot to 992 cubic feet for the late House speaker's collection—seven collections are larger than 100 cubic feet, not including nine recent accessions which also promise to be voluminous.[8] But size need not intimidate you. Collection guides and reference archivists can narrow the search. Of course it helps to have a disciplined research strategy, one tailored to the resources available at the repository you visit (see, for example, Frisch and Kelly 2003; Ryfe 2001). It's difficult for me to help someone who walks in and tells me, "I want to do something on Everett Dirksen." Do I turn them loose in the 1,600 linear feet of his papers?

WHY SHOULD YOU (A POLITICAL SCIENTIST) USE ARCHIVAL SOURCES IN LEGISLATIVE RESEARCH?

I am now skating on thin ice. Far be it from me to claim expertise in your discipline. My aim here is simply to suggest that members' collections contain information that will help you answer at least some of the questions your research about Congress addresses.

One of the themes of modern congressional studies is that the career goals and goal-seeking behavior of legislators greatly shape the nature of Congress as an institution. But scholars have difficulty in constructing or reconstructing the nature of careers. One of your colleagues has blamed the discipline's focus on Washington-centered, policy-centered, and increasingly party-centered approaches to research about Congress. Careers, however, are individual and respond to members' own special needs and circumstances, locally and regionally. "Comprehending the distinctive character of individual careers requires access to data that to many of us might seem almost mundane," Larry Dodd notes, "but such data can have significant implications for our interpretations of Congress as an institution and for careers within it" (Dodd 2004).

What we're really talking about here is congressional biography. Burdett Loomis has made the point that neither historians nor political scientists have produced much in the way of congressional biography. The careful examination of a single individual, Loomis writes, "may tell us as much as a data-rich, assumption-driven piece of analysis." And he issues this challenge to political scientists: "Moreover, the absence of biographies means that we have given up the telling of stories to others, who may well develop more cynical, less understanding studies than those who best understand the legislative branch" (Loomis 2000). In calling "for a return to the art of biography," Betty Koed, assistant historian of the U.S. Senate, reminds us: "Looking at the career of a specific member of Congress can also provide a glimpse into that difficult task of balancing state and national issues, defining political allegiance, and building a national legacy in harmony with local, constituent needs" (Koed 2000, 16). I can't think of one good reason why biography ought to be the exclusive province of historians.

What is it that we want to know about a member of Congress? It seems to me that substantial effort has been made over the past 30 years to refocus attention on the career of members in their districts, away from their role in Washington. Richard Fenno is largely credited with this shift to a study of "home style," an approach to congressional biography that incorporates what Dodd calls "mundane" data, or innocuous data. This stuff abounds in members' collections. Travel records, daily meeting schedules, information about local press appearances, lists of district friends (sometimes derived from Christmas-card lists), lists of charitable contributions made by the members, records of their membership in local organizations—unfortunately, this mundane data is often discounted in value and weeded from collections. But if Dodd is right about its value, then we archivists have made a mistake. Innocuous data can help us see the real nature of the legislative experience, understand the nature of congressional careers, see members' close attentiveness to their local districts, and appreciate the role of "home style" in the life of a legislator.

As significant as the study of "home style" has been as a corrective to a Washington-centric view of congressional biography and career, I am intrigued by the possibility of appraising congressional careers, of writing congressional biography, through a different lens, an adaptation of the framework Fred Greenstein (2000) uses to evaluate presidential leadership. He judges presidential success in terms of six factors: organizational capacity, political skill, public communication, cognitive style, vision, and emotional intelligence. My experience as an archivist suggests that a congressmember's collection provides vital information about each of these factors, and that a compelling congressional biography, or understanding of career, can result from consulting the archives using the Greenstein framework.

An office's personnel files, the office procedures manual, staff memoranda, the files of the chief of staff, even a legislator's correspondence can answer such questions as these: Does the member select able people? Does he or she fix what doesn't work in the office? Does he or she hold people accountable? Does he or she direct, delegate, and coordinate appropriately? The answers to such questions reveal a member's ability to rally the staff and structure their activities effectively, what Greenstein calls "organizational capacity."

How politically skillful is the congressmember? Does he or she have good political instincts? Does he or she grasp political implications? Does he or she set realistic expectations? Does the member get things done? The effectiveness of a congressmember depends to an important degree on his or her political skill: the ability to get elected in the first place and the ability to get things done once elected. The obvious archival sources for the first are the campaign and political files of a member, which contain strategy memos, evaluations by consultants and staff, polling data, and so on. Good sources for the second include clippings files (which document the media's evaluation of political skill), issue mail, personal and general correspondence, and files relating to the member's performance in ad hoc groups, leadership settings, and committees and subcommittees.

Somewhere along the line, successful members of Congress have to communicate in order to achieve reelection and exercise influence with colleagues, much as Dirksen did in the summer of 1964. Does the member have command of information? Does he or she appreciate the power of the position? Does he or she speak with conviction? Does he or she possess eloquence? Audiovisual sources in the archives are helpful here. The Dirksen papers, for example, contain fascinating information about Dirksen's appearances on the "Ev and Charlie" and "Ev and Jerry" shows, press conferences in the 1960s following the Joint Senate-House Republican Leadership meetings. Dirksen's performance in these settings elevated him to the national stage, gained him favor among journalists, and provided a woefully outnumbered Republican minority with a disproportionate influence on public policy. Naturally, the press secretary's files, news clippings, polling data, interview transcripts, speech files, and the like are rich sources, too.

A member's cognitive style deserves considerable attention. Can the member get to the central essence of issues? Is he or she open to new insights? Does he or she use accurate historical analogies? Does he or she exhibit intellectual strength across a broad range? What a member believes about how the world works and why it does so must count for a great deal in congressional biography. Here, the archival sources include family and personal records, correspondence with intimates, speeches and interviews, annotations on or reactions to briefing memos, and evaluations of voting records over time.

Greenstein accounts for vision, too, in evaluating presidents. The same might be applied to members of Congress. Does the member possess a set of overarching goals? Is he or she dedicated to the content of policies? Do the member's convictions set the terms of his or her interactions with colleagues in policy development? Does the member inspire? A strong archival collection, spanning more than a handful of years, can provide evidence of vision. The logical place to start is probably the public remarks a member makes—they all talk about their convictions, their goals, what inspires them (and ought to inspire you). But the key to learning about consistency lies in the archives. Does the "message" filter down to the staff in terms of how the office is structured, how constituents and colleagues are treated, in the work ethic of the member?

Finally, and most critically in my view, is emotional intelligence, the member's ability to manage his or her emotions and turn them to constructive purposes. Does the member have self-awareness? Is he or she able to accept criticism? Is he or she intellectually honest? Does the member exhibit strength of character? I have never seen a person write something that began "I know I am self-aware because . . . " Answering these questions will take some digging. One measure of a person's ability to accept criticism might be staff turnover. Also, character is tested in legislative battles. In that arena, did the member have the courage of his or her convictions? A member who actively seeks contrary views, who is comfortable with dissent in the office, who is decisive—congressional collections document these qualities.

Using archival materials created by a congressmember to answer the questions I have posed will not only tell the story of a life and career; it will be, as Barbara Tuchman once explained, a "vehicle for exhibiting an age."[9] Members of Congress don't exist in isolation any more than data do.

Here is a final reason to enliven political science research and writing about Congress by using archival sources. Political science journals publish prolifically the fruits of aggregate quantitative work and math modeling. Since I don't understand that research, I'm not in a position to discount it. But which of the following two examples stands a better chance of being read by people outside the discipline?

Example 1. The following appeared as part of an analysis of legislative bargaining.[10]

$$v_B = p \sum_{\sigma_B, \beta_B} \mu_B[\sigma_B, \beta_B](1 - \sigma_B x_S - \beta_B x_B)$$

$$+ (P - p) \sum_{\sigma_B, \beta_B} \mu_B[\sigma_B, \beta_B] \frac{\beta_B}{b-1} x_B + Q \sum_{\sigma_S, \beta_S} \mu_S[\sigma_S, \beta_S] \frac{\beta_S}{b} x_B$$

Example 2. Robert H. Michel, just elected leader of the House Republicans in December 1980 after a hard-fought contest with Guy Vander Jagt, spoke these words to his colleagues:

12/8/80

MR. CHAIRMAN, MY COLLEAGUES AND GUESTS OF THE CONFERENCE/

I COULD JUST ABOUT BREAK OUT INTO SONG! IF I DID, IT WOULD HAVE TO BE "~~THE LORD BE PRAISED~~" / FOR MY FATHER TOLD ME MANY TIMES AS A YOUNG MAN THAT WHEN ~~GOD~~ LOOKS WITH SUCH GOOD FAVOR UPON ME AS HE HAS HERE TODAY, I SHOULD FIRST PAUSE/ ACKNOWLEDGE ~~~~, GIVE THANKS AND THEN ~~GO FORTH~~ WALK~~ING~~ HUMBLY IN HIS SIGHT/

THAT IS WHERE I HAVE TO BEGIN MY STEWARDSHIP AS YOUR NEWLY ELECTED LEADER/

He continued:

How do I perceive my Leadership role? . . . I do not personally crave the spotlight of public attention. What I am interested in is seeing to it that the spotlight is focused on the vast array of individual talent we have assembled in this room. My job is to orchestrate your many talents in such a way as to give us the best possible overall performance rating.

To use the symphonic analogy, I know some of you prefer speaking softly as strings, others more vocally as woodwinds, some very loudly as brass and finally those boisterous ones for percussion, but in any event, the measure of our success will be how well we harmonize and work together.

Legislative bargaining or leadership style—the topic is almost irrelevant. The plain language of the historical record speaks more compellingly to me.

NOTES

1. Many of these organizations possess the papers of members of Congress. I conducted an informal survey of the ACSC (www.congresscenters.org) to determine the extent of political science use of their collections in 2004. The responses confirmed my suspicion. In the case of one repository, of the 192 uses of a single congressional collection, only 13 "might qualify" as political scientists; this from the most heavily used of the institutions which responded. Typical was this reply: "I can tell you none used ours, only historians. The local political science people claim they are only interested in statistical/graph type stuff (and we do have some things which would help them), so they have convinced themselves that congressional papers are of no use to them. Very frustrating."

2. For purposes of this chapter, a member's papers are defined as "all records, regardless of physical form and characteristics, which are made or received in connection with an individual's career in Congress." When I use "archives," I do not mean "data archives."

3. The advent of searchable finding aids and the online posting of selected portions of collections compromise the principle of original order to an extent.

4. In their guidance to senators and representatives, the Senate Historical Office and the Office of History and Preservation, Office of the Clerk suggest discarding such files as service academy applications not accepted, routine agency and department records, routine constituent correspondence and casework, certain categories of issue mail, declined invitations, outdated reference information, legislative files not related to the member's interests, nonsubstantive office files (including, curiously, financial records), and routine photographs. You are not likely to find these materials in congressional collections.

5. Among the reasons typically cited are these: longevity in office often means that early records "disappear"; a congressional office functions in the moment and discounts the importance of legacy; the member discourages preserving his or her records for any number of reasons; congressional offices often close quickly following death or electoral defeat.

6. The best way to evaluate a congressional collection is to see the finding aid, either by going online or by contacting the repository directly. The National Archives maintains a list of collections at congressional repositories at www.archives.gov/records of congress/repository collections/. The best printed sources for locating congressional papers are the *Guide to Research Collections of Former Members of the United States House of Representatives, 1789–1987*, H. Doc. 100-171 (Washington, D.C.: House of Representatives, 1988); and the *Guide to Research Collections of Former United States Senators, 1789–1995*, S. Doc. 103-35 (Washington, D.C.: U.S. Senate, 1995).

7. The Society of American Archivists Congressional Papers Roundtable maintains a list of institutions offering research funding; go to www.archivists.org/saagroups/cpr/grants.asp.

8. See www.ou.edu/special/albertctr/archives/collect.htm.

9. Quoted by Koed (Koed 2000, 17).

10. It is not important who published this equation, only that it represents a popular method of publishing research that is at odds with my preference.

BIBLIOGRAPHY

Dodd, Lawrence C. 2004. "Political Science and the Study of Congress: Trends and New Trajectories," www.congresscenters.org/dodd 2004.htm.

Frisch, Scott A., and Sean Q Kelly. 2003. "Don't Have the Data? Make Them Up! Congressional Archives as Untapped Data Sources." *P.S.: Political Science and Politics* 36(2):221–4.

Greenstein, Fred I. 2000. *The Presidential Difference: Leadership Style from FDR to Clinton*. New York: Free Press.

Koed, Betty K. 2000. "The Usefulness of Political Biographies," *LSS Newsletter, Extension of Remarks*, 23(1).

Loomis, Burdett A. 2000. "Editor's Note," *LSS Newsletter, Extension of Remarks*, 23(1).

MacNeil, Neil. 1970. *Dirksen: Portrait of a Public Man*. New York: World.

Ryfe, David Michael. 2001. "Visiting the Scene of the Crime, Or How to Interrogate a Presidential Archive," *PRG Report* 24(1):21–23.

29

Recovering History and Discovering Data in the Archives: An Alternative Mode of Research for Congress Scholars

Douglas B. Harris

> We are not talking here about a theory of politics. We are talking about a mode of research. But it is a mode of research which can—potentially at least—inform, enrich, and guide theories of politics.
>
> —Richard F. Fenno, "Observation, Context, and Sequence in the Study of Politics"

The fundamental test of any research approach in political science should be its ability to illuminate important empirical and theoretical questions about politics in ways that other research approaches cannot. Consider, for example, the unique descriptive and analytical contributions of the participant-observation "mode of research." The preeminent practitioner of this anthropological approach is Richard Fenno, whose fieldwork and "thick descriptions" of congressional politics provide scholars a mountain of anecdotes, descriptions, and data to better understand the politics, processes, and culture of the U.S. Congress (see Fenno 1973, 1978). Moreover, likely because his mode of research afforded him such an abundance of empirical information, Fenno's work is unusually rich theoretically. Not only did it open the U.S. Congress as a new empirical front to the Rochester School's rational choice theorizing, but it also brought such parsimonious theorizing into contact with the more interpretive and, in important ways, deeper and more enriching theories from across the social sciences.[1]

Previously published as "Recovering History and Discovering Data in the Archives: An Alternative 'Mode of Research' for Congress Scholars" in *Extension of Remarks* Legislative Studies Section, American Political Science Association (July 2005). Published with permission.

Recent scholarly interest in using archival methods to conduct research on Congress has opened the door to new sources of descriptive information and systematic data on topics as diverse as the organization and development of congressional campaign committees (Kolodny 1998), the contributions of notable figures in congressional history (Zelizer 1998), congressional committee assignments (Frisch and Kelly 2004; Lawrence, Maltzman, and Wahlbeck 2001), and congressional reform (Zelizer 2004). My own use of the archival method has been focused on two projects concerning congressional party leadership. The first, a study of House party leaders' uses of mass media strategies of legislative leadership, examines legislative leaders' most public and highly visible acts. The second, by contrast, analyzes the internal dynamics of intra-party races for elective leadership posts; because these are conducted by secret ballot, they are among the most private and ostensibly personal choices legislators make (Polsby 1969; Peabody 1976). In light of the inherent differences between studying both party leaders' most public and highly visible acts as well as the most insular choices legislators make, this chapter is a recommendation to colleagues in the study of Congress of the value of archival research as another mode of research that, like participant-observation, can address a broad range of questions, uncover new and illuminating descriptive information to expand our empirical understanding of Congress, and provide new opportunities for theory testing and refinement that only these kinds of empirical "finds" can allow.

RECOVERING THE HISTORY OF
CONGRESSIONAL MEDIA POLITICS

My archival research into House party leaders' media strategies has been set in the papers of every speaker of the House since Sam Rayburn.[2] Having completed my doctoral dissertation on the development of the public speakership and public congressional leadership without the benefit of archival research, in revising and expanding the project's scope, I planned to employ archival research methods to supplement existing data sources, refine the theoretical perspective, and fill in gaps that remained. Little did I realize the extent to which recovering the history and uses of congressional party communications would lead to a comprehensive revision of the work, with better examples, deeper insights, and a more complete understanding of not simply congressional media politics but congressional party leadership more generally.[3]

Given both my substantive concern with the underresearched topic of congressional party communications as well as theoretical questions regarding the causes and nature of institutional change over time, the first step toward better explaining the causes and consequences of the public speakership and public congressional leadership was to recover the history of their behavioral and organizational development that, due to the tendencies of political scientists and historians, was largely lacking in both scholarly literatures. Even historically oriented political scientists are more likely to zero in on pivotal moments for analysis or to pick and choose in American history for opportunities to test synchronic theories than they are to engage in research that is truly diachronic and developmental.[4] By the same token, because many historians are otherwise occupied with social and non-elite histories, and those that are interested in government and politics tend to search out every last nuance of the lives and careers of presidents, the history of the first branch has received considerably less attention (see Zelizer 2000).

Fortunately, important aspects of the history of congressional party communications were recoverable in archives. Minutes and notes from meetings, transcripts of leaders' press conferences and other media appearances, planning documents, poll and focus-group reports, and party talking points and message material were among the data used to shed unique light on how congressional leaders make the party messages that are so central to their influence in the contemporary Congress.

First, archival materials revealed how traditional House party organizations adapted to the new media imperatives of contemporary American politics. The ongoing, behind-the-scenes media efforts of (and increasingly formalized division of labor on media matters between) the speaker's office, the floor leaders and whips, the Democratic Caucus, and the Republican Conference were uncovered, as were the histories of the development of the Democratic Message Board and the Republicans' Theme Team and CommStrat as some of the more formalized extensions of party communications efforts in the House party hierarchy. If the documents cannot reveal a comprehensive history of all of the media activities of these party organizations, they nevertheless portray a congressional party leadership fundamentally transformed by media considerations and duties.

Second, the organization and activities of the litany of ad hoc media working groups from the last quarter-century of House history have also left a paper trail. Such informal organizations—including an Information Task Force headed by Chief Deputy Whip John Brademas (D-IN) in the 94th Congress, a series of Leadership Campaign Meetings in the 97th Congress, a leadership-directed Media Group headed by Representative Don Edwards (D-CA) in the 99th Congress, informal media planning groups under Minority Leader Bob Michel (that have been largely ignored by scholars drawing sharp contrasts between the styles of Michel and Gingrich) and Newt Gingrich's Conservative Opportunity Society, his communications-oriented "Strategy Whip" operation as minority whip, and his various media advisory teams and groups when speaker—have played key roles in organizing and implementing many of the House parties' media campaigns. In my disserta-tion research, I had seen mere mentions in secondary sources of informal party organizations and regular planning sessions in which leaders devel-oped party messages, made strategy for press outreach, and coordinated members' talk, but it was not until the subsequent archival research and the discovery of documents such as membership lists and meeting minutes from these organizations that my suspicion was confirmed that these rare outsider glimpses revealed public relations efforts that were increasingly routine in congressional leadership circles and pervasive of most of House leaders' activities.

Finally, pulling back the curtain, archival documents reveal that there is much artifice in congressional media politics: leaders choreograph floor politics and stage "pseudo-events" (sometimes even intra-party disagree-ments are staged for public consumption); they falsely deny in public the use of polls and media strategies; they disclaim efforts to politicize an issue but work behind the scenes to propel partisanship; they covertly delegate to other members or friendly outsiders certain messages that they would not themselves carry in public. Understanding that the history of congressional media politics is not only obscure because of a lack of scholarly attention but also because politicians often hide their attempts to manipulate press coverage and public opinion, uncovering documentary evidence of such be-haviors provides insights that perhaps no other research approach could.[5]

Taken collectively, these documentary "finds" reveal both the remark-able similarities in the public relations aims and efforts of Democrats and Republicans throughout the 1980s and 1990s and that the elements of "public congressional leadership" that were institutionalized during the O'Neill speakership had important antecedents in the 1970s.[6] Moreover, the closer look at the leader–follower relationship that archival research affords suggests that, like presidents, leaders "go public" to increase their leverage over their colleagues, exerting more autonomous influence than many theories suggest. The aims, if not the effects, of their media efforts are to change press coverage and public opinion in ways that pressure and, to a degree, manipulate their colleagues.

UNCOVERING THE INSULAR CONGRESS

My interest in a second project, examining the internal dynamics of intra-party leadership races, dates to my first days in graduate school when, as research assistant to Johns Hopkins political scientist Robert L. Peabody, I was deployed to "keep an eye on" emerging leadership races in the House and Senate. Too eager to realize that Peabody was telling me that he really had nothing for me to do and that I should instead focus on my first-year studies, I sought out every political science examination of leadership races. Through this research and innumerable conversations with Peabody, I became (and continue to be) intrigued by the choices legislators make at these key moments in congressional history. Still, because of the secret ballot in leadership elections (Polsby 1969), further analysis into the bases of support for particular leadership candidates, their campaigns, and the decisions of individual members to support one candidate over another has been stifled. As Peabody (1976) observed, "most of the variables [studies of leadership races] do not lend themselves to clear-cut isolation, easy operationalization, assignment of weights, or sophisticated causal orderings" (470).

Taking these lessons to heart, I held out little hope that any of the puzzles and questions remaining from Peabody's classic participant-observation study of the topic could be uncovered.[7] Nevertheless, whenever I ventured to a party leader's archive for the media study, I would also scour the collection's finding aid for any information on the person's leadership ambitions, races, and opponents. To my surprise, I found what I regard as new and important evidence on the concerns, strategies, and tactics that candidates for leadership posts employ. Expanding my purview to examine the papers of not only the winners but also their competitors and sometimes their campaign managers uncovered candidates' letters soliciting support (as well as responses from colleagues), written campaign plans and notes on strategy, and candidates' notes on conversations with colleagues. Most notably, in some instances archival work yields candidates' internal counts and tallies of supporters; although they must be used with care, these represent the best available sources of information we have on the coalitions of support for individual leadership candidates and individual legislator decision making in such leadership campaigns.[8]

This highlights a second potential use of archival materials: they can provide a window on a whole range of legislative behaviors about which scholars have little to no information. In congressional studies, there is no scarcity of data on members' official positions and acts—committee assignments and leadership posts, their speeches, bills introduced, amendments offered, and roll calls taken—which are meticulously recorded for posterity and available for analysis. Nevertheless, there are other kinds of behaviors, less observable from the outside, about which we know very little. Even though this behavior is more difficult to observe, it is no less important historically or less relevant for theories of politics. In the case of intra-party leadership races, we can choose either to remain in the dark or we can seek out and analyze, with due caution and in appropriate context, the best information available. Indeed, in these and other instances, evidence of such unofficial behavior is all the data we will ever have of key moments in congressional history. Consider Terry Sullivan's (1998) analysis of Democratic whip counts on whether or not to impeach Richard Nixon. Because Nixon's resignation precluded a floor vote on his impeachment, Sullivan's analysis represents the best available, systematic information on how Democrats might have voted in what was an undeniably important moment in American political history.

HISTORY FOR ITS OWN SAKE?

Am I advocating that political scientists study history for its own sake? Given the lack of political science and historical attention to Congress, what really would be wrong with that? It seems reasonable to encourage scholars of Congress to mine, recover, and produce new data sources that improve our understanding of the way Congress actually works. Setting aside broader debates on the value of counterfactual analysis, failing to recover the history or discover behaviors simply because they are more difficult to observe runs the risk of engaging in a kind of counterfactual analysis that no one would defend: that of making one's case unaware that the claims are, indeed, counterfactual.

Although it is tempting to rest on this first response, ultimately I, too, am advocating the recovery of congressional history for the sake of theories of politics. For example, historical institutionalists and others who study Congress diachronically will find much evidence to feed their theories in archives. As it stands, historical institutionalists are just as likely to use the work of historians as they are to do their own historical work, thus subjecting our analyses to the trends and dispositions of historiography (Lustick 1996). To minimize such difficulties (especially given the lack of attention to all but a few key moments in congressional history), and to the extent that we want to model development in Congress or test for the effects of institutional changes or reforms, we must do much of the historical work ourselves.[9] My experience suggests that historical-institutional theories informed by original research in the archives will produce models of institutional change that emphasize the importance of individual actors, the uncertainty of (and the importance of learning by) those actors, and their responses to multiple causes and stimuli promoting institutional change. Archival research likely will reveal that, far from being efficient and functional, institutional change is the product of many failed attempts and false starts (see also Zelizer 2004).

In addition to improving models of institutional change, archival discoveries might also find empirical answers to questions that previously have been argued on a theoretical rather than an empirical basis. For example, archival research into the behind-the-scenes activities of party organizations

have illuminated debates over whether parties "matter" in legislative decision making. My archival research of party efforts to coordinate members'
floor speeches demonstrated significant party effects on what was previously considered one of the more independent behaviors of members.
Those skeptical of the importance of party organizations might contend
that the confluence of members' speeches on a topic simply reflects the
similar dispositions of fellow partisans. However, evidence of party leaders'
planning of such message campaigns and members' post-hoc responses
lends empirical support to the theoretical view that the efforts of party leaders and organizations matter (Harris 2005a). Similarly, using the minutes
of Republican Conference and Democratic Caucus meetings, Richard Forgette (2004) has demonstrated that party coordination efforts affect party
unity. And we will surely gain deeper insights into party influence when
C. Lawrence Evans's archival research allows scholars to compare uncovered party whip counts on legislation to the stances members actually took
on roll-call votes.

More specifically, archival research can help solve puzzles related to our
principal–agent models of congressional party leadership. Principal–agent
models of congressional leadership often are concerned with the reciprocal
influence between leaders and followers. Who is leading whom? In making
such arguments, Congress scholars frequently make assumptions about the
goals and perspectives of leaders and followers and the sequence of events
that are crucial to teasing out these theoretical differences, but which our
dominant research methods leave us far too remote from our subject to
gauge. Though it is by no means perfect in this regard, archival research can
get us a bit closer to the subject matter and improve our understanding of
the timing and sequence of key events, and ultimately the complexities of
the leader–follower relationship.

For example, my research on media strategies exposed a pattern of House
leaders' poll use dating back to the early 1980s whereby, like Newt Gingrich
and the Republicans in the 1990s, House Democratic leaders made frequent
and sophisticated use of public opinion polls and focus-group methods. In
addition to correcting some mistaken impressions about Democrats' poll
use, this study also shed light on the causes of this change in leadership
style and the motivations of leaders' behavior. Whereas I had begun the
project expecting to find evidence that leaders' media activities (and, by
extension, poll use) would fit the model of conditional party government,
and that leaders would "go public" when the condition of intra-party agreement is met, I found that other factors such as interbranch conflict with
the White House and congressional recruitment patterns need also be considered to explain these changes in leadership style. Moreover, by pushing
more deeply into the complexities of this interplay between congressional
leaders and followers, archives also revealed a potentially much stronger

role for congressional party leadership organizations than is appreciated by most theories of leadership. Rather than merely trying to manipulate the range of preferences in Congress as reflective of district-based preferences, leaders framed media messages in attempts to change preferences of the public and, in turn, their colleagues in Congress (Harris, 2005b).

If our research agendas quite naturally show a bias toward analyzing behaviors that are easily observed, archival research yields a behind-the-scenes look at congressional politics that can help us account for biases and omissions in contemporary congressional research. For example, due to our focus on official sources, we see more of the "end products" of politics than we do politics in the making. This likely produces a bias in favor of assuming a clarity of purpose in political behavior and a certainty in politicians' actions. By the same token, our understanding of all manner of legislative choices will likely be enhanced by greater insight into the multiple considerations that go into legislator decision making, how legislators' preferences change over time, and the choices they make in the context of the alternatives they considered but did not select. We will surely know more about the politics of legislative committee assignments, for example, when we know not only the committees to which members were assigned but also the committee assignments they requested but did not receive (Frisch and Kelly 2004; Lawrence, Maltzman, and Wahlbeck 2001).

CAUTIONS AND CONCLUSIONS

Political scientists using archival research methods may often feel caught between the historians whose research approach we appropriate and the norms of our own discipline. First, given the practical limitations inherent in archival research, most notably the massive amounts of material in congressional papers, theory must guide the difficult choices political scientists make about where to look for evidence and what opportunities to forego. Historians may object that our research, being driven by social science theories, is too narrowly focused to fully capture the context and nuance of the events and individuals we study. Although we are not historians, political scientists' studies would be enriched by, at the very least, acknowledging our limitations in this regard. And political scientists should take care that their theoretical assumptions do not guide their choices in the archives too closely so as to preclude the possibility that their expectations will be disconfirmed. Though time-consuming and occasionally frustrating, casting a wide net in the archives provides a better context for understanding data and increases the possibility of serendipitous finds that might open doors to new theoretical insights.

By the same token, many political scientists will object to the necessarily interpretive nature of archival research. The more you conduct archival research, the more you are struck by the unevenness and omissions in the archival record, especially as you move from one collection to the next.[10] Sometimes doing archival research resembles Clifford Geertz's description of "doing ethnography," which he said "is like trying to read (in the sense of 'construct a reading of') a manuscript—foreign, faded, full of ellipses, incoherencies, suspicious emendations, and tendentious commentaries" (Geertz 1973, 10). But if archival research makes scholars more aware of the interpretive nature of their research, it is not to say that scholars using other approaches are spared such choices in interpretation. As with participant-observation, roll-call studies, or any empirical analysis, scholars of archival research must be careful not to overinterpret the data that come their way. But we should note that when data are scarce and lacking in context, we are most likely to overinterpret them. This then seems as much a prescription for more, certainly not less, archival research. To universalize the point: archival researchers would be prudent to marshal their archival finds in tandem with other sources of qualitative and quantitative evidence, just as participant-observers and those doing more quantitative empirical studies would likely benefit from consulting documentary evidence in congressional archives.

NOTES

1. In addition to exploring the three goals of members of Congress, Fenno's approach mirrored that of anthropologist Clifford Geertz (1973), and his analysis of legislators' interactions with their constituencies drew on sociologist Erving Goffman's (1959) concept of the "presentation of self" to portray legislators acting in complex, intersubjective human contexts.

2. This seems an appropriate place to express my gratitude to the Caterpillar Foundation and the Everett McKinley Dirksen Congressional Research Center, the Carl Albert Research Center at the University of Oklahoma, and the Department of Political Science, the Committee on Faculty Development, and the College of Arts and Sciences at Loyola College in Maryland. All of these organizations and the individuals who run them supported the travel necessary to conduct research in the papers of the John W. McCormack, Special Collections, Boston University; the Carl Albert Collection, Carl Albert Congressional Research Center, University of Oklahoma; Thomas P. O'Neill Papers, Special Collections, John J. Burns Library, Boston College; Jim Wright Collection, Mary Couts Burnett Library, Texas Christian University; Papers of Thomas S. Foley, Special Collections, Washington State University, Pullman, Washington; and Papers of Representative Newt Gingrich, Special Collections, University of West Georgia. In addition, the papers of Minority Leader Robert H. Michel at the Dirksen Congressional Research Center, and the papers of former Majority Whip John B. Brademas at Special Collections, New York University, have been invaluable in fleshing out the development of public congressional leadership.

3. The original research was based on a mix of secondary sources, systematic quantitative data on House party leaders' television appearances, and evidence of leadership staff allocations to press and communications responsibilities (see Harris 1998). This is not to discount nor disclaim that original research, the conclusions of which, I believe, largely have withstood this deeper look at the question; rather it is to point out that a better, more useful, and complete explanation of the subject could be found in the archives.

4. For example, it is not too much of an exaggeration to say that political scientists have devoted more attention to the three days in March 1910 that culminated in the revolt against Speaker Joseph Cannon than to the 20 years of congressional history that followed. On diachronic analysis, its aims and uses, see Cooper and Brady 1981.

5. This may be an instance where archival research might produce better descriptive information than interviews with political elites, who may be reluctant to reveal such efforts or may, in the case of media politics, continue to repeat party talking points. Notably, the best studies of presidential use of media and public opinion politics are based on intensive archival research (see, for example, Maltese 1994; Eisinger 2003; Jacobs and Shapiro 1995, 2000; Heith 1998).

6. The three aspects of public congressional leadership—enhancing leaders' media visibility, increasing access to political information (media expertise and polling), and coordinating messages emanating from party members—date to the Brademas Task Force in the mid-1970s. An outline of the activities of the task force revealed three chief intended functions; the group was to: (1) provide focal point for information, (2) promote exposure of leadership, (3) coordinate efforts to get information to members. Undated [likely late 1975] outline of Information Task Force functions, Folder "Information Task Force" Leadership Files, John Brademas Papers, Office of University Archives, Elmer Holmes Bobst Library, New York University.

7. Notably, the one study that had sought to get around these difficulties also employed documentary evidence; see Kelly 1995.

8. In addition to the archival resources cited above in note 2, information on leadership races has been garnered from examination of the papers of the House Democratic Caucus at the Library of Congress, the papers of Eddie Boland at Boston College, James G. O'Hara at the University of Michigan, the papers of Sam Gibbons at the University of South Florida, and the papers of Frank Thompson at Princeton University. This research, *The Austin-Boston Connection: Fifty Years of House Democratic Leadership* (Texas A&M University Press, forthcoming), was conducted in collaboration with Professors Anthony Champagne, Jim Riddlesperger, and Garrison Nelson; collectively we have examined dozens of archival collections, the historical scope of which extends from the late-nineteenth century to the late-twentieth century.

9. It has been suggested by historical institutionalists (see Skocpol 1984) that political scientists cannot (and in some instances need not) do their own historical work. Yet in those instances where we can do it (not to mention those where we must), our own historical work may well be worth the effort.

10. Archival researchers are subject to the recordkeeping of the politicians we study, their tendencies to put things on paper, the systematization of the processes we study, and the choices made in maintaining and organizing the archival collection. It is also true that scholars who analyze public opinion polls are subject

to the frequency with which polling organizations ask a particular question and change its wording, just as those who conduct roll-call analyses are subject to whether a particular issue comes up for a floor vote, if that vote is recorded, and the differences between the frequency of recorded votes in the "textbook" and post-reform Congresses.

BIBLIOGRAPHY

Cooper, Joseph, and David W. Brady. 1981. "Toward a Diachronic Analysis of Congress." *American Political Science Review* 75:988–1006.

Eisinger, Robert M. 2003. *The Evolution of Presidential Polling.* New York: Cambridge University Press.

Fenno, Richard F., Jr. 1986. "Observation, Context, and Sequence in the Study of Politics." *American Political Science Review* 80(1):3–15.

———. 1978. *Home Style: House Members in Their Districts.* New York: Harper Collins.

———. 1973. *Congressmen in Committees.* Boston: Little, Brown.

Forgette, Richard. 2004. "Party Caucuses and Coordination: Assessing Caucus Activity and Party Effects." *Legislative Studies Quarterly* 29(August):407–30.

Frisch, Scott A., and Sean Q. Kelly. 2004. "Self-Selection Reconsidered: House Committee Assignment Requests and Constituency Characteristics." *Political Research Quarterly* 57(2):325–36.

Geertz, Clifford. 1973. *The Interpretation of Cultures.* New York: Basic Books.

Goffman, Erving. 1959. *The Presentation of Self in Everyday Life.* New York: Doubleday.

Harris, Douglas B. 2005a. "Orchestrating Party Talk: A Party-Based View of One-Minute Speeches in the House of Representatives." *Legislative Studies Quarterly* 30(1):127–41.

———. 2005b. "House Majority Party Leaders' Uses of Public Opinion Information." *Congress and the Presidency* 32(2):133–55.

———. 1998. "The Rise of the Public Speakership." *Political Science Quarterly* 113(2):193–212.

Heith, Diane J. 1998. "Staffing the White House Public Opinion Apparatus, 1969–1988," *Public Opinion Quarterly* 62(Summer):165–89.

Jacobs, Lawrence R., and Robert Y. Shapiro. 2000. *Politicians Don't Pander: Political Manipulation and the Loss of Democratic Responsiveness.* Chicago: University of Chicago Press.

———. 1995. "The Rise of Presidential Polling: The Nixon White House in Historical Perspective." *Public Opinion Quarterly* 59(Summer):163–95.

Kelly, Sean Q. 1995. "Generational Change and the Selection of Senate Democratic Leader in the 104th Congress." Paper presented at the annual meeting of the Southern Political Science Association, Tampa, Florida.

Kolodny, Robin. 1998. *Pursuing Majorities: Congressional Committees in American Politics.* Norman: University of Oklahoma Press.

Lawrence, Eric D., Forrest Maltzman, and Paul J. Wahlbeck. 2001. "The Politics of Speaker Cannon's Committee Assignments." *American Journal of Political Science* 45(3):551–62.

Lustick, Ian. 1996. "History, Historiography, and Political Science: Multiple Historical Records and the Problem of Selection Bias." *American Political Science Review* 90(3):605–18.

Maltese, John Anthony. 1994. *Spin Control: The White House Office of Communications and the Management of Presidential News,* 2nd ed., revised. Chapel Hill: University of North Carolina Press.

Peabody, Robert L. 1976. *Leadership in Congress: Stability, Succession, Change.* Boston: Little Brown.

Polsby, Nelson W. 1969. "Two Strategies of Influence: Choosing a Majority Leader." In Robert L. Peabody and Nelson W. Polsby, eds., *New Perspectives on the House of Representatives,* 2nd ed. Chicago: Rand McNally.

Skocpol, Theda. 1984. "Emerging Agendas and Recurrent Strategies." In Theda Skocpol, ed., *Vision and Method in Historical Sociology.* Cambridge: Cambridge University Press.

Sullivan, Terry. 1998. "Impeachment Practice in the Era of Lethal Conflict." *Congress and the Presidency* 25(2):117–28.

Zelizer, Julian E. 2004. *On Capitol Hill: The Struggle to Reform Congress and Its Consequences, 1948–2000.* Cambridge: Cambridge University Press.

———. 2000. "Introduction to Roundtable: The U.S. Congress in the Twentieth Century." *Social Science History* 24(2):307–16.

———. 1998. *Taxing America: Wilbur D. Mills, Congress, and the State, 1945–1975.* Cambridge: Cambridge University Press.

Appendix: Chronology of Advances in Preserving the Documentation of Congress

1975   Senate Historical Office is established to serve as the Senate's institutional memory by collecting and disseminating information on important events, precedents, dates, statistics, and historical comparisons of current and past Senate activities; to administer the secretary of the Senate's responsibility for records disposition; and to advise on records management and disposition in members' offices.

1976   The Dirksen Congressional Research Center Symposium on Congressional Archives, Pekin, Illinois, sponsored by the Lilly Foundation, assembles initial advice on creating disposition guidelines. Summary of proceedings published in the *Congressional Record*, May 25, 1976.

1976   Conference on Access to Papers of Recent Public Figures, sponsored by the American Historical Association, the Organization of American Historians, and the Society of American Archivists (SAA), takes place in New Harmony, Indiana. Proceedings published.

1977   National Study Commission on the Records and Documents of Federal Officials, *Final Report*, recommends establishing presidential records as public records. For congressional papers, it states that the "public papers" of members of Congress should be the property of the United States.

1978   Conference on Research Use and Disposition of Senators' Papers is hosted by the Senate. Although panelists focus on research use and disposition issues, particularly those of constituent mail and staff files, related issues of ownership, access, and deposit of collections at research institutions also are discussed. Recommends the creation of a records management handbook. Proceedings published.

1980 S. Res. 474, 96th Congress, establishes uniform access policy for Senate committee records at the National Archives. Prior to that time, each committee controlled access.

1982 National Archives loans archivist to Senate. Archivist becomes a permanent position in 1984.

1982 House Bicentennial Office is created as a temporary office to plan and coordinate bicentennial celebrations.

1983 Ad Hoc Planning Group on a Manual for Congressional Papers submits a report to the SAA calling for a manual designed to help archivists with the decisions and procedures required to manage congressional collections. It is printed in Appendix D of the Harpers Ferry Report, available at the Congressional Papers Roundtable Web site (http://archivists.org/saagroups/cpr/projects.asp).

1984 At the SAA annual conference in Washington, D.C., 12 archivists involved with congressional collections meet informally "to share common concerns and get acquainted." The first official meeting of the Congressional Papers Roundtable is held in 1986 in Chicago at the SAA annual meeting. This network of archivists who collect congressional papers meets once a year to explore and resolve common problems and issues, produces a newsletter, and maintains the Web site: http://archivists.org/saagroups/cpr.

1985 Congressional Papers Conference sponsored by National Historical Publications and Records Commission (NHPRC) and the Dirksen Congressional Center convenes in Harpers Ferry, West Virginia. Establishes minimum and maximum standards for repositories and members' collections. Proceedings issued in 1986 by NHPRC as *Congressional Papers Project Report.*

1985 First edition of *Guide to Research Collections of Former United States Senators* facilitates access by identifying where the collections exist across the country. Information available at http://bioguide.congress.gov.

1985 First edition of *Records Management Handbook for United States Senators and Their Archival Repositories.* Solidifies a working definition of senators' papers within the Senate community, based on the functions of senatorial offices; sets forth detailed management and disposition advice for textual and electronic records; provides preservation advice for special media; and explains how to store, ship, and donate a collection. Updated and published periodically.

1985   Legislative Archives established as a separate unit within the National Archives (NARA). This is the first step in raising the status and visibility of the unit that administers the records of Congress at the National Archives.

1987   *Guide to Research Collection of Former Members of the U.S. House of Representatives* published. Facilitates access to collections.

1988   First edition of *Records Management Handbook for United States Senate Committees* published. Solidifies the definition of committee records within the Senate community, based on committee functions. Represents a consensus within the Senate regarding records disposition; provides management advice for textual and electronic records and advice on managing sensitive and classified records. Updated and published periodically.

1988   Center for Legislative Archives established. This is an important step in creating a more prominent and visible administrative unit for congressional records.

1988   H. Res. 419, 100th Congress, establishes uniform access policy for records of House committees and select officers at the National Archives. Prior to that time, access to the records was restricted for 50 years from the date of their creation unless the clerk of the House determined that access would be detrimental to the public interest.

1989   Publication of award-winning *Guides* to House and Senate Records at NARA facilitates research in committee collections. Available at http://www.archives.gov/legislative/.

1989   Understanding Congress: A Bicentennial Conference is held to explore the multidisciplinary nature of congressional research. Proceedings published as *Understanding Congress: Research Perspectives*, H. Doc. 101-241.

1990   Center for Legislative Archives is further developed at NARA. The status of the director is enhanced, a specialist in congressional history is added, and a public outreach program is initiated.

1990   The Advisory Committee on the Records of Congress is established (P.L. 101-509). This body meets twice a year to investigate and monitor issues affecting the preservation of the records of Congress. Chaired in alternating Congresses by the clerk of the House and the secretary of the Senate, it includes the House and Senate historians, appointees of the House and Senate leadership, and the archivist of the United States. The committee develops into the primary vehicle for addressing matters of documentation and preservation of records of Congress.

1991   *First Report* of the Advisory Committee on the Records of Congress focuses on preservation of Congress's holdings at the Center for

Legislative Archives and the development of the center. Report published.

1992   *The Documentation of Congress,* S. Pub. 102-20; Karen Dawley Paul, project director—report of the Congressional Archivists Task Force on Congressional Documentation that establishes model collection development policies for governmental and non-governmental institutions that focus on the documentation of Congress. Identifies critical archival sources contributing to an understanding of Congress and recommends strategies for their preservation. Many of the governmental recommendations are implemented by the Center for Legislative Archives. These are detailed in subsequent Advisory Committee on the Records of Congress reports. Individual repositories specializing in political documentation subsequently implemented numerous recommendations particularly in the collections development area.

1994   Congressional Papers Conference sponsored by Northwood University and the Margaret Chase Smith Library, Portland, Maine, contributes to increased understanding of the research value of congressional papers. Raises the issue of the research quality of legislative documentation in committee records, which is subsequently studied and monitored by the Center for Legislative Archives. Proceedings published.

1994   The Congressional Papers Roundtable, as part of the SAA annual conference in Indianapolis, sponsors its first workshop on the Acquisition, Processing, and Reference of Legislative Collections. Taught by Herbert J. Hartsook and Cynthia Pease Miller, it is subsequently presented five additional times over the next nine years at different locations around the country.

1995   *Second Report* of the Advisory Committee on the Records of Congress, S. Pub. 104-30, focuses on preservation of the records of congressional support agencies. Results in NARA preparing records schedules for these agencies for the first time.

1996   The House Legislative Resource Center is created under the Office of the Clerk, which combines many functions of the House, including the Office of Records and Registration which, since 1971, was responsible for archiving the records of the House.

1996   *Congressional Papers Management: Collecting, Appraising, Arranging, and Describing Documentation of United States Senators, Representatives, Related Individuals and Organizations* by Faye Phillips (Jefferson, N.C.: McFarland). Provides practical guidance to repositories developing their congressional holdings.

1998   First edition of *Checklist for Closing a Senate Office* published. A manual for closing a Senate office that provides advice on preparing a member's papers for donation to an archival institution. Emphasizes preparation of a collection for donation, gives a timeline, and facilitates the preservation of electronic records through a team approach that includes computer support analysts, vendors, and the archivist. Has resulted in many more collections of retiring members being inventoried prior to the office closing. Updated each Congress.

1998   *Biographical Directory of Members of Congress* is combined with bibliographic information and guides to research collections and goes online at bioguide.congress.gov.

2000   The House Department of Historical Services is created under the Legislative Resource Center, Office of the Clerk. Part of the mission of the department is to administer the clerk's role in records disposition and to provide records management and disposition guidance to House members' offices.

2000   *Third Report* of the Advisory Committee on the Records of Congress, S. Pub. 106-52, is the *first* report to focus on members' papers issues. Recommends the establishment of two task forces: one on records management and one on model repository guidelines. The records management task force produces baseline standards that administrative managers can use for a "self-assessment."

2001   Congressional Papers Forum on the *Third Report* sponsored by Congressional Papers Roundtable, S. Pub.107-42, recommends that offices hire archivists/records managers or provide staff with specific training at the NARA Modern Archives Institute. Advocates establishment of at least one congressional documentation center in each state as the most cost-effective way to preserve congressional documentation and the best way to facilitate research.

2002   First edition of *Opening a Senate Office Checklist* published and made available on a Transition Office Intranet site. Distributes baseline records management standards to the offices of newly elected senators during orientation, *before* they open for business.

2002   The House Office of History and Preservation is created as a separate office under the Office of the Clerk. Previously the office was the Department of Historical Services, Legislative Resource Center.

2003   A group of historians and archivists meet at the Robert C. Byrd Center for Legislative Studies, Shepherd University, Shepherdstown, West Virginia, to discuss ways to foster collaboration and communication among congressional study centers. The Association of Centers for the Study of Congress is established and meets for the first time in 2004. Supports a wide range of programs designed to inform and educate students, scholars, policy makers, and members of the general public on the history of Congress, legislative process, and current issues facing Congress. It encourages the preservation of members' papers and supports programs that make those materials available for educational and research use. Effectively furthers collaboration among historians, political scientists, archivists, and educators. Meets annually. See www.congresscenters.org.

2004   *Records Management Manual for Committees* published by the clerk of the House, U.S. House of Representatives.

2005   The John Brademas Center, New York University, Symposium on Presidential and Public Papers explores the history of the Presidential Records Act and current policy options and obstacles in archiving the papers of members of Congress. Recommends the development of a public policy for members' papers using the presidential libraries as a model. (Report "Preserving and Expanding Access to Public Papers" published March 2006, www.nyu.edu/ofp/brademascenter/events.html.) Panel discussions inspire drafting of resolution for preservation and donation of members' papers.

2006   *Fourth Report* of the Advisory Committee on the Records of Congress, H. Doc. 109-156, focuses on records management, access, and preservation as they relate to the records of Congress and the private papers of Members of Congress. The importance of electronic records management and preservation is highlighted.

2006   *Records Management Manual for Members* published by clerk of the House, U.S. House of Representatives.

2008   *Managing Congressional Collections* by Cynthia Pease Miller published by the Society of American Archivists. Funded by a grant from NHPRC, this guide for institutions that are developing congressional documentation collections helps to demystify the acquisition and management process. Available from SAA Web site, http://archivists.org.

2008   The House and Senate unanimously pass H. Con. Res. 307 urging the proper preservation of members' papers. The resolution recognizes these papers as documenting vital national, regional, and local public policy issues. It exhorts members "to take all necessary measures to manage and preserve" them, to arrange for their deposit or donation with a research institution that is properly equipped to care for them, and to make them available for educational purposes at a time the member considers appropriate.

2008   Capitol Visitors Center opens and prominently features congressional archival documents in the exhibit hall to tell the story of Congress.

Index

classified information in, 309–15, 317, 330–32; *Congressional Record* in, 4, 12, 37, 93, 122, 146, 153, 198, 326, 383, 392, 421; constituent correspondence for, 22, 38n17, 69–70, 149, 187–88, 235–36, 241–49, *246*, 250n7, 251n30, 264–65, 325, 327, 408–9, 416n1, 422, 436, 444n3; constituent issues and, 22, 38n13, 69–70, 149, 187–88, 235–36, 241–49, *246*, 250n7, 264–65, 325, 327, 408–9; constituent service records for, 22, 38n13, 69–70, 93, 148–50, 300–301; databases for, 70, 79, 85, 132–36, 208, *209*, 235–41, *238*, 243–44, 250n16, 257, 293, *294*, 328; discarded material from, 427n4; duplication in, 71, 147; as electronic, 2, 8, 11, 12, 21, 84–85, 100, 258–59, 265, 267–68, 272–73, 277n15, 320, 324, 325, 420; e-mail processing for, 136, 138–39, 324–25; expense of, 146; federal agency correspondence as, 300–301, 408–9; filing system for, 32–35, 55, 70, 149, 157, 186–89, 224–25, 234–35, 249n2, 265, 275, 328–29, 342n52; film in, 118, 420; finding aid for, 223, 228–29, 282, 295–98, *296*, 304–5, 306n7, 399, 427n3, 427n6; format of, 271; fragmentation of, 66; by function, 263–64, *266*, 267–68, *267–68*; handbook/pamphlets for, 69–70, 72; of high profile individual, 337–39; for historians, 4, 5, 65, 279; importance of, 1, 19; on Internet, 4, 12, 279–80, 299n2, 427n3; inventory for, 260–61, *261*; issue mail for, 155–56, 187, 204, 300, 327; LAN for, 134, 136, 239, 243–44; leadership studies in, 71–72, 73, 83, 439, 441, 444n6, 444n8; lobbyists/interest groups and, 66; location of, 56, 66, 256, 279, 392, 402; loss of, 3; management of, 8, 69–70, 146, 235, 249nn1–2; memoirs in, 258;

memorabilia in, 23, 188–89, 207–8, 218n1, 272, 274, 303; national subject base for, 293, 294, 300n11; newspaper clippings for, 158, 258, 327, 329; oral interviews for, 25, 31, 32, 82–83, 87, 115–16, 121, 129, 398–99, 444n5; ownership of, 2, 3, 4, 41, 65, 72, 89–92; personal files for, 92, 107, 154, 186, 256, 303; photographs for, 158–59, 272, 273–74, 303, 327, 420; policy books in, 258; preservation grants for, 5, 377n11; preservation of, 3, 19; press release for, 291, 297; privacy issues for, 3, 4, 31, 48, 65, 87, 101, 115, 138, 309, 332–33, 336–37; processing records for, 113, 258–59, 262–63, 269, 271, 279–80, 282, 303–4, 317, 319–23, 330, 341n33; processing vocabulary for, 260; protocol for, 5, 8, 19–20, 39–48, 49n1, 68–69, 82, 108–9; public *v.* private ownership of, 2–3, 4, 41, 65, 72, 100–101, 249n1; quality of, 183; redefining of, 161–62; research in, 69, 146, 160–61, 250n19, 280, 416n1, 422, 436, 444n3; responsibility for, 66–67; restrictions on, 115, 120n11, 160, 212, 247–48, 304, 317–18, 334–35; schedules for, 135; scope/content note for, 297; seminars for, 70; series scope notes for, 285–86, 296; size of, 27, 146, 159, 183, 249n1, 257, 269, 271–72, 277n16, 317, 319, 326, 329–30, 422, 442; speech notes/ recording for, 302, *302*; staff rosters for, 258; subgroup/series within, 264–65, *266*; subject guide for, 287; supplementary sources for, 121; technology and, 66; transfer case information for, 261–62; tri-fold brochure in, 290; trip files in, 303; uniqueness of, 421; value of, 145, 159, 326; variance in, 420; volume of, 3, 5, 27–28, 37n2; weeding of, 45–46, 147, 159–60, 326; working

Tribune Media, 361
Troubled Waters (Senate Public Works
　Committee), 397–98
Truman, Harry S., 9, 124
Truman and the 80th Congress
　(Hartmann), 382
Tuchman, Barbara, 425
Tunney, John, 396
two governor conflict, 52, 58n5. *See
　also* Talmadge, Herman E.
Tydings, Millard, 20

Udall, Morris, 289, 296, *296, 299*
UniAccess, 139
United States Capitol, 10
United States Capitol Historical Society,
　10
United States House of Representatives:
　Committee on House
　Administration for, 114; document
　responsibility as clerk of, 67, 70,
　74, 101–2; duties of, 148–51;
　Historical Office for, 7, 184;
　House Bicentennial Office, 7–8,
　19; House Concurrent Resolution
　307 by, 1, 100, 104–5; Office for
　the Bicentennial of the House of
　Representatives within, 19, 21;
　Office of History and Preservation
　for, 90, 91, 255–56, 300n5, 306n5;
　Office of the Clerk for, 67, 70, 74,
　101–2, 262; Office of the Historian
　for, 115; program for oral interviews
　by, 82; Public Works Committee
　for, 395; sergeant at arms of, 74;
　Telephone Directory for, 91
United States Mint, 8–9, 12–13
United States Senate: Archivist for, 90;
　Bicentennial Study Group for, 6–7,
　8; CapitolCorrespond for, 239, 243;
　CMS for, 114; Computer Center
　for, 239, 245, 248; databases for,
　235–41; document responsibility
　as Secretary of, 67, 103–4; duties
　of, 148–51; Historical Office for, 3,
　6–7, 8, 10, 21, 30, 91, 184, 255–56,
　300n5; microfilm service for, 33,

36, 38n18; Paul as archivist for, 2,
8, 21, 30, 31, 35, 37, 38n10, 38n12,
88n1, *109–12,* 109–16, 120n7, 182,
184, 195n8, 199, 245, 260, 272,
275, 301n12, 301n13, 326, 340n1,
341n39, 342n42, 369; Public Works
Committee for, 395, 397; Quick
Response for, 239; Quorum for, 239;
Select Committee on National Water
Resources, 393; Select Committee
on Presidential Campaign Activities
by, 2, 52; Select Committee to Study
the Senate Committee System of,
3; Select Ethics Committee for, 53;
sergeant at arms for, 74; Talmadge
investigation by, 53; *Telephone
Directory* for, 91; *Troubled Waters* by,
397–98
Unland, James, 4
*Unlikely Environmentalists: Congress and
　Clean Water, 1945-1972* (Milazzo),
　392, 398
USA Today, 337–38

Van Buren, Stephen, 272
Vermont, state of, 43–44
Vietnam War, 382–83
Vinson, Fred M., 121, 122, 126
Vogt, Sheryl, 340n1
Vogt-O'Connor, Diane, 273
volunteers, for political campaigns,
　112, 119
voters, education of, 117, 403–4

Wade, Rogers, 55, 56
Wahlbeck, Paul J., 410, 411
Walker, Steven, 46
Wallace, George, 116
Waller, Bob, 361–62
Walters, Charlotte, 416
Warner, Robert, 3, 146
Warren Commission, 124
Washburn, Wilcomb E., 212
Washington National Records Center,
　24, 261
Watergate Babies, 3
Watergate complex, 2–3

About the Authors
and Contributors

Patricia Aronsson served from 1979 until 1983 as the archivist for four United States Senators: Robert C. Byrd (D-WV), Wendell Ford (D-KY), Russell Long (D-LA), and Abraham Ribicoff (D-CT). She also served as archivist on the Hill for the Senate Sergeant of Arms, Howard Liebengood.

Richard A. Baker has directed the U.S. Senate Historical Office since 1975, when that office was created. Baker has taught courses in congressional history for Cornell University's Washington Semester Program and the University of Maryland. Before joining the Senate's staff, he served as a reference specialist in American history at the Library of Congress. Baker is the author of numerous articles related to congressional history and several books, including a biography of New Mexico Senator Clinton Anderson (D-NM) and *200 Notable Days: Senate Stories, 1787–2002*. He is a former president of the Society for History in the Federal Government and an occasional guest on C-SPAN.

Lauren R. Brown is curator, Archives and Manuscripts Department, University Libraries, University of Maryland, College Park, where he oversees five units: Historical Manuscripts, Literary Manuscripts, National Public Broadcasting Archives, Library of American Broadcasting, and University Archives. He is also an adjunct professor in the College of Information Studies on the University of Maryland campus.

Greta Reisel Browning is reference archivist/librarian in Special Collections at Appalachian State University in Boone, North Carolina. Previously, she worked at the Richard B. Russell Library for Political Research and Studies at the University of Georgia, where her primary duties included processing political collections. She has also held processing positions at the American Dance Festival Archives, the Missouri Historical Society, the Forest History Society, and North Carolina State University.

Elisabeth Butler has been archivist for the U.S. Senate Committee on Homeland Security and Governmental Affairs since 2004.

Paul I. Chestnut is retired from his position as head of the Preparation Section of the Manuscript Division of the Library of Congress. He served previously as head of the Reference and Reader Services Section of the Manuscript Division and as an assistant curator in the Manuscript Department of Perkins Library at Duke University and as assistant state archivist at the Virginia State Library and Archives. He is a member of various archival and historic preservation organizations and is a fellow of the Society of American Archivists.

James Cross is manuscripts archivist for the Special Collections Unit of the Clemson University Libraries. He was the Strom Thurmond archivist at Clemson and an archivist at the Richard B. Russell Memorial Library of the University of Georgia Libraries. Cross has given presentations at various professional meetings; writes a column on federal legislation, policies, and news for *SGA Newsletter*; is the author of several articles and reviews on archival and historical topics; and was a contributor to *The Encyclopedia of Cleveland History* (1996).

Scott A. Frisch is professor and chair of Political Science at California State University, Channel Islands in Camarillo, California. A former Presidential Management Intern and legislative aide to Senator Frank Lautenberg (D-NJ), he is the author of *The Politics of Pork* (Garland Publishing, 1998), and co-author with Sean Kelly of *Committee Assignment Politics in the U.S. House of Representatives* (University of Oklahoma Press, 2006) and *Jimmy Carter and the Water Wars: Presidential Influence and the Politics of Pork* (Cambria, 2008).

Connell B. Gallagher is retired after serving as University Archivist and Curator of Manuscripts and Head of Special Collections at the University of Vermont Libraries. He served as an archivist for U.S. Senators Robert T. Stafford (R-VT) and Patrick J. Leahy (D-VT) during a sabbatical year, 1988–1989, and he also served as an archivist for the U.S. Senate Judiciary Committee in the fall of 2007. Gallagher is a Fellow of the Society of American Archivists and of the Vermont Academy of Arts & Sciences. In 1999, he received the Distinguished Service Award from the New England Archivists.

Glenn R. Gray is archivist for the Central Valley Political Archive at California State University, Fresno. He worked briefly as archivist for the Senate Committee on Finance and as a records management analyst for the Board of Governors of the Federal Reserve System and served on the steering committee of the Congressional Papers Roundtable of the Society of American Archivists. He was awarded a Fulbright scholar grant to the United Kingdom in 2005 and 2006.

Mark A. Greene is director of the American Heritage Center at the University of Wyoming. He has been archivist of Carleton College, the curator of manuscripts at the Minnesota Historical Society (where he first worked extensively with congressional collections), and head of research center programs for the Henry Ford Museum. He has published 15 articles in the U.S., Canada, and Europe. Greene has served the Society of American Archivists as president and member of its governing council; he has also chaired its Manuscripts Repositories Section, Congressional Papers Roundtable, and Committee on Education and Professional Development. In 2002, he became an SAA Fellow.

Pam Hackbart-Dean is associate professor and director of the Special Collections Research Center at Southern Illinois University Carbondale. Hackbart-Dean previously served as director of the Southern Labor Archives and head of Special Collections and Archives at Georgia State University in Atlanta, as well as assistant department head/processing archivist at the Richard B. Russell Library, University of Georgia. She has chaired the Congressional Papers Roundtable, Oral History Section, and Manuscript Repositories Section of the Society of American Archivists.

Douglas B. Harris is associate professor of Political Science at Loyola College in Maryland. His research on Congress, political parties, and media politics has been published in *Political Science Quarterly, Legislative Studies Quarterly, Political Research Quarterly, American Politics Research, P.S.: Political Science & Politics, Congress & the Presidency, Presidential Studies Quarterly,* and *Extension of Remarks,* as well as in edited collections on congressional elections and public trust in government. He is co-author of *The Austin-Boston Connection: Fifty Years of House Democratic Leadership* (forthcoming from Texas A&M University Press).

Herbert J. Hartsook is director of South Carolina Political Collections, University of South Carolina, overseeing more than 85 manuscript collections documenting government, society, and politics in the post-World War II era. Previously, Hartsook served the South Caroliniana Library as director, curator of Modern Political Collections, and curator of Manuscripts, and, at the South Carolina state archives, supervised its Legislative Papers Project. Hartsook serves as the oral historian of the South Carolina Bar Foundation. He is active in the Society of American Archivists and has chaired its Manuscripts Section, Oral History Section, and Congressional Papers Roundtable. He conceived and presents a national training workshop for archivists who work with legislative collections.

Sean Q Kelly is associate professor of Political Science at California State University, Channel Islands in Camarillo, California. He previously taught at Niagara University in Lewiston, New York, and at East Carolina University. A former American Political Science Association Congressional Fellow and policy analyst for the Senate Democratic Policy Committee, he is co-author of *Committee Assignment Politics in the U.S. House of Representatives* (University of Oklahoma Press, 2006), *Campaigns and Political Marketing* (Haworth, 2006), and *Jimmy Carter and the Water Wars* (Cambria, 2008).

Alan Lowe, now director of the George W. Bush Presidential Library, was executive director of the Howard H. Baker, Jr. Center for Public Policy at the University of Tennessee. Lowe worked at the Ronald Reagan Presidential Library in Simi Valley, California, at the Office of Presidential Libraries at the National Archives and Records Administration in Washington, D.C., and served for a period as interim director of the Franklin D. Roosevelt Presidential Library in Hyde Park, New York. He served as the representative of Senate Majority Leader William Frist (R-TN) on the Advisory Committee on the Records of Congress, and was elected president of the Association of Centers for the Study of Congress in 2008.

Frank H. Mackaman is director of the Dirksen Congressional Center in Pekin, Illinois. He is also adjunct professor of Political Science at Bradley University. Previously, he was the director of the Gerald R. Ford Library and Museum, and professor of history and visiting lecturer in political science at the University of Michigan. He is the author of many articles and monographs on archival and historical topics and has served the Society of American Archivists in many capacities. Mackaman is a founding member of the Association of Centers for the Study of Congress. His extensive civic service includes an 18-month term as mayor of the City of Pekin after being drafted by the city council upon resignation of the incumbent.

Mary McKay is university archivist at Willamette University in Salem, Oregon, where she manages several congressional collections. Her previous positions include serving as head of the arrangement and description department at the Richard B. Russell Library for Political Research and Studies at the University of Georgia and as processing archivist for the

Ann Richards papers at the University of Texas. She has served on the steering committee of the Congressional Papers Roundtable of the Society of American Archivists.

L. Rebecca Johnson Melvin is librarian and coordinator of the Manuscripts Unit in Special Collections, University of Delaware Library. She was project archivist for the papers of Senator John J. Williams (R-DE) and has supervised numerous congressional and other processing projects at Delaware. She is a past chair of the Congressional Papers Roundtable of the Society of American Archivists and served on the grant-writing and editorial committees of *Managing Congressional Collections* (SAA, 2008).

Paul C. Milazzo is associate professor of history at Ohio University with areas of concentration in American politics, political institutions, and federal policy, particularly after 1945. His recent research and publications have focused on environmental policy making in the United States Congress. Milazzo is the author of *Unlikely Environmentalists: Congress and Clean Water, 1945-1972* (University Press of Kansas, 2006).

Naomi Nelson is coordinator for Research Services in the Manuscript, Archives, and Rare Book Library, Emory University. In her previous position as modern political collections archivist at Emory, she developed expertise with electronic records in congressional offices. She has chaired the EAD Roundtable as well as the Congressional Papers Roundtable of the Society of American Archivists.

Karen D. Paul has served as Senate Archivist since 1982 and is responsible for planning, implementing, and directing a comprehensive archival management program for the U.S. Senate. She is a founding member of the Congressional Papers Roundtable of the Society of American Archivists and serves on its steering committee. She edited *The Documentation of Congress* (1992), which resulted in the creation of records disposition schedules for the congressional support agencies, offered a road map for developing the programs of the Center for Legislative Archives, and provided a collection development model for repositories specializing in congressional documentation. She is a founding member of the Association of Centers for the Study of Congress and serves on its executive committee.

Faye Phillips is associate dean of libraries for special collections at Louisiana State University. Previously, she served as a contract archivist in the United States Senate and as an archivist working with political collections at various other institutions. Political and congressional papers collections continue to be a research interest for Phillips and these materials, particularly the Long family papers (Huey P., Earl K., Russell B., and others), are a part of the LSU Libraries' Special Collections. Phillips is the author of *Congressional Papers: Collecting, Appraising, Arranging and Describing* (McFarland, 1996).

Sara Roberson Kuzak is an archivist at the California State Archives in Sacramento. As a graduate student at California State University, Sacramento, her master's thesis was based on an internship at the California State Archives, where she processed the papers of State Senator Robert Presley.

Jill Severn is head of Access and Outreach at the Richard B. Russell Library for Political Research and Studies, University of Georgia Libraries. Prior to this, she held other positions at the Russell Library and worked as a project curator at the McKissick Museum at the University of South Carolina. Severn is a member of the University of Georgia's Foot Soldier Project for Civil Rights Studies Faculty and is the director of the Russell Forum for Civic Life in Georgia. She has written and lectured widely on outreach and access issues, her main research interest.

Jeffrey S. Suchanek is head of the Public Policy Archives at the University of Kentucky Libraries, where he previously worked as a political papers archivist and oral historian. He is co-author of *Time on Target: The World War Two Memoir of William R. Buster*. In the Society of American Archivists, he has chaired the Congressional Papers Roundtable and the Oral History Section, and served as a member of the Education Committee. He also served on the board of directors of the Kentucky Council on Archives.

Sheryl B. Vogt is director of the Richard B. Russell Library for Political Research and Studies at the University of Georgia Libraries. She currently holds appointments to the Advisory Committee on the Records of Congress and the Georgia Historical Records Advisory Board. She is president of the Association of Centers for the Study of Congress, and was the 2004 recipient of the Scone Foundation's Archivist of the Year Award. She is active in the Society of Georgia Archivists, where she was editor of the society's peer-reviewed journal, *Provenance*, for ten years, and the Society of American Archivists, where she chaired the Manuscripts Repositories Section and the Congressional Papers Roundtable and co-chaired the 2008 Program Committee. She is the author of various articles and national conference papers on congressional archives and holdings of the Russell Library and is a Fellow of the Society of American Archivists.

Larry D. Weimer was project archivist for the papers of Senator Harrison A. Williams, Jr., (D-N.J.) at Special Collections and University Archives, Rutgers University. He has spoken about the reference use of congressional collections for local and social history before the New Jersey Library Association and the Association of Centers for the Study of Congress. Weimer is the curator of "Crossroads: Harrison A. Williams and Great Society Liberalism, 1959-1981," an exhibition on display in 2009 at Special Collections and University Archives, Rutgers University.

Karyl Winn is retired from a career as curator of manuscripts at the University of Washington Libraries. She acquired and directed processing of papers from numerous members of Congress from Washington State, notably the papers of Henry "Scoop" Jackson (D-WA) and Warren Magnuson (D-WA). She is a founding member and former chair of the Congressional Papers Roundtable of the Society of American Archivists. Post retirement, Winn has advised Gonzaga University on processing the papers of former Congressman George Nethercutt (R-WA).

Nancy Beck Young is professor of history at the University of Houston, after teaching at McKendree College in Lebanon, Illinois, and the University of Texas at Austin. Her interests include Congress, the presidency, and first ladies, though she is also a student of Texas political history, especially Texans in Washington. She has published several books, including biographies of Congressman Wright Patman (D-TX) and First Lady Lou Henry Hoover. She is currently writing a manuscript entitled "Why We Fight: Congress and the Politics of World War II," which is under contract to Princeton University Press, and editing an encyclopedia on the U.S. presidency. Young was a Woodrow Wilson Center Fellow in 2003–2004.